A NOBLE COLLECTION

A NOBLE COLLECTION:
THE SPENCER ALBUMS OF
OLD MASTER PRINTS

Marjorie B. Cohn

FOGG ART MUSEUM

HARVARD UNIVERSITY ART MUSEUMS

1992

EXHIBITION SCHEDULE

Elvehjem Museum of Art, University of Wisconsin, Madison
March 14–May 17, 1992

The Saint Louis Art Museum, Saint Louis
June 30–September 8, 1992

Spencer Museum of Art, University of Kansas, Lawrence
October 18, 1992–January 3, 1993

Fogg Art Museum, Harvard University, Cambridge
March 22–June 13, 1993

This catalogue was made possible by support from the National Endowment for the Arts,
a federal agency, as well as several Harvard Museum funds—the Andrew W. Mellon Publication Fund,
Henry P. McIlhenny Fund, Carola B. Terwilliger Bequest, and Edward A. Waters Publication Fund.

ISBN 0–916724–80–8

CONTENTS

DIRECTOR'S PREFACE

AMONG THE most important work of recent art history has been the study of patronage and collecting. It has provided us access to how specific works of art have traveled in space and through time, from one collection to another, and a vivid sense of how such works were valued in their own and subsequent times. This is particularly true with regard to the history of prints, which as objects of multiple production were often dispersed far and wide, exerting their influence in numerous and differing social circumstances and historical periods.

Marjorie B. Cohn, Carl A. Weyerhaeuser Curator of Prints, has previously contributed to the study of collecting with her pioneering work on the early American collector and benefactor of Harvard University and its fine arts collections, Francis Calley Gray, published in 1986 and entitled *Francis Calley Gray and Art Collecting for America*. With the present catalogue, however, and its associated exhibition, Marjorie Cohn has turned her attention to a European collection of prints, the so-called Spencer Albums, formed in the early years of the eighteenth century by Jean and Pierre-Jean Mariette, the premier print dealers in Europe, and most recently owned by the eighth Earl Spencer of England. Her distinguished connoisseurship, thorough and detailed archival research, and sensitivity to the material and technical aspects of works of art have illuminated the historical importance of these albums and the aesthetical qualities of the prints which they comprise. That she accomplished this feat with characteristic grace and high standards while serving for a good bit of the time as both curator of prints and acting director of the Harvard University Art Museums, is typical of her commitment to scholarship and to the affairs of the Museums, and we are most grateful to her.

We are grateful, too, to Melvin R. Seiden for the purchase of the albums with the Harvard University Art Museums in mind. He and the investment firm Vermeer Associates, for which he is a consultant, have insured the albums against the fate suffered by so many others. They will remain intact and available for study and appreciation by students and scholars, now and forever.

Members of the Museums' staff were also instrumental in the acquisition of the Spencer Albums and should be acknowledged here. These include, besides Marjorie Cohn, John Rosenfield and Edgar Peters Bowron, who during much of the acquisition period were acting director and director of the Museums, respectively; Henri Zerner and Konrad Oberhuber, who were curator of prints and drawings, respectively; and, most importantly, David P. Becker, who as acting curator of prints of the Fogg Art Museum from 1987 to 1989, undertook the thorough cataloguing of the prints in the albums, thus providing Marjorie Cohn with the essential foundation on which she subsequently built the structure of her research.

Numerous other colleagues contributed much to the realization of this project and are appropriately thanked by the author. I wish only to acknowledge the directors of the institutions participating in the tour of this exhibition—Russell Panczenko of the Elvehjem Museum, University of Wisconsin at Madison; James D. Burke of the Saint Louis Art Museum; and Andrea S. Norris of the Spencer Museum, University of Kansas at Lawrence—and the National Endowment for the Arts and the Andrew W. Mellon Foundation for their support of this project and the scholarly mission of the Harvard University Art Museums.

James Cuno
ELIZABETH AND JOHN MOORS CABOT DIRECTOR

ACKNOWLEDGMENTS

A N E V E N T such as the publication of the Spencer Albums and production of the associated exhibition has both proximate and ultimate causes, and we must thank many people who have assisted us at every stage. Above all, our gratitude goes to Melvin R. Seiden for the purchase of the albums and his generous collaboration in their aquisition by the Harvard University Art Museums. All of us, Mr. Seiden included, have been determined that they should not be dismantled. The albums' acquisition partially through the gift of Mr. Seiden and partially by purchase, was completed by David P. Becker and Edgar Peters Bowron, building upon the work of Henri Zerner, Konrad Oberhuber, and John Rosenfield. Originally this publication and exhibition were conceived of as a collaboration between Mr. Becker and the present author; although this did not in the end prove feasible, I and my fellow catalogue entry writers have benefited in particular from the impeccable cataloguing of the prints undertaken by Mr. Becker.

Many colleagues have given us great assistance in the course of our research. We should like to thank in particular those in Europe: Marian Bisanz-Prakken and her assistant at the Albertina, Vienna; David W. Riley of the John Rylands University Library of Manchester; Anthony Lister of Cheshire; Antony Griffiths and Martin Royalton-Kisch of the British Museum, Mirjam Foot of the British Library, and Adrian Eeles of Artemis, Ltd., London; Françoise Viatte and Rosaline Bacou of the Louvre and Laure Beaumont-Maillet and Maxime Préaud of the Bibliothèque Nationale, Paris; Marcia Fialetti and her assistants at the Pinacoteca Nazionale, Bologna; John T. Spike of Florence; Leonardo Selvaggio of the Biblioteca Nazionale Universitaria di Torino, Turin; Michela Perale of the Museo Correr, Venice; Silvia Chico and Marie-Thérèse Mandroux-França of the Academia Nacional de Belas-Artes, Lisbon. Elsewhere in the United States, Sue Welsh Reed at the Museum of Fine Arts, Boston; Kristin Spangenberg of the Cincinnati Art Museum; Thomas Rassieur, then of the Metropolitan Museum of Art, and Stephanie Wiles of the Pierpont Morgan Library, New York; Alvin L. Clark, Jr., of The Yale University Art Gallery; and David Acton, now of the Worcester Art Museum, have been most helpful. Finally, our research was facilitated here at Harvard by our Fogg colleague William W. Robinson and also by staff members of many of the university libraries, in particular Dennis Marnon and Eleanor Garvey of the Houghton Library, Frank Trout of the Map Collection, Carolyn R. Fawcett of Widener Library, and Thomas Batchelder, then of the Fine Arts Library.

As principal author of the catalogue I should like especially to thank my co-authors, whose contributions to the publication often extended far beyond their individual entries. In particular, David P. Becker advised and assisted on all phases of catalogue preparation; Shelley R. Langdale undertook research in Italy and Portugal on many entries besides those for which she is

9

the signed author; Anne Summerscale collated technical data and advised on several entries; Andrew C. Blume pursued bibliographic data; and he and Kristina Hartzer Nguyen proofread part of the Checklist. Alexander Nagel, a doctoral candidate in fine arts, also proofread a portion of the Checklist and assisted in other ways. Alvin L. Clark, Jr., Sue Welsh Reed, and William W. Robinson read many of the entries in their particular specialties, and Kristina Hartzer Nguyen and Anne Summerscale read the Introduction; I have benefited greatly from their suggestions. I should also like to thank Porter Mansfield for her assistance.

The publication of this catalogue by the Harvard University Art Museums was ably forwarded by Peter Walsh and Evelyn Rosenthal, and we are all deeply grateful for the care taken with its production by The Stinehour Press. All arrangements for the exhibition were capably accomplished by Jane Montgomery and her associates in the Museums' registrar's office, Anne Driesse and Ellen Young in the conservation department, and Danielle Hanrahan and her associates in the exhibitions department.

Finally, I should like to thank my colleagues at the three other museums who from the first have committed themselves and their institutions to this exhibition and publication: Andrew Stevens of the Elvehjem Museum, University of Wisconsin at Madison; Barbara Butts and James D. Burke of the Saint Louis Art Museum; and Stephen Goddard and Andrea S. Norris of the Spencer Museum, University of Kansas at Lawrence. Their support and that of the National Endowment of the Arts, a federal agency, as well as several Harvard museum funds—the Andrew W. Mellon Publication Fund, Henry P. McIlhenny Fund, Carola B. Terwilliger Bequest, and Edward A. Waters Publication Fund—have allowed us to realize our ambition to bring the Spencer Albums, their contents and significance, to a wider audience.

INTRODUCTION

Si celles cy [pages] vous ennuyont vous est le maistre de les laisser, mais pour moy de ne plus me refondre à quitter la plume . . . Je continueray, s'il vous plaist, à vous parler d'estampes. Pierre-Jean Mariette to Jean Mariette, Vienna, 20 October 1718[1]

PRINT COLLECTIONS and collecting have been, increasingly, the subject of scholarly attention in the last twenty years. This interest is but one part of a sharpening focus upon the magpie urge of mankind to collect. It may signal the maturity, even the lush over-ripening, of the institutionalization of this urge; many recent catalogues have been spawned by the centennials and other anniversaries of the founding of museums. A spate of exhibitions honoring collectors has been matched by a rush of publications analyzing the motives that lie beneath the personal and cultural valuation of art en masse.

Within this larger picture, prints have been both neglected and favored. As that art form traditionally least worthy in the hierarchies of art academies and trade, their presence in collections has typically been ignored or relegated to accessory status, along with drawings, in overviews of a period or nation's collecting habits. Print production alone, especially in the era of reproductive engraving when the subjects of the prints would indicate the tastes of their purchasers, has been of particular interest. On the other hand, the peculiar capacity of print collections themselves to expose the turn of mind toward classification to which all collectors seem prone has caused these collections, or their catalogues, to become the touchstone of analyses of whole eras and cultures.

Pressures of the market, of later cataloguing systems according to art historical conceptions, and of print preservation practices have, unfortunately, forced us to rely upon published catalogues and surviving manuscript indices and inventories, and even upon earlier authors' theoretical constructs for collections, rather than upon collections themselves. Only rarely has the collection, together with its original catalogue, survived to speak for itself. Even in the instance of the Spencer Albums, survival is only partial. What remains, however, is sufficient to suggest new perspectives on a moment of special importance in the history of print collecting—that moment when, in the eyes of their possessors, prints of the most prestigious sort ceased largely to be bear-

1. MLMS BS/b9/L37. I should like here to express my deepest appreciation to Rosaline Bacou, former curator of the Cabinet des Dessins, and Françoise Viatte, curator of the Département des Arts Graphiques, Musée du Louvre, for permitting me to study and quote from letters exchanged between Pierre-Jean Mariette and his father Jean Mariette, now in the collection of the Louvre. The full publication of these letters by Mlle Bacou, projected for 1993–1994, will add greatly to our knowledge of the Mariettes.

11

ers of information about other forms of knowledge and began explicitly to convey their own messages, about art and about the artists who had created them.[2]

The collection at issue here, which survives in nine volumes containing 3,588 late sixteenth- and seventeenth-century Italian, French, Dutch, and Flemish etchings and engravings (and one mezzotint), is of added importance in that it was assembled by the leading professional print connoisseurs of seventeenth- and eighteenth-century Europe, the Mariettes. Its particular character is distinctly different from other known surviving collections associated with this Parisian family who collected, made, published, and sold prints through four generations. It is the intention of this publication to explain that difference in terms of the circumstances of the print-collecting world of the early eighteenth century. While this Introduction will serve to set the scene, catalogue entries discuss aspects of the Mariettes' expertise, perspective, and accomplishment with more specific reference and in greater detail. The entries are integral to the argument.

Nowhere, however, does the Mariette name appear on the Spencer Albums or in their documented provenance. The only identifying mark on the volumes is a label pasted inside each front cover which says "Althorp." This is the seat of the Earls Spencer in Northamptonshire, England; and, indeed, it was the eighth earl, Edward John Spencer (b. 1924), who in 1983 sold the nine albums to Artemis, Inc., of London. They were resold in 1984 to Vermeer Associates, for which Melvin R. Seiden is a consultant;[3] and then in 1987 and 1988 they were acquired, partly by purchase and partly through the gift of Mr. Seiden, by the Harvard University Art Museums. They have been accessioned into the print collection of the Fogg Art Museum.

The sale of nine print albums by the eighth Earl Spencer was only the most recent in a centuries-long sequence whereby the Spencers have sold collections of prints, drawings, manuscripts, and books almost as rapidly as they accumulated them. Although it is the Spencer painting collection, which still largely remains at Althorp, that has defined the family's taste in the public eye, in fact it was those collections of works on paper, now virtually entirely dispersed, that were its more distinctive achievement. Fortunately, records survive in auction and library catalogues, enabling us today to estimate the original scope and context of the set of albums of which nine now form part of the Fogg print collection. Before defining that scope and context, however, it will be useful to describe the albums themselves, both to establish the role of the Mariettes in their formation and to limit as much as possible the parameters of their acquisition by the Spencer family, who collected fine art and books on a grand scale from the mid-seventeenth century through the early nineteenth.

2. See Timothy Riggs, "Michiel Hinloopen's Collection." *Print Quarterly* 4, no. 4 (1989):445–47, especially p. 446.

3. Mr. Seiden, a graduate of Harvard College and Harvard Law School, has been a longtime supporter of the University's art museums. With regard to the Spencer Albums he has written, "In terms of their value to the Fogg, I thought that they would add tremendous strength to an already outstanding collection and make the Museum a center for the study of early printed material. . . . I saw the albums at the Artemis Gallery in London and arranged to have them sent to the Fogg for examination. Both Bill Robinson and Henri Zerner were of great help in making the judgment to go forward with the acquisition. I'm most grateful to them" (letter of 29 August 1991).

The albums are very large. In vertical format with a cover size of almost 22½" by 16" (568 x 410 mm), their double-page spread is three feet wide. The largest contains 188 numbered folios plus title page, a table of contents, and end sheets, and weighs thirty pounds (13.5 kg); the others are only somewhat less bulky. They are bound in red morocco leather with gilt tooling and page edges and opulent marbled endpapers (see *fig. 1*).[4] In every aspect the style of the bindings exactly conforms to that typical of the end of the seventeenth century and the first half of the eighteenth century among the most prestigious Parisian bookbinders.[5] I refer even to such details as the shape of the spines; to quote a historian of French binding practices, "The rounded form of the spine of the volumes is always the result of the *endossure* [the particular technique of shaping the spine], a skill in which the French workers, it seems, were the experts."[6] Plate 4 of this history, which reproduces a binding of 1730, shows virtually the identical system of tooling on the spine as seen in two versions on the Spencer Albums; according to the accompanying text, "Toward 1740, the central floral ornament of each panel between the cords of the spine was replaced by a single flower, with stem and leaves...."[7] This development has not yet occurred on the Spencer Album bindings.

Also reproduced in this history of French bookbinding are two other volumes which are closely comparable to the Spencer Albums. These were bound by Luc-Antoine Boyet, who was named *relieur du roi*—binder to Louis XIV—in 1698.[8] His work as described by both this and another authority was noted for the great solidity of the book's structure:

> The bindings attributed to him are very plainly tooled, the ornamentation generally consisting only of a rectangular fillet of gold lines, with some slight decoration at the angles, but they are distinguished by their solidity and the finish and excellence of the forwarding.[9]

It should be noted that the tooling of the Spencer Albums' covers is exactly as described above,

4. There are two schemes of tooling on the bindings; see fig. 1 and the Description of the Albums. The four albums containing mixed assortments of prints (s1, s2, s5, s6) and the two albums of Tempesta prints (s8, s9) carry one design, and the two albums of Callot prints (s3, s4) and the one of della Bella prints (s7) carry the other. All of the albums have silk markers bound in; albums s1, s3, s4, s5, and s6 have pale blue ribbons, and albums s2, s7, s8, and s9 have dark blue ones.

5. See Devauchelle 1959–1961, vol. 2, pp. 21–24. His descriptions were confirmed by a survey of late seventeenth- and early eighteenth-century French bindings in the collection of The Houghton Library, Harvard University, kindly facilitated by Eleanor Garvey. Mirjam

Foot of the British Library has tentatively concurred with this attribution on the basis of photographs of the Spencer Albums' bindings (letter of 5 December 1989).

6. Devauchelle 1959–1961, vol. 2, p. 17: "La forme arrondie du dos des volumes était toujours le résultat de l' 'endossure', tour de main dont les ouvriers français, paraît-il, avaient la spécialité."

7. Devauchelle 1959–1961, vol. 2, p. 24: "Vers 1740, le fleuron central de chaque entre-nerfs fut remplacé par une fleur, avec tige et feuilles ..."

8. Devauchelle 1959–1961, vol. 1, pl. 84, 87; Boyet is discussed in vol. 2, pp. 146, 148, where he is described as having died in 1733.

9. Fletcher 1895, p. 53.

Fig. 1. Spencer Albums 4 (Callot, vol. 2) and 6 (Italian), bindings. The photograph shows the two systems of spine decoration found among the nine albums and the tooling of the covers, which is the same on all nine. It also shows one of the paper labels which survive, either intact or as a residue, on all of the albums, and which probably indicate an eighteenth-century shelving system. (Photograph by Michael Nedzweski)

and that the particular system of sewing lends special solidity to the structure of the volumes and is a mark of great expense.[10]

Apart from the evident close resemblance of Boyet's work to the Spencer Albums, he is of particular interest because his only son, Etienne, admitted as a master by the Parisian bookbinder's guild in 1709, left France in 1713 to enter the service of Prince Eugene of Savoy in Vienna, for whom he would bind 335 folio volumes of prints largely purchased from the Mariettes. The bindings (and the prince's collection) survive to this day in the Albertina, and are close in size, structure, format, style, and materials to those of the Spencer Albums.[11]

A feature common to both sets of albums is the inclusion within the original binding of elaborate title pages and tables of contents written in an elegant French whose style and orthography identify it as early eighteenth century (see *fig. 2, 3*).[12] In the case of the Spencer Albums, the tables of contents exactly specify the actual contents of the albums, or at least all the spaces on all the pages on which prints are now or once were mounted. A few prints have been removed (see below and also Cat. 35), but none has been added. Indeed, with the possible exception of Album 7, devoted to the works of Stefano della Bella, the tables of contents are so closely written that little room was left for additions, although the albums themselves contain frequent blank leaves (see below).[13] In any case, it appears that the nine albums remain essentially as they were created.

It should be noted that the tables of contents refer to page numbers which were applied to the folios prior to the albums' being bound. In several instances the trimming of the page blocks of the albums sheared off the upper portion of these numbers, and they were reinscribed below in another hand.[14] This accident provides objective proof of the deduction that the prints were selected, arranged, and mounted prior to binding. It would have been physically impossible to

10. I am grateful here and throughout in all matters concerning the bindings for the advice of Dennis Marnon.

11. See James et al. 1991, fig. 91a–b. The tooling of the boards is more elaborate than that of the Spencer Albums, which do not have armorial bearings, but the tooling on the spine is somewhat simpler. Boyet fils returned to Paris only on the death of the prince in 1736. See Devauchelle 1959–1961, vol. 2, p. 148; Braubach 1965, p. 104. See also below, note 71, for reference to another album produced by Jean Mariette, which is in a binding with very similar tooling patterns to those of the Spencer Albums, although it is much smaller and in mottled brown calf. This album postdates 1702 and probably antedates Jean's sale of his stock of topographical engraved plates in 1733.

12. The exception to this rule is Album 5, of Dutch and Flemish prints, which contains no title page or table of contents. There are no page stubs to indicate that these have been removed, and the folios were not originally numbered. In every other aspect the materials and tech-

nique of the volume's construction are the same as the other eight volumes. Comparable title pages and tables of contents were included in albums made for Prince Eugene and João V of Portugal; see Mandroux-França 1986, fig. 4, for reproductions of the bilingual Portuguese title pages. It should be noted that any of the various early eighteenth-century British peers who might have been the patron of the Spencer Albums would have been able to read their French tables of contents.

13. In the case of the single album surviving from the collection of the king of Portugal, many blank leaves are included at the end of the folios on which prints are mounted, and there are also blank pages left after the table of contents, as if additions were anticipated. For this and subsequent technical information on this album, I am grateful to Shelley Langdale for her close examination of the album in Lisbon, which was facilitated by the kind offices of Silvia Chico and Marie-Thérèse Mandroux-França.

14. My thanks to Arthur Vershbow, who first pointed out an instance of this on folio 122 of Album 7.

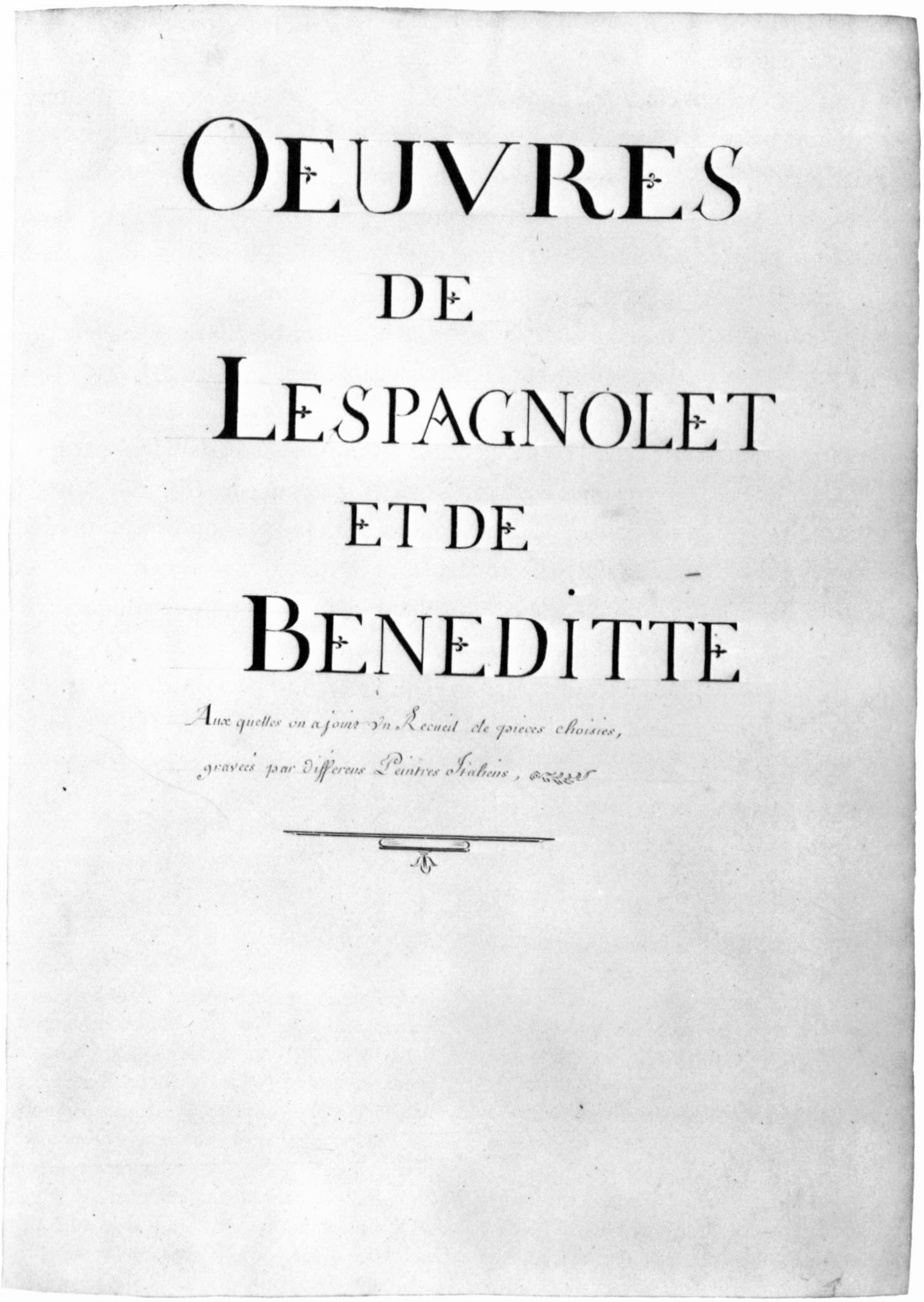

OEUVRES
DE
LESPAGNOLET
ET DE
BENEDITTE

Aux quelles on a joint Un Recueil de pieces choisies,
gravées par Differens Peintres Italiens,

Fig. 2. Spencer Album 6, the title page. (Photograph by Michael Nedzweski)

16

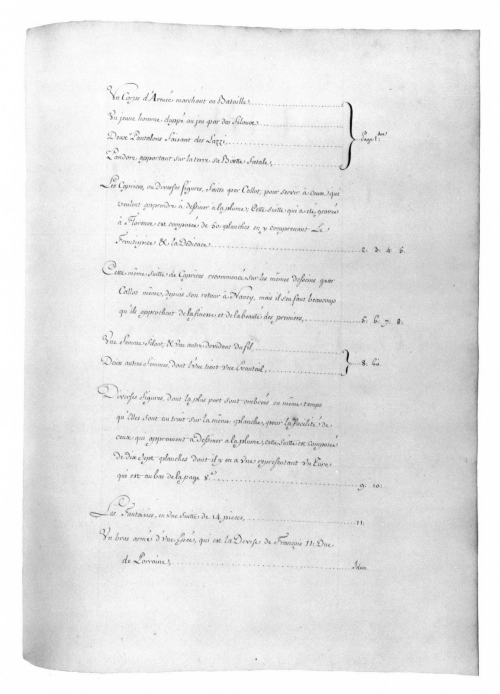

Fig. 3. Spencer Album 4 (Callot, vol. 2), the first page of the table of contents. In this instance, the suffix "bis" after folio 8 indicates prints added to complete a page partially filled with prints by Callot which conclude a set that continues from previous pages. Other instances of "bis" in the albums usually designate pages additional to the consecutive pagination, but in every instance the additions are integral to the albums and are included in the tables of contents. (Photograph by Michael Nedzweski)

17

align and paste the prints into the albums once the latter had been constructed, especially in the case of larger sheets which extend deep into the gutters of the volumes.

All of the pages of the Spencer Albums are composed of two French manufacturers' versions of *colombier*, or dovecote, paper (*fig. 4, 5*).[15] The name refers to the paper's watermarks, and was stipulated by French law for paper of a certain size and weight.[16] The paper manufacturers' monograms are found on the folios' countermarks. One, P G separated by a heart, is that of Gourbeyre;[17] the other, T D separated by a well-head (*puits*), is that of Dupuy.[18] Standard dictionaries of watermarks date them to the later seventeenth century. The same countermarks are found in a few of Prince Eugene's albums, notably one of Rosa and Ribera etchings (vol. HB 42), where Gourbeyre paper of chaplet size (slightly smaller and much lighter than dovecote) is used throughout. The same countermarks are also found among those in the single surviving Mariette album from the collection of the king of Portugal, where grand-eagle paper (slightly larger than dovecote) is used. They are also commonly found on French maps of the largest sizes which were published in the late seventeenth and early eighteenth centuries.[19]

In four of the Spencer Albums, Dupuy paper is used throughout.[20] In the other five albums, the alternating use of the two papers is of significance, given the single characteristic that differentiates them: the paper made by Gourbeyre is thinner than that made by Dupuy, a difference which averages about 20 percent when the thickness of the sheets is measured with a micrometer and which is distinctly palpable upon leafing through the albums. Practically without exception, Gourbeyre is used for the blank sheets separating groups of prints within each album and for title pages and the tables of contents, and Dupuy is used for the print-mounting sheets.[21] Pre-

15. One exception must be cited: in Album 8 (the second volume of prints by Antonio Tempesta), folio 14 bears a chaplet watermark. The sheet is much lighter in weight than the dovecote papers, and it atypically retains its deckle fore-edge. Folio 14 holds a single print, the last of a series of twenty-four Old Testament battles, which is listed in ordinary style in the table of contents and is definitely not a later addition.

16. Joseph-Jérome Le François de LaLande, *Art de Faire le Papier* (Paris:, n.p., [1776?]), pp. 525–26, where an "Arrêt du conseil d'état du roi en interprétation de l'arrêt du 27 janvier 1739" is quoted in full. The paper is more fully titled grand-dovecote or imperial, and its size is, of course, double the size of the Spencer Albums as one sheet makes up a double-page spread. James et al. 1991, p. 49, provides a useful table with the names, sizes, and weights of all sizes of paper as regulated by the French in the mid-eighteenth century.

17. Heawood 1321, grand-eagle paper from a book dated 1685.

18. Heawood 1322 and Churchill 445, grand-eagle paper, on undated architectural engravings by Guérard.

19. Such as in the *Atlas françois* published in Paris by Alexius Hubertus Jaillot in 1695, maps of France and of the diocese of Narbonne published by Guillaume de l'Isle in 1703 and 1704, and the maps *Direction du Mans* and *Directions des Traittes de Laval* published by I. B. Nolin in 1727. Some of the maps in the 1695 atlas are dated 1696. The marks on these papers are chaplet and grand-Jesus (IHS), indicating smaller sizes than dovecote. I am very grateful to Frank Trout, curator of the Map Collection, Harvard College Library, for his willing assistance in my examination of the collection's many large seventeenth- and eighteenth-century French maps.

20. Albums s7 devoted to della Bella, s3 and s4 devoted to Callot, and s9, the second one devoted to Tempesta. It should be noted that the two paper-use systems do not coincide with the two tooling systems; see note 4.

21. One of the most significant exceptions is the print by Monogrammist GpP (Cat. 30), which is mounted at the very top of a Gourbeyre page immediately preceding blank folios also with a Gourbeyre mark (as would be expected). The atypically uncentered mounting suggests that this very rare print was added as an afterthought, but it is included in the table of contents.

sumably, the heavier paper, but of the same dovecote size, was desired for the mounting sheets in order to compensate for any distortion induced over time by the superimposed prints. Not incidentally, an identical distinction was observed in the selection of papers for an album of prints in Prince Eugene's collection now in the Albertina (vol. HB 103), where a chaplet paper was used. Again, Dupuy was selected for mounting pages and Gourbeyre for blank pages and the table of contents.

This technical detail is typical of the extreme attention to the mountings and bindings as working mechanisms in the Spencer Albums. After almost three hundred years, the prints and pages remain virtually undistorted, and the albums open and close perfectly. The perfection of the preservation of individual impressions is a measure of our loss in so many old-master prints that were removed from the sheltering pages of albums, the typical storage format of print collections until the nineteenth century, and remounted, often with bathings and pressings along the way. It must be admitted, however, that very few other albums of any period provided the quality of mounting papers and techniques, the safe protection of ample margins, and the sheltered circumstances which the Spencer prints still enjoy.[22]

A passage from a manuscript dictionary of artists which was written by Pierre-Jean Mariette on the basis of generations of expertise indicates the Mariette family's enormous appreciation for old-master prints in superb condition. In this case Pierre-Jean is referring to a Dürer collection assembled by Ortelius in the sixteenth century and later owned by Burgomeister Willem Six, which had been purchased by his father Jean Mariette from the Six sale. The prints had been protected in an album. The passage also gives the best possible sense of the commitment to prints of Jean and Pierre-Jean Mariette, father and son, which reached far beyond merely commercial interests.

> Many [Dürer] prints have passed through my hands, . . . but it is only by pure chance that they are of good quality. It was the same with my father, who was even crazier about them than I, and I never saw him happier than when he made the acquisition of a beautiful collection of these prints, which today forms the basis of my holdings, and which I rank among the rarest that I have. Every time I look through them, I feel myself taken by a new pleasure, which is only matched by my surprise to find brought together so large a num-

22. Not every print in the album is in superb condition, and the exceptions are interesting in themselves. Many among the long run of landscape etchings by Anthonie Waterloo are discolored in a distinctive blotchy pattern so severe that it has discolored the blank facing pages against which the prints close (and which are otherwise undiscolored throughout the albums). The identical kind of discoloration is seen in Waterloo impressions in the Mariette albums assembled for Prince Eugene of Savoy, as if the firm had recourse to a particular edition that was printed on unsound paper or paper that had been treated in some way to predispose it to discoloration. Given the otherwise impeccable standards of both the Spencer Albums and those of the prince, it is inconceivable that this discoloration would have been evident in the early eighteenth century. Among the Spencer della Bella prints, there are also a few where the paper has become very friable, to the point of breaking down; it would have been impossible to mount them in this condition and so they too must have deteriorated over time from some inherent vice. For further discussion of damaged prints in the albums, see Cat. 2 and Cat. 31, n. 11.

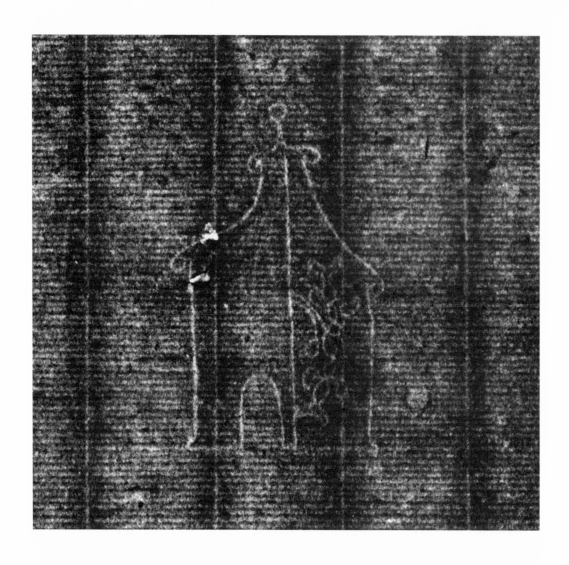

Fig. 4. Mark and countermark of Gourbeyre dovecote paper, from Spencer Album 6.
(ß-radiograph, actual size, by Anne Driesse)

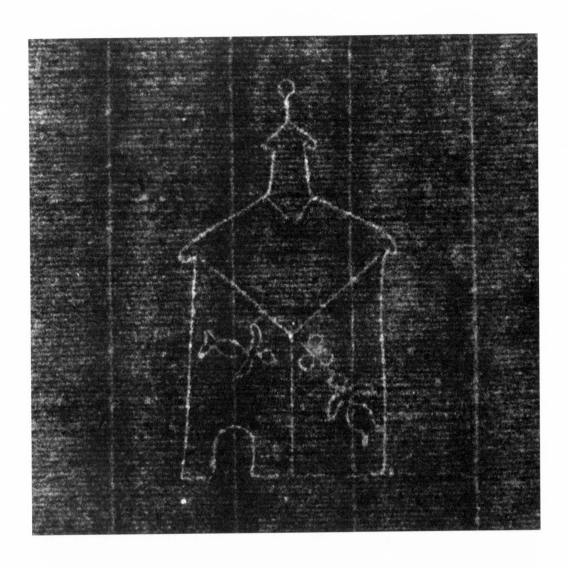

Fig. 5. Mark and countermark of Dupuys dovecote paper, from Spencer Album 6.
(ß-radiograph, actual size, by Anne Driesse)

21

ber of such early impressions, and to see them in such perfect condition. All of them retain their first freshness. . . .[23]

⁂

Even more than the evidence of the bindings, close attention to the watermarks provides additional proof of the Mariettes' role in the albums' formation.

There are a number of very large prints in the collection. Many were drum-mounted into the album's usual mounting paper and backed at their centerfolds by a guard, whose stub was sewn in. Two large prints had strip margins applied to make up the album's page size.[24] It is interesting to note that both of these are edged with identical paper, with a chaplet and not a dovecote watermark, and that both bear the signature and dating (1660, 1668, 1670) of Pierre Mariette II, as if strip margining, rather than drum-mounting, was the preferred method of the later seventeenth-century Mariette shop.

But from the perspective of the Mariettes' production of the Spencer Albums, by far the most interesting solution to the problem of bringing large prints "up to size" is seen on nine impressions of plates by two seventeenth-century French etchers, Sébastien Bourdon's seven *Acts of Mercy* (s5.59–65) and Michel-Ange Corneille's *Flight into Egypt* (s5.98) and *Christ and the Virgin Appearing to Saint Francis* (s5.101).[25] These impressions, exceptionally among all of the prints in the albums, have wide margins and were bound into the album without auxiliary mounting papers (although the Bourdons, which are double-page spreads, were of course guarded so that the centers of their compositions would not disappear into the sewing). Among all of the thousands of prints in the albums, only these are printed on the identical papers that comprise the albums—the Bourdons on dovecote sheets with Dupuy's mark and the Corneilles on dovecote sheets with Gourbeyre's mark. The Bourdon plates are so large that their printed surfaces fold onto themselves and ink transfer is not discernible, but the Corneille plates face onto the blank

23. Mariette 1851–1860, vol. 2, p. 156: "Il m'est passé bien des estampes par les mains, . . . mais c'étoit un pur hasard si elles se trouvoient de bonne qualité. Il en est arrivé de même à mon père, qui en a manié encore plus que moi, et jamais je ne le vis plus content que lorsqu'il eût fait l'acquisition d'un beau receuil de ces estampes, qui fait aujourd'hui le fond de celui que je possède, et que je mets au rang de ce que j'ai de plus rare. Toutes les fois que je le parcours, je me sens pénétré d'un plaisir nouveau, qu'égale ma suprise de trouver rassemblées un si grand nombre de pièces d'une date si ancienne, et de les voir d'une condition si parfaite. Toutes ont leur première fraîcheur. . . . "

The manuscript is now in the collection of the Cabinet des Estampes of the Bibliothèque Nationale, Paris. A large part has been published, and in this case the quotation is taken from that publication. This catalogue will also quote extensively from the manuscript itself, especially from passages which have not been published, and also where Mariette's editing is of interest.

24. Jan de Bisschop, *Joseph Distributing Grain in Egypt* (s5.42); Giovanni Battista Vanni, *Christ at the Wedding of Cana* (s6.8). Within the albums, the prints have been assigned accession numbers according to folio and placement on the page reading from left to right and top to bottom. Thus s5.42 is the forty-fifth page of Album 5. When there is only one print per page it is not designated (in this case) s5.42.1.

25. See the previous note describing the accessioning system.

GENEALOGIES OF THE MARIETTE–LANGLOIS AND SPENCER–CHURCHILL FAMILIES

MARIETTE AND LANGLOIS FAMILIES

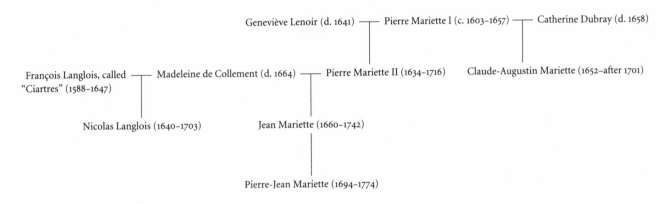

Geneviève Lenoir (d. 1641) —— Pierre Mariette I (c. 1603–1657) —— Catherine Dubray (d. 1658)

François Langlois, called —— Madeleine de Collement (d. 1664) —— Pierre Mariette II (1634–1716)   Claude-Augustin Mariette (1652–after 1701)
"Ciartres" (1588–1647)

Nicolas Langlois (1640–1703)   Jean Mariette (1660–1742)

Pierre-Jean Mariette (1694–1774)

NOTE: Only persons associated with the contents and the early history of the Spencer Albums are included in these family trees.

SPENCER AND CHURCHILL FAMILIES

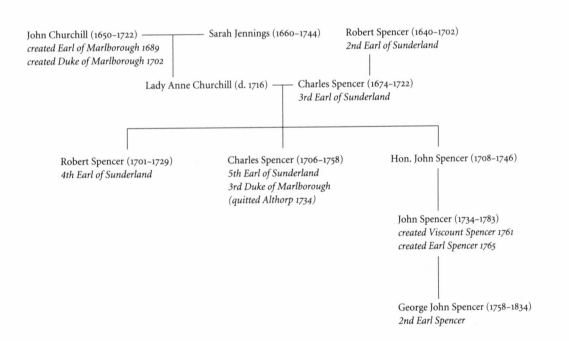

John Churchill (1650–1722) —— Sarah Jennings (1660–1744)   Robert Spencer (1640–1702)
created Earl of Marlborough 1689   *2nd Earl of Sunderland*
created Duke of Marlborough 1702

Lady Anne Churchill (d. 1716) —— Charles Spencer (1674–1722)
                                 3rd Earl of Sunderland

Robert Spencer (1701–1729)   Charles Spencer (1706–1758)   Hon. John Spencer (1708–1746)
4th Earl of Sunderland   *5th Earl of Sunderland*
                                  3rd Duke of Marlborough
                                  (quitted Althorp 1734)

John Spencer (1734–1783)
created Viscount Spencer 1761
created Earl Spencer 1765

George John Spencer (1758–1834)
2nd Earl Spencer

reverse of pages. There is a significant amount of black printing ink offset onto these facing sheets, as if the impressions were very fresh when the volumes were bound. The publisher's address on each plate proves that these nine impressions were printed by the Mariettes.[26] The implication is obvious: when the albums were being compiled, these impressions were struck for inclusion in them.

Although the Mariettes' names do not appear *on* the albums, they are frequently encountered, as indicated above, *within* the albums. The Mariettes published a number of the impressions, especially of French prints but also of etchings by Jan Both, which is perhaps to be expected considering the size of their business in the late seventeenth and early eighteenth centuries. The family firm often purchased plates that had already been issued by the artist or by another publisher; the Mariette-printed impressions in the Spencer Albums are of later states. Generally speaking, the plates remained in good condition and were impeccably printed.

Conforming to the consistently high quality of impressions throughout the albums, it is notable that there are many cases of early states of prints that were later republished by the Mariettes. For example, the horizontal plate of Testa's *Garden of Love*, included in Album 2 in its first state, acquired the inscription "P Mariette excud" in its second state. Even more interesting, the series by della Bella of *New Inventions for Cartouches* is included in its first state as published by the widow of François Langlois prior to her marriage to Pierre Mariette II and his ensuing acquisition of the plates, at which time the inscription was changed to "Chez Pierre Mariette le fils . . ." (see Cat. 57).[27]

Perhaps more important, the preparation of this exhibition has made it evident that the stock of prints collected by Pierre Mariette II was liberally drawn upon when the albums were compiled. Even prior to the point when prints selected for exhibition were removed from the albums, it was recognized that several bore the characteristic signature and dating of Pierre II.[28] Some were inscribed on their front surfaces, and others, among those large prints in the albums whose versos are visible, were easily seen to have been inscribed on their backs. Among the smaller prints, which are tipped down to the mounting sheets by their corners and at points along their edges, no inscriptions on the reverse could be discerned because of the thickness of the albums' pages. When the prints selected for exhibition were removed, however, eleven were

26. Beginning with the estate of Pierre I, Mariette inventories list presses, so there is no doubt that the firm actually printed the plates that they published. The Bourdon prints, which were probably created c. 1661–1664 (see Fowle 1970, vol. 1, p. 51) bear the publisher's inscription "Pierre Mariette rue S. Jacques à l'esperance." This address was used after 1637 by Pierre Mariette I when he acquired the firm at this address from Jean Messager, and by his successors Pierre II, Jean, and Pierre-Jean Mariette. The Corneille prints bear the publisher's inscription "chez Mariette rue S. Jacques aux colonnes d'Hercules." This address was used by 1657,

after the marriage of Pierre II to the widow of François Langlois and his acquisition of the capital goods of the latter's firm at this address (Mandroux-França 1986, p. 54, n. 12). The inscriptions were not necessarily changed with the passing of the Mariette generations. The only other impression of these prints on Dupuy or Gourbeyre paper that I have located is one of Corneille's *Flight into Egypt* in the Albertina, which bears a Dupuy dovecote watermark.

27. See also DE.V.-M., vol. 1, p. 156.

28. See Lugt 1788–1790.

found to be inscribed by Pierre II on their reverse; this number includes two that were already known to have his signature on the front, with different dates (Cat. 8, 10). Presumably the signatures and differing dates signal the prints coming twice into his hands as a print dealer rather than as a private collector, and their inclusion at much later dates into the Spencer Albums simply fulfilled their destiny as dealer's stock.

A Mariette signature has been construed by posterity as a guarantee of quality, representing personal connoisseurship of the highest order. Conforming to this conception, it must be admitted that the works selected for exhibition were chosen for their importance as prints or the beauty of their impressions, with rarity or representativeness of the Spencer Albums only a secondary consideration. Thus it was not surprising that among seventy-odd old-master prints a number turned out to have been inscribed in his hand. Yet surely the proportion is too great to be coincidental, especially when one considers the very probable presence of more signatures on the reverse of all the prints which remain in the albums. In fact the number of prints with Mariette inscriptions in the Fogg's nine Spencer Albums is known to have once been larger by two: a Ribera and an Agostino Carracci, sold by the sixth Earl Spencer in 1919 along with many other prints also bearing Pierre II's signature.[29]

All of the prints that were discovered to have inscriptions on their reverse are Italian, as defined either by the birthplace of their artists or the place of their creation. Letters exchanged between Pierre-Jean Mariette and his father Jean, when the former was in Vienna from late in 1717 until early in 1719 to complete the cataloguing of the collection of prints largely purchased by Prince Eugene of Savoy from Jean Mariette, inform us that the prince had also just acquired a group of Italian prints from a Bolognese source.[30] Further, Prince Eugene agreed to turn over to the Mariettes duplicates generated by this additional purchase. From the letters and from many other sources, it is evident that the Mariettes endeavored through the generations to accumulate the best possible collection of prints. This might be considered a personal collection, but it is probably better construed as a reference library, to be consulted for pleasure and, more important, for information essential to the Mariettes' trade as print dealers in the era before the publication of authoritative oeuvre catalogues. One small fragment of this reference library survives —an album of the prints of Parmigianino and his school sold in 1775 after Pierre-Jean's death and now in the Metropolitan Museum of Art, New York (see Cat. 8). Pierre II had died in 1716, and his prints—whether considered as a personal collection or as dealer's stock—were inherited by his son Jean; thus any new acquisitions of fine and rare Italian impressions that came into the Mari-

29. Christie 1919 no. 34, 151. Prints sold in 1919 were stamped with the mark Lugt 1532. Lugt also registered three other Spencer marks, 1530, 1531, and 2341a. This last mark is found on old-master prints from Althorp purchased in 1983 by Artemis, Ltd., apart from the nine Spencer Albums, as evidenced by impressions of two Rosa etchings, *The Fall of the Giants* and *The Crucifixion of Polycrates*, now in the collection of the National Gallery of Art, Washington, and impressions of prints by Villamena, *The Brawl*, Salimbeni, *Baptism of Christ*, and Vignon, *Saint John the Baptist*, in the Museum of Fine Arts, Boston. The Villamena print bears a Mariette signature dated 1667. None of the prints in the Spencer Albums bears any of the Spencer stamps.

30. See Cat. 2, n. 4–6.

ettes' possession c. 1720 could produce disposable duplicates from among the prints now in Jean's hands.

There is no reason to suppose that the Spencer Albums predate those of Prince Eugene (or, for that matter, the 150 albums of French prints compiled by the Mariettes for João V of Portugal through the years c. 1721–1728).[31] Indeed, an attribution of a print to "Le Golbo" in the table of contents of Spencer Album 1, that is, to Pietro Paolo Bonzi, "Il Gobbo de' Carracci," suggests that the Spencer Albums postdate Prince Eugene's collection, for it was apparently among the Mariette notes in Vienna that Adam Bartsch found an attribution of this print to Cavedone.[32] It is the Bonzi and not the Cavedone attribution which is now accepted for the print, and presumably the revised attribution represented by the Spencer Album entry postdates that in Prince Eugene's collection.

One might, of course, adduce the attribution to Bonzi coupled with the Viennese Mariette note on Cavedone as proof that the Spencer Albums were *not* compiled by the Mariettes. Yet the physical evidence implicating their authorship is overwhelming, and it is more reasonable to ascribe the attribution to "Le Golbo" as testimony to continuously improving connoisseurship. It is but a single instance of the astounding accuracy by modern scholarly standards of the Spencer Albums' tables of contents as a whole. More than physical evidence, this thoroughgoing expertise identifies the Mariettes, father and son, as the compilers of the albums, which by their nature had to have been assembled at one time under a single authority. No other such universal connoisseurs are known among the print collectors, publishers, and dealers of early eighteenth-century France.

※

The evidence of the bindings, watermarks, and inscriptions, plus the lack in the Spencer Albums of any prints themselves which, by authorship or even date of printing as indicated by publishers' addresses, could postdate c. 1740, generates a period of about thirty years—c. 1710–c. 1740—during which these albums must have been produced. Certainly they could not antedate 1707, the date inscribed by Pierre Mariette II on at least three of the prints; and it is, as indicated above,

31. One album, the second of two of the prints of Jean Berain, survives in the library of the Academia Nacional de Belas-Artes, Lisbon. The print collection of João V, with particular reference to the French albums compiled by the Mariettes, has been the ongoing study of Marie-Thérèse Mandroux-França. See especially Mandroux-França 1986, p. 50. This article, p. 54, n. 15, gives a fascinating summary of the costs of production of such albums as represented in surviving invoices. The albums were bound not by Boyet but by Antoine-Michel Padeloup, another important Parisian binder who described himself in 1733 as "Relieur ordinaire du Roy de Portugal"

(Fletcher 1895, p. 67). The cover of the surviving album is reproduced in Mandroux-França 1986, fig. 3; it is much more elaborately tooled than the Spencer Albums. A complete description and discussion of the print collection of João V will be published by Mme Mandroux-França in 1993; I am most grateful to her for sharing the fruits of her research preliminary to this publication.

32. B.XVIII.331–2, in reference to *Madonna and Child with Saints Anthony and Catherine* (TIB40.249.2). See Cat. 30.

26

probable that the albums postdate 1720. At this time Jean Mariette was head of the family firm. It was to Jean that the letters and manuscripts of his son Pierre-Jean and every other surviving document accord the palm as the preeminent print connoisseur of his day.

Pierre-Jean Mariette is today more renowned than his father in the larger world of art historians, curators, and collectors, because of his later associations with important drawing cabinets (including his own), print production enterprises, and a much more active mid-eighteenth-century art market throughout Europe. These associations have led even so sophisticated a scholar as Francis Haskell to ascribe to the son, in his youthful years in Vienna working for Prince Eugene, an expertise in prints that Pierre-Jean would never have claimed for himself.[33] Published analyses of surviving manuscripts in the Bibliothèque Nationale, Paris, and the Biblioteca Nazionale Universitaria, Turin,[34] that relate to the prince's collection identify Jean as their principal author (though their scribe was Pierre-Jean); and the letters between Mariette *père et fils* confirm this.

In his letters from Vienna, Pierre-Jean constantly referred to Jean's manuscript notes on Prince Eugene's collection as his guide. When new problems in cataloguing were presented, as, for instance, by the newly arrived Italian collection, he sought his father's advice, all the while presenting as knowledgeable a front as possible to his princely patron. Nothing is more amusing, and touching, than Pierre-Jean's response to his father's offer to send to Vienna his, Jean's, catalogue of the oeuvre of Raphael, to clarify some issues with regard to sixteenth-century reproductive prints that perplexed Pierre-Jean:

> Do you know how you have exposed me, in a flash have demolished all my little fortune, for the Prince is clearly going to recognize the difference between the good and the mediocre, that is, between the work of the father and of the son. . . .[35]

And equally touching is the evidence in the letters of the son's growing expertise in print connoisseurship and his pleasure in communicating to his father some advance he has been able to make on the latter's cataloguing.[36]

All of the letters from Vienna concern prints and not drawings. Only after he left Vienna for Italy did Pierre-Jean show the beginnings of that interest in drawings which would eventually es-

33. Haskell 1988, p. 20.

34. Mandroux-França 1986, p. 54, n. 26; Paris 1967, pp. 173–74, where Gérald Burdon is the author of the essay and catalogue entry on the manuscript in the Biblioteca Nazionale Universitaria, Turin (Ms L² I 2).

35. MLMS BS/b9/L17 (Vienna, 27 February 1718): "Scavez vous à quoy vous m'avez exposé, en un moment vous avez detruit tout l'edifices de ma petite fortune, car le Prince est aller clairvoyant pres s'appercevoir de la difference qu'il y a entre le bien & le mediocre, je veux dire entre le travail du Pere & du fils . . ." Also, in another let-

ter, Pierre-Jean alludes to his late grandfather, finding a likeness in an elderly Venetian collector: ". . . la mesme humeur & le choix & la connoissance des Estampes, celuy cy ne veut asolument que ce qui est de plus beau & de plus rare" (MLMS BS/b9/L42, Venice, 30 December 1718).

36. See, for example, MLMS BS/b9/L34 (Vienna, 31 August 1718), MLMS BS/b9/L35 (Vienna, 16 September 1718), and MLMS BS/b9/L37 (Vienna, 28 October 1718), which concern the works of the Carracci and their school.

tablish his larger reputation,[37] and even there, as he made the acquaintance of Italian collectors and librarians, he was primarily concerned for the family's principal occupation—the buying and selling of prints. In Bologna he found that all the prints had been "destroyed by the painters or carried off by foreigners,"[38] and in Rome he found intense competition from English buyers, already a presence in Paris, "who buy everything here—even all the bad things—with gold pounds."[39] Alert to the success of the Rossi print publishing firm, his father's Roman competitor whose successive catalogues, published since 1677, had shaped collections as far away as England,[40] he urged the production of a Mariette catalogue: "It is essential to make a catalogue of your stock like that one made by Rossi, I see now more than ever the necessity, everyone in Italy has asked me for it. . . ."[41]

Probably Jean Mariette had himself intended to travel to Vienna to complete the cataloguing of what must have been the Mariettes' most important print sale in their history, but in 1716 the death of Pierre II, the head of the family firm, required that Jean remain in Paris as its new head. And so the next year, with hope and some trepidation, he had sent his twenty-two-year-old son across Europe as his representative.[42] In 1720 or 1721 that son returned, mature and alert to his commercial responsibilities; soon afterward the firm received from João V of Portugal almost as important a commission as the one they had earlier successfully carried through for Prince Eugene (who would remain their loyal customer at least into the mid-1720s[43]). We know from a letter from an English dealer requesting advice about prints from father and son sometime after

37. Jean cautions his son to be concerned for quality and not quantity of drawing acquisitions and to take special care to obtain the best advice (MLMS BS/b10/L21, Paris, 20 February 1719).

38. MLMS BS/b9/L44 (Bologna, 2 February 1719): ". . . tout les estampes de ce pays ont eté en detruittes par les Peintres ou enlevées par les etrangers."

39. MLMS BS/b9/L46 (Rome, 10 March 1719): ". . . les Anglois qui sont si tracaffiers chez nous, achettent icy tous au poids de l'or & toutes mauvaises choses. . . " The letters and manuscripts of Pierre-Jean Mariette betray a lifelong disdain for the English as connoisseurs and a competitive anxiety about their lavish spending on art. Late in life he undertook to learn the language in order to read the works of Horace Walpole, which he decided had not been worth the effort.

40. See Waals 1984, pp. 239–41, for a perspicacious analysis of how the practicalities of collecting, in this case the assimilation of prints from the Rossi 1699 catalogue into the collection of Samuel Pepys, could inflect collection arrangement systems, which scholars usually tend to interpret only as theoretical constructs.

41. MLMS BS/b9/L46 (Rome, 10 March 1719): ". . . j'entends par la qu'il faudroit faire necessairement un

catalogue de vostre fonds comme la fait Rossi, j'en vois à present plus que jamais la necessité, mille gens en Italie me l'ont demande . . ." Earlier in Vienna Pierre-Jean had served as the intermediary between his father and the Austrian general Count von Wackerbarth, to execute a subscription from the latter to publishing ventures. For a time it seemed as though the general would defraud the Mariettes, and Pierre-Jean agonized over his having been duped and having put his father at financial risk: "La supercherie que Mr. de Wackerbaart m'a faitte pour vous obliger en quelque facon, a luy procurer un sous-scription du livre du Pere Montfaucon, ainsy je ne vous le repeteray point" (MLMS BS/b9/L35, Vienna, 16 September 1718). The matter was resolved within two months (see MLMS BS/b9/L38, Vienna 25 November 1718), and no doubt the son learned an important commercial lesson.

42. Jean's letter to Pierre-Jean of 6 January 1718 is a moving specimen of the sort of advice any father would write to a son away from home for the first time. In this case, of course, the son's situation was complicated by the fact that he was the father's "customer's man" to one of the most powerful princes in Europe (MLMS BS/b10/L9).

43. Henderson 1964, p. 264.

1727 that they were considered very much a team and the court of last resort in this field of expertise.[44] Thus the picture we have established of the two Mariettes working together as the premier print dealers of Europe in the period from c. 1720 through c. 1740 sustains our attribution of the Spencer Albums to them both, with Jean taking the lead in their production if the albums' date falls at the earlier limit and Pierre-Jean assuming more responsibility if it is later. Jean sold the bulk of his stocks as a print publisher in 1733–1734; he would die in 1742 at the advanced age of eighty-two.[45]

On the chance that the albums are still earlier—after 1707 but prior to 1720—one must make mention here of the intimate friendship between Prince Eugene of Savoy and John Churchill, duke of Marlborough. The two were Europe's first generals, whose combined armies defeated those of Louis XIV in a series of epochal battles at the beginning of the eighteenth century. "I do not only estime but I really love that prince," exclaimed the duke to his duchess Sarah in 1706.[46] The duke and prince were also art-collecting companions, with the prince depending upon the duke's contacts among English picture dealers.[47] On his visit to London in 1712, the prince was entertained by Marlborough's son-in-law Charles, third earl of Sunderland, who had been the British envoy to Vienna in 1705 and who was a great book collector. His surname was Spencer and his sons would inherit the titles and property of the duke and duchess of Marlborough.

Surely Prince Eugene and his closest associates in war and diplomacy would in their many visits together have relaxed in discussion of their collections and acquisitions, and surely the project of Prince Eugene to acquire tens of thousands of prints from the Mariettes originated prior to 1712; it would have taken at least five years simply to select so many impressions, one would think, even if they were already gathered together in the stock of Pierre Mariette II. Did Marlborough or Sunderland, then or later, turn to the Mariettes in emulation of their friend Prince Eugene? Or did the prince see in one of his English companions' libraries a ready-made collection that excited his admiration? Or was it only a perfectly predictable coincidence that the surviving Spencer and Savoy collections were formed by the same preeminent Parisian firm? Marlborough, Sunderland, and Savoy dedicated their lives to the defeat of the French. It is one of the ironies of culture and history that the provenances of surviving monuments to the consummate knowledge of the Mariettes bear their names.

The descent of property through the Churchill and Spencer families in the early eighteenth century is a particularly tangled tale. It must be told, but not until surviving catalogues and in-

44. "Voici, Monsieur, le détail de ce que M. Pond m'a écrit que vous aurés la bonté d'examiner à votre loisir. Il n'y a qu'à Monsieur votre père et à vous que nous pouvons avoir recours, parce que la décision d'un autre ne suffiroit pas dans cette occasion" (Mariette 1851–1860, vol. 2, p. 354). The question concerned Parmigianino prints, and the reference to Arthur Pond, who first met the Mariettes in 1727, provides the *terminus post quem*. See Lippincott 1983, pp. 24–25.

45. Préaud 1987, p. 230. Jean Mariette remained active as a collector at least through 1734 when he purchased from the Willem Six sale a collection of Dürer prints that had been formed by Ortelius. See Mariette 1851–1860, vol. 2, p. 147. Not incidentally, 1740 is also the time point of a short-term rupture in cultural relations between France and England, when the countries again went to war against one another. See Lippincott 1983, pp. 83–84.

46. Snyder 1975, vol 2, p. 681 ([15]26 September 1706).

47. Braubach 1965, p. 99.

ventories[48] are consulted in order better to define the Spencer collection of prints and thus, perhaps, to estimate with greater accuracy the relative probability of each of five candidates as its purchaser: the first duke of Marlborough (d. 1717); the dowager duchess of Marlborough (that is, Sarah, duchess of Marlborough, after the death of the duke; she died in 1744); the Marlboroughs' son-in-law the third earl of Sunderland (d. 1722); his second son the Hon. John Spencer (d. 1746), who was heir to all of his grandmother the dowager duchess's personal property; and John Spencer's son John, the first Earl Spencer.

⁂

On the flyleaf of each Fogg Spencer Album is a number written in brown ink. This number is recorded in the shelf-list that served as the inventory of the Althorp library sold to Mrs. John Rylands in 1892.[49] After each of the numbers in the list that matches one inscribed in the Spencer Albums is written, "Collection of engravings. Left at Althorp." These numbers are clustered together in a section of the shelf-list that groups together volumes whose contents are prints, apparently reflecting the organization of the Althorp Library. All those with no contrary indication were received by the Rylands Library. This section in full:

8037 Mrs Rylands [meaning that she kept this] Gori Mus. Etrusc.
8038 Collection of engravings. Left at Althorp. [*Spencer Album 6*, mixed Italian]
8039 Collection of engravings. Left at Althorp. [*Spencer Album 2*, mixed Italian and French]
8040 [page broken off, not legible]
8041 Dorigny. Pinotheca Hamptoniana
8042 Aquila. Imagines Farnesiani
8043 Collection of engravings. Left at Althorp. [*Spencer Album 1*, mixed Italian, specifically Bolognese]
8044 Collection of engravings. Left at Althorp.
8045 Collection of engravings. Left at Althorp.
8046 Collection of engravings. Left at Althorp.
8047 Collection of engravings. Left at Althorp. [*Spencer Album 7*, della Bella]
8048 [not filled up]
8049 [not filled up]
8050 Work of M. Antonio, Fol.

48. Apart from the 1882 shelf-list and the 1740 inventory quoted at length below, the most useful documents are the catalogue for the auction sales of 1919 (prints, Christie 1919) and 1811 (drawings, Philipe 1811). This last collection is believed to have been consigned by the second Earl Spencer, according to an inscription by Campbell Dodgson in the catalogue copy in the British Museum. I am grateful to Antony Griffiths for this information.

49. Mrs. Rylands donated the library, including the shelf-list, to the city of Manchester as a memorial to her husband. In 1972 the Rylands Library was acquired by the University of Manchester. My thanks to David W. Riley, keeper, who gave every assistance to this research.

8051 Collection of engravings. Left at Althorp. [*Spencer Albums 8 and 9*, Tempesta]

8052 Collection of engravings. Left at Althorp.

8053 Collection of engravings. Left at Althorp. [*Spencer Album 5*, mixed Dutch and Flemish]

8054 Collection of engraved portraits [Dutch and French]

8055 Collection of engravings. [Dutch]

8056 Collection of engravings. Left at Althorp.

8057 Collection of engravings. Left at Althorp.

8058 Collection of engravings. Left at Althorp.

8059 Collection of engravings. Left at Althorp.

8060 Rubens. Luxembourg

8061 Collection of engravings. Left at Althorp.

8062 Collection of engravings. Left at Althorp. [*Spencer Albums 3 and 4*, Callot]

8063 Mellan. Coll. of engravings.

8064 Mrs. Rylands [meaning that she kept this]. Hogarth Coll. of Prints

8065 Disegni di diversi pittori Italiani.

This list permits several significant deductions, the most obvious and important being that at least nine albums—"collections of engravings"—in addition to the nine now in the Fogg Museum collection remained at Althorp after the 1892 sale of the library.[50] That the volumes represented by the shelf-list, both those left at Althorp and those sold to Mrs. Rylands, seem to have been shelved by nationality, leads to the deduction that the now-missing and untraced albums were roughly divided between Italian and Northern prints. There is also the possibility that the Rubens "Luxembourg" album (about which see below) represented a transition between the Netherlandish and the French sections, and so there would have been one additional album of French prints shelved immediately before the two volumes of the works of Callot now at the Fogg.

The 1919 auction sale catalogue supports the above sketch of the putative contents of the complete Spencer print collection, although it also offers some new puzzles to replace those it resolves. The most prominent feature of this auction was a long run—ninety-one etchings in eighty lots—of prints by Rembrandt, including many of his most important compositions. No fewer than twenty-eight of these carried the signature of Pierre Mariette II, and the conclusion is inescapable that another Dutch album with a substantial section of Rembrandt prints was part of the set compiled by the Mariettes in the early eighteenth century.[51] Nine other prints bearing Mariette signatures that are not identifiable from the tables of contents as having been removed

50. As the nine extant Spencer Albums were given only seven shelf-list numbers, the two sets of two volumes containing the works of the same artist being assigned only one each, it is possible that more than nine additional albums were left at Althorp. Of course not all of the albums left at Althorp were necessarily part of the Mariette set.

51. There were also two Rembrandts signed by Claude-Augustin Mariette. See Cat. 43 concerning this member of the family.

from the Fogg's nine albums were also sold in this auction. They were by Martino Rota,[52] Ferdinand Bol, Bercham, Dujardin, and Van Dyck, confirming the guess that both Italian and Netherlandish albums would have been among those no longer accounted for.[53] The present somewhat patchy representation of the Dutch school in particular would probably have been more comprehensive, and comparable to that which remains of the Italian schools, especially the Bolognese. Regrettable as the fact of incompleteness is, it is reassuring to our theory of a commercially produced survey collection to suppose that the Mariette-made set of albums was once more systematic.

The sale in 1919 of twenty-one engravings by Albrecht Dürer implies a German album; the dearth of Mariette signatures among them does not necessarily insure that it would not have been part of the same set as the albums now at the Fogg, in that relatively few Mariette signatures figure among the Dutch, Flemish, or French prints in the Fogg Spencer collection, although all nine volumes are manifestly a (partial) set. Many prints in the auction without Mariette inscriptions can be identified as having been cut out of the Fogg albums.[54] The presence in the auction of twenty-four engravings by Marcantonio Raimondi suggests that the Marcantonio album, which was accessioned into the Rylands Library but which is not now available for inspection, might have a rash of cut folios comparable to that in the Claude section of the Fogg's Spencer Album 2. However, there are other indications of provenance among both the Dürers and the Marcantonios that virtually preclude the Mariettes as the source of the albums from which they were removed.

The albums at the Rylands Library that are now available present an interesting complement to the Spencer collection at the Fogg. First, none of the Rylands volumes are from the shop of the Mariettes. The three that present comparable print collections—of portraits by Sadeler, Morin, Lutma, Nanteuil, and others (8054), of the works of Claude Mellan (8063), and of mixed Dutch and German landscape and animal prints, including works by Hollar (8053)[55]—are in identical eighteenth-century English bindings (although the mounting pages are French papers, and one sheet among all of the hundreds of pages even bears a Gourbeyre dovecote watermark).[56] A note

52. Rota was represented by two engravings after *The Last Judgments* by Michelangelo and Titian (?) (TIB 33.36.28, TIB33.37.29). These reproductive prints, dated 1569 and 1576, are anomalous in the context of the albums preserved at the Fogg. One must postulate either that a different kind of album was included in the original set or that these prints are comparable to the one signed by Mariette included in an album from Althorp now in the Rylands Library (see below).

53. Dutch and Flemish work was generally not separated until the later eighteenth century; see Pomian 1982, p. 23.

54. See the Checklist, in which the prints cut out of the albums and sold in 1919 are identified with an asterisk.

55. The other artists in the album include Dujardin, Vadder, Uden, Vlieger, Ruisdael, Roos, Dassonville, Bega, Cortese, Kabel, Bramer, Begeyn, and Wierix, the last being a later addition. The Vlieger impressions and some of the Roos are particularly remarkable.

56. Most of the mounting pages of these albums, which are 475 x 400 mm, are chaplet papers with the countermark B*C*R, with a lunette below the oblong cartouche which contains the monogram. There are also a very few Gourbeyre grand-eagle papers. The binding is in brown calf with rather coarse gilt tooling. The page edges are reddened and not gilded, and the marbled endpapers are pieced together rather than being composed of a single sheet, as in the Fogg Spencer Albums. Altogether these albums give the distinct impression of a

on the reverse of one of the mounting sheets in the Dutch and German album that sounds like one an English dealer might have written—"14. Prints of Villemena the very best Impressions Cost 50 Louis."—extends so deeply into the gutter that the volume must have been made up after the annotation, and the titles stamped on the spines of two of the books are in English: "P O R - T R A I T S / B Y / S A D L E R / M O R I N /& C" and "W O R K / O F / M E L L A N."[57]

Among the hundreds of prints included in these three albums, one has a visible Mariette inscription, which is no less than one would expect in an eighteenth-century collection of excellent impressions of earlier prints.[58] Nine prints in the portrait and in the Dutch and German albums bear the stamped mark "NH," as do four among the prints sold in 1919 (but, significantly, none among the Rembrandts or those by any other artist that also bear Mariette inscriptions).[59] Further, the one print included within the nine Fogg albums that was not actually mounted into a volume and listed in its table of contents but was laid loosely between the pages, Camillo Procaccini's *The Stigmatization of Saint Francis* (Cat. 5), also bears this mark.[60] And finally, Adrian Eeles, director of Artemis, Ltd., reports that in 1983, at the same time his firm purchased the nine albums from the eighth Earl Spencer, they also acquired about one hundred prints that were found unmounted at Althorp; at least one of these bore the NH mark.[61]

Lugt tentatively identified the mark as that of Nathaniel Hillier (1707–1783).[62] The sale of Hillier's drawings and prints took place in 1784, a critical date if this mark was applied by his estate, as was often the case with collector's marks.[63] The first Earl Spencer died in 1783, and so it would have been the newly titled second earl, George John Spencer, who made purchases from the Hillier sale. This Earl Spencer became famous as a collector on the basis of his great library, which featured incunabula and which was the treasure sought by Mrs. Rylands; and he was apparently the vendor of a superb collection of drawings sold in 1811, presumably to finance his

---

less expensive production, although the impressions themselves are often superb. I am grateful to Mirjam Foot of the British Library, who confirms the eighteenth-century English provenance of these bindings (letter of 5 July 1990).

57. The other album's title—M.V. ENDEN / PO. V. WIN-GARDE. / K DU. IARDIN / &C.—does not reveal its nationality. There are no title pages or tables of contents in these albums.

58. "P. mariette 1666" inscribed on a portrait by Aegidius Sadeler of Elias Schmidgrabner (H.XXI.70.324).

59. A few of the prints sold in 1919 also bore the mark of Sir Peter Lely, whose sales took place in the late seventeenth century, further arguing for an English provenance for some of the Spencer collection; see Lugt 2092–2094.

60. This is the only stamp visible on any of the Fogg Spencer prints; Mariette inscriptions are otherwise the sole indications of provenance.

61. Letter of 28 September 1989. The NH mark is on Salimbeni's *Baptism of Christ*, acquired by the Museum of Fine Arts, Boston. The rest of these prints found loose at Althorp included many Italian and Northern sixteenth-century works prior to the era of the Carracci, a period unrepresented in the Spencer Albums (with the exception of a few etchings after Titian landscapes). At least one, *The Brawl* by Francesco Villamena, now in the collection of the Museum of Fine Arts, Boston, bears a Mariette inscription, dated 1667.

62. Lugt 1974. See also James Byam Shaw, *The Italian Drawings of the Frits Lugt Collection,* 2 vols. (Paris: Institut Néerlandais, 1983), vol. 1, pp. 31–32, 446–47, 459, for further information about the identification of this mark with Hillier. I am grateful to Carlos van Hasselt for drawing this reference to my attention.

63. As for example with the Lely mark seen on a number of Spencer prints; see Lugt, p. 388.

book acquisitions.[64] His activity as a print collector is doubtful both because of his willingness to sell the drawings and because his library, as reported in its shelf-list, is devoid of later eighteenth-century albums of prints or print reference material.

Lugt described Hillier as a "marchand d'estampes," and so it is possible that if the stamp was Hillier's, he applied it much as Pierre Mariette II inscribed his name. In that case, with Hillier having been born in 1707, the Spencer collection prints bearing the mark could have been acquired earlier in the century, at about the same apparent date of the albums now at the Fogg and the three English albums of prints now at the Rylands Library as indicated by their bindings and watermarks.

One other album of prints now in the Rylands Library is so astonishing a conception in itself and bears so strongly on any characterization of the Spencer Albums now at the Fogg that it must be described in full. This is "La Gallerie du Palais DV LUXEMBOURG PEINTE PAR RUBENS, Dessinée par Les Sr Nattier, et gravée Par Les plus Illustres Graveurs du Temps. Se Vend A Paris Chez le Sar Duchange Graveur du Roy . . . rue St Jacques au dessus de la rue des Mathurins," to quote its title page, which bears the date 1710. It is self-evidently not a publication of the Mariettes, but it is also bound in red morocco, tooled in much the same style though not the same hand as the Fogg albums, and its grand-eagle-sized folios are Gourbeyre papers. These are, however, the images' printing papers and not mounting papers; the impressions comprising the album are directly bound in.

The prints reproduce the famous suite of paintings by Rubens celebrating Marie de' Medici and her son Louis XIII. Each painting is represented by two impressions. One is a superb impression of the actual print, with its descriptive title engraved below, which reverses the composition of the painting; it was bound into the volume so that it forms the left side of a double-page spread, with the folio at the right being blank. Upon turning this page, whose reverse is also blank, one sees the same print again but this time in reverse, in other words, as the composition was painted; but the engraved descriptive caption remains conventionally legible from left to right. Close inspection reveals that this was accomplished by printing a counterproof of the print and *also* an impression of the inked plate, having masked out everything but the lettering, all in perfect registration. Nothing could be more luxurious than this volume, yet although it is a tour-de-force of printing, it refers more clearly to a great painter than to the printmakers who have concocted it. If one turns, then, to the nine Fogg Spencer Albums, one sees an extension of this attitude.

⁂

Unlike the other Mariette-made print collections that survive, notably the collection of Prince Eugene of Savoy, the Spencer Albums are about painting. It is true that Prince Eugene's collection

64. Philipe 1811.

34

attempts to comprise the complete oeuvre of an artist, including reproductive prints after his painted compositions. It is true that this collection formed the basis for Adam Bartsch, its curator in the early nineteenth century, in his production of *Le Peintre Gravure*, which he opens with a ringing defense of prints by painters as the key to understanding them *as* painters.[65] But the inclusion in the Vienna albums of so many duplicate prints that provide touched proofs, variations of state, and even counterproofs makes them in the end about painters as printmakers and about printmaking itself (see Cat. 10).

The Spencer Albums are a greatly concentrated version of Prince Eugene's collection, with almost everything that relates to printmaking boiled away and everything that pertains to painting distilled into its essence. Perhaps the single exception to this generalization is the inclusion of a very few duplicate prints in the albums. Two, of an Ostade (s5.12.4, s5.16.6) and a Grimaldi (see Cat. 31), are printed in different colored inks on differing papers, as if to illustrate a point peculiar to the reproduceable image that is a print. But these are truly exceptional within the albums and otherwise there are no counterproofs and no variations of state, nor is there any attempt, even in the huge compilations of works by Callot, della Bella, and Tempesta, to provide the complete works of a printmaker. Even among artists with more manageable oeuvres, characterization rather than comprehensiveness seems to be the goal. This means that artists are represented by their most important works, and among their prints within the albums, their masterpieces are usually the finest impressions. The Spencer Albums, then, like the Rubens volume from the Spencer collection, are luxurious even if one discounts the splendor of their papers, calligraphy, and binding, and they are anything but haphazard.

What painters are represented? Those for whom the French and, even more, the English in the early eighteenth century had a notorious passion.[66] Generally speaking, they are the Italian painters of the Bolognese and Roman Baroque school established by the Carracci;[67] other seventeenth-century Italian artists whose works usually featured a landscape or genre component; Dutch and Flemish painters of landscape, genre, and lowlife subjects; and French and Lorrainese artists who, again, produced a significant number of landscape and/or genre subjects among their prints. The presence of so many works by della Bella, Callot, and Tempesta extends the concept of albums of works by painters, of course, as these artists were preeminently printmakers. Perhaps the definition of the Spencer Albums should itself be extended to claim that they are

65. B.I.iii–iv: ". . . les estampes gravées par les auteurs, c'est-à-dire, par les peintres mêmes, ont presque toujours l'avantage sur celles des graveurs . . . nous n'y rencontrons rien qui soit étranger à leur auteur, nous y retrouvons celui-ci tout seul, et nous n'y remarquons que le talent et l'esprit qui lui sont propres et particuliers."

66. See Pears 1988, passim and pp. 168–70 in particular, about English collecting tastes. Herrmann 1972, pp. 70–73, 201, gives amusing extracts from disparaging nineteenth-century writings by Mrs. Jameson, Gustav

Waagen, and Thomas H. Woods, senior partner at Christie's, when English taste had turned from Guido Reni and Carlo Maratti.

67. See Hale 1954, pp. 66–71, for a discussion of the English literature on Italian painting leading up to the writings of eighteenth-century connoisseurs such as Richardson, which promoted Baroque as well as Renaissance masters; see Lipking 1970, pp. 3–126, for the continuation and expansion of this discussion into the eighteenth century.

about *art*, the art of the late sixteenth and seventeenth centuries in Continental Europe, that is, the great art movement that was based upon the accomplishment of the Italian Renaissance and was reformed by the Carracci and other Baroque painters. If anomalies like Tempesta and Callot and a pure etcher like della Bella were included, it was perhaps because they were too famous to be ignored, in France and in England, where they were mentioned in dealers' advertisements and auction catalogues as early as the seventeenth century.[68] The emphasis by these artists on landscapes, the hunt, and other subjects for which the British had particular fondness was also in their favor. Notable in the collection of the British Museum today are particularly superb Tempesta impressions deriving from the seventeenth-century collection of Sir Peter Lely.

It should not, however, be assumed from the foregoing that the albums present a secular view of seventeenth-century painting. Because of the strong representation of Italian Baroque artists, a very large number of prints with religious subjects are provided, and the doctrines expressed or implied are Roman Catholic. This does not preclude the possibility that the albums were commissioned by a Spencer or a Churchill (who of course were Protestant), for virtually at the time of the album's production, print collecting had been transformed. The principles which had guided collection organization had shifted from a primary interest in the subjects of the works to an attention to the individual style of their artists as a part of a larger shift in taste, notably in England.[69] The attitude of Adam Bartsch in 1803, that prints could reveal "talent and spirit" that was "individual and particular" to each painter-printmaker, had already been expressed by Jonathan Richardson the Elder, specifically with regard to Italian artists in the early eighteenth century:

> The prints etched by the masters themselves; such as those of Parmeggiano, Annibale Carracci, and Guido Reni (who are the chief of those of whom we have works of this kind) are considerable upon the same account; not for the handling, but the spirit, the expression, the drawing, and other the most excellent properties of a picture....[70]

Only recently, now that the classification of print collections has become a subject of scholarly interest, have we begun to realize the substantial revolution in attitude that this represents.[71]

68. See Ogden and Ogden 1955, pp. 96, 108; Rostenberg 1963, pp. 46, 51. The latter is interesting in that it emphasizes the availability in London of prints by Italian Baroque artists such as Maratti and Castiglione.

69. It should be noted that the Portuguese commission to the Mariettes was for a print collection arranged by subject, and that by 1725 it was agreed that it would be arranged historically, by artist (Mandroux-França 1986, p. 50); thus the English taste conformed to the forefront of fashion as exemplified by Europe's most important print dealers.

70. Richardson 1792, p. 167.

71. For information on earlier print collection classification schemes, see Balsiger 1970; William W. Robinson,

"'This Passion for Prints': Collecting and Connoisseurship in Northern Europe during the Seventeenth Century," pp. xxvii–xlviii, in Ackley 1981; and Pomian 1982. For particular earlier collections, see J. A. de Lasarte and A. Casanovas, "Catálogo de la Colección de Grabados de la Biblioteca de la Escorial," *Anales y Boletin de los Museos de Arte de Barcelona* 16–17 (1963–1966); Peter W. Parshall, "The Print Collection of Ferdinand, archduke of Tyrol," *Jahrbuch der Kunsthistorischen Sammlungen in Wien* 78 (1982):140–84; Waals 1984; Véronique Meyer, "The Inventory of Gilles Rousselet (1610–1686). *Print Quarterly* 2, no. 4 (1985):299–308; Jan van der Waals, *De Prentschat van Michiel Hinloopen* (Amsterdam: Rijksmuseum, 1988); Alexander de Bruin

It paralleled the development of the taste in England for Italian Baroque painting and the ancillary, practically frantic need felt by the English to acquire quickly standards of connoisseurship that would prevent their being duped by Italian and French picture dealers. This development in English taste was certainly an outcome of generations of "milords" traveling to the Continent, under the variety of circumstances that can be imagined given the wars and dynastic transformations to which seventeenth-century England had been subjected. This is no place to recapitulate that development, save to note that customs duties on imports were dropped by the island nation in the 1680s, with a resultant boom in the painting market,[72] and that after 1720 religion, which had been the single most divisive force in the previous hundred and more years, suddenly became a politically dead issue.[73]

The substitution of "taste" and the exercise of connoisseurship as primary cultural values among the English peers and wealthier members of the middle class, which relegated the subjects of prints (and paintings and drawings) to secondary status at exactly the point when Roman Catholicism ceased to be a *causus belli* in British domestic politics, is probably more than a remarkable coincidence. It was indubitably associated with British military triumphs over the French, whose menace in the later seventeenth century and patronage of the Stuart pretenders had caused Louis XIV, the most threatening representative of Catholic absolutism, to figure prominently in satires and mob violence directed against popery.[74] Suddenly after the Peace of Utrecht, the peaceful ascension of the Hanovers to the throne, and the rise in power of the Whigs, we find newly titled nobles such as the first duke of Chandos, with a fortune freshly minted in Marlborough's campaigns, constructing a chapel with a program "that would not have been out of place in any Catholic church."[75]

---

et al., "Conservatie, restauratie en onderzoek van een-zestiende-eeuws prentenboek: het *Heemskerck-album*," *Bulletin van het Rijksmuseum* 38, no. 3 (1990): 173–214.

It should be noted that the Mariettes produced collections of prints compiled by subject as well, notably in that area—architecture and topography—which has remained popular as a category in which to collect prints into albums to this day (with photographs being substituted for engravings in the nineteenth and twentieth centuries, generally speaking). The National Gallery of Art, Washington, holds two albums which contain virtually identical series of impressions from the same plates. One is titled on its spine *Vues par Perelle* and the other *Vues de France*. Not surprisingly, it is the second binding, which defines the volume by its subject, that is original to the album; the first binding, which defines its contents by artist, is from the nineteenth century, well into the age of art history.

The actual dates of the albums, however, reverse this order. *Vues par Perelle* contains states of plates that lack any inscriptions whatsoever or else they bear the address

of the publisher Nicolas Langlois. These same plates, substantially more worn and with the address changed to that of Jean Mariette, appear in the volume with the earlier binding, and this binding is close in style to that of the Spencer Albums. In 1702, shortly before his death, Nicolas Langlois gave his assets as a print publisher to his half-brother Jean Mariette (Préaud 1987, p. 229).

72. See Pears 1988 and also Pears 1982; Ogden and Ogden 1955, passim but especially p. 91; Denvir 1983, p. 7.

73. Holmes 1986, especially p. x.

74. See Holmes 1986, p. 188; Ewald 1978, p. 72. The latter quotes a description from the London paper *The Flying Post* for 7–10 February 1712/13 of the burning of effigies: "... the Pope dress'd in his Pontificalibus ... and the Pretender on his Left, in a French Dress ... Instead of laying any Marks of State upon his Shoulders, 'twas thought more proper to have a little French Ware strung about his Neck ... "

75. Haskell 1980, pp. 280–81, this quote from p. 280. By the late nineteenth century, such taste, which had descended through all ranks of society through the mecha-

So warmly was Italian painting embraced, and its subjects defused sufficiently to be comic, that when British satirical pens turned to joshing the new fad for "taste" it was specifically foreign Catholic iconography that characterized pretentions and foolishness. To quote Samuel Foote in his play *Taste*, c. 1752, where a fatuous British patron, an artist, and "two art market types" are conversing about some paintings: "It is, my lord, St. Anthony of Padua exorcising the devil out of a ram-cat; it has a companion . . . which is the same saint in the wilderness reading his breviary by the light of a glow-worm."[76]

In his catalogue of the works of Guido Reni, D. Stephen Pepper has correctly interpreted the crucial importance to subsequent art history of this new eighteenth-century English dominance of the practice of connoisseurship as opposed to seventeenth-century concern with the relationship of subject, form, and style—in particular, the new disregard of subject as a criterion of value.

> In the history of criticism it is the dilettanti, especially the English, who precisely at this time succeed the French theorists in dominating European thought. In this process the French academic emphasis on a theoretical system, rational in nature, gives way to a strictly empirical inquiry into the appearance of the work: not to trace the source of the passions, but to establish criteria of identification (connoisseurship) and of appreciation (aesthetic judgement). . . . The immediate effect of this decoupling of ideas from appearance is seen in a commentary by Sir Robert Strange written in 1769. . . . He describes a painting by Guido of the *Virgin and Child* . . . to which he applies the title "The Offering of Love": "I will not take upon me to dispute the intention of the painter in the subject of this picture; but it is not characterized with any particular marks of divinity, and as we have rather a supernumerary quantity of Madonnas, I judged it no impropriety to engrave it under the preceding title."[77]

Both the play by Foote and the commentary by Strange betray a continuing British nervousness about a Catholic subject which, perhaps, *required* the cover of connoisseurship to legitimize a regard for images of saints and madonnas.

Ultimately the new system was derived from Italy, from the example of Italian drawing collections and from works such as Vasari's *Lives of the Most Eminent Painters, Sculptors, and Archi-*

nism of reproductive prints, was advanced as evidence of high culture in contrast to taste that preferred native British subjects; "[It is] a good sign of the mental condition of the inmates of a country mansion when we have been greeted in the hall with chromolithographs of Annunciations, Nativities, Crucifixions and Ascensions. We need not say that such themes show a family to be better read and more widely travelled than the households who use as wall furnishings horses by Stubbs [or] pigs by Morland . . ." (*Saturday Review*, 1874, quoted in Lambert 1987, p. 193).

76. Quoted in Sutton 1981, p. 81. See Sutton 1981, p.

325, for an often quoted diatribe by William Hogarth against "dead Christs, Holy Families, Madonas and other dismal Dark Subjects," which is in fact explicitly a screed against imported paintings and not against Roman Catholicism. Doubtless his choice of examples added to the resonance of his argument.

77. Pepper 1984, pp. 48–49. See Filipzcak 1987, pp. 130–38, for a penetrating analysis of this development, which was truly Europe-wide, as it related not to English taste and Italian art but rather to developments in the North and South Netherlands.

tects (which was, of course, "illustrated" by his own collection of drawings, the exemplar for the organization of an art collection by school and artist rather than subject).[78] The *Lives* was amplified in Italy by subsequent histories and biographies that also read art in terms of the development of painting through the careers of individuals within local schools, and that began to approach problems of connoisseurship.[79] Of particular concern was not the differentiation of one great artist from another but the distinction of originals from copies, and to that end certain criteria were elevated to, in Jeffrey Muller's words, "the authority of a hard-and-fast law. . . . Authenticity was identified with the free play of the artist's hand and mind. Caprice, fantasy, will, boldness, resolution, and spirit characterized an original."[80] These were exactly the characteristics that, in the opinion of theoreticians and connoisseurs of prints in the seventeenth and eighteenth centuries, distinguished the process of etching from that of engraving;[81] and it was etching and not engraving that was the print process universally employed by the Italian painters such as Parmigianino, Annibale Carracci, and Guido Reni whom connoisseurs were so eager to separate from their copyists. Thus the rise in interest in artists' etchings more generally is easily explained, and the presence practically exclusively of etchings (as opposed to engravings or woodcuts) in the Spencer Albums is accounted for.

By the time the Spencer Albums were organized, the original artist-etcher within the context of his national or regional school offered the natural pattern into which to fit individual prints. Thus in the album devoted to the Carracci, not only are the sections of works by the three Carracci themselves, Guido Reni, and Cantarini followed by a section *Pieces des Eleves des Carraches* to illustrate the later development of the school, but even within the earlier sections school compositions are included to exhibit more fully the range of the Carracci, Guido, and their closest disciples. Classification was still in transition, however, and subject was not entirely abandoned as a criterion. Once the first priority—the determination of the identity of the artist

78. See Karpinski 1989, especially pp. 105–6, concerning this Italian sixteenth-century conception of prints. See James et al. 1991, pp. 3–13, for a succession of sixteenth- through eighteenth-century historically arranged Italian drawing collections. The Resta collection found in Italy c. 1710 by John Talman, which was purchased by Lord Somers and which eventually fell into the hands of Richardson the Elder, was described by Talman: "It consisteth of sixteen volumes in folio, gilt on the back and sides, and most of them bound in red turky leather. . . . The design of this work is to shew the rise and fall of painting in divers periods of time" (quoted in Herrmann 1972, pp. 108–9).

79. Enggass and Brown 1970, pp. 34–35, quotes an interesting passage of proto-Morellian attribution technique by Guilio Mancini (1588–1630), from his *Considerazioni sulla pittura* written c. 1617–1621.

80. Muller 1989, p. 144.

81. See Le Comte 1702, vol. 1, pp. 131–32, where his praise of etching should be understood as a compliment indeed, as he was a partisan of engraving: "Entrons dans le détail de ses qualitez particulieres, pour en connoître la vertu. C'est par le moien de cette Eau si merveilleuse qu'on pousse les sujets au de-là même du naturel; elle agit avec tant de vivacité, qu'elle égale celle du Pinceau, & ne laisse pas refroidir le genie de l'Auteur . . . " See also Johnson 1982, pp. 195–96, where he quotes the *Encyclopédie*, vol. 1, p. 205: "Les eaux-fortes des peintres sont quelquefois plus recherchées que les plus belles estampes des graveurs"; and Denvir 1983, pp. 234–35, where he quotes Gilpin's *Essay on Prints*: "Etching, on the other hand, is more particularly adapted to sketches, and slight designs; which, if executed by an engraver, would entirely lose their freedom; and with it their beauty. Landskip too, in general, is the object of etching. The foliage of trees, ruins, sky and indeed every part of landskip requires the utmost freedom."

as an individual and a school member—was established, the prints that fell within any given class were arranged according to subject, whether it was the two full volumes of the works of Tempesta (see Cat. 23) or the very few prints by an artist such as Michel-Ange Corneille. In the case of prints by and after an artist such as Castiglione, for example, they were arranged in subject order independent of the individual plates' authorship (see Cat. 48, 50).

What is the general concept that underlies the ordering of the prints? For subjects regarded by the compilers as historical, which included the events and personages of the Christian religion beginning with the creation of the world, the order is generally chronological. What one might think of as set pieces, such as the many representations of the Madonna and Child that are devoid of specific references to the actual circumstances of the Nativity, are usually placed after the narratives from which they derive, in this case the Gospels. Pagan mythology follows Christian religion, but sometimes, as in the case of the Tempesta albums, historical events and personages of the ancient world continuing into those of the modern precede mythological subjects.[82] All prints that reflect narrative or the characterization of historical personages take precedence over genre, landscape, and ornament, in that order.[83]

There are exceptions to this classification scheme. There is, for instance, sometimes the desire to represent an artistic entity constituted by several prints. Thus in the case of works by and after Maratti the sequence begins, correctly, with the very large etching "*Heliodore frappé de Verges dans le Temple, ou il etoit entré dans le dessein de le piller, gravé par Carle Maratte, d'ap. le merveilleux tableau de Raphael, qui est au Vatican,*" to quote the table of contents. Next comes a group with the general subject of the Life of the Virgin, among them an Adoration of the Kings. These are followed by seven prints representing "*Les Peintures d'une Chapelles de l'Eglise de S! Isidore, a Rome,*" again in the words of the table of contents. (We give these in full to indicate, by the way, the attentiveness of the compilers to their audience's need to know both the artist and the subject of the prints in the albums.) That group contains an Adoration of the Shepherds, manifestly out of correct order within the entire context of the works of Maratti, but indicating the desire to retain the unity of the cycle of paintings.

The more frequent cause of the disruption of rigid order is the wish, realized in so many ways throughout the albums, to present the prints as attractively as possible. The closest attention was given to their arrangement on the page, with everything carefully planned. In the prints in Al-

82. But see Cat. 22, n. 4.

83. See the Description of the Albums, which presents a running summary by subject type of the contents of the albums.

The oeuvre catalogues of Adam Bartsch, who worked from the Mariette albums of Prince Eugene of Savoy, perpetuated into the early nineteenth century this hybrid system in which a residue of formerly absolute subject classification was retained, subordinated to classification by artist. The problem of the organization of a print collection was a topic of heated debate through the nineteenth century as connoisseurship continued to develop; see Marjorie B. Cohn, *Francis Calley Gray and Art Collecting for America* (Cambridge: Harvard University Art Museums, 1986), pp. 54–63. Only with the maturing of art history in the early twentieth century would some oeuvre catalogues shed the last vestiges of subject classification and resort to pure chronology within an artist's career as their organizing principle.

bum 6 on folio 10 (*fig. 6*), for example, *Doubting Thomas* by Palma the Younger precedes—that is, is mounted to the left of—*Saint John the Baptist*, which figures in the Gospels at an earlier point. This choice was apparently dependent upon the complementary gestures of Christ and the saint in the two prints, which frame the lower extent of the folio attractively, more so than they would were they mounted in other positions.

An interest in the decorative effect of the complete page is especially obvious in the cases of long sequences of prints, such as della Bella's sets of instructional cards for the young Louis XIV (s7.10.1–s7.24.12). The total number of prints in the series was tabulated and the individual pages were laid out so that the end of the series would coincide with the bottom of a page. The individual pages could not usually be uniformly dense with prints, and so elaborate schemes, all bilaterally symmetric, were worked out so that the flow of the series would appear uninterrupted. The della Bellas, for example, have several systems of four rows per page: one with four, three, three, and four prints per row; another with three, three, three, four; yet another with four in every row; still another with three. Mounting locations were carefully spaced, measured, and marked beforehand with pencil ticks. (This system is used throughout the albums, even where only one print is mounted per page.) Occasionally the mounter would get confused and mark off the wrong system (as on s7.16); he would correct himself using both prick marks and ticks, as if he had resort to a template produced from another page.

On the pages where each series begins, the title page, which in the case of the della Bella card sets is horizontal although the format of the cards themselves is vertical, is invariably mounted at the center top to preserve the symmetrical aspect. The series is automatically "out of order" in that one reads the playing card mounted first, at the top left, before the title. More interestingly, plates of an identical format are sometimes mounted out of numerical order if the visual balance of the page is enhanced. Thus in *The Game of the Kings of France*, only a rough approximation of the reigns' sequence, which is clearly specified on the cards in large numerals, is preserved. In a three-card row at the bottom of folio 19, for example, *Louis the Fat* (40) is at the left and *Philippe the Handsome* (46) at the right. They are equestrian portraits, facing in opposite directions, and thus provide a symmetric and substantial closure to the page.

An even more striking "out of order" series is found on the page that holds Callot's *Military Exercises* (s4.12.1–s4.12.12, s4.12.14). The set shows various positions of pikemen, halberdiers, and riflemen, and the management of cannon firing ("ready," "aim," "fire"). The series of thirteen tiny plates was not deemed sufficient to fill the page, nor could it easily be divided into symmetric rows. Therefore two additional prints of cavalry engagements, of greater visual weight, were added at the lower left and right at the bottom, making five rows of three prints.[84] The battle

---

84. The cavalry battles (L.1313–1314) are catalogued by Lieure as a separate series from the military exercises (L.1320–1332). He described them, however, as "Deux petites estampes, que les collectionneurs ajoutent généralement aux *Exercises militaires*" and noted that in

their second state the publisher Fagnani added the numerals 13 and 14 to the plates to enforce the connection. The Spencer Album impressions of the battles and the exercises are first states, without numbers. The table of contents considers them a single series but remarks

scenes fulfill much the same closure function as the equestrian portraits described above. The single print from the *Exercises* positioned between them is of drummers, an anomalous subject among the rest of the plates representing weaponry, and a subject that neatly balances the iconography of the title page, mounted directly above four rows up, which shows another drummer, a piper, and two trumpeters. The "out of order" aspect of this page that most clearly runs against the grain of the subject for the sake of decorative symmetry is the row of three plates of cannon firing. "Fire" is at the left, "Aim" is at the right, and "Ready" in the center, a complete scrambling of functional sequence in order to point at each other the two cannon barrels that are aggressively pointing, past the central image in which the cannon is aimed more obliquely into the distance.

Decorative beauty in all the pages of all the albums is entirely in terms of symmetry. This accords with the aesthetic of collection presentation more largely in the seventeenth and early eighteenth centuries. Gallery paintings, that is, paintings of the galleries in which important collections were installed (a new genre of painting in this period), show close-packed symmetrical arrays, with the works often arranged by subject. Thus in the representation by Panini of the gallery of Cardinal Valenti-Gonzaga, portraits are clustered in rows around history and religious paintings. The dense mounting of the pages of the Spencer Albums is comparable; that it was not a measure for the sake of economy is obvious when one contemplates the lavish expanse of blank paper, the verso of each mounting sheet, which faces each page of prints.[85]

Paintings were often given standard frames by their owners (including the Spencers at Althorp[86]), and there was a vogue for "formatizing," that is, trimming the paintings to the appropriate shape and size to conform to the larger decorative symmetry of a wall arrangement.[87] In the Spencer Albums almost all of the prints are trimmed close to or within their platemarks, and many have lost their lower margins, which contained texts, as if the visual image and not its verbal gloss was the essential (see Cat. 58). While not as destructive as formatizing, this close trimming is a further indication that the albums are art collections and not essentially print collections, for even in the eighteenth century a diehard print collector would always prefer the untrimmed impression to the trimmed.

A writer on the architecture of the period also remarks on the contemporary standard of symmetry, which was imposed upon buildings that were intended to convey prestige and communicate status. A full quotation is irresistible, partly because the passage indicates the extent to

---

upon the battles as a separate subject: "Les Exercises Militaires en Quinze pieces, dont il y en a deux qui representent des Batailles."

85. This expanse of white was considered a serious distraction by some seventeenth- and eighteenth-century connoisseurs. See Ris 1877, p. 112, quoting the abbé de Marolles ("vis-à-vis une page blanche qui ne servioit qu'à choquer la vue et à multiplier mal à propos les volumes d'un grand receuil"), and Denvir 1983, p. 74.

86. Notably Robert Spencer, the second earl of Sunderland, who "spent a small fortune" on uniform frames for his painting collection (Pears 1988, p. 157).

87. See Von Holst 1963, p. 153, fig. 167, for a reproduction of the Panini, and pp. 161–62 for a discussion of formatizing. Filipczak 1987 provides an excellent overview of gallery painting as a genre, especially as it developed in Flanders in the seventeenth century.

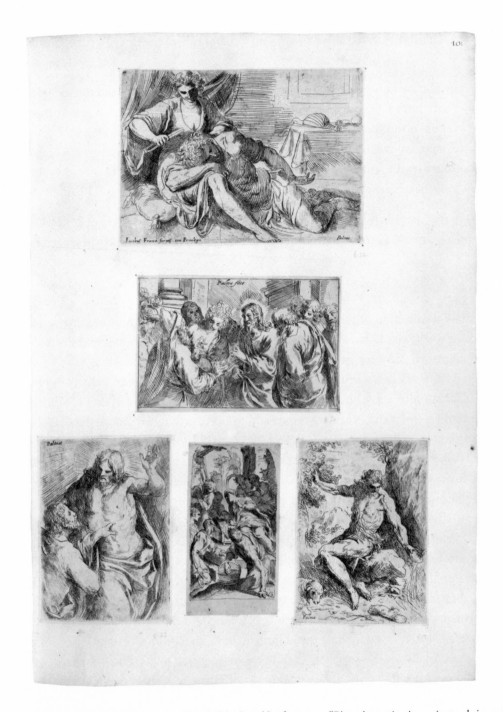

Fig. 6. *Spencer Album 6, folio 10. The prints as described in the table of contents: "Pieces inventées & gravées par le jeune Palme . . . Dalila coupant les cheveux de Samson, Jesus Christ jugeant la femme adultere, S! Thomas mettant le doige dans le côté de J:C., Les Pasteurs adorants l'Enfant Jesus, S! Jean Baptiste dans le desert, —10:" Visible below the bottom row of prints are pencil ticks and paper residues which indicate that at first only the two outside prints were mounted in this row and that they were later lifted and the center print (now considered a copy after Palma) was inserted. The appearance of the page with only two prints in the bottom row would have conformed more closely to the usual somewhat vertical aesthetic of page arrangements in the Spencer Albums, but as all of the prints now on the page are listed in the table of contents, there is no doubt that all are original to the album. The Bartsch numbers were added by a later Spencer owner. (Photograph by Michael Nedzweski)*

which this standard permeated all art forms, but also because of the three particular examples it cites:

> The formal house flourished because it reflected absolute monarchy and the society that went with it. In the late seventeenth and early eighteenth century, when absolute monarchy was at its most powerful, saloons between matching apartments were springing up from Russia to America, and from Sweden to Sicily. The immense prestige of Louis XIV and his court set the fashion, but it was imitated by the opponents of France as well as its allies—by Prince Eugene at the Belvedere and the duke of Marlborough at Blenheim.[88]

As we see in the Spencer Albums and in those of Prince Eugene, the pages of collections organized by Jean Mariette, a Frenchman of the age of Louis XIV, echoed a much larger aesthetic.

❧

Thus we have a collection of nine or more albums that present the most admired, prestigious artists whose works would have been available to and desired by the wealthy collecting class of the early eighteenth century in France and England. The albums are that era's commercial equivalent of a lavish late-twentieth-century "coffee-table" collection of French Impressionist painting shading into early Picasso and Matisse (with Callot and Tempesta also included as equivalents to Daumier and Whistler). As the albums were produced prior to the availability of a repertoire of reproductive engravings, to say nothing of photomechanical reproductions, information about personal and school style was conveyed largely by means of original etchings, which in any case were believed to provide the most accurate, evocative characterizations. Impression quality and condition of the prints in the albums is of the highest quality, and presentation is lavish: these books were expensive.

It is difficult to believe that although the albums were manifestly a commercial enterprise, they were produced on speculation. Although they are without idiosyncracies that would lead to the conclusion that a particular customer with highly developed taste had exactly specified their contents, they seem simply too expensive to have been made up without having been bespoke. The present-day superb condition of the albums' bindings and pages make it unlikely that their owners particularly enjoyed looking through them, and, to continue the analogy with many of today's deluxe art tomes, it is probable that they were acquired to decorate the shelves of a great library because it was thought suitable that they should. We must now face the question of who first held this opinion, proceeding from the assumption that the volumes had no earlier owner than a member of the Spencer or Churchill families, because the albums themselves give no indication of any other provenance.

Thus the case is also prejudiced against the first Earl Spencer, who arrived on the collecting

---

88. Girouard 1978, p. 144.

scene too late to have commissioned the albums, although the nature of his taste as known through his paintings and drawings would otherwise have virtually guaranteed him to have been the Mariettes' patron. We are left with three members of the family as principal candidates, more by reason of their life dates than known proclivities for exactly the art represented by the albums. These are, in order of increasing likelihood, Charles Spencer, third earl of Sunderland, his son the Hon. John Spencer, and his redoubtable mother-in-law Sarah, duchess of Marlborough. One additional candidate, John, duke of Marlborough, is eligible strictly and solely on the basis of life dates, and the tale should begin with yet another, even though his early death excludes him as a possibility; for Robert, second earl of Sunderland, was the first great art collector among the Spencers.

Robert Spencer was the son of a Cavalier killed in battle for Charles I and a Sidney, one of the leading Puritan families. He became lord president and secretary of state to James II, but in the words of his descendant Winston Churchill, "he lured his master to his follies and his fate. . . . Certainly no man played a greater part in the downfall of King James, except King James himself. . . ."[89] Another biographer has characterized him as "that rare phenomenon in the Spencer family, a bad man. . . . Of all the admirable qualities which he should have inherited . . . he possessed only two, genuine artistic appreciation and a good brain. . . ."[90] Sunderland was educated in Italy and on his many later travels abroad in a diplomatic capacity he acquired major works by contemporary French painters such as Sébastien Bourdon and by Italian painters such as Annibale Carracci. In Rome in 1662 he had his portrait painted by Carlo Maratti (see Cat. 13).[91] He died in 1702, out of political favor despite a career notorious for its flexibility, and his painting collection, rich in exactly the kinds of works exemplified by many of the prints in the albums, descended to the next proprietor of Althorp, his son Charles, third earl of Sunderland.

Charles was also educated abroad. In 1688 after the death of James II and the ascension of William and Mary, his father had found it convenient to leave England for a while, and the family lived in Utrecht where their son, evidently a talented scholar, studied at the university. After 1702, the son quickly assumed the political mantle of his late father, becoming envoy extraordinary to Vienna in 1705, secretary of state south from 1706 until 1710, lord-lieutenant of Ireland in 1714, and then successively lord privy seal, joint vice-treasurer, secretary of state, lord president of the Council, first lord of the Treasury, and one of the five lords of the Junto under Queen Anne. Despite what was by all accounts an unattractive personality,[92] Sunderland's position, intelli-

89. Churchill 1938, vol. 1, pp. 275, 276.

90. Battiscombe 1984, p. 50. See below for a description of his collecting, and see the provenances of paintings catalogued in Garlick 1976 for those remaining at Althorp which are known to have come from him.

91. Garlick 1976, no. 437, pl. 10.

92. "He had none of the insinuating charm and genial courtesy of his incomprehensible father. He was an ultra-Whig of the straitest and most unbending type. . . .

this young prig and coxcomb . . . The arid, pedantic Sunderland . . ." (Churchill 1938, vol. 2, p. 199; vol. 3, p. 175; vol. 6, p. 30; Sunderland was not Winston Churchill's favorite ancestor); "a plump unlovely young man of an earthy quality" (Peter Smithers, *The Life of Joseph Addison*. 2nd ed. [Oxford: Clarendon Press, 1968], p. 113). His mother-in-law Sarah Churchill came to think even worse of him—"a furious Madman, without any Principle" (BLMS Add.61439, fol. 139). Charles's affectionate

gence, and political talents were sufficient to insure a distinguished career; but it was certainly advanced by his marriage (his second) in 1700 to Anne Churchill, daughter of the earl (later duke) of Marlborough, at a time when her mother was the intimate confidant of Princess Anne, soon to become queen.

Sunderland participated in the various artistic endeavors of his time, being a subscriber to the formation of the Royal Academy of Music, for example,[93] but it was to the collecting of books that he was truly dedicated in temperament and purse. The formation of libraries was a favorite avocation of the nobility under Queen Anne, but Sunderland's voraciousness was notorious: "When, for example, the agent of the earl of Sunderland secured for his master the Zarottus Virgil . . . Wanley bitterly complained that such competition was sending up book prices to unreasonable heights."[94] In his diary for 6 February 1703, the bishop of Carlisle noted that the master of Trinity College had ridiculed "the Expensive humour of purchaseing old Editions of Books at Extravagant Rates; a Vanity to which the present earl of Sunderland [is] much subject."[95] Certainly the earl would have known of the Mariettes, because of his close association with Prince Eugene of Savoy at exactly the time that the prince was making his acquisitions from them; and one can imagine the easy attractiveness to the earl of commissioning handsome volumes that would provide evidence of his awareness of the most fashionable art without going to the obsessive (and expensive) lengths represented by the prince's hundreds of albums. Yet an order to the Mariettes for the Spencer Albums would have been somewhat uncharacteristic given his antiquarian and, apparently, unartistic tastes. In any case the albums would have had to have been purchased during the earlier, less likely portion of the span of years (c. 1710–c. 1740) that I have identified as the period of the collection's formation, for Charles Spencer died in 1722.

One would assume that the earl's famous library was the one sold in 1892 from Althorp to Mrs. Rylands, but in fact at least a very large portion of it was sold earlier, in 1881 and 1882, and not from Althorp but from Blenheim, the palace of the duke of Marlborough.[96] Sunderland in his will confirmed

letters to his third wife, however, whom he married after the death of Sarah's daughter (hence one source of Sarah's enmity), show a very appealing side of his personality.

93. Foss 1971, p. 156.

94. Duncan 1975, p. 263; see also pp. 260–61.

95. William Nicolson, *The London Diaries of William Nicolson, Bishop of Carlisle, 1702-1718.* Eds. Clyve Jones and Geoffrey Holmes (Oxford: Clarendon Press, 1985), p. 199.

96. See the sale catalogue for the contents of the library as sold: Puttick and Simpson, *Bibliotheca Sunderlandiana. Sale Catalogue of the truly important and very extensive library of printed books known as the Sunderland or Blenheim Library* (London, sold in five portions, December 1881, April 1882, July 1882, November 1882,

March 1883, plus June 1883 [returns and addenda]). A notice of the sale from the London bookseller Bernard Quaritch is bound into the copy in the Harvard College Library; it describes the collection: "The Library contains about 20,000 volumes, the larger portion of which consists of the Works of the ANCIENT GREEK and ROMAN CLASSIC WRITERS. These are found either in the first or very early editions . . . or in special editions produced by celebrated printers. . . . Many of them are printed upon vellum, and nearly all are of a very high degree of rarity. Another principal and important feature in the Library is the large number of EARLY PRINTED and RARE BIBLES. . . . The Editions in English comprise those of 1541 and 1549, 1595 (Q. Elizabeth's copy), 1619 (James I.'s copy on large paper [thus King James's copy of King James's Bible. The catalogue, p. 112,

all the Deeds of Settlement made on my several Marriages and the Gifts and Appoint-
ments of the Pictures and Furniture of my House at Althorp . . . and of my House in
Picadilly. . . . I give and bequeath the Rest of my personal estate in manner following. . . .
All the rest and residue . . . to my eldest Son and Heir the Lord Spencer. And my will is,
that all my ready money [etc.] be in the first place applied [for cash legacies] before any
Sale of my Plate, House-hold Goods or Books.[97]

His eldest son Robert Spencer, the dissipated, unmarried fourth earl of Sunderland, died
only seven years later. In settlement of a debt of £6000 he had given the books to his brother
Charles, now fifth earl of Sunderland, who also became the duke of Marlborough in 1733 because
the first duke and duchess of Marlborough and their eldest daughter had no surviving male
heir.[98] At least some of the Sunderland books were moved to Blenheim and were installed in a
huge room originally intended for a picture gallery, where together with a presiding bust of the
third earl, they became a high point of nineteenth-century tours of the palace.[99] One source
maintains that the larger portion remained at Althorp, but its share in the collection that eventually would be sold to Mrs. Rylands will be forever unclear because it was submerged some seventy-five years later by the still more splendid and copious acquisitions of the second Earl
Spencer, "the real founder of the magnificent Althorp library."[100]

One must raise the question here of why at the sale of that library to Mrs. Rylands the Spencer
Albums were "left at Althorp." Was it because they were perceived as art and not books? Probably
not, in that other comparable albums were sold to Mrs. Rylands. Was it because they were known
in the family to have a different provenance than the bulk of the collection, because they descended from the Sunderland line or even Marlborough? At one point in the sale negotiations,
sometimes difficult, the agent reported to the fifth Earl Spencer, "I think everything will go
smoothly now that I have shown them that your Lordship will not except from the sale any books
but those especially connected with the family."[101] Two months later Spencer reported to his wife
that "The Book people have discovered that it will cost more to pack and carry a good many

---

suggests that it is the printer's presentation copy to the
King]). Of Dante there are about a Hundred Editions,
dating from 1472 to 1583. . . . There are numerous rare
Works relating to America . . . A vast number of Tracts
relating to England and France in the Sixteenth and Seventeenth Centuries . . ."

Manchester 1864, vol. 2, p. 144, describes the library as
containing seventeen thousand volumes; accessions
made in the eighteenth century are not sufficient to account for the difference. It should be noted that most of
these accessions, as described in the sale catalogue, were
books containing plates, usually in proof impressions.

97. BLMS Add.61439, fol. 166–167.

98. See a letter from Sarah, dowager duchess of Marlborough to the earl of Godolphin, 16 April 1728 (BLMS
Add.61439, fol. 170).

99. William Eccles. *A New Guide to Blenheim Palace*,
11th ed. (Woodstock: William Eccles, 186[?]), pp. 32–34.

100. Battiscombe 1984, pp. 72, 76, 80. In 1892, the year
of its sale, the library was "housed in eight main rooms
at Althorp: the Long Gallery, Long Library, Breakfast
Room, Domenichino Room, Raphael Room, Old Book
Room, Billiard Room and the Ante Billiard Room." A
total of 43,331 books were sold to Mrs. Rylands (Gordon
1986, pp. 20–21).

101. E. G. Hodge, of Sotheby, Wilkinson and Hodge,
auctioneers, to Lord Spencer, 10 August 1892 (Gordon
1986, p. 203).

more books than they are worth, so they propose to leave books like the Annual Registers, R. Agric. Soc. Reports and similar books, also all Novels."[102] Surely the volumes of prints would have been worth packing if they had been made available by Spencer!

Lady Spencer's diary in 1893, after she had busied herself refilling some of the gaping shelves, offers yet another option:

> We settled that only the Long Library, which was the original Library of the House, should be re-planted with Books and remain the Library. . . . I had nearly finished filling the Library in 4 months after the Books were taken away with the help of *Edinburgh* and *Quarterly Reviews* which were in the Picture Gallery. . . . These books were not wanted and were left when the other Books were sold.[103]

Could the albums of prints also have been shelved in the Picture Gallery, as would have been appropriate, and been somehow overlooked? This is improbable but cannot be known; one may as well suppose that the matched set of red morocco bindings particularly suited the decor.

Taking the slim clue that the albums might have been construed as having a provenance that the family valued in particular, one must turn from the third Earl Sunderland, who was basically a book and not an art collector, to the Marlboroughs, who decidedly were art collectors and who were the most glamorous and wealthy ornaments on the Spencer family tree.

One cannot overestimate the position of the duke of Marlborough in early eighteenth-century Britain. To quote Trevelyan, "At the top of the social hierarchy stood the Duke, who would in any other land have been styled a Prince, and whose manner of life outdid in magnificence the courts of allied monarchs drawing England's pay."[104] A component of this life was the acquisition of important paintings, which sometimes were received as tribute from client states. Certainly the duke took advantage of his Continental campaigns to purchase or receive paintings, especially the works of Rubens and his school, of which the duke was especially fond.[105] He also owned a suite of paintings then thought to be by Titian, on the subject of the Loves of the Gods, which were engraved as early as 1708–1709.[106]

102. Gordon 1986, p. 205, n. 2.

103. Gordon 1986, pp. 204–5, quoting an undated entry from June 1893.

104. Trevelyan 1930, p. 28.

105. "In the War of the Spanish Succession Max Emanuel of Bavaria fought on the side of France and could not prevent the imperial troops and their English allies from occupying Munich. On this occasion the Duke of Marlborough obtained Rubens' Venus and Adonis (now in the Metropolitan Museum, New York) and van Dyck's large Charles I on Horseback . . . (now in the National Gallery in London)" (Von Holst 1963, p. 166). "Marlborough's favorite master was Rubens. After the Duke's victories over the French various Flemish cities, as well as the Hapsburg Emperor, presented him with examples of the master's work. . . . Marlborough also owned . . . a group of 120 paintings by David Teniers, reproducing the Archduke Leopold William's Collection. . . . Marlborough had a sharp eye for pictures . . . [and] on returning from [sic] England, his baggage contained five cases of pictures" (Sutton 1981, pp. 322–23). One thinks immediately of the Rubens album now in the Rylands Library; this would have been a suitably deluxe presentation copy for the duke, although presumably it would have received a special dedicatory binding.

106. Griffiths 1989, p. 256.

It was at this period that the duke was particularly busy about the decoration of the yet-un-finished Blenheim Palace, the gift of a grateful England after his victories over the French Catholic foe. His letters to Sarah record the purchase of "glasses," that is, mirrors, from Paris in 1707, which he wanted to have transshipped from Brussels along with "hangings," the famous Alexander tapestries that he commissioned from De Vos.[107] One wonders if he also ordered prints from Paris in 1707 from the Mariettes, whom he would have heard about from his dear friend Prince Eugene. The hegemony that Paris held in luxury goods, furnishing, and fashion is nowhere better exemplified than in the purchases made by the conquerors of the army of Louis XIV.

Sarah was as attentive as her husband to the furnishing of Blenheim, although it seemed to daunt even her at times. In 1715 in an inquiry on the prices of featherbeds, she railed at "all such things as will be wanted in that wild, unmercifull house."[108] For procurement, such was her political and personal power that she could require "the man who had been missioned to circumvent France now [to] condescend to go shopping. . . ."[109] This man was the fourth earl, later first duke, of Manchester. Thus on 16 March 1707, Manchester wrote to Sarah from Venice,

I find the velvets are better at Genoa, but for damasks here [I shall send] to your Grace three patterns in damask of different colours, and what they will cost. . . . I have bespoke some for myself, and have so managed that the person who provides me does get but sixpence in a yard: this method I thought would be the more properest, that you might be at a certainty, as also not be deceived in the price.[110]

A response from the imperious Sarah on 1 August 1708 was typical:

I desire your Lordship will be pleased to give directions for to have made the quantity of damasks and velvets that I have put down, in English measure—of the green damask, 1,300 yards; yellow damask, 600 yards; crimson damask, 600 yards; scarlet plain velvet, 200 yards; plain blue velvet, 200 yards; scarlet damask, the same colour as the velvet, 100 yards; blue satin, same colour as the velvet, 200 yards. [These quantities give one an appreciation for the enterprise that was Blenheim Palace.] Notwithstanding all this that I have troubled your Lordship with, I believe I shall be forced to trouble you again for a vast deal I shall want to furnish that house. . . . 't is the common way of the world to consider one's self in the first place, so you will not wonder at me having drawn this trouble on yourself.[111]

It is exactly the dynastic character of the investment into Blenheim Palace that makes the descent of the print albums less likely through the duke of Marlborough and more likely through his

---

107. Snyder 1975, vol. 2, p. 826, letter of [19]30 June 1707.

108. Quoted in Cowles 1983, p. 393. Blenheim Palace would be completed only after the death of the duke.

109. Manchester 1864, vol. 2, p. 321.

110. Manchester 1864, vol. 2, p. 323.

111. Manchester 1864, vol. 2, pp. 388–89.

duchess. The property of the duke, in particular the palace and its appurtenances, was subject to entail and primogeniture, the system of inheritance which the British peerage of the eighteenth century regarded "almost as a fundamental law of nature."[112] Ultimately, as we have seen, his estate devolved to the Spencer heir who bore that family's hereditary title, the fifth earl of Sunderland. In accepting the enormously wealthy dukedom, an agreement had earlier been reached whereby the property entailed in the Spencer line, notably Althorp and its picture collection, would be settled upon Sunderland's younger brother the Hon. John Spencer.[113]

This development is not extraneous to a discussion of Sarah because even before the death of her son-in-law the third earl of Sunderland she had been outraged by his remarriage after the death of her daughter to a woman not of her choosing[114] and by the marriage of his heir also to a woman whom she had not selected.[115] After the deaths in 1722 of her husband and in 1733 of her daughter Henrietta, duchess of Marlborough, she embroiled herself in endless action against the expenditures of the new duke out of the Marlborough Trust, a legal entity set up by her late husband in order, in her words, "to hinder his Posterity from being disinherited by a Spendthrift Heir," the class to which she clearly believed her elder surviving grandson belonged.[116]

Sarah had quite another opinion of his younger brother John, however, who had always been her favorite since she had undertaken to raise the Spencer boys after the early death of their mother and who in 1734 complaisantly married the woman she chose.[117] Writing to the long-suffering trustee the earl of Godolphin just months before her own death in 1744, she characterized her two grandsons' relative avariciousness:

> Howeveras I am packing up to be gone [that is, to die], I have a Mind to inform your lordship of something that is possible may be of some use to the two Sons of my Lord Sunderland's ... now nobody has any Title to [his legacy] but the three children ... now living,

112. G. C. Broderick, "The Law and Custom of Primogeniture," in *Systems of Land Tenure in Various Countries*, ed. J. W. Probyn (London, 1881), p. 105, quoted in *Family and Inheritance: Rural Society in Western Europe, 1200–1800*, eds. Jack Goody et al. (Cambridge: Cambridge University Press, 1976), p. 377.

113. "On Tuesday last the estates of his Grace Charles Duke of Marlborough, in Northamptonshire [Althorp] and Bedfordshire, together with Sunderland House in Piccadilly, were in due form conveyed to the Hon. John Spencer, his Grace's only brother, pursuant to the last will and testament of the late Duke of Marlborough—that then, in that case, he would recommend it to the Duke of Marlborough to settle such estates he was before in possession of on his younger brothers or brother, or give them or him an equivalent of money in lieu thereof, within three months after the acquisition of those honors. . . . We hear that the Duchess Dowager of Marlborough hath settled 5000*l.* per annum on the Hon. John Spencer, her grandson, and his heirs for ever"

(*Daily Courant*, 21 January 1734, quoted in Delaney 1861–1862, vol. 1, p. 430).

114. See Battiscombe 1984, pp. 67–68, where the financial settlement over Sarah's grandchildren is identified as the principal issue.

115. See Cowles 1983, p. 413, for an account of this affair which estranged Sarah from her daughter Anne Lady Bateman. The ultimate source of Sarah's rage is laid to political grudges.

116. BLMS Add.61439, fol. 123v.

117. "Yesterday, the Hon. John Spencer, Esq., brother to his Grace the Duke of Marlborough, and grandson to her Grace the Duchess-dowager of Marlborough, was married at St. George's, Hanover Square, to the third daughter of the Right Hon. the Lord Carteret, a beautiful young lady, with a fortune of 30,000*l*" (*Daily Courant*, 15 February 1734 [thus they were married on Valentine's Day], quoted in Delany 1861–1862, vol. 1, p. 427, n. 1).

that is, the two Brothers and Lady Bateman. John Spencer will want none of it, the duke of Marlborogh will always want whatever he has. What I write is to prevent any Mischief that I can....[118]

Realizing that despite all the mischief she herself had made, she could not recover the Marlborough fortune for her favorite, she made him sole heir to her personal property, a not inconsiderable consolation. Sarah, duchess of Marlborough, "had the reputation of being the richest woman in Europe, worth nearly £2,000,000 and enjoying an income of £40,000 in the commanding currency of the day."[119] Of great interest to this investigation, her personal property included prints. Their mention in an inventory of the contents of Blenheim and Marlborough House, London, undertaken as part of the endless litigation she instigated over the Marlborough legacy, is the only mention at this period of prints in the hands of the family that I have been able to locate.[120]

In October 1740 the duchess and a secretary toured every room of Blenheim Palace. Mostly they recorded furniture, and so conscientious was the identification of property that upholstery, which was often very valuable, was separated from the frames it covered: "Seven Square Stools The frames only belonging to the Trust and the upper Cases, but the Covers that are Rich Gold Embroidered upon Blew are the Dutchess of Marlbro's own furniture."[121] Some paintings were itemized: "A List of the Pictures. In the Long Closet. A Madonna of Raphael very fine which Cost Six Hundred Pistoles, [etc.]" but after a while the secretary often resorted to reference: "Lesser Pictures of different Sizes One Hundred and twenty-Six all of Great Masters and Gold Frames. There is a Printed Book which tells who are the Masters..."[122] If, however, the painting was the personal property of the duchess it was specified:

A Small Madona with a Child in a Gilt Eight Square Frame is the Dutchess of Marlboroughs and likewise the Murder of the Innocents and the Madona over the Chimney at length with Angels peircing the Serpent is hers bought of my Lord Banbury . . . Fyshes Picture at length over the Chimney done by Seeman is the Dutchess of Marlboroughs. [Etc.][123]

Then the pair came to "the Room before the Bed Chamber." Here were hanging "Thirty five Prints which are the Dutchess of Marlboroughs."[124] "In the waiting Room between the two Appartmts" were "Nine Prints by the best Hand which are the Dutchess of Marlboroughs."[125] Again

118. BLMS Add.31439, fol. 172, letter of 3 August 1744.
119. Cowles 1983, p. 405.
120. BLMS Add.61473, Blenheim papers vol. 373. A label on the inside front cover is inscribed "Inventory of Blenheim and Marlborough House signed by S. Duchess–1740." On folio 10, Sarah makes the statement, moving in its awareness of the significance of Blenheim as a unity: "The Reason that I distinguish what is mine at Blenheim is because the Hous is now Compleat and to take them away would lessen the Beauty of it which I have no mind to do. For perhaps I may alter my Mind and leave the Things at my death that are...my own."
121. BLMS Add.61473, fol. 3.
122. BLMS Add.61473, fol. 1.
123. BLMS Add.61473, fol. 2.
124. BLMS Add.61473, fol. 8.

and again the pattern repeats in successive rooms that are evidently not public spaces or state apartments:

> Belonging to the Appartm! with Arched Callico Furniture.
>
> In the Room next to the Dressing Room.
>
> Fourteen Arm Chairs Cover'd with Caffoy Yellow Ground & Crimson flowers
>
> One Window Curtain of Gold Colur'd & White Striped Burdet.
>
> Nineteen prints of the best hands which are the Dutchess of Marlbro's
>
> In M! Spencers Appartm! in the first Room.
>
> Blue Camblet Hangings
>
> A press Bed like a Cabinet
>
> A large Wainscot Stand
>
> Two Coffoy Chairs
>
> In the Bed Chamber
>
> A Blue Bed and Hangings
>
> A Wainscot Table two Stands
>
> Six Walnut Tree Chairs with blue Camblet Seats
>
> Twenty three prints that are the Dutchess of Marlbro's
>
> In the Closet
>
> Blue Camblet Hangings
>
> Four Walnut tree Chairs with Camblet Quilted
>
> A Walnut tree Chest of Drawers
>
> Two Dimity Window Curtains
>
> A Dressing Glass
>
> Fifteen Prints which are the Dutchess of Marlboroughs. [Etc.][126]

Every single print listed in this inventory is described as being the property of the duchess.[127] One wonders, of course, what they were—who were the "best hands"?—and one senses that the prints' description as such was written at the prompting of the ancient but formidable woman who stood at the secretary's elbow. In any case, they were certain to have been framed and hung as decoration, and thus, given the custom of the period, they were probably engravings and mezzotints and not the kinds of etchings which predominate in the Spencer Albums.

Apart from the evidence of the inventory, Sarah is known to have been, herself, a picture collector. In his catalogue of paintings at Althorp, Garlick identifies seventeen canvases apart from family portraits as having been hers.[128] Most of these are Dutch or German, and thus if she had purchased the Spencer Albums they would not have been an expression of personal taste.

125. BLMS Add.61473, fol. 8v.

126. BLMS Add.61473, fol. 9v.

127. No prints were listed in the inventory of Marlborough House.

128. Garlick 1976, nos. 2, 15, 46, 48, 70, 95, 100, 114, 133, 337, 432, 446, 519, 550, 551, 552, 613.

Certainly she did not hesitate in pronouncing opinions on her "spendthrift" grandson's Dutch pictures; she visited Charles in his home in the Little Lodge, Windsor Park, where she saw, as she said,

> pictures of horses and dogs and some old sort of Dutch pictures as I took them to be, with vast heavy carved frames almost as large as the cornice on the outside of a house, all gilt. I dare say they cost a great deal of money, and are worth a great deal more to those that like such things than the pictures that are in them, most of which I believe are very indifferent paintings.[129]

She is also suspected of having been a drawing collector, as the prior owner of drawings that were the property of her grandson and heir the Hon. John Spencer, as recorded in an Althorp inventory of 1756, which included works by works by Bellini, Carracci, Dürer, Raphael and Rembrandt.[130]

This inventory, which I have been unable to locate among microfilms of the Spencer-Churchill papers now on deposit in the British Library, could provide the missing clue to the *terminus ante quem* of the acquisition of the albums; for the source that reports on Sarah as a possible drawing collector goes on to say that some of the "works" "were sold at Philips in 1811 and others, years later, at Christie's in 1919." This is of vital importance in that only prints, including prints from the Spencer Albums, were sold in 1919. If the implicit identification of the presence of prints with a provenance from the Hon. John Spencer is correct, then the purchase of the albums antedates his son the first Earl Spencer, an avid collector of exactly the sort of art represented in them, who was born only in 1734 and thus could not have begun his collecting career until the 1750s.[131]

A few painting purchases by the Hon. John Spencer are known. A Rembrandt painting *The Circumcision*, now in the collection of the National Gallery, Washington, was bought at auction in 1744/45 "by Crisp for Mr. Spencer £55.13s," to quote the annotation in the copy of the sale catalogue in the Victoria and Albert Museum.[132] Garlick lists among the pictures still at Althorp a Dolci *Marriage of Saint Catherine* bought in 1740, two Panini architectural fantasies bought in 1745, and two hunting subjects by John Wootton bought as early as the mid-1730s, when Spencer had just come into his inheritance.[133]

---

129. Rowse 1958, p. 36.

130. Sutton 1981, pp. 323–24. Garlick 1976, pp. 94–105 gives an inventory of paintings at Althorp and Wimbledon "belonging to the late Honble Mr Spencer" and dated 25 October 1746. Most of the pictures had been received by him through inheritance. Seven framed drawings (nos. 160, 397) were recorded.

131. Also among the drawings sold in 1811 was lot 747, a drawing by Sir James Thornhill of "The ceiling of the hall at Blenheim—masterly pen and bistre—very fine." This could provide another link to a possible drawing collection which could only have descended through the Hon. John Spencer from the duchess of Marlborough.

132. Pears 1988, p. 245, n. 120; p. 246, n. 127.

133. Garlick 1976, nos. 130, 488, 489, 702, and 703. Nos. 704–712 in this catalogue, also purchased by the Hon. John Spencer, are also hunting, dog, and horse paintings which, because of the people in them, would have functioned as family portraits, such as nos. 331 and 333. It should be noted that Wootton was an extremely expensive taste; see Deuchar 1988, p. 140.

These purchases are the only indication of his artistic taste (unless we assume that he had *asked* his grandmother to hang so many prints in his "appartm^t"). The Hon. John Spencer, born in 1608, was educated abroad at his grandmother's expense. Perhaps she sensed in him an inclination toward art; his (and his brother's) cicerone on the Continent reported him "very eager in his desires to see Italy."[134] Her instructions to the tutor expressed strong sentiments against the acquisition of "taste":

> I never had any taste for curiosities and I think they are of little value further than that they serve to kill time while you have nothing better to do and that it is not proper to be in England. Useful learning is what I have always earnestly recommended and next to that, to be sure, good company. . . . [She then runs through speaking foreign languages well, dancing, and fencing.] As to medals and antiquities, painting and sculpture, I don't look upon that to be the most useful knowledge to anybody, and much less to younger brothers who will have no money to lay out on such things.[135]

This last disingenuous comment about the eighteen-year-old John, whom she doted upon, came true in a way, for he died at age thirty-eight after enjoying her legacy for only two years. He goes practically unmentioned in family histories, and the one briefly vivid characterization I have found gives little hope for him as a sustained collector: "the reprobate Jack Spencer, the adored and distracting grandson of Sarah Jennings [Duchess of Marlborough]."[136]

We move on, then, to his son John, who thoroughly enjoyed the wealth and paintings that came as his inheritance. Prohibited by the terms of his great-grandmother's legacy from an active role in politics, he worked effectively enough behind the scenes to be created Viscount Spencer in 1761 and Earl Spencer in 1765.[137] He had become a familiar figure in the sale rooms by the 1750s; in 1758 he paid £2,200 for a Sacchi and a Guido Reni.[138] Some of the other most important paintings at Althorp today were also his purchases, including Gaspard Dughet's *Landscape in the Roman Campagna, with Figures* also bought in 1758, Rosa's *Witches and Their Incantation* bought in 1761, and a Rosa pair, *Cincinnatus Called from the Farm* and *Diogenes*, bought in Florence in 1764. He commissioned horse and dog portraits from Stubbs[139] and in 1771 in Rome commissioned *Agrippina with the Ashes of Germanicus* from Gavin Hamilton.[140] According to an in-

134. Rowse 1958, p. 16; to complete the passage: "Mr. [Charles] Spencer had very little curiosity and looks upon all travelling as a very insipid entertainment, and thinks of Italy with a great dread as having no taste to the things he expects to see there. But Mr. John is far from being in the same case; he thinks of seeing France with pleasure enough, but he is very eager. . . . "

135. Rowse 1958, pp. 18–19. Sarah was outraged at the frivolous expenses for which their tutor asked repayment, "all those extravagancies of music, treats, allowances to the footmen and feathers, notwithstanding that I writ positively that I would not allow of it" (p. 10).

136. Villiers 1939, p. 2, n. 2.

137. Garlick 1976, p. xiv. This source, pp. xiii–xiv, gives the most intelligible summary of the descent of property through the Churchill and Spencer lines. With regard to Spencer's politicking, "When he entertained the voters at Althorp he stationed footmen at the main door holding plates of sandwiches. Each guest took one, and biting into it, found his teeth meeting a golden guinea" (Battiscombe 1984, p. 76).

138. Garlick 1976, nos. 579 and 521.

139. Garlick 1976, nos. 622–623.

140. Garlick 1976, no. 261.

scription on a copy of an 1811 auction catalogue, he was also the collector of several hundred old-master drawings whose attributions exactly coincide with the generally fashionable taste expressed by the Spencer Albums.[141] There is no doubt that if he did not purchase the albums, at least he would have appreciated them. And the first Earl Spencer was not unknown as a library purchaser, although his inclinations were slight compared to those of his grandfather and son.[142] That he purchased books en bloc indicates by analogy, perhaps, a readiness to buy a preassembled print collection. Certainly, however, he could not have commissioned the Spencer Albums, which had to have been produced prior to his tenth birthday.

❧

In sum, I believe Sarah, duchess of Marlborough, to have been the most likely patron of the Mariettes. I consider her grandson the Hon. John Spencer a close second possibility, and I reserve the outside chance of her son-in-law Charles, third earl of Sunderland, having commissioned the Spencer Albums. And I must always concede that any member of the family, from Charles down to the book-mad second Earl Spencer, could have purchased the albums ready-made.

The frustration at not being able to identify with certainty the first owner of these volumes should in no way, however, compromise our appreciation of their status as surviving evidence of the preeminent expertise of the Mariettes and the fact of their patronage at the highest levels. Just as silks, porcelains, or furniture set standards of design, craftsmanship, and luxury that made French decorative arts the conventional language of gift and display across Europe, the connoisseurship of prints as practiced by the Mariettes resulted in tangible products—sets of print albums—which probably far exceeded their immediate purchasers' appreciation, yet which provided these patrons with demonstrations of a sensibility toward costly, rare, and fashionable art. That the Spencer Albums were commercial products and not the piece-by-piece accumulation of an amateur makes them all the more precious testimony to the taste of their time, the time of taste.

141. Philipe 1811. See above, note 48.
142. Battiscombe 1984, p. 75, where a purchase of a library of five thousand volumes, largely Elizabethan works, is mentioned.

CATALOGUE

OF THE EXHIBITION

Note to the Catalogue

The prints have been measured to their plate marks, where visible; otherwise, the sheet size is given. Generally speaking, the prints in the Spencer Albums have been trimmed very close to the plate marks or within them. Height precedes width.

Where no watermark is described, none was found.

References to multiartist, multivolume standard print catalogues are abbreviated, using the initial or name as indicated in the Bibliography followed by the volume number, the page number, and the catalogue number, each separated by a period. No attempt has been made to list every published catalogue reference for each print.

The accession number was assigned to each print according to its place within the Spencer Albums. Thus, a print with the accession number s3.49.4 would be from Spencer Album 3; it would have been mounted on the forty-ninth folio, and would have been the fourth print on that page, reading from left to right and top to bottom. All prints will be remounted in the albums after exhibition.

The authors of the catalogue:

DPB David P. Becker
ACB Andrew C. Blume
CB   Cammy Brothers
MBC Marjorie B. Cohn
SRL Shelley R. Langdale
KHN Kristina Hartzer Nguyen
AS   Anne Summerscale

Index of Artists in the Exhibition

GIOVANNI BATTISTA D'ANGOLO DEL MORO

Verona c. 1515 – c. 1573 Venice

1 *Landscape with Saint Theodore and the Dragon*, after Titian, 1560s

etching and engraving

197 x 326 mm

inscribed in plate, lower right: *Apresso Gio'a Franc.º Camocio.*[1]

drawing on verso, black chalk, of a hand, and, red chalk, a tracing of the hill and buildings of the print on the recto

B.XVI.99.5 (Titian), TIB32.149.5 (Titian)

Francis H. Burr Fund, s6.3.1

Cataloguers of this etching have always recognized its relationship to the work of Titian; in fact, it closely copies a drawing from the Venetian master's late period, now in the Janos Scholtz Collection of the Pierpont Morgan Library, New York.[2] The etching was given in print in the late eighteenth century to Titian himself,[3] but in manuscript Mariette had already doubted an unequivocable attribution:

> This work . . . passes for being, not only the invention of Titian, but also his print. However, even though this work has been done with considerable skill and precision and even though one could not better imitate the manner of Titian, it seems to me that one cannot say that it was engraved by this capable painter. Rather, I believe it to be by one of his disciples who has engraved all the other landscapes whose execution is attributed to Titian. . . .[4]

In the table of contents of Spencer Album 6, the compiler, whom we propose to have been Pierre-Jean Mariette (together with his father), was equally circumspect: "Two Landscapes, invented by Titian, & which are supposed also to be engraved by him. . . . "[5] This caution contrasts with his description of the two preceding plates as "invented & engraved by Titian."[6]

Bartsch, in his introduction to the few etchings that he lists under "Titian," was equally dubious about the attribution and bluntly stated his basis:

> Many of our readers will be astonished to find our catalogue of the work of *Titian* consisting of only eight pieces; and in our opinion, even these did not come from the needle of this painter. It is more than likely that *Titian* never engraved anything. . . . In inserting these prints in our work under the heading of *Titian*, we have only wanted to avoid the reproach . . . which would have been made to us by amateurs who took these prints to be productions of the needle of this great artist, and who . . . paid dearly for them.[7]

Bartsch went on to comment that the various sixteenth-century etchings after Titian landscapes must have been the work of several hands. Their attributions have been much discussed over the succeeding years, and we concur with the ascription of this particular plate to Giovanni Battista d'Angolo del Moro.[8]

Battista was born in Verona c. 1515, where he worked until 1557, when he and his son Marco went to Murano to work on the decoration of the Palazzo Treviso, where Paolo Veronese, Alessandro Zelotti, and others also worked. He apparently remained in Venice until his death c. 1573. He was a prominent figure among a number of etchers in the Veneto in the mid-sixteenth century, including Battista Pittoni, Giovanni Battista and Giulio Fontana, Paolo and Orazio Farinati, and Angiolo Falconetto. Although these artists worked primarily as painters, they produced a steady succession of prints from the early 1550s through the end of the century.[9] Apart from the woodcut, etching was the preferred medium in Venice. It allowed a delicate touch and muted, even tonality which could approximate the colorism of Venetian painting without resorting to the complex pictorialism often employed to achieve similar effects in engraving.

The wide range of styles and techniques through which Battista progressed has led to confusion among the cataloguers of his etchings, which has been compounded by the many ways he signed his plates, using initials and variations of his name and nickname.[10] Sometimes he did not sign at all, as seen in this print. His work of the 1550s shows influence of both Titian and Battista Franco in the use of unmarked areas of paper and more regular systems of hatching (e.g.,

61

TIB32.298.25, TIB32.305.32). Battista's production of a number of landscape prints at this time further indicates his interest in Titian.[11] His figures, however, in their bulging muscles and diminutive extremities relate more to the work of Veronese than to Venetian styles. Both these influences are evident in this print. In composition and detail, the etching is quite faithful to the drawing, except for some areas of cross-hatching and most obviously the addition of the funneling cloud of smoke that fills the left corner. This raises an interesting iconographical issue, but first the history of the saint must be told.

Most early cataloguers of this print, including Mariette, gave it a descriptive title such as "Landscape with Dragon." Others assumed it to be a depiction of Saint George. Nancy de Grummond first recognized the subject as an event from the life of Saint Theodore, an obscure fourth-century saint who was the patron saint of Venice from the sixth century until the body of Saint Mark was brought to the city from Alexandria in the ninth century.[12]

According to de Grummond, the representation of Saint Theodore in the Morgan Library drawing (and thus this print) relates most nearly to a story told by Dionysius Draconarius. Briefly, Christ appears to the sleeping warrior-saint and orders him to slay a dragon which has been terrorizing the city of Euchaita. At the time of Saint Theodore's summons, the young son of a poor Christian widow had been selected for sacrifice and is tied up before the city, waiting for the dragon's approach. Saint Theodore arrives and, encountering the beast, orders it to halt in the name of Christ. The dragon falls at the feet of the saint, who pierces it through with his lance. In this print, triumph over the dragon occurs essentially as a result of the saint's command, the lance serving as an auxiliary prop which he will then use to finish off the monster. In the background, the group of buildings represents the city of Euchaita and in the middle distance under a tree, a tiny seated figure may portray the child.

The killing of the dragon by weapon alone is a far more frequent representation of Saint Theodore in the literature on the saint and in Venetian images prior to the sixteenth century. De Grummond suggests that a shift in interest in the depiction of Saint Theodore and the dragon occurred in response to the rise of the cult of Saint George, who shares the attribute of the slaying of a dragon while on horseback, traditional also to Saint Theodore. Hence the absence of a horse in Titian's drawing and this print, and the inclusion of the more obscure reference to the saint's verbal challenge to the dragon. Note the gesture of command in the raised hand (which has also been interpreted as fright and abhorrence: Mariette said that the soldier regards "avec frayeur un horrible dragon"[13]).

The presence of the smoke could be explained by another incident in Saint Theodore's life. Such conflations of stories in one image are not unusual, and it may have served here to clarify the identity of the saint as Theodore rather than George. In a tale typical of Christian martyrdom, Theodore refuses to sacrifice to idols and is apprehended and interrogated (and eventually martyred). The authorities give him a few days respite to change his mind, during which he uses his freedom to set fire to the pagan temple. De Grummond has suggested that the smoke rising from the hills in Battista's print may allude to this.[14]

The swirl of smoke, however, is an engraved addition to what is otherwise a pure etching. One impression is known "before the smoke," in the Gabinetto degli Uffizi, Florence (inv. no. 2619). Whether the smoke was added to fill an area which appeared empty once the composition was reversed in the print or whether a further identification of the scene with the story of Saint Theodore was desired is moot. It is not surprising that engraving was chosen for the supplementary work; multiple biting of plates is virtually unknown in Italian etching until the work of Barocci in the 1580s. In any case, the impression in the Spencer Album would thus be a third state, as there are several known impressions before the addition of the publisher's name but with the smoke.

SRL & MBC

1. Giovanni Francesco Camoccio was principally a book and print seller, but he also worked as an artist and published books and prints of his own work in Venice between 1550 and 1570. His address also appears on the Venetian prints of Martino Rota and Etienne Dupérac. See Reed and Wallace 1989, p. 83, n. 2.

2. Inv. no. 1977.46. The authorship of the drawing, no less than that of the etching, has been debated, but recent scholars agree on the attribution to Titian. For the history of the attribution, which includes the suggestion that the drawing itself was by Battista, see Chiari Moretto Weil 1989, no. 32. For additional discussion of the drawing see Harold E. Wethey, *Titian and His Drawings, with Reference to Giorgione and Some Close Contemporaries* (Princeton: Princeton University Press, 1987), pp. 52, 164. The date currently accepted for the drawing is c. 1560.

3. Heinecken 1778–1790, vol. 3, pp. 542–44.

4. Mariette 1851–1860, vol. 5, pp. 331–32: "Cette pièce, qui est gravée à l'eau forte, passe pour être, non seulement de l'invention de Titien, mais encor de sa graveure.—Cependant, quoyque cette pièce soit touchée avec autant d'art que de précision et qu'on ne puisse mieux imiter la manière du Titien, il me semble qu'on ne peut pas dire qu'elle soit gravée par ce savant peintre. Je la crois plustost d'un de ses disciples qui a gravé tous les autres paysages dont l'on attribue la gravure au Titien. . . ." Mariette goes on to propose an artist: "et je tiens que c'est celuy qui a marqué quelques unes de ses pièces de la marque D. B." He assembles a small oeuvre for "D. B.," whom he suggests (p. 339) could have been Dirck Barentsz., a Dutch pupil of Titian. However, "D. B." would seem to be correctly identified by Nagler as Donato Bertelli, who with his younger relative Domenico Bertelli was a printmaker and publisher in Venice in the second half of the sixteenth century (Nagler 1858–1879, vol. 2, p. 384, nos. 973, 974).

5. "Deux Paysages, inventés par le Titien & que l'on pretend aussi etre gravés par luy . . ." The other print is *Landscape with a Swineherd* (TIB 32.150.6), now attributed to an anonymous sixteenth-century artist after Titian.

6. ". . . inventé & gravé par le Titien." The landscapes are *The Flautist* (TIB 32.151.7), now attributed to an anonymous sixteenth-century artist after Titian, and *Landscape with Nymphs and Satyrs* (TIB 42.51.44), now attributed to Giovanni Francesco Grimaldi. Curiously, another etched copy after the Titian drawing that was the model for the latter print has been attributed to del Moro (Chiari 1982, p. 65).

7. B.XVI.95: "Plusieurs de nos lecteurs seront étonnés de ne trouver notre catalogue de l'oeuvre du *Titien* composé que de huit seules pièces; et suivant notre opinion, encore celles-ci ne viennent elles pas de la point de ce peintre. Il est plus que probable, que *Titien* n'a jamais rien gravé . . . En insérant ces estampes dans notre ouvrage sous l'article du *Titien*, nous n'avons voulu par là qu'eviter le reproche . . . que nous auroient fait ceux des amateurs qui prennent ces estampes pour des productions de la pointe de ce grand artiste, et qui . . . les auront peut-être payées chèrement."

8. The attribution was first proposed by Nagler and is confirmed by Chiari. See Chiari 1982, p. 64, for a summary of proposed attributions, which include Battista's son Marco.

9. See Reed and Wallace 1989, pp. 32–33, where the biography of Battista is by David Acton. See also Terence Mullaly, "Battista del Moro in Perspective," *Print Quarterly* 4, no. 4 (1987):403–7, where three more prints are added to his oeuvre.

10. Battista was the son-in-law and pupil of the painter Francesco Torbido, called Il Moro, from whom he took his nickname. See Giorgio Vasari, *Le vite de piu eccelenti pittori scultori ed architetti* (Florence, 1568), ed. Gaetano Milanesi (Florence, 1878–1885), vol. 5, pp. 296–98.

11. Wilhelm Schmidt describes fifteen landscape etchings by Battista in Meyer, vol. 2, p. 38, nos. 33–47.
12. Grummond 1972, pp. 6, 11–12, 25.

13. Mariette 1851–1860, vol. 5., p. 331.
14. Grummond 1972, pp. 24–25.

AGOSTINO CARRACCI

Bologna 1557 – 1602 Parma

2 *The Madonna of St. Jerome*, 1586, after Cornelis Cort after Correggio

engraving

482 x 328 mm

watermark: six-pointed sun-shape in circle with crown above

inscribed in plate, lower right of design area: *Aug. Car. Bonon. ᵉincidit et impressit / 1586 / Venetiis Donati Rasciotti formis;* lower margin: *TYBERIO DELPHINO PHISICAE PERTISS.ᵒ ET C./ OPTIME MERITO / INVENTIONEM HANC EXIMII PICTORIS ANTONII CORREGIENSIS GRATI ANIMI ERGO DICAT SACRATQ. / AVGVSTINVS CARRATIVS.*
inscribed in brown ink, verso: *P. mariette 1679*

B.XVIII.87.95 iii/iii, TIB39.134.95, Bohlin 142 iii/iv.

Alpheus Hyatt Fund, S1.10

The Spencer Album entitled "Works of the Carraci and of Several Painters of Their School"[1] opens with a long sequence of the prints of Annibale, Agostino, and Lodovico Carracci, the three Bolognese painters who, by their energetic reform of the Mannerist style they found prevalent in Bologna and Rome, established the basis for the seventeenth-century North Italian Baroque style. Especially important in this regard, with influence reaching far beyond their century and locale, were two achievements of the Carracci apart from their paintings: their foundation of an enduring art academy at Bologna based upon the study of the live model, and the proliferation through prints of compositions, their own and others, that embodied the principles of naturalistic and ample form, space, and design, which were their specific concern.

The selection of seventy-five Carracci prints in the Spencer Albums is just that, a selection. The graphic oeuvres of Annibale, Agostino, and Lodovico are much larger;[2] and if one takes into account the traditional understanding of the "oeuvre" of an artist as represented in prints, one would have to assemble a full album for Lodovico and no less than seven for Annibale and Agostino together, which is in fact the number of volumes of prints by and after the Carracci arranged by the Mariettes for Prince Eugene of Savoy and described in the manuscript catalogue now in the Bibliothèque Nationale.[3]

To this day the oeuvre of a painter is understood to comprise all of his compositions, and

Aug. Car. Bonon, incidit et impressit.
1586.
Venetiis Donati Rascicotti formis.

TYBERIO DELPHINO PHISICÆ PERITISS. ET C.
OPTIME MERITO
INVENTIONEM HANC EXIMII PICTORIS ANTONII CORREGIENSIS GRATI ANIMI ERGO DICAT SACRATQ.
AVGVSTINVS CARRATIVS.

until the late nineteenth century, that is, until photographic reproduction devalued the reproductive engraving, the oeuvre was represented by prints executed after his compositions. It was this kind of oeuvre of the Carracci about which the Mariettes, father and son, corresponded at length in 1717–1719, when Pierre-Jean, who had been sent to Vienna to catalogue the collection of Prince Eugene of Savoy, found that the prince had acquired a large group of Italian prints that had originally been assembled by a Bolognese painter. Jean Mariette suggested that the group had once belonged to the seventeenth-century Bolognese biographer and art historian Malvasia. It was especially rich in works by and after the Carracci.[4] Pierre-Jean wrote his father, "However, I find them excellent and, it appears to me, of an extraordinary rarity."[5] The "However" refers to his distress at the prints' condition; as he explained in another letter, "these are prints which belonged to painters that is to say very poorly preserved . . . it's a great pity. . . ."[6]

The Spencer Album selection of the oeuvre of the Carracci concentrates practically entirely upon prints from the hands of the three artists. Those few prints after their works that it includes are etchings by the Carracci's immediate followers, such as Coriolano's *Christ Crowned with Thorns* after Lodovico (TIB41.133.1)[7] and Brizio's *Holy Family Returning from Egypt* after Lodovico (TIB40.114.2) and *The Virgin and Child Beneath a Tree* after Agostino (TIB40.115.3). This does not mean, of course, that there are not many reproductive prints among the Carraccis in the album, for a few of Annibale's prints and many of Agostino's, including this one, reproduce the works of others.

Agostino was principally a reproductive engraver, at a time when this was as honored a profession as that of *peintre-graveur*, as a later century would denominate the printmaker who works from his own original designs. *The Madonna of Saint Jerome*, as this Madonna and Child with an angel and Saints Jerome, Mary Magdalen, and the youthful John the Baptist is known, is ostensibly a reproduction of the painting by Correggio which, in the sixteenth century, was in the church of S. Antonio in Parma (and is now in the Galleria Nazionale, Parma). Yet despite the inscription on the print crediting the composition to Correggio, in fact there is no doubt that Agostino copied the image from its reproduction in an engraving by Cornelis Cort (H.V.45.50).[8] This was suggested by cataloguers as early as Malvasia, and Bohlin argues the case convincingly. Her concluding suggestion—"Since the painting was probably in a dark church interior and because Agostino usually worked after drawings, it may have been a convenience to use Cort's engraving as a model"—is eminently sensible.[9]

What is curious is the Mariettes' disregard of the intermediary model by Cort. In the Mariette manuscript in the Bibliothèque Nationale, the print is listed as "after the famous painting by Correggio which is at Parma." The writer goes on to say, "Agostino Carracci made few works so well drawn and handled with such skill, it makes one wish that he had engraved many others after the great Painter whose graces are so sensitive and lively."[10] What is even more curious is the marginal note in Pierre-Jean Mariette's hand: "The landscape is an addition which is not in the painting."[11] It is exactly this landscape, copied directly from Cort, which distinguishes the Cort print from the original picture.

Pierre-Jean Mariette recognized Agostino as a copyist of Cort: the Bibliothèque Nationale manuscript identifies the *Rest on the Flight into Egypt* (Bohlin 39), which reproduces a composition of Passari, as a copy of Cort's engraving of that subject.[12] And the Mariettes also compiled an extensive catalogue of the works of Cort, whose prints filled two volumes.[13] Pierre-Jean's opinion of the Cort print, however, was prejudiced by his evaluation of the signature "C. Cart" which is found on this engraving and on others by the Netherlandish artist who worked in Northern Italy. With reference to a print of Saint Nicholas, Mariette wrote:

> ... this print and the others which are in his oeuvre with this same name, *C. Cart.*, are not by the celebrated engraver C. Cort. He never did anything in Italy with such inflexibility of line, and we have here a new and unknown engraver, of whom it seems I have made the discovery. ... This same C. Cart also made a copy of the Virgin, accompanied by Saint Jerome and Saint Magdalen, engraved by Agos. Carracci, after Correggio. ...[14]

No subsequent scholar has acknowledged the existence of C. Cart. This is among the very few errors of attribution or judgment which can be found among the prints catalogued by the Mariettes.

Perhaps the Mariettes' conception of the Cort as an inferior product was influenced by the advance in engraving technique by Agostino Carracci from Cort signaled by the former's copy of the latter's work. If one compares the line structure of Agostino's *Madonna of Saint Jerome* to that of the Cort original, one sees, especially in the close cross-hatching, an abandonment of moiré effects, which had been cultivated by Mannerist engravers to the point of making them positive pictorial devices. Hatchings in the print by Agostino, while no less disciplined than those in Cort's, produce even in the relatively late impression on exhibition a full, plastic effect without calling attention to the actual engraved surface. This advance toward an appearance of naturalism would have been very much to the taste of the Mariettes. That this particular impression, which is in a superb state of preservation, was not scorned by them is indicated not only by its inclusion in the Spencer Album but also by the signature of Pierre Mariette II on its reverse.

MBC

1. *"Oeuvres des Carraches et de Quelques Peintres de Leur Ecole."*

2. See Bohlin for their complete production of prints. This exemplary catalogue gives twenty-two plates to Annibale, with three rejected; 213 plates to Agostino, with an additional twenty-one questioned and fifty-nine rejected; and four plates to Lodovico, with one rejected.

3. BNMS R065733, R065770, R065778, R065793, R065800, R065808, and R065855 are the frames in which the description of each album begins.

4. The letters from Pierre-Jean Mariette in Vienna to his father Jean Mariette in Paris that contain discussions of the Italian prints in this particular collection are MLMS BS/b9/L6, L8, L12 (to Baron G. W. von Hohendorff, diplomatic adviser and artistic agent of Prince Eugene in Paris), L34, L35, and L37. The letter from Jean Mariette to his son that mentions the possibility that the prints belonged to Malvasia is MLMS BS/b10/L11.

5. MLMS BS/b9/L6: "J'y en trouve cependent d'excellentes & que me parroissais d'une rarité extraordinaire" (n.d., 1717).

6. MLMS BS/bp/L12: "ce sont des estampes qui ont appartenu à des peintres c'est à dire forte mal conservées ... c'est grand domage ..." (Pierre-Jean Mariette to Baron von Hohendorff, Vienna, 15 December 1717). An intriguing possibility is raised by the poor condition of

the superb first-state impression of Agostino's *Pietà* (Bohlin 102) included in the Spencer Album, which is disfigured by having been heavily squared for transfer, a typical abuse through use at the hands of a painter. In their correspondence Pierre-Jean indicated to his father that Prince Eugene would turn over to the Mariettes duplicates from his collection created by the assimilation of this Italian collection; one wonders whether this print was among them.

7. In fact the print is after a drawing by Cavedone after the painting by Lodovico.

8. Hollstein identifies the subject as the Madonna and Child with Saints Catherine and Jerome.

9. Bohlin, p. 244.

10. BNMS R065741: "La Sᵗᵉ Vierge accompagnée de Sᵗ Jerosme debut & de Sᵗe Magdaleine qui adore à genoux l'enfant Jesus. Cette excellente estampe a eté gravée a Bologne en 1586 d'après le fameux tableau du Correge qu est à Parme. Augustin Carrache a fait peu de pieces, aussy bien desinnées & touchées avec autant d'art que celle cy, il feront a souhaiter qu'il on en gravé plusieurs autres d'après le grand Peintre dont les graces sont si

sensibles & si piquantes." It is interesting to note that Bartsch followed the Mariettes here as in so many other things, in ignoring the existence of the intermediary of the Cort print.

11. BNMS R065741: "Le paysage est une addition qui n'est point dans le tableau."

12. BNMS R065740. See Bohlin, p. 137, for a discussion of the competitive relationship of Agostino and Cort as reported by Malvasia, at this early stage of the former's career.

13. BNMS R066180 is the first frame of the Cort catalogue.

14. Mariette 1851–1860, vol. 2, pp. 16–17: ". . . cette pièce cy et les autres qui sont dans le cours de l'oeuvre avec ce mesme nom, *C. Cart*, ne sont point du célèbre graveur C. Cort. Il n'a jamais rien fait en Italie de si roide pour la conduite des tailles, et voicy un nouveau graveur qui n'estoit pas connu, dont il me semble avoir fait la découverte. . . . Ce mesme C. Cart a fait aussy une copie de la Vierge, accompagnée de Saint Jérosme et de sainte Magdaleine, gravée par Aug. Carrache, d'après *le Corrége* . . ."

ANNIBALE CARRACCI
Bologna 1560 – 1609 Rome

3 *Saint Francis of Assisi*, 1585

engraving

145 x 106 mm

inscribed on plate, lower center: *1585*; on a rock, lower left: *Ani Ca / in fe.*

inscribed, verso, brown ink: *P. mariette 1691*

B.XVIII.191.15, TIB39.402.18, Bohlin 7

Alpheus Hyatt Fund, s1.30.1

Annibale Carracci is arguably the leading figure in the reform of painting initiated in Bologna at the end of the sixteenth century. He and his brother Agostino, along with their cousin Lodovico, founded an academy of painting there in 1582 that taught art based on the models of the High Renaissance and classical antiquity. They encouraged drawing from life and the painting of compositions that would be more understandable to the beholder.

The major printmaker of the family was not Annibale. That honor belonged to Agostino, to whom 231 prints can be securely attributed.[1] Malvasia, the seventeenth-century biographer and

historian of Bolognese art, tells us that Annibale learned printmaking from Agostino, and Bohlin has returned several Agostino-like prints to Annibale's early years as a printmaker, around 1581.[2] Agostino's graphic language is one that is consistently orderly and rational. Hatching always follows the contour of forms, the compositions are carefully worked out with a great deal of attention paid to detail, and, as Bohlin has remarked, his lines are "juxtaposed in a careful progression."[3] Annibale was more interested in the intrinsically artistic possibilities of the medium. Where Agostino worked to translate the effects of oil painting, Annibale sought to create independent works of art that exploited the possibilities of the medium. Annibale's prints are sketchier and looser than his brother's, and his forms often disintegrate into the background, creating a sense of atmosphere and light.

These are some of the elements that we see in this small *Saint Francis*. The print was probably intended as a portable devotional image, the subject of which does not seem to appear in any of the Franciscan legends and is clearly not intended as a narrative but rather as an exemplum of a certain kind of personal spirituality. *Saint Francis*, dated 1585, is similar in format and scale to three representations of saints that Agostino executed around 1583. Agostino's prints—*Saint Francis Receiving the Stigmata, Saint Jerome*, and *Saint Francis Adoring the Crucifix*[4]—are executed in a tight, careful manner; all show the respective saint half-length, with his attention fixed within the picture. The person who would be contemplating the image is not engaged by the saint or made to feel as if he could enter the picture's space. All of the figures have been brought right up to the front of the picture plane, and the object of their contemplation has been moved to the edge of the scene. The beholder is asked to look at the saint as an emblem and is not invited to participate in his meditation.

Annibale, on the other hand, by allowing us to see the saint from straight on and by placing the skull in his lap, gives the viewer access to the same experience as the saint. Francis becomes not only the object, but the mediator of our devotion. Our focus—created by the intense light of the white of the paper around Francis's head—is, however, still on Francis's own ecstatic experience as he embraces the cross while looking down at the skull, a symbol of both sin and death. His profound absorption was recognized even in the seventeenth century, by Giovanni Bellori in his biography of Annibale: "St. Francis clasps the Crucifix to his breast and in his heart contemplates death . . ."[5]

The burin work is very loose, and Annibale seems to be trying to do something new with the medium. Instead of exploring engraving's expressive possibilities as developed by Mannerist engravers, by using calligraphic swelling lines and networks of close hatching to build up forms, he varies the length of his lines and avoids hard contours and edges. He achieves a certain sketchy quality, especially in his rendering of Francis's hair and the landscape in the background, that is not inherent in engraving. He reaches a height of naturalism, spontaneity, and light in the figure of the saint, especially in the intensity of his expression. The saint has been rendered so as to give a maximum of expressive effect by stressing his face, crabbed feet, and gnarled hands contrasted with the relative simplicity of the robe, which acts as a foil for the fall of light and shade. Some of the lines are so undisciplined and seemingly effortless that it is almost as if this engraving were an etching. Even Malvasia was fooled: he mistakenly referred to the print as an etching.[6] Clearly Annibale was trying to exploit these effects, and by the 1590s, he began to use etching more and more in his prints.

ACB

1. See Bohlin passim.

2. Bohlin, pp. 37, 422–30. The prints in question are *The Crucifixion*, signed and dated 1581 (Bohlin 1) and *The Holy Family with Saints John the Baptist and Michael*, signed and dated 1582 (Bohlin 2).

3. Bohlin, p. 39.

4. Bohlin 124–26, repro. p. 221.

5. Bellori 1968, p. 74.

6. Bellori 1968, p. 434.

PIETRO FACCINI

Bologna c. 1562 – 1602 Bologna

4   *Saint Francis Holding the Christ Child in the Presence of the Virgin*

etching

361 x 245 mm

inscribed, verso, brown ink: *P. mariette 1668*

B.XVIII.272.1, TIB40.144.1, TIB4004.270.001

Alpheus Hyatt Fund, S1.31

It is hard to know where to place Pietro Faccini among the artists who emerged in Bologna towards the end of the sixteenth century. By the time he had reached his mid-twenties, Faccini seems to have established himself as a rather prosperous merchant who, as Malvasia tells us, "attired himself nobly, treated himself well, and lived in the grand manner, being able to live on his income when he took up painting."[1] Malvasia's remarks lead us to believe that Faccini did not begin his career as an artist but probably took up painting in the late 1580s, around the time he is known to have joined the Carracci academy.

The paintings of Faccini, such as the *Martyrdom of Saint Lawrence* for the Ferri Chapel of S. Giovanni in Monte at Bologna,[2] a commission of 1590 that came through his contacts with the Carracci, are executed with a monumental sense of scale and a clarity of narrative that seems to reflect Venetian influences. The artist has combined these elements with a typically Bolognese figure style, which comes down through Parmigianino, and a looseness of handling, which might find its precedents in Ferrarese painting and would later appeal to young artists of the next generation such as Guercino. The ideas that seem to underlie his traditionally Emilian yet reform-minded style must have their roots prior to his first formal contact with the Carracci academy. Although Faccini seems to have had no direct followers or pupils, his works left their mark on the history of Bolognese painting in other ways. Guercino, for example, had access to some of the drawings of the older artist, whose style is evident in the early work of the younger master.[3]

The Vision of Saint Francis, the only Faccini print in the Spencer Albums, is one of four etchings Bartsch attributed to the artist.[4] The print illustrates a popular Franciscan legend with no precise literary source. Although the story of Saint Francis receiving the Christ Child appears in Lucas Wadding's *Annales minorum* of 1625, there seems to be no previous text of the legend. It might very well have had its origins in a tale from the *Little Flowers of Saint Francis*, which tells of such an event happening to a certain Brother Conrad of Offidia. It is likely that in the search for new Franciscan imagery after the Council of Trent, the miracle became associated with the saint himself and not his lesser-known companion.[5] The earliest known pictorial representation of

71

this new subject is Lodovico Carracci's painting of 1583–1584[6] (Rijksmuseum, Amsterdam), which might very well have been known to Faccini while he was associated with the Carracci academy.

The composition of this print probably records a now lost painting of the subject that was painted for the Church of the Cappuccini in Bologna[7] which we know also from three drawings, in the Fogg, in the Ashmolean Museum, Oxford, and in the Louvre.[8] The Christ Child lies precariously balanced in the saint's arms, almost forgotten as the composition focuses on the relationship between Saint Francis and the Virgin. These two protagonists look directly into each other's eyes, locking in the diagonal composition that is created by the reciprocal kneeling poses of their figures. Among the drawings, only the Louvre version places the saint in this relationship with the Virgin. The Oxford sheet appears to be dependent upon Lodovico's composition. Here the Virgin stands on the ground (with no angels) next to the saint, who looks at the child as he cradles him in his arms. The Fogg drawing is a kind of *via media* between the two. Here the saint looks neither at the Child nor at his mother, who is still on the ground but now has a prominent halo.

In the print, Faccini has used the white of the paper contrasted against the wedges of quickly etched lines to create the aura surrounding the Virgin and saint. Francis's companion, who shades his eyes from the light, watches the scene from below, outside of this glow. The careful cross-hatching of Francis's robe describes both its texture and the fall of light and shade, making him a remarkably solid and earthy figure. The Virgin's draperies, on the other hand, seem to dissolve into the light that surrounds her. Faccini has etched the Virgin so as to anchor her feet and legs into the diagonal of the composition by using a graphic language similar to that which he has used throughout the figure of Francis. Her upper body, however, is etched much more loosely and the lines have a freedom not found elsewhere in the print. While maintaining the stability of the composition, Faccini has differentiated between the two worlds of the Virgin and the saint.

It has been suggested that the general format of the composition, especially the pose of the Virgin, derives from Agostino Carracci's engraving after Tintoretto of the *Madonna Appearing to Saint Jerome*.[9] If this is the case, Faccini has transformed a rather grandiose and impersonal composition, in which the main characters are separated by a gulf of space, into a scene of high tension and great emotion by placing the main protagonists in proximity to each other towards the front of the picture plane and by reducing the setting to a bare minimum.

ACB

1. Malvasia 1841, as cited by Mario di Giampaolo in Washington 1986, p. 129.

2. Washington 1986, pp. 129–30, cat. 43.

3. See De Grazia 1984, p. 375.

4. B.XVIII.270–73, TIB40.144–46. Veronika Birke excludes all but *The Vision of Saint Francis* from Faccini's oeuvre in TIB4004.269.

5. See Andrew Blume, "*A Vision of Saint Francis* in the Wadsworth Atheneum," *Master Drawings* 29 (1991): 52–54.

6. Gail Feigenbaum suggests this date in her forthcoming monograph on Lodovico (Bologna: Nuova Alfa). The painting is illustrated in *The Age of Caravaggio* (New York: Metropolitan Museum of Art, 1985), pp. 120–21, cat. 28.

7. De Grazia 1984, pp. 386, 388. Malvasia says that Fac-

cini executed a "San Francesco che receve Cristo Bambino nelle braccia" (Malvasia 1841, vol. 1, p. 400).

8. Reproduced in De Grazia 1984, pp. 386–87.

9. Reed and Wallace 1989, p. 115. Agostino's print is illustrated and discussed in Bohlin 146.

CAMILLO PROCACCINI

Bologna? c. 1555 – 1629 Milan

5   *Saint Francis of Assisi Receiving the Stigmata*, 1593

etching

512 x 338 mm

inscribed in plate on rock, lower center: *Camillo procacino / Bol inuent: Incid: / 1593*; lower margin: *Signasti Domine Seruum Tuum Franciscum Signis Redemptionis Nostrei.*

stamped in black, lower left: NH[1]

B.XVIII.21.5, TIB9.40.5

Bequest of Agnes Goldman Sanborn, by exchange, s2.40A

Procaccini was born into a family of painters and probably began his career at an early age. By 1571 he had entered the Bolognese guild of painters and by 1580 he was executing independent commissions. He is thought to have visited Rome and is known to have been to Parma in 1585. As well as being affected by Bolognese Mannerist artists such as Pellegrino Tibaldi, his work also shows the influence of Taddeo Zuccaro, Correggio, and the Carracci. Towards the end of the 1580s he, along with other artist members of his family, moved to Milan, where his brother Giulio Cesare was instrumental in founding a Baroque style that had little effect on Camillo.[2]

This print, one of six attributed by Bartsch to Procaccini, is the only print in all of the Spencer collection now at the Fogg to have been inserted loosely into the albums (see the Introduction). Mounted into Spencer Album 2, however, are four other prints by the artist, including his enormous *Transfiguration* in its first state (TIB39.39.4).

Procaccini is an interesting printmaker in several respects. He created some of the most monumental printed religious images of his time, even though these very prints suffer from technical difficulties that seem to be a result of the printing and etching process. As well as suffering from foul-biting throughout the plate, his *Saint Francis* is overbitten; this accounts for its overall gray tonality. All known impressions exhibit the same problem. This particular impression also suffers from the plate having slipped in printing, so that many of the lines are doubled. These defects may well be the result of the artist's decision to use such a large plate. One further peculiarity seems to be the consequence of the artist's deliberate technical manipula-

Signasti Domine Seruum Tuum Franciscum Signis Redemptionis Nostre.

tion: at the right center to the edge there appears a large semicircular area which roughly defines the farther spaces of the composition in which both the line and the background tone are lighter than in the rest of the plate. This seems to be some kind of attempt, through burnishing perhaps, to achieve atmospheric perspective to aid the recession into space. The identical effect occurs in other impressions and so must have been generated from the plate and not from manipulation during printing. This solution was not particularly effective since part of the area of lightening is in the middle distance of the panoramic landscape.

The print's subject is taken from one of the great scenes from the life of Saint Francis: his stigmatization. The representation of this event was popular during the Franciscan reforms of the 1570s and 1580s because it stresses the saint's personal, ecstatic relationship with Christ and with Christ's sufferings.[3] Accordingly, in order to make the vision more immediate to the beholder, Procaccini has brought the figure toward the front of the picture plane and drawn him on a very large scale, allowing us not only to see his expression but to have a good look at his gruesome, newly acquired stigmata, pierced welts which seem to incorporate the nails of the Passion within the wounds. The figure's naturalism and immediacy are heightened by the relatively large scale of its hands and feet, as well as by the prominence given to the tattered robes held in place by a cinture to which is attached a cross and skull—images associated with the Capuchin Franciscans. The potential drama created by the composition's diagonal construction—from the saint's leg at the lower left through his wounded torso up to the seraph at the upper right, and all reinforced by the bending tree at the center—is undermined by the failure of Procaccini's technique to render exciting effects of light and shade. The overall gray tone of the print deprives the image of the focus it deserves.

Stylistically, Procaccini has achieved an uneasy mixture of post-Tridentine naturalism with Mannerist landscape conventions and elegance of graphic presentation. This kind of elegance, however, is not an inherent trait of etching. The swelling and tapering line and the use of networks of expressive parallel hatching are really to be associated with engraving which Procaccini seems, in many passages of the *Saint Francis*, to be trying to imitate. By not fully exploiting his actual medium, he has considerably reduced the naturalness of his presentation.

Overall immediacy is further undermined by placing this large-scale scene uncomfortably in a panoramic landscape with a long vista that recedes too quickly into the distance. The landscape itself is full of different, often disparate, elements. The houses in the middle distance on the right clearly derive from Venetian prints by Titian and Campagnola, while the apparently fictitious city in the far distance is much more a creation of this phase of late Mannerism. Also in stark contrast to the fairly naturalistic figure of Saint Francis is his companion, seated behind the trees, reading. This figure has been drawn with an elegance not seen in the larger figure. His hands have been elongated and are reminiscent of Parmigianino's work. The folds of his draperies, particularly the cap he wears, seem to have a life of their own and do not really conform to the figure.

The 1586 engraving by Agostino Carracci of the same subject (Bohlin 140) might very well have been known to Procaccini. Agostino's print has a unified style and a convincing recessional space. Procaccini seems not to have been completely comfortable with this new naturalistic vocabulary, which became current in Emilian painting at this time, although he was clearly affected by it.

A C B

1. Lugt 1974. Lugt associates this mark with Nathaniel Hillier (1707–1783), a London print dealer whose collections were sold in London on 16 February and 15 March 1784. See the Introduction.

2. See Nielson 1979; De Grazia 1984, p. 343; Reed and Wallace 1989, p. 74.

3. Askew 1969, p. 281.

LODOVICO CARRACCI

Bologna 1555 – 1619 Bologna

6   *The Holy Family under an Arch*, c. 1588

engraving

270 x 331 mm

blue paper; watermark: illegible device within a shield

inscribed in plate, lower left: *Lodovicus Carraccys. / in. fe.*

B.XVIII.26.4, TIB39.46.4, Bohlin 1

Alpheus Hyatt Fund, s1.11

Lodovico Carracci, the older cousin of Agostino and Annibale, executed only four prints (all included in Spencer Album 1). Presumably he made them in emulation of the graphic achievements of his cousins, who were expert and prolific printmakers. As might be expected from such a limited production, Lodovico did not perfect his graphic techniques, although he was sufficiently experimental to attempt a drypoint (TIB39.45.3). His lack of practice as an engraver is evident in the inflexible and unsophisticated engraved line of the print on exhibition.

The Spencer Album impression of *The Holy Family under an Arch* is one of three known examples of the first state of this engraving that are printed on blue paper. In her discussion of the two impressions known to her, Bohlin suggests "that the artist himself was attempting to expand the possibilities of tonal ranges in the graphic medium";[1] and indeed, the Carracci were accustomed to use blue paper in their drawings. It was also employed in a 1590 edition of *La Gerusalemme liberata* illustrated with prints by Agostino,[2] and it was, more generally speaking, in wide use in Northern Italy by the end of the sixteenth century, over a century since its introduction into Europe by Venetians who had first encountered it in their trade with the Arab world.[3]

The blue paper may have been an expedient adopted by Lodovico for this engraving when he perceived that the originally rich tonal qualities inherent in the fresh burin line had begun to wear: the impression of the first state on white paper at the Bibliothèque Nationale, Paris, which can be directly compared to the first-state impression on blue paper in the same collection, is far richer. The impression in the Spencer Album compares closely in quality to the blue-paper example at the Bibliothèque Nationale and also to a first-state impression on white paper at the British Museum.

Two drawings are associated with the print, one recently on the London art market for the Madonna and Child[4] and another in the collection of the Ashmolean Museum, Oxford, for the figure of Saint Joseph.[5] The latter is a study of a young male model who holds exactly the pose seen in the print. The former, however, shows both the Madonna and Jesus in subtly but significantly different poses. In the drawing the Madonna clasps her child only with her right arm (her left in the print, which reverses the drawing); and rather than a loving embrace, her pose gives the sense merely of her steadying him as they both gaze down at the viewer with apparent superiority in the figurative as well as literal sense. This dominating quality is reinforced by the Christ Child's posture, which is more firmly upright, his leg extended vigorously forward in support of his body, and by his gesture, which is much more explicitly one of blessing. In the drawing Christ has assumed the authority of the Salvator Mundi. The position of the feet of the Virgin is also somewhat changed in the print from the drawing. Indeed, the only aspects that remain truly constant are the expression of the Virgin and the substantial absence of her body: any sense of the structure of her form is absorbed into a tumble of drapery in both drawing and print.

With regard to her expression, the elegant arched eyebrow is much more effective in the drawing than in the print, given her superior, outward gaze. It is as effective in Lodovico's *Bargellini Madonna*, an altarpiece of the Madonna and Child with saints now in the Pinacoteca Nazionale, Bologna, which is dated 1588. The painting, which resembles the engraving only in the head of the Madonna (even to representing her facing left rather than right, as in the drawing), thus provides us with an approximate date for the print.

It was presumably this altarpiece, one of Lodovico's most important, which was among the works that so impressed the young Pierre-Jean Mariette upon his visit to Bologna in 1719. He declared to his father that Lodovico was "my hero, his noble genius, his grand design, his awesome manner of composition charm me."[6] And in the manuscript now in the Bibliothèque Nationale he especially praised this print for its qualities of design (while criticizing its technique):

It is the only [print by Lodovico] which he engraved entirely with the burin and where one sees no trace of etching, doubtless following the example of Annibale, he was spurred to try the burin which Agostino had employed with so much success, but if he did not succeed in [equaling *crossed out*] engraving this print as freely as Agostino would have done, there is by way of compensation a taste in composition so excellent and graces so like those of Correggio that one would [easi *crossed out*] take it to be after him if one did not know that L. Carracci had equalled and even surpassed him sometimes. As well, it is extraordinarily rare to find this print in a good impression and without having been [retouched *crossed out*] reengraved....[7]

MBC

1. Bohlin, p. 480.

2. See Bohlin, p. 272. The principal illustrator was the printmaker Giacomo Franco, with both artists working after drawings by Bernardo Castello.

3. Meder 1978, vol. 1, p. 141.

4. Trinity Fine Art Ltd./Compagnie des Beaux-Arts Ltd. *An Exhibition of Italian Old Master Drawings, 1500–1800.* London: Harari & Johns Ltd., 30 Nov.–14 Dec. 1990, no. 22, repro. p. 55. The drawing is also reproduced in Bohlin, p. 482, fig. 1b.

5. Reproduced in Bohlin, p. 481, fig. 1a.

6. MLM BS/b9/L44 (Bologna 2 February 1719): "mon heros, son genie noble, son grand dessein, & sa manniere terrible de composer me charment."

7. BNMS R065858: "C'est l'unique qu'il ait gravé entirement au burin et ou l'on ne remarque aucun trace d'eau forte, sans doutte qu'a l'exemple d'Annibal il se sera piqué de manier le burin dont Augustin se servont avec tout de succés, mais s'il n'a pas reussy à [egaler *crossed out*] graver cette estampe aussy librement que

l'auroit fais ce dernier, il y a mis en recompense en gout de dessein si excellens & des gracer sui semblables à celles de Correge que l'on la prendroit [aisem *crossed out*] pour estre d'après luy si l'on ne scavoit que L. Car- rache l'a egale & mesme surpassé quelquefois. Au reste il est extraordinairement rare de trouver cette estampe de bonne impression & sans estre [retouchée *crossed out*] regravée . . ."

ANNIBALE CARRACCI
Bologna 1560 – 1609 Rome

7   *Mary Magdalen in the Wilderness*, 1591

etching and engraving

220 x 161 mm

watermark: triangle with the upper, horizontal edge echoed within the form by a concave line

inscribed in plate, at left on rock: *Carra:in.*; at lower edge, center: *1591.*

inscribed on verso in brown ink: *P. mariette 1668*; in another hand, in graphite: *Dormril* (?) *1613LU*; in brown ink: *16#; 15#*

B.XVIII.191.16 i/ii, TIB39.403.16, Bohlin 12 i/iv

Alpheus Hyatt Fund, s1.36.2

This representation of the penitent Magdalen falls into the same class as Annibale's *Saint Francis* (Cat. 3). They, and many other small prints produced by Annibale and his brother Agostino con- forming to instructions to artists issued subsequent to the Council of Trent, are devotional im- ages designed to inspire private meditation on repentance and salvation. Their subjects allude to Christ's sacrifice for sinful man, either by presenting the dead Christ himself or through the de- vice of a representation of a crucifix, as here. They often refer to death, the inevitable fate of man, as embodied by a skull. When the principal subject of the print is a saint, that holy person is in- variably shown in a state of such consuming spiritual concentration that he or she personifies the intensity of contrition and adoration which the print is designed to inspire.

Mary Magdalen was a beautiful prostitute whose reform was effected by Christ during his life on earth and who was present at his crucifixion; it was she who, going to his tomb to anoint his corpse, discovered his resurrection. According to the legend generally accepted by the beginning of the seventeenth century, after the events of the Gospels she, Mary Martha, and several other early Christians settled in what is now France. She sought solitude in a mountainous wilderness in Provence, where she ended her life in ascetic meditation. As a sinner whom Christ himself had saved, her continuing mortification was an especially exemplary source of inspiration; to quote Emile Mâle, "Magdalen in the desert thus became for Christian art the symbol itself of repen- tance. That beauty which gradually faded far from the gaze of men . . . was the most pathetic im-

age imaginable of penitence."[1] Annibale has provided his Magdalen with her usual attributes: the crucifix and jar of ointment symbolizing her presence at Christ's death and her continuing contemplation of its mystery, the skull symbolizing Golgotha and man's mortality, and the reed mat and disheveled hair, which grew to a miraculous length to cover her nakedness in the wilderness, symbolizing her eremitic isolation.

The artist has used stippling to render the suggestively glimpsed bosom of the former prostitute. Amid all the wiry dashes, lines, and hatchings of the print, this is the only region of shadowed softness. The late twentieth-century connoisseur conceives of this as an ironical commentary on the redeemed fallen woman, now so excessively modest that she hides her fleshly beauty even in a wilderness where male eyes cannot penetrate; but to the devout late sixteenth-century artist, which Annibale certainly was, this allusion to the Magdalen's earlier allure would only have heightened his expression of her later piety.

The print is juxtaposed in catalogues and also in the Mariette manuscript at the Bibliothèque Nationale with Annibale's etching of the penitent Saint Jerome (TIB39.400.14).[2] Diane De Grazia Bohlin, author of the authoritative catalogue of the Carracci's prints and drawings, has suggested that the two form a pendant pair;[3] however, the differences in size and technique—*Saint Jerome in the Wilderness* is a significantly larger, more freely sketched, and comparatively blond work— militate against such a close relationship. The two plates may not even be so closely associated chronologically as Bohlin, who dates *Saint Jerome* c. 1591, suggests, for there is a significant ripening of technical skill between the two prints. Compared to *Saint Jerome*, *Mary Magdalen* remains self-conscious and unsure in its hatching structure, most notably in the rendition of the saint's proper left leg. Evidently Annibale, having determined the point of greatest projection of the knee, decided that the form of the leg could be best expressed by concentric lines expanding from that point down the leg; yet they get progressively straighter as they approach the ankle and thus awkwardly transform the system from a topographical to a tonal one in the course of a single, small element of the design.

The "contour map" approach to hatching, typical of Mannerist engravers, would have to have been more consistently pursued to be effective. Annibale's brother Agostino, following the lead of Cornelis Cort, had already developed hatching systems which, while conforming to the topography of form, minimized the projection of points and emphasized the juncture of planes in space (see Cat. 2). Rather than ever becoming accomplished in their systems, however, Annibale moved beyond them in the directions he himself had initiated in his engraved *Saint Francis* (Cat. 3), with its expressive sketchiness, and in other areas of this print, such as the Magdalen's softly swelling breasts and the feathery landscape in the distance. His *Saint Jerome* presents a far more advanced moment in this great printmaker's education.

MBC

1. Mâle 1932, p. 69: "Madeleine au désert devint donc dans l'art Chrétien le symbole même du repentir. Cette beauté qui s'evanouissait peu à peu loin des regards des hommes . . . était l'image la plus pathétique de la pénitance qu'il fût possible d'imaginer." See pp. 67–68 for a general discussion of her cult after the Council of Trent.

2. BNMS R065879. Pierre-Jean Mariette added a note in the margin: "M. Crozat a le dessein originale à la sanguine." This preparatory drawing, now in the Louvre, is reproduced in Bohlin, p. 441, fig. 12b. The Carracci's early biographer Bellori juxtaposed the two prints in his list of Annibale's oeuvre (Bellori 1968, p. 74).

3. Bohlin, pp. 440–43.

VESPASIANO STRADA

Rome c. 1582 – 1622/4 Rome

8   *Mystic Marriage of Saint Catherine*

etching

174 x 125 mm

watermark: fragmentary

inscribed in plate, design area, lower left: *Nic. Van Aelst. formis Roma*; lower right: *·VESPASIANO·STRADA·I·F·*

inscribed in brown ink, recto: *P. mariette 1666*; verso: *P. mariette 1667*

B.VII.309.16, TIB39.353.16

Francis H. Burr Fund, s6.42.3

Spencer Album 6 contains eleven prints by Strada, about half of the complete etched oeuvre of this minor early seventeenth-century painter of the Roman school. All of his prints can be categorized as private devotional images—Madonnas, saints, the dead or captured Christ presented as an object of pity. Only an Annunciation and several incidents from the lives of saints, such as the Stigmatization of Saint Francis and this Mystic Marriage of Saint Catherine, can be said to have narrative implications, and in each case the "story" is presented as a visionary moment conveyed by the pose and relationship of figures rather than by any intimation of continuing action.

The first account of the Mystic Marriage of Saint Catherine, in which the infant Christ presents a wedding ring to the saint, appeared in the 1483 English translation of the *Légende dorée*.[1] The sixteenth and early seventeenth centuries saw the blossoming of this incident within the larger cult of the saint, who was by legend an ancient Alexandrine princess, the daughter of the king of Cyprus (hence the crown she wears in Strada's representation of her). While one could attribute the popularity of the Mystic Marriage to a general Counter-Reformation emphasis upon the ecstatic experience of the love of God, recent scholarship has located its special rele-

Nic. Van Aelst. formis Rome P. mariette. 1666 VESPASIANO·STRADA·I·F.

vance to Italy at this time within a more secular development: the concentration of inheritance increasingly upon the eldest son through developing concepts of lineage and associated mechanisms of primogeniture and entail.[2]

The particular expedient adopted by fathers for daughters of marriageable age, who would have to be provided with dowries if they married and who in any case would continue the lineage

84

if they produced children, was to cause them to enter convents. The glamorizing of marriage to Christ has been construed as one aspect of a societal campaign to make this alternative to earthly marriage acceptable to whole generations of nubile girls:

> ... the popularity of the scene increased as female monastic incarceration became a standard tool of lineal survival. As patrician daughters slipped into her clothes, the Alexandrian saint ... became ever more fashionable and her relationship with the infant Christ ever more tender.[3]

In his rendition of the Mystic Marriage, Strada has focused the attention of all participants except that of Catherine, who modestly casts down her gaze from the materialization of the Holy Family before her, upon the ring, the symbol of marriage. The printing of this particular impression, an exceptionally rich one, further enhances our concentration upon the sacred ring by means of a patch of heavy plate tone that floats above the chain of hands of the three protagonists: Mary who holds Jesus, who extends the ring to Catherine, who raises her hand at his touch to receive it. The plate tone, somewhat attenuated, extends throughout most of the sheet, covering its entire surface except the figures of Mary and Catherine and the upper left corner, the radiant heavenly source of legions of cherubim who bring the princess the laurel wreath and palm of triumphant martyrdom.

As noted by Mariette, who considered this etching to be "one of the most beautiful of V. Strada," the artist has here "affected the manner of Parmigianino."[4] Adam Bartsch, in his entry on the print, quotes Mariette almost exactly, adding "the works of," omitting the "V.," and qualifying the extent of Parmigianino's influence to "un peu," thus pedantically rendering Mariette's perceptions into more orthodox catalogue entry style.[5] This dependence of Bartsch upon the several lifetimes of connoisseurship represented by the surviving Mariette manuscripts now in the Bibliothèque Nationale, Paris, and the collection of Prince Eugene of Savoy now at the Albertina, Vienna, may be seen throughout his volumes. He does not forfeit his status as the first to make available to the print-collecting world at large resources for the systematic assessment and classification of old-master prints; however, credit is owed to the basis of his accomplishment.

The value to us today of Bartsch's volumes and their ever-multiplying progeny of oeuvre catalogues, and the quite different nature of the expedient to which a pre-Bartsch-era print connoisseur had perforce to resort, is defined by the circumstances of an impression of this same Strada print now in the collection of the Metropolitan Museum of Art in New York. It is mounted in an album deriving from the estate sale of the collection of Pierre-Jean Mariette in 1775. This album, entitled *Oeuvre de Parmessan Tome I*ʳ, contains prints by Parmigianino and in his style; given Mariette's analysis of Strada's *Mystic Marriage of Saint Catherine*, the print logically finds its place here, specifically on folio 26 in a section devoted to the prints of Schiavone (Andrea Meldolla, 1510–1563).

Strada's etching is pasted onto the lower right corner of folio 26; Schiavone's version of the same subject is mounted at the lower left. When the folio is turned, however, we do not proceed to another subject by either Schiavone or Strada; on folio 27 are mounted four more Mystic Marriages, and all four compositions are closely, even deceptively, derived from the Strada etching. What this album seems to present, therefore, is a small portion of the library required in the pre-Bartsch age for a professional connoisseur of prints, sufficient for that connoisseur to assemble a collection such as that represented by the Spencer Albums, where there are virtually no duplicates of compositions and no inclusions of copies or derivative images when the "original" was intended.

One cannot doubt the prodigious visual memories of men such as the Mariettes, grandfather, father, and son. But one also cannot minimize the role that must have been played by many volumes, such as that single one still fortunately preserved at the Metropolitan, in their continuing self-education and also in their commercial lives. We should think of this volume of the etchings of Parmigianino and his school as a pre-Bartsch reference book. We know that it was assembled by Pierre-Jean Mariette because many of the impressions bear his signature, with appended dates ranging through the middle third of the eighteenth century. Many other impressions, however, bear the characteristic signature and seventeenth-century dating of his grandfather Pierre Mariette II and so must have been selected for inclusion in this album from the family print stocks in much the same way as were the many impressions in the Spencer Albums that display Pierre II's signature. What is significant, however, is not the similarity of the signatures in these albums but the apparent difference of the purposes of the albums themselves.

The impression of the Strada *Mystic Marriage of Saint Catherine* from the Spencer Albums, which was also signed by Pierre Mariette II, leads to further reflection on the commercial basis and function of the Mariettes' centuries-long tradition of print connoisseurship. This impression is signed "P. mariette 1666" on its front and "P. mariette 1667" on its back. It is one of four prints from the Spencer Albums known to bear two different dates inscribed by Pierre Mariette II. As the reverse of so few of the prints in the albums can be inspected and as so many carry Pierre Mariette's dated inscriptions on their obverse, it seems probable that in fact a number of others also bear two dates.

Any interpretation of this double dating must be speculative, but one could be, simply, that the print came into Pierre Mariette's hands more than once in the course of his trade in prints. Certainly, a collector would be as likely to sell to him, the leading dealer in old-master prints in Paris, as to buy from him, especially if Mariette had already established his interest in a print by offering it for sale at an earlier date. An argument against this hypothesis is that the paired dates are never many years apart, yet there would seem to be little reason for Mariette repeatedly to re-date a print if it remained in his collection continuously.

In any case, the discovery of impressions like this one, with two dates, requires that we re-think the conventional ascription of a place within Mariette's personal collection to all impressions bearing his signature. There is no doubt of the high quality of this impression; on the other hand, that quality may simply represent the standard of the commercial stock of the Mariette firm.

MBC

86

1. Réau 1955–1959, vol. 3.1, p. 268.

2. Hughes 1988, p. 26.

3. Hughes 1988, p. 28.

4. BNMS R069357: "Cette piece est une des plus belles

de V. Strade, il y a affecté le gout du Parmesan."

5. B.XVII.309: "Cette pièce est une des plus belles de l'oeuvre de *Strada*. Il y a un peu affecté le gout du Parmesan."

GUIDO RENI

Bologna 1575 – 1642 Bologna

9 *Angels in Glory*, 1607, after Cambiaso

etching

410 x 275 mm

inscribed in plate, lower left, design area: *LUCAS CANGIASIUS INV.*; in lower margin: *IV-BILEMVS DEO SALVTARI NOSTRO. / Per Ill.ri Domino Dño Vido Taurelio Parmensi Viro insigni, ac bonarum Artium amatori et obseruantice et grati animi ergo· Petrus Stephanonius Vicentinus Dicebat / Romae Anno Domini MDCVII. Superiorū permissu. Cū Priuilegio.*

inscribed in brown ink, verso: *P. mariette 1668*

B.XVIII.299.45, TIB40.196.45, TIB4005.327.028 S3/3

Alpheus Hyatt Fund, S1.74

The artistic training and career of Guido Reni took numerous turns, from his early apprenticeship to Denis Calvaert, a Flemish Mannerist painter of great importance in Bologna in the late sixteenth century, through work in the more progressive Carracci academy in the mid- and later 1590s, to practice as an independent and highly successful painter in Rome at the beginning of the seventeenth century. In 1607, the year of this etching, Reni received the first in a series of commissions from the powerful Roman family the Borghese, whose head was Pope Paul V.[1] Eventually in 1614 Reni would return to Bologna and become that city's most important painter and printmaker, with patronage throughout Europe.

Reni's path from Calvaert to the Carracci can be understood as an artistic journey toward increasing naturalism (despite the sense, as reported by Malvasia, that he had not rejected Calvaert's manner sufficiently to suit the Carracci).[2] Upon his arrival in Rome, Reni seems to have been immediately, albeit briefly, drawn to the even more aggressively realistic works of Caravaggio; and this etching, after the earlier Genoese painter Luca Cambiaso, may be seen as a continuation of this concern in its bold chiaroscuro and the dramatic perspective of the tumbling cascade of cherubim. Especially in comparison with the sketchy style of most of Reni's etchings, as represented by the *Holy Family* in this exhibition (Cat. 12), the rich, systematic shading, which makes the forms so tangible, is an anomaly among his prints.

IVBILEMVS DEO SALVTARI NO STRO.

Per Ill.ᵐDomino Dño Vido Taurelio Parmensi Viro insigni, ac bonarum Artum amatori et obseruantiæ et grati animi ergo Petrus Stephanonius Vicentinus Dicabat
Romæ Anno Domini MDCVII. Superiorũ permissu . Cũ Priuilegio.

Reni has, however, abandoned Caravaggio's earthbound repertoire of subjects in his selection of this "jubilation of angels," as the print has been titled.[3] Veronika Birke has perceptively observed that all of the various versions of the traditional title, which incorporate "angels," must be incorrect because the lowest cherub is not an angel in that he has no wings.[4] She posits that the omission cannot be accidental because the babe is conspicuously positioned with his back turned to the viewer; she speculates that the true subject of the image refers to the striving of the innocent human soul toward heaven, which is suggested by the pose of the figure's legs, braced to boost him into the realm of angels.

When we turn to the Cambiaso drawings which, one or more,[5] are the presumed source for the print, we see that the angel with his arm upraised above the head of the wingless putto also lacks wings, which Reni has conscientiously supplied in the print. Cambiaso often drew celestial appearances and assumptions with a central holy figure supported by wingless putti,[6] and so the omission in this case could be fortuitous. In any case, Birke is correct in distinguishing the lowest babe as the focus of the print.

The more significant deviation of the print from the drawing(s) lies in Reni's plastic modeling of the forms. Some of the drawings are in Cambiaso's typical outline style, in which the draftsman's preternatural skill in foreshortening establishes the remarkable sense of bodies' free fall in space. They are unshaded and thus would have offered no guidance whatsoever to Reni.[7] At least two drawings, in the British and Cincinnati Museums, are washed to provide the sensation of strong illumination, but the specific patterns of shading are not identical to that in the etching by Reni.

In fact, the most interesting drawing related to the print is by Reni himself, a red chalk study (Collection of the Dukes of Devonshire, Chatsworth) in which some of the passages of modeling, such as the buttocks of the wingless putto, even surpass the etching in concern for form-enhancing chiaroscuro devices such as reflected internal highlights.[8] This drawing, as well as the print, demonstrate that Reni, here working as a reproductive printmaker of the early seventeenth century, thought in terms of his prototype's compositional and iconographical intent and not his personal style and technique.[9] It would not be until the early eighteenth century, most relevantly in the so-called *Cabinet Crozat*, whose first volume was edited in 1729 by Pierre-Jean Mariette, that a systematic attempt would be made to reproduce in prints the hand as well as the conception of an earlier draftsman.[10]

MBC

1. See Reed and Wallace 1989, p. 123; Los Angeles 1988; and Pepper 1984, for the artist's biography.

2. Los Angeles 1988, p. 148.

3. Sopher 1978, no. 59. Turner 1989, p. 194, titles it *Glory of Child Angels*. In the seventeenth century, Malvasia called it *La Gloria d'angeli* (Malvasia 1841, vol. 1, p. 93).

4. Albertina 1988, p. 36. The Spencer Album 1 table of contents titles the print *Un Grouppe d'Anges*.

5. There are references in the literature to five drawings, in the Uffizi, Florence; the Pinacoteca Nazionale, Bologna; the British Museum, London; the Academia de San Fernando, Madrid; and the Poole Collection, Cincinnati Art Museum, Cincinnati (see TIB4005.326 and Sopher 1978, p. 43). The Harvard Fine Arts Library Visual Collections files hold photographs of the draw-

ings in London and Bologna and of another in the collection of the Earl of Plymouth, Oakley Park, Ludlow. How many of these are by Cambiaso is unclear.

6. See for example the *Assumption of the Magdalen* (Victoria and Albert Museum, inv. no. 9060B), *Assumption of the Virgin* (Mathias Komor, repr. Finch 1968, no. 40), and *Madonna in Glory* (H. Schickman Gallery, repr. Finch 1968, no. 69).

7. The drawing in Bologna, usually identified as the specific model for the print, is one of the sheets that lack any shading whatsoever.

8. See in this connection putti painted by Reni in fresco in 1613 (S. Maria dei Servi, Bologna, now detached; repro. Los Angeles 1988, pp. 195–96), where form revealed by strong illumination, here from below, is rendered with equal sensitivity.

9. There exists in the British Museum (inv. no.

1869–12–12–412) an impression of the etching printed in brown ink, which has been retouched with pen; it simulates a drawing perfectly. Because the margin has been trimmed, it is impossible to determine the state.

10. The *Cabinet Crozat* was formally titled *Recueil d'Estampes d'après les plus beaux Tableaux et d'après les plus beaux Desseins qui sont en France dans le Cabinet du Roy . . .* The king's collection was given precedence, but in fact the majority of the examples, which were drawings, were in the collection of Pierre Crozat, who together with Mariette and the comte de Caylus undertook the publication. See Lippincott 1983, p. 24, and Paris 1967, pp. 179–80, for accounts of the drawing facsimile publications in which Pierre-Jean Mariette was involved and their influence on English and Italian developments.

JUSEPE DE RIBERA

Játiva, Valencia 1591 – 1652 Naples

10   *The Martyrdom of Saint Bartholomew*, 1624

etching and engraving

321 x 238 mm

watermark: illegible figure (human?) within a shield

inscribed in plate, lower margin: *Dedico mis obras y esta estampa al Serenismo: Principe Philiberto me Señor / en Napoles año 1624.*; lower right: *Iusepe de Rivera spañol*

inscribed in brown ink, lower right: *P. mariette 1667;* verso, in brown ink: *P. mariette 1670*

B.XX.81.6; T1B44.274.6; Brown 12 i/ii.

Francis Burr Fund, s6.49

The Mariette manuscript entry on Ribera that precedes the tabulation of Ribera prints in Prince Eugene of Savoy's collection suggests that the Spanish artist "could perhaps [be] considered as a Neapolitan painter," and it remarks upon the "spirit" of his etchings.[1] This appreciation explains Ribera's inclusion in Spencer Album 6, otherwise entirely devoted to Italian artists. Many of them could be described (using an anachronistic vocabulary) as romantic, notably Salvator Rosa (see Cat. 47) and Giovanni Benedetto Castiglione (see Cat. 14, 48, 53). Album 6 also contains the one etching usually attributed to Michelangelo Merisi da Caravaggio, the late-sixteenth-century

D. mariette 1667

Dedico mis obras y esta estampa al Sereniss.mo Principe Philiberto mi señor
en Napoles año 1624.

Iusepe de Riuera spañol.

painter who by the psychological directness of his works and the tempestuous conduct of his life set the canon for the romantic personality in centuries to come. The etching by Caravaggio, *The Denial of Saint Peter* (DeV.1), is mounted on the same page as two of the prints traditionally ascribed to Ribera, *Centaur and Triton Fighting* (TIB44.279.11) and *Cupid Whipping a Satyr* (TIB44.280.12), anticipating the advice given in the late eighteenth century by Karl-Heinrich von Heinecken for the organization of collections that would contain both original prints and also prints reproducing the oeuvres of painters: "*Guiseppe* RIBERA . . . etched for his [own] amusement. If you do not want to form a separate section of the works of this artist, you can add him to *Michelangelo da Caravaggio*."[2]

In this Spencer Album, which does include some reproductive prints (largely after Castiglione), Ribera predominates over Caravaggio; yet the compiler's intention—to represent the *artist* by a virtually complete array of his prints[3] rather than the *printmaker* by a complex array of various states and counterproofs—is indicated by a comparison of the selection of etchings by Ribera in the Spencer Album with those by him in the album compiled by the Mariettes for Prince Eugene.

In Prince Eugene's album, both of the Ribera prints on exhibition here are also presented in counterproofs, and *Silenus* is also given in its first state, without inscription, as well as in its published state. The studies of eyes, ears, and noses and mouths by Ribera (TIB44.284–6.15–17) are represented in Prince Eugene's album by early impressions from the uncut plates; in the Spencer Album the impressions are after the plates were cut in half. In fact, only one Ribera in the Spencer Album is in a rare first state: the *Large Head with Grotesque Growths* (TIB44.277.9). This impression, exceptionally, is in poor condition; all of the other Spencer Riberas are in fine condition and in splendid impressions from the published states, printed on the somewhat grayish paper which Ribera's cataloguer identifies as requisite to an appreciation of his etchings at their best. In relation to *The Martyrdom of Saint Bartholomew* he writes, "To be fully appreciated, this print must be seen in an early impression when grayish paper was used and before the shallow-bit lines had begun to fade."[4] In the Spencer *Saint Bartholomew* the balance between the deeply etched and more lightly etched areas of hatching is perfectly preserved, achieving a virtually coloristic effect enhanced by the subtle plate-wiping that the impression displays. Note especially the sense practically of two tones of ink in the head of the shattered idol at the left (the miracle worked by Bartholomew that so enraged the pagan ruler that he ordered his martyrdom by flaying).[5]

The subject was a particular favorite of Ribera; the cataloguers of his paintings list four autograph versions and another produced by a collaborator. They also list twelve copies, including three that are closer in composition in reverse to the print than any extant autograph painting, suggesting a lost original of which the print is a virtual reproduction.[6] That Ribera painted and etched the subject in response to demand is not in doubt; the taste for martyrdoms of the most brutal or pathetic kind has been noted in Italian Counter-Reformation art,[7] and plague-ridden Naples has been singled out as favoring Saint Bartholomew because of the "popular tradition [which invoked him] against convulsions and nervous illness in general."[8] This print, in 1624

Ribera's first multifigural etching, was dedicated to Prince Philibert of Savoy, the viceroy of Sicily, indicating that the artist (or his publisher) believed that an auspicious debut could be made at the highest levels of patronage with such a subject. Ribera's interpretation of the martyrdom is especially poignant, suggesting how willingly the saint went to his painful and gruesome death. Whether through ecstatic obliviousness or stoic restraint, the old man does not flinch: the hand actually being skinned is only loosely knotted with a flimsy cord to a dead twig which would have snapped at the least tug.

There is no doubt of the Mariettes' appreciation of Ribera prints. François Langlois, called Ciartres, the first husband of the wife of Pierre Mariette II, published a collection of twenty-two plates engraved by Louis Elle after compositions by Ribera, largely in the format of body parts isolated as instructional images for draftsmen. These plates passed into the hands of the Mariettes, who republished them with two additional plates; the images included, on plate 12, portions of Saint Bartholomew. Subsequently either Pierre I or Pierre II published a reproduction of the entire composition.[9]

The etchings' modern cataloguer has compiled a listing of Ribera impressions known to him that were signed by Pierre Mariette II; the dates Mariette inscribed span the period 1661–1669.[10] These impressions plus those included in the Mariette-compiled albums now at the Albertina and the Fogg total twenty-four and include seventeen of the eighteen prints ascribed to Ribera and his school.[11] As is usual in modern print connoisseurship, the presence of Mariette inscriptions was used by Ribera's cataloguer to identify impressions of outstanding quality. Typically, this observation has led to an appreciative definition of the status of the Mariettes as collectors. However, the fact that this Spencer Album impression of *The Martyrdom of Saint Bartholomew* was signed by Pierre II twice, and with two different dates,[12] points to an interpretation of his signature as an indication that the print entered his commercial inventory more than once. The high quality of the impression thus would refer to the standard that he maintained as a print dealer.

MBC

1. BNMS R068638: "L'Espagnolet peut etre considéré comme peintre napolitain...beaucoup d'Esprit."

2. Heinecken 1771, vol. 1, p. 132.

3. Lacking is the very early and atypical *Saint Sebastian* (TIB44.2702) and two later commissions, an equestrian portrait (TIB44.283.14) and a coat of arms (TIB44.287.1, known in only two impressions), relating to contemporary personages and thus also atypical of Ribera's work as a history painter.

4. Brown, p. 18.

5. See Brown, p. 28, and Wegner 1989 for a full exposition of the subject.

6. Pérez Sánchez and Spinosa 1978, nos. 24, 34–36, 200, 259–71.

7. Mâle 1932, pp. 127–28, where Ribera's *Saint Bartholomew*s in particular are cited as an expression of the times and not of any peculiar "sombre génie espagnol."

8. Wegner 1989, p. 53.

9. Brown, pp. 39, 83.

10. Brown, p. 39.

11. The one that is missing: *St. Jerome Reading* (Brown 13).

12. This is known to be the case also with three other prints in the Spencer Albums. See Cat. 8.

LUCA GIORDANO

Naples 1634 – 1705 Naples

11   *Saint Anne Received into Heaven by Christ and the Virgin*, c. 1660

etching

256 x 331 mm

watermark: P V surmounted by a trefoil

inscribed in plate, design area, lower edge, center: *Lucas Iordanus*; lower margin, center: *Sancta Anna*

B.XXI.177.6 i/ii, TIB191.6, TIB4717.006 s2/4

Richard Norton Fund, s6.57

The most recent, authoritative consideration of the small print oeuvre of Luca Giordano assigns the six etchings that are known and generally accepted as his work (TIB47.186–191.1–6) to the artist's first period in Naples as an independent artist.[1] Born in Naples, Giordano had received some of his early training from Jusepe Ribera and had then traveled to artistic centers in central and northern Italy. Upon his return to Naples in the early 1550s, renewed contact with the work of Ribera seems to have inspired him to create these few etchings. This early impression of his *Saint Anne* is printed with a considerable amount of gray tone, which simulates the grayish cast of many of Ribera's best impressions (see Cat. 10). And perhaps Giordano used the tone to conceal a fine cracquelure bitten into the surface of the plate, the result of a faulty ground, which is visible in early clean-wiped impressions of the print.[2]

While the somewhat haggard facial types of Saint Anne and the Virgin and the peculiarly flattened, banded drapery patterns in this print hark back directly to Ribera etchings,[3] these characteristics and also the larger conception of the composition are close to several of Giordano's own major paintings of the later 1650s. The altarpiece dated 1657 of *Saint Anne and the Virgin* in the church of the Ascension in the Neapolitan district of Chiaia is comparable; even closer is the figure of the Virgin, apparently a fragment of a larger composition, which in 1966 was in the collection of the Newhouse Galleries, New York. With the exception of the direction of her gaze, the gesture of her right hand, and a more collapsed posture, this Virgin essentially duplicates in pose, proportion, and style the figure of the Virgin in the print. The painted Virgin, who is in an attitude of adoration, is supported by a putto with the same elongated torso and protruding belly as those in the etching.[4]

Oreste and Scavizzi, the cataloguers of Giordano's paintings, have dated the fragment to c. 1660; and they have associated it with another fragmentary painting, of the resurrected Christ, now in the collection of the Museo de Arte, Ponce, Puerto Rico, suggesting that the two canvases may once have formed parts of a much larger composition.[5] The physical and facial type of

Lucas Iordanus.

SANCTA ANNA

Christ in this painting is also very close to that in the print, although Christ holds an entirely different pose; the putti surrounding him are likewise comparable. When one turns to paintings of similar subject and composition from Giordano's later career, such as the *Virgin Appearing to Saint Francis* of c. 1680 (Private Collection, Paris)[6] or the *Dedication of the Virgin* of c. 1685 (S. Maria in Campitelli, Rome),[7] the affinity of the pictures from about 1660 with the etching of *Saint Anne* is even more apparent.

The subject of the print, while easily read, is somewhat mysterious in that the usual histories of the life of Saint Anne, the mother of the Virgin Mary, end with her death (which was singularly merciful through the intercession of her grandson Christ, so that she became the patroness of "the good death"[8]). Typically in artistic representations she is shown alive, often in narrative scenes referring to the conception, education, and youth of the Virgin. She is also often shown as an aged woman in the company of her daughter and infant grandson.[9]

Saint Anne became immensely popular in Europe only during the late Middle Ages and Renaissance, as a part of the general rise of mariolatry, and her cult underwent great ramification. Accretions to her history, such as a total of three marriages and other children and grandchildren (who purportedly included five of the apostles) were suppressed by the Counter-Reformation Church. Her feast, initiated in 1584 and then deleted from the saints calendar by Pius V, was reinstated in 1621.[10]

One of the continuing centers of devotion to Saint Anne seems to have been Naples, and particularly the waterfront district of Chiaia, where a little sixteenth-century church, "una chiesetta," was dedicated to her by the fishermen,[11] and where two of Giordano's important altarpieces in other churches represent episodes from her life.[12] Finally, there may have been a personal component to Giordano's choice of subject for the etching, which, unlike those of altarpieces, would probably not have been determined by a patron: he was baptized in the parish of S. Anna a Palazzo in Naples.[13]

MBC

1. See TIB4717.292–302. The author, Paolo Bellini, has also published a separate study of the prints of Giordano, "Contributi a Luca Giordano," *Il conoscitore di stampe—Print Collector* 36 (1977):17–36. See also Ferrari and Scavizzi 1966, vol. 1, pp. 18–19. *Christ and the Adulteress* (TIB47.190.5), Giordano's only dated print, is from 1653.

2. As seen in the superb impression in the National Gallery of Art, Washington (inv. no. 1973.56.1). The pattern is noticeable at the upper edges and sides of the plate in the sky. Another impression of this print in the same early state as the Spencer Album impression and with an overall grayish tone was offered by Colnaghi's in 1986.

3. Notably Ribera's two versions of *Saint Jerome in the Wilderness* (TIB44.272.4 and TIB44.273.5). The body types of the putti can also be usefully compared to those in Ribera's *Coat of Arms* (TIB44.287.18).

4. Ferrari and Scavizzi 1966, vol. 2, pp. 71–72; vol. 3, fig. 119.

5. Ferrari and Scavizzi 1966, vol. 1, p. 61; vol. 2, pp. 70–72; vol. 3, fig. 118.

6. Repr. Ferrari and Scavizzi 1966, vol. 3, fig. 181.

7. Repr. Ferrari and Scavizzi 1966, vol. 3, fig. 279–81.

8 Réau 1955–1959, vol. 3.1, pp. 93, 95.

9. See P. Beda Kleinschmidt, *Die Heilige Anna* (Düsseldorf: L. Schwann, 1930), which reproduces hundreds of Saint Anne images but does not give the Giordano plate or any other of its subject.

10. Réau 1955–1959, vol. 2.2, pp. 141–42; Mâle 1932, p. 347.

11. The church, S. Maria delle Neve, has since been

rededicated to the Virgin. See Vittorio Gleijeses, *Il Borgo di Chiaia* (Naples: Edizioni Scientifiche Italiane, 1970), pp. 189–90.

12. *Saint Anne and the Virgin*, 1657 (Church of the Ascension, Chiaia, repr. Ferrari and Scavizzi 1966, vol. 3, fig. 57, and *Saint Anne, the Virgin, and Saint Joachim*,

1664 (S. Teresa, Chiaia, repr. Ferrari and Scavizzi 1966, vol. 3, fig. 108). *An Education of the Virgin* in the church of S. Giuseppe, Chiaia, has also been attributed to Giordano (see Ferrari and Scavizzi 1966, vol. 1, p. 214).

13. TIB4717.292.

GUIDO RENI

Bologna 1575 – 1642 Bologna

12 *The Holy Family with a Scene of Moses Striking the Rock*, c. 1597

etching

229 x 146 mm

watermark: elongated shield with an illegible device, identical to that on an impression in the British Museum (inv. no. U–3–37)

B.XVIII.275.9 i/ii, TIB40.157.9, TIB4005.287.004 s1/2

Alpheus Hyatt Fund, s1.63.4

Beginning on folio 58 and continuing through folio 65 of Spencer Album 1, which is devoted to the Carracci and their Bolognese followers, one faces a barrage of Madonnas. All but one of the twenty-four prints on these eight openings include Mary and Jesus; of these, fifteen are Holy Family scenes. By far the largest number are by Cantarini,[1] whose seven representations of the Rest on the Flight into Egypt form a class of their own; but six, including this etching, are by Guido Reni—or at least are traditionally ascribed to him.

As Birke, the most recent cataloguer of Reni's prints, has remarked more generally about Reni's etchings, "The representations of the Madonna and Child become a repetitive type."[2] This repetitiveness, which is exaggerated by the arrangement of Spencer Album 1, is embodied in this particular print and two others (TIB40.158.10 and TIB40.159.11) in which the form of the Madonna is virtually identical. These three etchings are mounted on the same folio of the album (together with a fourth print by Reni of Mary, Jesus, and Joseph [TIB40.147.1]); it is obvious that the compiler of the album, as well as Bartsch and all other subsequent cataloguers, recognized the three compositions' intimate connection.

What has gone unnoticed is the fact that the figure of the Madonna was drawn to exactly the same internal dimensions on all three plates; the distance from the tip of her nose to the tip of her prominently extended big toe, for instance, is 141 mm. The version on exhibition here has always been given priority in the series. The outline of the figure of the Madonna in the other two

etchings, which are both in reverse of this composition, may well have been traced onto the plate from an impression of this print, a process that would explain their reversal.

The head of the Madonna, with its elegant coiffure and affecting turn toward the young Christ, epitomizes the strong influence on the young Reni of the works of Parmigianino noted by all commentators, which has been used by Birke to date this print to an early stage in the Bolognese artist's career as a printmaker. And as early as the eighteenth century, it was "the airs of his heads (in the gracious kind)" which for the pioneering English connoisseur Jonathan Richardson the Elder "had a delicacy in them peculiar to himself, and almost more than human."[3] Using Reni as a principal example, Richardson went on to discuss the value of etchings as records of the hand of the Italian masters, for use in forming a connoisseur's eye, with particular emphasis on the head as a locus of characterizing expression:

> The excellence of a print, as of a drawing, consists not particularly in the handling; this is but one, and even one of the least considerable parts of it: it is the invention, the grace, and greatness, and those principal things that in the first place are to be regarded. . . .
>
> The prints etched by the masters themselves, such as those of Parmeggiano, Annibale Carracci, and Guido Reni (who are the chief of those of whom we have works of this kind) are considerable upon the same account; not for the handling, but the spirit, the expression, the drawing, and other the most excellent properties of a picture, or drawing, though by the nature of the work, they are not equal to what they have done in those ways of working.
>
> And it is further to be observed, that as prints cannot be so good as drawings they abate in the goodness they have by the wearing of the plate; they thus become to have less beauty, less spirit, the expression is fainter, the airs of the head are lost. . . .[4]

Richardson's denigration of the handling in the etchings of Reni and also Parmigianino refers to the uninflected line and cursory passages of cross-hatching, so different from the highly developed graphic systems of engraving and etching that had evolved through the seventeenth century. Yet this etching by Reni is not, in fact, so spontaneous an expression of draftsmanship nor so close an imitation of Parmigianino's single-bite technique as it might first appear. There are extended passages of burnishing on the left pilaster and on the block of stone supporting the Madonna's extended arm. A brief notation of the block's texture over this burnished area indicates that the plate was subjected to a second bite, belying its apparent technical simplicity.

Likewise, the iconography of the image is not simply a Holy Family. A bas-relief above the heads of Mary and Jesus represents the Old Testament episode of Moses striking the rock and bringing forth a spring, the Israelites having "murmured against Moses, and said, Wherefore is this that thou hast brought us up out of Egypt, to kill us and our children and our cattle with thirst?"[5] The reference to the return from Egypt directs us to look again at the etching's characterization of Jesus, who is in fact not an infant but a toddler, capable of standing on his own feet. According to the Gospel of Matthew, Mary, Jesus, and Joseph had gone to Egypt and remained there so "that it might be fulfilled which was spoken of the Lord by the prophet, saying, Out of Egypt have I called my son."[6] Reni's Jesus is the older boy who is seen in representations of the return of the Holy Family from Egypt. And the visual reference to the spring of fresh water, the salvation of the nation of Israel, may clarify his ambiguous gesture raising his mother's mantle, perhaps to draw attention either to her breasts or to her womb, the nourishing spring or the source of the Salvator Mundi. It should be noted, however, that in traditional typological interpretations of the Old Testament, the spring freshened by Moses refers not to Mary but to Christ himself, whether to his institution of the sacrament of baptism or to the water and blood that issued from his side, pierced by the lance of Longinus.[7]

The scene of Moses striking the rock is omitted from the two etched repetitions of the composition, and other figures are added—baby angels showering Christ with flowers in one and a young Saint John the Baptist adoring the Virgin in the other. These scenes, then, are more typical of devotional images of the Holy Family; and their banality of thought, as well as coarseness of line, may justify Birke's doubts about their authenticity.[8]

MBC

1. Simone Cantarini, Guido Reni, Lorenzo Loli, and Flamino Torri are the four artists whose etchings of Mary and Jesus, with or without Joseph, saints, and angels, are grouped together on fol. 58–65.

2. Veronika Birke, in TIB4005.279. Her essay (TIB 4005.277–79) provides the most current overview of Reni's activities as an etcher. The catalogue which follows (TIB4005.280–371) proposes a chronology of prints by Reni, of copies after him, and of prints traditionally ascribed to him.

3. Richardson 1792, p. 152.

4. Richardson 1792, pp. 166–67.

5. Exodus 17:3. I am indebted to Greg Thomas for his identification of the subject of the bas-relief, which is called "a scriptural scene" in the traditional title of the print.

6. Matthew 2:15.

7. Réau 1955–1959, vol. 2.1, p. 201.

8. TIB4005.287.

CARLO MARATTI

Camarino 1625 – 1713 Rome

13   *The Holy Family with Angels*, c. 1647

etching

174 x 129 mm

B.XXI.90.4, TIB47.14.4, TIB4703.27.004 S1/3

Alfred Jaretzki Fund, S1.111.1

Carlo Maratti was the leading painter in Rome at the end of the seventeenth century; he achieved great fame as the last major exponent of the High Baroque style. He came to Rome at an early age and was apprenticed in the workshop of Andrea Sacchi, where he is said to have re-

mained for twenty-two years.[1] In Sacchi's studio he studied drawing and copied the work of the great artists of the High Renaissance and early seventeenth century, including Raphael, Polidoro, Annibale Carracci, and Domenichino.[2] He became an independent master shortly before Sacchi's death in 1661, was admitted to the Academy of Saint Luke, the painter's guild, in 1662, and assumed its presidency in 1664, eventually being named president for life in 1701. Maratti received many important commissions, including works for Popes Alexander VII (1655–1667), Innocent XII (1691–1700), and Clement XI (1700–1721).[3] Clement thought him worthy to undertake the restoration of Raphael's Vatican Stanze, which also suggests that he was the leading "establishment" painter of his day.[4]

Paolo Bellini has proposed that most of Maratti's etchings date from before 1660, that is, during his time in Sacchi's workshop when he was "confined to the exercise of drawing."[5] Spencer Album 1 contains twelve of the fourteen prints attributed to Maratti by Bartsch as well as ten after Maratti compositions.

Maratti's nickname was "Carluccio delle Madonne," and this applies quite aptly to his activity as a printmaker. Of the prints attributed to him by Bartsch and Bellini, five take as their subjects scenes from the life of the Virgin, and four depict the Madonna and Child. The latter four, which are all in the same dimensions and oval format, form a kind of series. Their specific iconographies, objectively defined, are quite different, and for this reason they are separated in Bartsch's catalogue and thus have not been formalized as a set. Their consonance in size, style, and subject considered more largely, however, is evident. Each print represents the adoration of the Christ Child. In this etching we see angels at the Nativity responding to the divine light that pours out from above. In the others Maratti depicted *The Mystic Marriage of Saint Catherine* (TIB47.20.10), *The Magdalen Anointing the Sleeping Christ* (TIB47.16.6), and *The Madonna and Child with the Infant John the Baptist* (TIB47.19.9). In their second states, these four prints acquire inscriptions, and one, *The Madonna and Child with the Infant John the Baptist*, which is inscribed in the plate in a different script, is dated 1647—Maratti's only dated print. As these added inscriptions are in a later state, it is impossible to be sure that the other three are from the same year, but their affinities make this likely.

The unity of the series was tacitly recognized by the compiler of the Spencer Album. In the table of contents they were described as "four works in oval format representing subjects of the Virgin, or Holy Family, invented & engraved by Carlo Maratti,"[6] and they were mounted on the same folio. The compiler clearly took great pains to put these prints together since each of the four Spencer Album impressions differs greatly in state and quality, and they must have been assembled substantially after their printing. This print is a particularly fine early impression of the rare[7] first state, before the addition of any of the inscriptions. The richly inked and clean-wiped plate energizes the drama of the scene and makes clear the intended effect of radiant, celestial light.

ACB

1. Paolo Bellini in TIB4703.21.

2. Maratti made etchings after the work of each of these masters, prints that Bellini believes were executed during his stay in Sacchi's studio; see TIB4703.21.

3. Paolo Bellini in TIB4703.21.

4. Maratti was also a portraitist and he painted Robert Spencer, second earl of Sunderland, in 1662; see the Introduction.

5. Paolo Bellini in TIB4703.22.

6. "Quatre pieces de forme ovale, representant des Sujets de Vierge, ou Ste Famille, inventés & gravés par Charles Maratte."

7. Paolo Bellini in TIB4703.27.004.

GIOVANNI BENEDETTO CASTIGLIONE

Genoa 1609 – 1664 Milan

14   *Nativity with God the Father, the Dove of the Holy Spirit, and*
     Two Angels Adoring the Christ Child, c. 1645

etching

295 x 202 mm

B.XXI.15.11, TIB46.25.11, TIB4602.23.011 S2/2, Percy E 6

Richard Norton Fund, s6.87.2

Spencer Album 6 is devoted to prints by the Spaniard Ribera ("Lespagnolet" on its title page) and Italian artists (see Fig. 2). Among the Italians, Castiglione takes pride of place, both on the title page, where as "Beneditte" he is the only one listed by name, and in the album itself, which contains forty-eight of his etchings, virtually all of those which are now securely attributed to him.[1] Missing are two portraits of contemporaries (TIB.46.58.56, 57), whose absence is not surprising given the Spencer Albums' dearth of portraits. Also missing are ten tiny landscape and figure sketches, marginalia cropped from the plates of the series of heads (TIB.46.59–60.58–67), and a late, apparently unfinished Nativity with angels (TIB46.22.8). Indeed, the compiler of the Spencer Albums has made every effort to characterize Castiglione by finished and fulsome compositions; for, exceptionally among the many printmakers included within the albums who were primarily painters, Castiglione is also represented by a long series of unabashedly reproductive engravings (see Cat. 50) and even by a reproductive mezzotint, unique within the albums (Cat. 49).

This etching of the Nativity typifies almost all of the Spencer Album Castiglione impressions in several ways. It is an exceptionally good impression, taken from the fresh, unworn plate, and it has been printed with a significant amount of tone which, together with Castiglione's clouds of nervous cross-hatching, defines the miraculous subject: the apparition of God the Father and the Holy Spirit hovering within an arm's embrace of the baby Jesus. The plate tone is subtle—a haze of gray—but inspection of all edges of the impression reveal it to have been carefully applied everywhere except in those areas that spatially would logically be illumined by the radiant dove: Mary's face, Jesus, the veil Mary draws back to reveal him to his father, the loose straw in the manger, and the ancient paving and toppled column before the tableau, symbolizing the overthrow of the old dispensation. It is interesting to note that in this system of illumination the face of God is darkened by hatching, doubtless to focus attention on Jesus but also to permit God's halo to be perceived by contrast. Yet his halo remains merely an attribute; it is the brilliant emanations from the Holy Spirit that literally and figuratively permeate Mary and the infant Christ.

The artist's fascination with the subject of the Nativity, a nocturnal scene in which the sacred, unexpectedly revealed in the most mundane circumstances, could best be embodied in bursts of

light, is closely bound up with his innovative development of the monotype technique, especially the so-called "dark field" monotype. To create such a print, thick pigment is wiped over an un-etched plate—essentially an opaque layer of the same plate tone Castiglione manipulated so tellingly on his etched plates. The layer of wet pigment is brushed and scratched to create a design in light strokes and patches, and then it is offset onto a sheet of paper by passing plate and paper together through a press, much like printing an etching. As the artist works from dark to light, the technique is peculiarly suitable for nighttime moments of radiant revelation such as the Annunciation to the Shepherds and the Nativity, the subjects of dark-field monotypes by Castiglione now in the collections of the Albertina (TIB46.61.1 and TIB46.62.2), Windsor (TIB4602.99.126), and the Gabinetto Nazionale, Rome (TIB4602.102.128).

A version of our etching, God the Father adoring his newborn son, was also executed by Castiglione in monotype. It survives in both a first and a second, paler impression, in the collections of the Bibliothèque Nationale, Paris (TIB4602.100.127 s1) and Windsor (TIB4602.100.127 s2).[2] The dove of the Holy Spirit is not actually delineated in this representation, but the radiance emanating from wavy lines drawn across God's belly can be construed as its equivalent. The sheet bears every sign of the artist's haste to describe the main protagonists—Mary, Jesus, God, two angels—before the fluid dark field dried. The only carefully detailed portions of the composition are the facial expressions of the four adorers of the infant and also the body and gaze of Jesus. As in the etching, the simple, precise draftsmanship which defines the pudgy limbs and ingenuous regard of the newborn child contrasts with the surrounding disheveled graphism.

Pierre-Jean Mariette prized Castiglione's willingness to sacrifice draftsmanship to dazzling effect as the artist's distinctive artistic contribution. With reference to his drawings, which were apparently relatively numerous in early eighteenth-century Parisian collections, he wrote, " . . . one could scarcely want anything more beautiful. They are studies for his paintings, where the effect of light and dark makes the whole effect; for it is that to which this artist seems to have limited himself in these drawings. There is no point in looking for regularity of form, it is entirely neglected."[3]

This impression of *The Nativity with God the Father, the Dove of the Holy Spirit, and Two Adoring Angels* is characteristic of the Castigliones in Spencer Album 6 in yet another way: it is in exceptionally fresh condition. Indeed, most of the nine albums' prints are clean, unpressed, and unabraded. Their state of preservation is a testimony to the virtues of the old way of storing print collections in albums and to the exemplary materials and techniques of mounting and binding used by the Mariettes in these compilations.

One physical feature of the surface of this print provides our assurance of its pristine condition: in the forearm of the adoring angel at the right, a white hair is caught by a few strands of paper fiber. The hair is a detached residue of the wooly felts between which the sheet of paper was pressed during its manufacture; a single felt hair was overlapped by the wet paper pulp and incorporated into the sheet. Although a printer often inspects the surface of his paper carefully for such defects before passing the dampened sheet and inked plate through the press, this hair eluded any such search. More remarkably, the operation of printing and the later vicissitudes of the impression—it was sold in Italy, carried to France, and eventually mounted in this album—also did not detach the hair. A sheltered life has preserved it. Had the impression suffered the usual fate of old-master prints that have survived into the late twentieth century, of being mounted and remounted, bathed and pressed, scuffled between one sheet of paper after another, this telling hair would surely have been lost.

MBC

1. For authoritative discussions of Castiglione as a printmaker, see Percy 1971; Charles Dempsey, "Castiglione at Philadelphia," Burlington Magazine 114 (Jan. 1972):117–20; Bellini 1982; and Paolo Bellini's edition of the Castiglione section in TIB4602.13–127, which includes an extensive bibliography.

2. The monotype is signed "Gio Benedetto Castiglione Genovese." This self-description of the artist as coming from Genoa is traditionally interpreted as having been adopted by Castiglione after his move to Rome c. 1647, and is thus often used to assign a *terminus post quem* to any given work. The etching of the same subject is unsigned; the composition relates to a painted altarpiece of 1645 in San Luca, Genoa. Thus either the monotype postdates the etching by several years or the etching, despite its lack of any indication that Castiglione executed it after his arrival in Rome, postdates the painting. Bellini dates the etching 1645–1647 on stylistic grounds (TIB4602.23.011).

3. Mariette 1851–1860, vol. 1, p. 334: "Les dessins de Benedette Castiglione qui sont ici [Paris], sont très considérables, et l'on n'en peut guères désirer de plus beaux. Ce sont des préparations pour ses tableaux, où le clair obscur fait déjà tout son effet; car c'est à quoi cet auteur paroît s'être borné dans ces desseins. Il n'y faut par chercher la régularité des formes, elle y est entièrement négligée."

GIULIO CARPIONI

Venice? 1613 – 1679 Vicenza

15 *The Agony in the Garden*

etching

327 x 223 mm

watermark: three-lobed design surmounted by an illegible device; countermark: V C surmounted by a trefoil

inscribed in plate, lower margin, left: *Matio cadorin forma In Padoa*

B.XX.178.2, TIB45.68.2, TIB4504.95.002 S2/3

Francis H. Burr Fund, s6.24

Contemporary with Castiglione as well as with P. Testa, Simone [Cantarini] da Pesaro and Salvator Rosa, Carpioni has points of contact with all of them, but he, best of all four, succeeds in grasping the essentials of the painter's use of etching, which is not a sketch nor yet a picture, neither too summary nor too conscientious.[1]

Matio Cadonn Forma In Padoa

It is hardly accidental that the four other seventeenth-century Italian etchers cited by Augusto Calabi in his praise of Carpioni are also represented by outstanding impressions in the Spencer Albums. The nine surviving Spencer Albums feature such works if only, perhaps, because in the nineteenth and twentieth centuries, when the Earls Spencer sought to realize some of the value accrued in their ancestral collections, more money could be raised by selling prints of Dürer, Marcantonio, Rembrandt, and other seventeenth-century Dutch artists (see the Introduction). Over the past 150 years, seventeenth-century Italian prints have been, and continue to be, comparatively undervalued, especially when one considers the esteem with which they were regarded in the seventeenth and eighteenth centuries. At that time, seventeenth-century Italian pictures were avidly collected throughout Europe, and connoisseurs collected prints by the favored painters as a useful supplement to drawings, with both being guides to the appreciation and attribution of paintings.[2]

Spencer Album 6 is devoted to a mélange of Italian prints whose common characteristic is painterliness (e.g., works by Barocci, Castiglione, Grimaldi, Ribera, and Rosa but not the Carracci, Maratti, or Testa). Among them are four by Carpioni out of the twenty-four attributed to him without qualification in the most recent catalogue of his etchings.[3] Judged by the standard evoked by Calabi, Carpioni's works stand out even in Spencer Album 6, which is distinguished by many superb examples of Ribera and Castiglione etchings, although the compilers have restricted their choice to Carpioni's larger religious compositions and neglected his mythological pieces and bacchanals. The latter would have provided even stronger testimony to the artist's debt to sixteenth-century Venetian painting and would also have reinforced the immediate recognition this *Christ on the Mount of Olives* provides of his influence on eighteenth-century Venetian art. Indeed, this print has been cited as the model for a painting by Giovanni Battista Tiepolo now in the Bottacin Collection, Museo Civico, Padua.[4] More generally, the spindly crossed tree trunks filling a composition's corner, the diagonal gaze leading to a populated expanse of radiant sky, and the large, somewhat bland bare limbs will be seen again in countless religious and secular works of the Tiepolos.[5]

But the religious content of the print by Carpioni is particular to its own time. As etchings in this exhibition by Faccini and Procaccini demonstrate (Cat. 4, 5), the holy figure whose ecstatic prayer is consummated by mystical revelation or even a miracle became a stock in trade of Catholic Counter-Reformation imagery, in order to inspire comparable, personal, fervent devotion among the faithful. Typically the episode would take place out of doors, usually in a rustic setting, and the holy figure would sometimes be accompanied by unwitting companions. Only the most rudimentary knowledge of the Gospels suggests the paradigm of such scenes: the night of anguish suffered by Christ prior to his crucifixion, which he spent in the Garden of Gethsemane on the Mount of Olives with several disciples, who slept rather than kept watch with him. It was only after the Council of Trent that the parallel, specifically between the Agony in the Garden and the Stigmatization of Saint Francis, was drawn; and the Gospel episode is believed to have had a formative influence in representations of the later miracle.[6]

MBC

1. Calabi 1924, pp. 138–40. See Cat. 14, 17, 28, 29, 47, 48, and 53 for prints by the other artists mentioned.

2. See Cat. 12 for the opinion of Jonathan Richardson the Elder, a pioneering early eighteenth-century connoisseur, on these matters. Pierre-Jean Mariette's opinion of Carpioni's prints was appreciative although qualified. Note how he, too, stresses their attractiveness to the collectors of his time: "Il a gravé lui-même à l'eauforte quelques-uns de ses desseins, et ces estampes sont recherchées; elles sont touchées avec esprit. L'auteur, sans être correct, a de la grâce . . . " (Mariette 1851–1860,

vol. 1, p. 310).

3. TIB4504.93–113.

4. Pilo 1961, p. 81.

5. This general compositional scheme was reused frequently by Carpioni, in prints in his *Madonna and Child with Saint John the Baptist* (TIB45.74.7), *Nativity* (TIB45.75.8), and *Penitent Magdalen* (TIB45.77.10). The *Madonna and Child with Saint John the Baptist* served as a model for works by Antonio and Francesco Guardi (TIB4504.99.007).

6. Askew 1969, pp. 292, 294.

FRANCESCO CURTI

Bologna 1603 – 1670 Bologna

16a   *Bust of a Young Woman Facing Left, Her Hair Loose on Her Shoulders*, after Guercino

engraving

165 x 225 mm

Bologna 517

William M. Prichard Fund, s1.97.1

OLIVIERO GATTI

Piacenza 1579 – after 1628 Piacenza

16b   *Two Legs of a Man in a Kneeling Position*, plate 10 from *Book of the Principles of Drawing*, 1619, after Guercino

engraving

143 x 208 mm

inscribed in plate, lower right: *10.*

B.XIX.31.127, TIB41.118.127

William M. Prichard Fund, s1.103.3

One can view the print collection that is the Spencer Albums and also the print collection comprised of the sets of engravings after Guercino by Oliviero Gatti and Francesco Curti found on folios 86–103 of Spencer Album 1 as instructional manuals. They were assembled in France and,

insofar as is known, received in England in the early eighteenth century. By this time, a taste for Italian painting had developed among British royalty, nobility, and the higher middle class. Italian paintings were collected and they were imitated, by professional artists serving these classes and also by amateurs among them. Contemporary diaries and other writings betray a real anxiety about acquiring the sophisticated knowledge necessary to purchase and produce the sorts of paintings that were the common currency of Continental high culture.

On the periphery of Europe, England was in much the same position as Spain (although its base of art patronage was certainly broader and more highly educated), and the comments of Antonio Palomino (1655–1726) in his life of Murillo are apposite: "The fact is that foreigners do not want to concede fame to any Spanish painter who has not passed through an Italian customshouse. They do not take into account that Italy has come to Spain by means of statues, famous paintings, prints, and books."[1]

The "prints" specified by Palomino as instructional for Spanish painters would have been any prints that represented Italian art and style, including reproductive engravings of entire compositions and also original etchings by Italian masters such as those which dominate Spencer

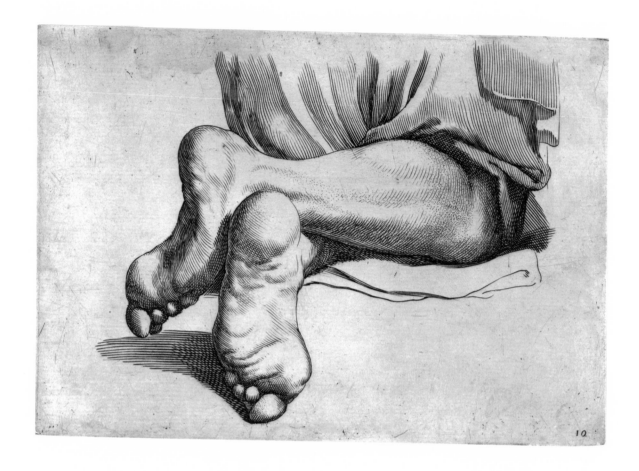

Albums 1, 2, and 6 and those regarded so favorably as conveyors of personal style by Palomino's English contemporary Jonathan Richardson the Elder (see Cat. 12), who wrote the first self-help manual for connoisseurs.

The "books" referred to by Palomino were probably also prints, gathered into bound volumes for instructional purposes. Some of these gatherings were after the fact; that is, they would have been comparable to a posthumous edition of etchings by the Dutch landscape etcher Anthonie Waterloo, whose title page makes their intended use explicit: "Very useful for landscape painters and lovers of drawing."[2] By Palomino's time, the same time as the compilation of the Spencer Albums, "books" would also have comprised artists' manuals, some of which were entirely made up of prints conceived and executed explicitly for the instruction of artists. These took two forms, the drawing book and the model book, which have been conscientiously defined by Bolten:

> . . . the term "drawing book" is employed to describe those printed didactic works . . . in which the instruction makes use of the visual, rather than the verbal medium. . . . In contrast, the model book is merely a storehouse of iconographic and formal elements . . . a

thesaurus of wide-ranging categories of image and form, intended for the artisan. The drawing book, on the other hand, is designed to provide instruction in the creation of images and is designed for the use of painters, graphic artists and . . . sculptors.[3]

The early history of the drawing book in particular has been described in an admirable chapter by Amornpichetkul within a larger publication on sixteenth- and seventeenth-century artists' education.[4] Both of these recent publications locate the conceptual source of the drawing book within the work of the Carracci, in their method of artistic training embodied by the life-drawing classes which they instituted within their Bolognese academy and in the drawings of body parts, studies in contour and modeling, which were Agostino Carracci's particular, practically compulsive specialty.

It is prints after drawings such as these that John Elsum, an early eighteenth-century English writer on painting in the Italian manner, especially recommended as the basis for the study of drawing. He cited yet another late sixteenth-century Italian painter as his authority:

> 1. I set my self to Discourse of *Drawing*, and I find it best described, by *Cavalier Frederico Zuccharo* in his Treatise of Ideas, . . . who says, *That Drawing is terminated in the Object understood, by which the understanding knows the thing that is represented to it,* and is of two sorts, *Internal* and *External.*
> 2. The *Internal* is the Idea. The *External* is the Copy of that Idea, and is of 2 sorts, *Interious* as the inner lines, and *Exterious* as the Out-lines. . . .
> Now as to the several ways of Drawings, the *first you must know, is that which is made with the Pen,* and consists chiefly in imitating a Print.[5]

It was, perhaps, only a few years after Elsum's recommendation that the Spencer Albums came to England. They contain entirely or in part at least five Italian drawing manuals that were explicitly published as such,[6] as well as a separate instructional plate,[7] plates from a manual that was never completed (although they were copied and issued as a manual by François Langlois, called Ciartres, and his successors, the Mariettes),[8] and plates from print series by Callot, whose didactic function is implicit in the figures being first etched in contour only and then repeated in fully modeled versions standing side by side.[9]

Besides the inclusion of so many drawing manuals in this particular collection, there is far more evidence of late seventeenth- and early eighteenth-century English interest in teaching devices derived from Italian academic practice. British artists and connoisseurs scrambled to provide themselves a remedial education once Restoration society found itself prepared to accept the luxuries of Continental visual culture.[10] In England a touring German could report that he had visited "a mechanician, Jackson, who has has all manner of curious inventions to his credit, such as . . . a special kind of casts of limbs for painters and sculptors, etc.,"[11] and, also in England, the drawing book by Gatti, a plate from which is on exhibition here, was plagiarized in 1663, twenty years after it had been pirated by the Mariettes in Paris.[12]

The engravings by Gatti and Curti derive from a booklet of drawings prepared by Giovanni Francesco Barbieri, called "Il Guercino" (1591–1666), for the instruction of beginning draftsmen. At the time, Guercino, a largely self-taught painter from Cento, in Emilia, was at the beginning of his long career. He was very much under the artistic influence of the Carracci, emulating them even to their system of education, and he founded his own drawing academy in 1616. On a trip to Venice in 1618, Guercino and his drawn drawing manual were introduced to Palma the Younger, who had already published his own etchings for the same purpose (impressions of which are included in Spencer Album 6). Palma's warm appreciation of Guercino's efforts apparently encouraged the production of plates after Guercino's designs by Gatti and Curti, which, though issued separately, were often conflated into a single series such as the one we find in Spencer Album 1.

Of the two engravers, Curti is more pedantic in technique, pricking a dot inside every lozenge as appropriate and never allowing two, or a row, to soften the linear discipline. But he is also much more expert an engraver than Gatti: observe the curling tendrils of loose hair over the girl's shoulder and the loose back-and-forth curve that marks her inner elbow, and note how it swells to a blunt end to simulate the positive stop of a pen. Gatti is sketchier in technique, especially in the diffuse stippling and delicate burin strokes that shade the swelling calf. Neither printmaker was necessarily betraying his model, however, for Guercino himself sometimes drew in a combination of line and stipple. This drawing technique, so distinct that Guercino's cataloguer has denominated it the artist's "gravure style," is seen most frequently in complete compositions. It is assumed to have been adopted by Guercino for the benefit of his engravers.[13]

MBC

1. Enggass and Brown 1970, p. 200, quoting Palomino's *Museo pictórico y escala óptica. III. Parnaso español pintoresco laureado.*

2. Quoted in Freedberg 1980, p. 56. Freedberg attributes the motive of model-making to the artists of the many uniform Dutch landscape print series of the seventeenth century, and not merely to later editors. Not incidentally, a very long series of prints by Waterloo occupy fol. 59–78 of Spencer Album 5; they would undoubtedly have been to the taste of both English and French eighteenth-century connoisseurs who were, perhaps, amateur draftsmen.

3. Bolten 1985, p. 11.

4. Amornpichetkul 1984, pp. 108–18.

5. Elsum 1704, pp. 5–7.

6. By Gatti (s1.86–87, 98–103), Curti (s1.88–95), Palma the Younger (s6.9–14), della Bella (s7.152–54, 156, 161–64), and an anonymous seventeenth-century Italian artist (s1.67.2). See Amornpichetkul 1984 and Bolten 1985, and also Stone 1989, pp. 273–77, concerning these drawing manuals.

7. By Valesio (Cat. 20).

8. By Ribera (s6.55–56); see Brown, pp. 39, 69–70, concerning this project in all its phases.

9. s4.9–10. The series were recognized by the Mariettes as instructional prints: "Les Caprices, ou diverse figures il y en a qui sur la mesme planche sont ombrées & vis a vis au simple trait pour la facilité de ceux qui commencent à dessiner à la plume" (BNMS R065626). They are similarly described in the album's table of contents: "Diverse figures dont la plus part sont ombrées en même temps qu'Elles sont au trait sur la même planche, pour la facilité de ceux qui apprennent a dessiner a la plume..."

10. The first English drawing manual, which pirated plates by Odoardo Fialetti, was published by Alexander Browne in 1660, the year of the Restoration. Previously, a London publisher had issued plates by Wenzel Hollar, a Bohemian-born printmaker in the employ of the Royalist earl of Arundel, whose subject and format indicates their intended use by student draftsmen. See Rostenberg 1963, pp. 39–40, concerning these and other early

British drawing manuals. It should be noted that the large expenditures by Charles I on Italian paintings, often of Catholic subjects, was a significant issue prior to his deposition, and that as early as 1626, two Guercino paintings had entered the British royal collection.

11. Uffenbach 1934, p. 171.

12. See Amornpichetkul 1984, p. 112, n. 23, and Bolten 1985, pp. 277–78, for the history of copies of the Gatti manual. Rostenberg 1963, p. 53, reports that as early as 1655 *A Book of Portraiture*, a collection of plates after

Guercino, was published in London. Pierre-Jean Mariette himself noted with reference to the great popularity of prints after Guercino drawings that the British "sont passionés pour les desseins de Guerchin" (Mariette 1851–1860, vol. 1, p. 74).

13. Stone 1991, pp. 26–28. The introduction to this catalogue, especially pp. xi–xix, provides a brief overview of Guercino's career. There is also a useful discussion of the appreciation of Guercino in eighteenth-century England, pp. xxv–xxvii.

SIMONE CANTARINI

Pesaro 1612 – 1648 Verona

17   *Fortuna*, after Reni, c. 1636

etching

236 x 145 mm

watermark: arms of Amsterdam, similar to Heawood 348, 349 (n.p., 1676, 1684)

B.XIX.143.34, TIB42.109.143, Bellini 5 i/ii

William M. Prichard Fund, S1.71.2

Simone Cantarini is represented in the Spencer Albums by twenty-two of the thirty-seven prints attributed to him by Bartsch, including all seven of his etchings of the *Rest on the Flight into Egypt*, that subject which the compiler of the albums seemed so to dote upon.

Cantarini, known as "Il Pesarese" from his birthplace, received his first training from a local artist and then around 1635 entered the studio of Guido Reni, the most eminent follower of the Carracci still working in Bologna. During his brief association with Reni (which ended bitterly in 1637 with Cantarini apparently feeling exploited by demands that he reproduce works by Reni),[1] the younger artist produced several prints that reflect not only the master's compositions but also his graphic style. This print of *Fortuna* is derived from Reni's painting now in the Vatican Pinacoteca, and its blunt linear systems, open hatching, and overall blond tonality closely follow Reni etchings such as the Holy Family also in this exhibition (Cat. 12). Indeed, in its second state *Fortuna*, like several other Cantarini etchings from the period when he worked with Reni, acquired the legend "G. Renius. in. et fec."

The Cantarini prints so inscribed in their later states were traditionally ascribed to Reni, but Mariette, in his table of contents for Prince Eugene's album, already recognized Cantarini's au-

114

thorship. In his commentary on the artistic differences between Cantarini and Reni as reflected in the etched version of Fortuna by Gerolamo Scarsello (TIB42.258.6), which follows the original Reni painting far more literally, Mariette acknowledged the virtue of Cantarini's direct approach. Mariette's assertion of the authorship of Cantarini in the first case and his reattribution of the second print to Scarsello in the following quotation indicate the evolution of print connoisseurship reflected throughout the ten manuscript volumes now in the Bibliothèque Nationale, which would be codified in the next century by Adam Bartsch:

> f.59. Fortuna represented by a woman standing on a globe, who empties a purse filled with money while an amor tries to restrain her by the hair. This piece is invented and etched by Il Pesarese, he has made it corresponding to that of Guido his master [which *crossed out*] is on this same page, [also *crossed out*]
>
> An impression of this same print on which has been engraved at the bottom the name of Guido but for no other reason than to give it greater value. . . .
>
> The same subject treated differently by Guido and etched by one of his disciples, [believed to be Elisabetta Sirani *crossed out*] Gerolamo Scarsello, with respect to the comparison one can make by means of these two prints between master and disciple, it seems [that there is more grace in *crossed out*] that the figure of the woman is more graceful in that of [the master *crossed out*] Guido and the pose of the child is much more lively in that of [the disciple *crossed out*] Pesarese.
>
> f.60 . . . Fortuna engraved in wood by Barthelemy Coriolano . . .[2]

Mariette's reference to Coriolano's woodcut reminds one of that other great early seventeenth-century woodcut that represents an amor airborne beside a triumphant deity, Christopher Jegher's brilliant interpretation of *Hercules Slaying Discord* by Peter Paul Rubens (H.IX.187.15). Despite their differing techniques, Jegher's *Hercules* and Cantarini's *Fortuna* exploit comparable technical devices: the amor in Hercules is carved with notably more delicate lines than those which represent the bludgeoning giant; the amor in Fortuna, while etched in the same bite as the striding goddess, has been burnished to lighten and blur the lines. In both cases, the artists' ambition, to evoke an infant hovering as delicately as a hummingbird above a representation of omnipotent force, is brilliantly achieved.[3]

Although Cantarini's etched oeuvre contains several prints with landscape settings, most notably *Mercury and Argus* (Cat. 29), his capacity to represent space is realized even in this print where only a blank globe lies below a vertical screen of cloud. An admirer of Cantarini's art has located this capacity in his brilliantly illuminated figures rather than in their settings: "In Cantarini's work there is a simple spirit, enthused by the sunlight that blesses everything, radiantly resting on bodies and giving that heady ecstatic sense of space that makes men happy."[4]

MBC

1. For further biographical information on Cantarini, see Reed and Wallace 1989, p. 128.

2. BNMS R068573: "f.59. La Fortune representée par une femme qui est debout sur un globe, qui renverse une bourse rempli d'argent pendent qu'un amor l'efforce de la retenir par les cheveux. Cette pièce est inventée & gravée à l'eau forte par le Pesarese, il l'a fit en concurrance de celle de Guide son maistre [qui *crossed out*] est sur cette mesme feuille, [aussy *crossed out*]

Une epreuve de cette mesme estampe ou l'on a gravé au bas le nom de Guido mais sans autre raison que pour la rendre du meilleur debit. . . . Le mesme sujet traitté different par le Guide & gravé à l'eau forte par quelqu'un de ses disciples, [l'on croit que c'est Elisabeth Siriani *crossed out*] Jerosme Scarselli, a l'egard du jugement que l'on peut porter sur ces deux pieces faites en concurrance pas le maistre & par le disciple, il semble [qu'il y a plus de grace dans *crossed out*] que la figure de femme est plus gracieuse dans celle du [maistre *crossed out*] Guido & l'attitude de l'enfant est beaucoup plus spirituelle dans celle du [disciple *crossed out*] Pesarese.

f.60. . . . La Fortune gravé en bois par Barthelemy Coriolan . . . "

3. For an extended discussion of the developing iconography of Fortuna in the sixteenth and seventeenth centuries, with reproductions of many engravings and etchings of the subject, see Russell 1990, pp. 204–20.

4. Benvenuto Disertori, "The First Century of Etching," *Print Collector* 12 (March–April 1975):6–13, p. 8.

AGOSTINO CARRACCI

Bologna 1557 – 1602 Parma

18 *Venus*, c. 1590 – 1595

engraving

inscribed in brown ink, verso: *P. mariette 1666*

B.XVIII.108.129, TIB39.171.129, Bohlin 181

Alpheus Hyatt Fund, s1.46.3

In the authoritative modern catalogue of Carracci prints, this engraving bears the expanded title *Venus or Galatea Supported by Dolphins*.[1] I prefer the identification of Venus, which is traditional for the print, because this beautiful and beguiling young woman rides on the shell so long associated with the birth from the sea of the goddess of love, and because she is crowded round with amorini. In fact, however, the conception is indebted to Marcantonio Raimondi's engraving after Raphael of Galatea (TIB27.47.350), and the question cannot be settled here.

What is evident is the artist's delicate play with the sensuousness of his subject. Particularly evocative is the soft brush of feathers against the breast of an appreciative Venus. One is reminded of the many engraved representations of Leda and the Swan, where the act of copulation is embodied in the caress of Leda's buttocks by the swan's feathered tail. Centuries of connoisseurs have enjoyed the piquant touches in Agostino's print; it is rare to find it in as fine an impression as that from Spencer Album 1.[2]

Venus comes from the series known from the erotic content of its fifteen prints as the *Lascivie*. In fact, as Bohlin makes clear, the series is a creation of posterity: the variety of formats militates against it having been conceived as a single coherent group.[3] Separating the prints out by specific subject and size, one can assemble a set of goddesses in relatively chaste situations (Bohlin 178–183), a set of nymphs and satyrs who are anything but chaste (Bohlin 184–188), two complementary Old Testament subjects (*Lot and His Daughters*, Bohlin 177, and *Susannah and the Elders*, Bohlin 176), and two interior scenes in particularly debauched taste, which match even to their inclusion of a cat in the one and a dog in the other (although it must be admitted that the sizes of these last two prints differ somewhat and that the imagery of *Gold Conquers Everything* [Bohlin 190] is more conventional than that of *The Satyr Mason* [Bohlin 189]).

The Spencer Album devoted to the prints of the Carracci and their school includes only four of these, all mounted on a single page (*Orpheus and Eurydice* [Bohlin 178, s1.46.1], *Andromeda* [Bohlin 179, s1.46.2], *Venus* [Bohlin 181, s1.46.3], and *The Three Graces* [Bohlin 183, s1.46.4]). With the possible exception of the right-most of the Three Graces, whose hand covering her genitals has strayed, these four engravings provide the least titillating imagery of the entire fifteen; there is no doubt that the Spencer Album presents a censored version of the *Lascivie*. This is hardly surprising given Pierre-Jean Mariette's undisguised distress at Agostino's capacity to make obscene prints. He discussed *A Nymph and Satyr Embracing* (Bohlin 187), admittedly the most explicit among the fifteen, in the following terms:

> I have seen impressions of it with the date 1559, and this date appears to have been en-graved on the plate by Carracci himself. He put it there, undoubtedly, to make the change, to make believe that this abominable work, for no one could ever [do] anything more lascivious, was not his, because it would bear a date prior to his birth; but this expe-dient would be useless; his style would be there, more certain and more than enough than anything [else] which he could have done to identify himself. Anything that a painter might make, he always manifests himself in spite of himself, even when he takes the greatest pains to dissemble; it would be best to produce nothing that one could not declare oneself the creator of without blushing.[4]

That Mariette was not simply embarrassed for one of the artists whom he esteemed most highly is indicated by comparable comments he made about Romeyn de Hooghe, hardly one of his favorites: "He was accused of having engraved obscene images, of having spread them abroad, and having, in imitation of Aretino, given youth lessons in debauchery worthy of the greatest reproof."[5]

What is striking, however, in Mariette's discussion of Agostino's erotic print is not his prud-ery but his resigned yet ringing affirmation of the supreme power of connoisseurship. Although he validates his own métier in terms of the artist's inability to conceal his hand, in fact Pierre-Jean Mariette is presuming an audience, at least of one, capable of recognizing this hand no mat-ter what the expedient to which the skillful artist might have resorted.

MBC

1. Bohlin, p. 295.

2. Bohlin, p. 289. That this impression is from the col-lection of Pierre Mariette II is not irrelevant considering his grandson's opinions (see below), but no Mariette would have knowingly abridged an artist's oeuvre for prudish reasons.

3. Bohlin, pp. 289–90, provides an overall assessment of the series, with its critical history. The prints them-

selves are described and reproduced on the following pages, pp. 291–305.

4. Mariette 1851–1860, vol. 1, p. 316: "J'en ay vu des épreuves, avec la datte 1559, et cette datte paroissoit avoir été gravée sur la planche par le Carrache même. Il la mit, sans doute, pour donner le change, en faisant croire que cette abominable pièce, car on ne peut rien de plus lacif, n'étoit pas de luy, puisqu'elle portoit une date antérieure

à celle de sa naissance; mais cet expédient étoit inutile; il y avoit mis sa manière, plus certaine et plus suffisante que tout ce qu'il auroit pu y mettre pour se faire connoistre. Quelque chose qu'un peinte fasse, il se manifeste toujours malgré luy-même, lors même qu'il prend plus de tâche de se contrefaire; le mieux est de ne rien produire, dont on ne puisse se déclarer l'auteur sans rougir." Bohlin suggests that the date, which only appears in the second state of the print, may have been added by a later publisher "in ignorance of its actual publication date. On the other hand, Agostino himself, after having been rebuked by the pope [Clement VIII],

may have felt it necessary to disavow authorship of the engraving" (Bohlin, p. 301).

5. Mariette 1851–1860, vol. 2, p. 379: "Il fut accusé d'avoir gravé des images obscènes, de les avoir répandues dans le public, et d'avoir, à l'imitation de l'Aretin, donné à la jeunesse des leçons de débauche dignes de la plus grande répréhension." Mariette deplored de Hooghe's *The French Reign of Terror in the Dutch Villages Bodegraven and Zwammerdam* (H.IX.120.89–96), the Dutch counterpart of the French artist Callot's two series on the horrors of war, which Mariette applauded.

ODOARDO FIALETTI

Bologna 1573 – 1638 Venice

19a *Ornament with a Triton Embracing a Nereid Seated on a Sea Monster, a Putto and a Dragon Above, after Giancarli*

etching

234 x 145 mm

inscribed in plate, lower left margin: *Polifilo Giancarli In*; lower right margin: *OF* [superimposed] *inc*

B.XVII.280.52, TIB38.242.52

Francis H. Burr Fund, s6.31.3

19b *Ornament with a Triton and Four Putti Carrying Off a Dolphin, after Giancarli*

etching

234 x 145 mm

inscribed in plate, lower left margin: *Polifilo Giancarli In*; lower right margin: *OF* [superimposed] *in*

B.XVII.280.48, TIB38.238.48

Francis H. Burr Fund, s6.31.4

These are two of the nine designs which, together with a title page, comprise one of the few complete suites of ornament prints in the Spencer Albums (TIB38.233–242.43–52, s6.29.3–s6.31.4).

Their only competitors for this classification are etchings by Stefano della Bella (see Cat. 55a–d). A set of trophies by Galestruzzi (see Cat. 54a–b) only marginally falls in this category because it in fact reproduces paintings.

Scarce as ornament prints are in the albums, which largely feature the work of history and landscape painters,[1] they form a numerous class in printmaking from its earliest beginnings through the eighteenth century.[2] Among the various subdivisions of the genre, this series by Fialetti may be described as foliate grotesque.[3] The term "grotesque" derives from a major source for ornament in the Renaissance and after: the newly discovered subterranean (thus *alla grottesca*) remains of ancient Roman structures that were often lavishly decorated with ornamental composites of human, animal, and plant forms in bas-relief, mosaic, and mural painting.

Among these designs and also among the survivors of antique monumental architecture,[4] patterns of acanthus foliage and other blossoming vines were one of the major conventions for decorating panels which could not be left bare and yet which were to remain subsidiary to realistic representations (that is, depictions of complete or at least plausibly excerpted natural forms in space). The plant forms, neverending tendrils ever renewed with fresh growth, were of course more than a space-filling device. Their inherent iconographic potential is understood when one recognizes the descendants of this Roman motif in the spandrels of Romanesque cathedrals in Milan and Palermo, to give but two examples. Nor can the page surrounds in illuminated medieval manuscripts be omitted from even this briefest of descriptions of the genre that one might describe as inhabited foliage. Although a specific form of the ancient grotesque may have awaited rediscovery by Renaissance artists, it had proliferated, transformed, in Christian and Islamic art in the intervening millennium.

Even more than the plant forms, the creatures that clamber and swing among Fialetti's leaves and blossoms refer to the antique inheritance rejuvenated in sixteenth-century Italy. Apart from the ubiquitous putti, Fialetti's etchings swarm with dolphins, nereids, tritons, and even more fanciful sea monsters. Their individual forms and their disconcerting habit of metamorphosing from foliage bespeak the peculiar hold on our imaginations that has always been exerted by aquatic creatures, who gracefully populate a medium in which we humans cannot survive and who are prone to inconceivable transformations—think of the tadpole!

Parallel to the sixteenth-century rise of the ornament print in all its hybrid forms was the increasing popularity of Ovid's *Metamorphoses*, whose tales, narrative equivalents of the plotless episodes of ornament, also often feature sea life—divine, human, and bestial—in combination and constant flux. A summary of but one of the stories from *Metamorphoses* demonstrates their consonance with prints such as these by Fialetti:

. . . the maiden Scylla was bathing naked in the sea when Glaucus, himself recently transformed from a mortal to a sea god, saw her and loved her. He approached her and pleaded his love, but she fled, wondering at his monstrous appearance. To win her, Glaucus went to Circe to beg for a love charm, but he was received by the enchantress with

Polifilo Giancarli In.

Polisilo Giancarli Inu

declarations of her own love for him. He refused it and in her wrath she revenged herself on her rival by poisoning Scylla's bathing pool with evil roots so that when she entered the water her loins were transformed into barking doglike monsters. . . .[5]

Not only the specifics of form—even the aquatic roots have their analogue in Fialetti's dragon-infested vines—but also the action driven by love, lust, wrath, and revenge is comparable, with the prints and the tales equally distempered by the genial conventions of their respective arts.

The great difference between the prints of Fialetti and works by his immediate predecessors and contemporaries, such as Vico (see TIB30.290–297.451–464), Pittoni (see Berliner 1926, cat. 202), Ciamberlano (see TIB44.190–201.3), and Falcone (see TIB44.307.19), is that these others, and ornament printmakers more generally, respected the convention of the plane surface it was their intention to decorate.[6] Many compositions even indicate by a shaded ground their common inheritance from antique architectural bas-reliefs. But Fialetti's forms are often sharply foreshortened and richly shadowed; they move in and out of brightly illuminated space. In this he betrays his descent and that of his draftsman Giancarli[7] from the great painters of the Venetian Renaissance, in particular Tintoretto.

Although Fialetti was born in Bologna and always retained something of the lessons of the Carracci,[8] he spent his working life in Venice and copied a number of the compositions of Tintoretto.[9] His huge etching of the latter's *Wedding at Cana* (TIB38.200.2) is also included in Spencer Album 6. The kinship of Fialetti's decorative prints with the painter's compositions on themes drawn from antique myth, such as *Mercury and the Three Graces*, *The Birth of the Milky Way*, and *The Marriage of Bacchus and Ariadne*, is striking. Tintoretto's serene, sky-spanning gods and goddesses ornament the entire expanse of their canvases with much the same spatial pressure that we see in these minor, yet still fecund, variations on the lives and lusts of lesser gods.

MBC

1. The lack of ornament prints in the albums conforms to the concept of the high status of history painting. The Mariettes were deeply involved in the publication of ornament prints since the mid-seventeenth century (see Weigert 1953, p. 186), as they were in the publication of topographical views, but examples of either of these genres would have been unsuitable for inclusion in volumes such as the Spencer Albums except as they might be associated with important painters, as prints by Fialetti were.

2. See Berliner 1926 for a comprehensive survey of the genre.

3. See Ward-Jackson 1967 for an enlightening cruise along "the main streams and tributaries" of ornament prints. See also Brown/RISD 1980 for discussion of Renaissance ornament prints of this general type and their relation to architecture. Fialetti etched another set after Giancarli, in a horizontal format (TIB38.243–249.53–65)

4. The Ara Pacis and the altar or base dedicated by

Gnaeus Domitius Ahenobarbus on the Campus Martius are two major Roman monuments that together could provide inspiration for the Fialetti ornaments, foliate designs from the former and putti, tritons, nereids, etc., from the latter. As with all derivations from the antique, however, one must always ask, "What did he know, and when did he know it?" I am not suggesting direct borrowing.

5. Wallace 1979, p. 48.

6. A large number of ornament prints by Northern sixteenth-century engravers, notably Hans Sebald Beham and Heinrich Aldegraver, could also be included in this category.

7. Giancarli (also spelled Zancarli) is scarcely known except through the two sets of prints after his drawings by Fialetti. He is believed to have worked in Venice at the end of the sixteenth century.

8. One of Fialetti's major and most influential print series was a drawing book modeled after the instruc-

tional scheme of the Carracci academy (TIB38.315–337.198–243). See Amornpichetkul 1984, Bolten 1985, and David Rosand, *Palma Giovane and Venetian Mannerism*, Ph.D. dissertation, Columbia University, 1965, pp. 263–341.

9. See Amornpichetkul, 1984, pp. 112–13, and Reed and Wallace 1989, p. 248, for summaries of what little is known of Fialetti's life and career. Of interest is Carlo Ridolfi's note that he went to Venice in order to study the works of Tintoretto.

GIOVANNI LUIGI VALESIO

Correggio? 1583? – 1633 Rome

20   *Twelve Principal Movements of the Head*

engraving

207 x 139 mm

inscribed in plate below image: *Dodici principali mouimenti della Testa, per chi / desidera intenderli nella pittura* [*The twelve principal movements of the head, for him who wishes to understand them in painting*]; at lower right: *Il Valesio inv. f.*

B.XVIII.216.7, TIB40.18.7, TIB4002.144.167

William M. Prichard Fund, S1.79.1

Valesio's engraving is a distillation and inflection toward decorative ends of the type of pedagogical prints that were gathered together in what have been described as "exercise books" or "academic drawing books."[1] Such books came into their own in the wake of the Carracci reform of painting and, as an offshoot of the analytical approach to drawing taught in the Carracci academy, constitute a crucial document.[2] Characteristic of such prints was the presentation in successive sheets of studies of parts of the body. The goal was not so much to gain an understanding of anatomy, as would have been the case in the sixteenth century, as to discover principles underlying the representation of the visible world. In a particular sheet, some part of the body would be analyzed graphically: it would first be reduced to a minimal number of graphic signs, usually a contour outline, and then be repeated on the same sheet with further graphic systems to indicate light, movement, and three-dimensional form.

Valesio was one of the first to produce such a drawing book—*Primi elementi del disegno, in gratia de i principianti nell'arte della pittura, fatti da Gio. Valesio l'Instabile, Academico Incaminato di Bologna*—which has been dated to the years 1606–1616 on the basis of its dedication.[3] It is possible that this engraving was made as a kind of comment on the series, a transition between pedagogy and art poised at the threshold of history painting, which is the artist's final goal. Although the print is not known to have been part of such a book, it clearly acknowledges the genre in its inscription and also in the ostensibly academic juxtapositions of the differing poses.[4] At the same time, it draws on the idealizing effects of antique models, such as heads found on

Dodici principali mouimenti della Testa, per chi
desidera intenderli nella pittura.

Il Valesio inu. f.

antique gems and coins to which Agostino Carracci turned in some of his drawings. It is possible that Valesio derived the bearded male head from such a drawing in which a remarkably similar head appears.[5]

Since Agostino was particularly interested in engraving and brought that art to a new level of perfection (see Cat. 2), this print of twelve heads by an artist who had been a student in the Carracci academy suggests a specific indebtedness. A tenet of Carracci teaching was that twelve figures should suffice for most history paintings, a doctrine reported to Malvasia by the painter Garbieri.[6] Valesio's bold handling of the burin (his *franco bolino*) and coloristic effects, which are remarked upon by Malvasia[7] and exemplified by this engraving, also tie him to the Carracci academy and specifically to the graphic style of Agostino. More generally, there was, perhaps, associated with the academy a contemporary vogue in Italy among literati and dilettanti for the collecting of prints and drawings and particularly those with a pedagogical aspect, together with a proliferation of informal drawing classes attended by prominent persons.

An unpublished drawing attributed to Valesio in the Uffizi, *Roundel with Heads* (inv. no. 4272s), is clearly associated by format and subject with this engraving, although it is not a preparatory drawing for it. The drawing presents twenty classicizing heads of men and women, all turned in profile counterclockwise and arranged, overlapping, in a circular band. Reminiscent of designs for ceremonial plates or shields, it is more formal and decorative than the print, and flatter in that it makes less use of effects of light. But both drawing and engraving manifest the dual aspect of such works: as self-acknowledged descendants of academic studies and as collectible artistic productions in their own right.

Valesio is thought to have been born around 1583 and thus of a slightly younger generation than the Carracci. He was a latecomer to painting and printmaking, having started out in Bologna as a teacher of fencing and dancing (which he accompanied on the lute). He then joined his brother in a shop specializing in calligraphy, and he was a poet who came to know all the important poets in the city—Cesare Rinaldi, for example, who was a close friend of Agostino Carracci.[8] Early sources report that at the late age of thirty Valesio entered the Carracci academy, where Lodovico Carracci gave him an accelerated course in the elements or "principles" of art. It may be that the master construed Valesio's work in calligraphy as preparation for drawing, since the analytic aspects of learning to write letters and learning to draw had been emphasized at least since the time of Alberti.[9]

Although Valesio is known to have executed painting commissions, his growing reputation as an artist rested on his draftsmanship and printmaking. Unlike Agostino, whose graphic work represented an immense range of subjects, Valesio in the main produced engravings for court and ecclesiastical ceremonies, for title pages (three of which are also included in Spencer Album 1), and for illustrations of dramatic texts or books of poetry. He had an extended network of friends among the most refined and avant-garde literary circles and was a member of the literary academies of the Torbidi and the Selvaggi.[10]

Valesio was a passionate advocate of the poetry of Giovan Battista Marino, the greatest poet of the century, who in turn expressed his admiration for the art of Valesio. In 1620 the poet complained to his publisher that no one in Paris could illustrate his *Sampogna*: "There are not to be found anywhere any Tempestis, Renis, Valesios, or Morassonis."[11] Marino honored Valesio even further by including poems describing works by Valesio (now lost) in his *Galeria*[12] and by mentioning Valesio in his great epic poem, the *Adone.*[13]

Malvasia, the seventeenth-century biographer of Bolognese artists, presents Valesio as a many-faceted minor poet and artist who received inflated praises during his lifetime, declined in his last decade in Rome, and was quickly forgotten after his death.[14] Perhaps Malvasia overstates this last point, since Marolles mentioned him in his *Livre des Peintres*,[15] and the very inclusion of Valesio's prints in the Spencer Album suggests a continuing appreciation of his work. In the long view, however, Malvasia was right, in that Valesio is barely known to modern students of the seventeenth century and was not mentioned in Wittkower's survey. The scholarly account of this painter-poet is far from complete.[16] For instance, we learn from an eyewitness report that Valesio produced two chiaroscuro paintings for the funeral celebration for Marino mounted by the Academy of the Umoristi in Rome in 1625.[17] A fuller account would explore the ways in which poetry and art merge both in his life and his productions and would perhaps show him to be a representative figure of his time.

A S

1. See Bohlin, p. 57; Bolten 1985, pp. 243ff; Veronika Birke in TIB4002.144; Amornpichetkul 1984, pp. 108–18. In her discussion of Valesio's drawing book, Birke (in translation) used less suitable phrasings such as "instructional patterns" and "model book" (TIB40002.144).

2. See Bohlin, and Dempsey 1977, passim, and his commentary on this engraving p. 79, n. 21. See also Dempsey's "The Carracci Academy," pp. 33–43, in *Academies of Art between the Renaissance and Romanticism*, ed. A. W. A. Boschloo, *Leids Kunsthistorisch Jaarboek* (1989), especially p. 39.

3. TIB4002.144.

4. In his mention of this print, Malvasia, the seventeenth-century biographer of Bolognese artists, substitutes "*introdursi*" for "*intenderli*" in the inscription, which changes the meaning slightly, giving the inscription a practical inflection by directing it more to beginning artists and amateur painters rather than including collectors or connoisseurs as well. Malvasia's manuscript notes transcribe the inscription correctly in one instance and incorrectly in another; perhaps when he chose among his notes for publication he did not have the print before him. See Malvasia 1841, vol. 1, p. 92, and for Malvasia's manuscript notes see Marzocchi 1983, pp. 345, 361.

5. See for example the *Sheet of Studies (Venus and Adonis, Putti, Heads, Caricatures, and a Hunt)* (Windsor inv. no. 2001 recto; repr. in Wittkower 1952, pl. 35), or

Head of a Faun in a Concave Roundel (National Gallery of Art, Washington; repr. in Bohlin, p. 459).

6. Malvasia 1841, vol. 2, p. 216. More obviously, Valesio's design improved upon the crude lining up of heads found in drawing books in a typical print of parts of the body.

7. Malvasia 1841, vol. 1, pp. 90, 92. Malvasia has very little to say about Valesio's relation to Agostino except a brief mention of Valesio's move from drawing to engraving (vol. 2, p. 96).

8. See Malvasia 1841, vol. 2, pp. 95–103, for biographical details.

9. For Valesio as a calligrapher see Giovanni Fantuzzi, *Notizie degli scrittori bolognesi* 9 vols. (Bologna: Stamperia di S. Tommaso d'Aquino, 1781–1795), vol. 2, p. 134. For Alberti, see Lorenzo Battista Alberti, *De pictura*, ed. Grayson (London: Phaidon, 1972), pp. 96–98, and recent discussion of this tradition in David Rosand, "The Crisis of the Venetian Renaissance" *L'Arte*, pp. 13, 45; Bolten 1985, p. 192; Charles Dempsey, "Introduction," *Gli scritti de' Carracci*, ed. G. Perini (Bologna: Nuova Alfa, 1990), pp. 12–13.

10. Malvasia 1841, vol. 2, p. 100.

11. M. Guglielminetti, ed., *Lettere di G. B. Marino* (Turin: Einaudi, 1966), p. 257: "Ma qui ha pochi maestri, che posseggano eccellenza di disegno: ed infine non si ritrovano per tutto i Tempesti, i Reni, i Valesi, ne' i Morazzoni . . ." (letter to G. B. Cotti, Paris, January 1620).

12. Reprinted by Malvasia in his life of Valesio (Malvasia 1841, vol. 2, p. 98).

13. Giovan Battista Marino, *Adone* canto 5, 55: "E to Michel, di Caravaggio onore, / per cui del ver piu bella è la menzogna, / mentre che creator più che pittore, / con l'angelica man gli fai vergogna; e voi, Spada e Valesio, il cui valore / fa de' suoi figli insuperbir Bologna; / e voi, per cui Milan pareggia Urbino, / Morazzone e Serrano e Procaccino."

14. As Malvasia himself states in his manuscript notes, he is drawing a parallel between the unmerited good fortune of Valesio and that of Pinturicchio as presented by Vasari in his *Lives* (Marzocchi 1983, pp. 358, 360).

15. Marolles 1855, p. 68. Valesio is listed in the section on Italian draftsmen.

16. Veronika Birke, in her commentary for *The Illustrated Bartsch* vol. 20, did add a substantial number of prints to Valesio's oeuvre originally catalogued by Bartsch, and she has established the year of his death as 1633 and not in the 1620s, as previously thought (TIB4002.144).

17. Borzelli, Angelo. *Storia della vita e delle opere di Giovan Battista Marino*. (Naples: Tipografia degli Artigianelli, 1927), pp. 259–64.

ANTONIO TEMPESTA

Florence 1555 – 1660 Florence

21a *Canto XV from Torquato Tasso*, La Gerusalemme liberata *(Third Series)*

etching

273 x 203 mm

inscribed in plate, upper center in plaque: *Del buon ueglio seguendo il san consiglio / Trouano i duo guerrier la fida scorta / Che gli accoglie nel picciolo nauiglio / E per l'alto Ocean ratta gli porta, / E sempre doue scorge ogn'hora il ciglio / Sembra al ueloce pin la strada corta / Passan l'armi d'Egitto, e in strana terra / Hor crudi, hor uaghi uolti gli fan guerra*; lower edge, center: *XV*.[1]

B.XVII.177.1242, TIB37.126.1242

Gift of Melvin R. Seiden, s8.86.1

21b *Canto XV from Torquato Tasso*, La Gerusalemme liberata *(Second Series)*

etching

145 x 180 mm

inscribed in plate, lower center of design: *XV*; below design, left: *Poi che la Coppia de' Messaggi arditi / Del buon ueglio sequi l'orme, e i consigli; / Di mirabil nochiero a i fidi inuiti / Varca su cauo legno onde è perigli,—*; and right: *Ma già scorge, che ingonbre arene, e liti / Han de l'Egittio Re tende e nauigli, / Poi giunti al fin del corso, armano il petto / Hor cótra ū fero, Hor cótra ū dolce aspetto.*[2]

B.XVII.177.1222, TIB37.106.1222

Gift of Melvin R. Seiden, s8.86.2

Del buon ueglio seguendo il san consiglio
Trouano i duo guerrier la fida scorta
Che gli accoglie nel picciolo nauiglio
E per l'alto Ocean ratta gli porta
E sempre doue scorge ogn'hora il ciglio
Sembra al ueloce pin la strada corta
Passan l'armi d'Egitto, e in strana terra
Hor crudi hor uaghi uolti gli fan guerra

XV

XV

Poi che la Coppia de' Massimi ardita
Del buon ueglio segui l'orme, e i consigli
Di mirabil nochiero a i chi inuia
L'arca su cauo legno onde è perigli

Ma più scorge, che ingombra arene, e lit
L'Un de l'Egitto Re gioie e nauigli
Poi giunta al fin del corso, impugno il peso
Hor contra il fero Hor contra il dolce aspetto

Tempesta's oeuvre is characterized by large series of prints, often repeated in only slight variation and almost exclusively illustrative. In addition to battles and hunts, these include, among others, the months, seasons, wonders of the world, and literary works. His earliest master was the Flemish emigré to Florence Stradanus (Jan van der Straet), also a prolific designer of print subjects. Tempesta also studied with Santi di Tito, the teacher of many Florentine painters of the early Baroque. From 1575 Tempesta worked mainly in Rome, but continued to enjoy considerable Florentine patronage. His work influenced the young Jacques Callot (see Cat. 24, 52). Tempesta probably learned etching in Rome in the 1580s,[3] quickly adapting its ease of execution to his fluid draftsmanship and inventive, if somewhat predictable, designs. His dated etchings range from 1589 to 1627 and were mostly published in Rome, with some commissioned by publishers in Florence and the Netherlands.

The enormously popular epic *La Gerusalemme liberata (Jerusalem Delivered)* by Torquato Tasso (1544–1595) was first published in 1581. The first illustrated edition appeared in Genoa in 1590, with engravings after drawings by the Genoese painter Bernardo Castello (1557–1629). Giacomo Franco and Agostino Carracci executed the engravings for that edition, consisting of twenty full-page plates, one preceding each canto.[4] Castello designed two additional series of illustrations for *La Gerusalemme liberata* in smaller and larger format, issued in Genoa in 1604 and 1617.[5]

Aside from a small anonymous series of 1598, Tempesta's Tasso designs were the next to appear. Interestingly, he also designed and etched three separate sets of illustrations, which, like those of his predecessors, contain twenty plates each, in varying formats (small vertical, medium horizontal, and larger horizontal within elaborate vertical decorative borders).[6] The latter two series are present in the Spencer Albums and are represented here by one plate from each, illustrating the fifteenth canto.

The internal precedence of Tempesta's three series is difficult to determine. The smallest set (not present in the albums) seems to have appeared first in Rome in 1607, and also clearly depends upon the 1604 "miniaturized" set by Castello, as it contains virtually the same figural elements in similar scale, at times only reversed or rearranged. The two larger Tempesta sets are not dated, and are less obviously dependent upon the Castello illustrations in larger format. In comparison, Tempesta has heightened the action and drama, both in terms of the more "life-size," volumetrically defined figures and a more effective disposition of light and shadow by skillful use of hatching. Often the same elements are present in all versions of an illustration but are rearranged in terms of placement and relative scale.[7] The precise degree to which the Castello designs served as prototypes for Tempesta remains unclear, but the question serves as a typical case study for his utilization of earlier illustration cycles in issuing his own versions. These were often reprinted until the plates literally wore out, their ubiquitous presence in turn influencing later works of illustration and decorative art throughout Europe.

This canto concerns a rescue mission by two knights in search of their compatriot Rinaldo, who has been imprisoned in Armida's palace on the island of Teneriffe. They are sent on their way by an old wizard and conveyed in a boat steered by a mysterious oarswoman. Arriving at the island, they must face the wild beasts and resist the proffered delights of nymphs bathing in the Fountain of Laughter in order to reach the palace. The depiction of these several incidents, all displayed in the etchings exhibited, reflects a long tradition in manuscript and book illustration of showing a progression of events within a single frame. For his two versions, Tempesta has switched the arrival and departure scenes between foreground and far distance. Here Tempesta has not relied on Castello's 1590 illustration, which depicts only the boat voyage and a vista of a large armed fleet.

Particularly for the larger plate, Tempesta has indulged his fantasies in delineating the dragons and other beasts facing the two knights; a hint of his predilection for detailed battle scenes is visible in the middle distance at left. Essentially a highly glorified epic of the Crusades, *La Gerusalemme liberata* gave the artist ample opportunity for showing sieges, cavalry charges, massed encampments, and pitched battles.

Both plates include different verses; in the case of the larger, these are framed by elaborate ornamental frames. The addition of verses directly on the etching plate indicates that Tempesta intended his sets of illustrations to stand alone, without being bound into letterpress editions of the text.[8] In this respect his editions of illustrations to famous literary texts resemble today's comic books, a shorthand route to the classics. Etching was not a common medium for illustrating printed editions of such epics as Ovid, Tasso, Ariosto, or Dante at this time. These serious works, intended for learned audiences, were more often reserved for the more tightly controlled, "higher" technique of engraving. Including other series in addition to the Tasso, such as illustrations for Ovid's *Metamorphoses* and the Old Testament, Tempesta's works served to popularize such epics and their imagery.

DPB

1. "Following the sound advice of the venerable seer, the two warriors find their faithful escort, who takes them onto a little ship and rapidly carries them across the high seas; and whenever they see the shore, the fast ship makes the long journey seem short. They sail past the Egyptian army, and, in a strange land, ugly and lovely faces in turn battle with them."

2. "After following the directions and advice of the good seer, the pair of daring, trustworthy messengers, together with their admirable pilot, overcome waves and danger on their ship. But already they see the shores and beaches occupied by the Egyptian king's tents and ships. Then upon reaching the end of the journey, they arm themselves to fight with figures of either fierce or gentle aspect." My thanks to Giuseppa Saponara and Anne Summerscale for this and the preceding translation.

3. Reed and Wallace 1989, p. 217.

4. See Bohlin, nos. 155–64. For a survey of illustrated editions of Tasso, see Ferrara 1985, pp. 85–131.

5. See Ferrara 1985, nos. 4, 7.

6. Respectively, TIB37.87–90.1188–1207, TIB37.91–111.1208[1]–1227, and TIB37.112–131.1228–1247. As the Ferrara catalogue noted (Ferrara 1985, p. 100), the illustrations in *The Illustrated Bartsch* for the first series are reproduced out of proper order.

7. Castello's two Tasso series exhibit considerably more different features between them than Tempesta's two. Castello increased the scale and dramatic action of his figures for his later set of 1617, perhaps reflecting some reverse influence from Tempesta.

8. See Ruth Mortimer, *Harvard College Library Department of Printing and Graphic Arts Catalogue of Books and Manuscripts—Italian 16th Century Books* (Cambridge: Harvard University, 1974), p. 681, for examples of separate issues of the 1590 Castello Tasso plates. With no verses included in the plates, however, it is clear they were commissioned and executed for a printed book. Though in all probability intended to stand alone, Tempesta's larger series of Tasso illustrations were published in conjunction with a complete printed text of *La Gerusalemme liberata* in 1735 in Urbino.

ANTONIO TEMPESTA

Florence 1555 – 1660 Florence

22   *The Exterminating Angel Slays the Army of Sennacherib,*
     plate 21 from *Old Testament Battles,* 1613

etching

198 x 282 mm

watermark: anchor [?] within a circle

plate inscribed within design area, lower center: *. 21 .;* lower right: *AF* [monogram]; in lower margin, in cartouche below design: *CLADES SENACHRIB.;* to left of cartouche: *Quis cladem illius noctis, quis funera dicat? / Quot duce cum foedo millia casa· cadant?;* to right of cartouche: *Non hominū uires, haec numinis edidit ira / Se scelerū ultorem praebuit ipse Deus.*

B.XVII.131.256, TIB35.82.256

Gift of Melvin R. Seiden, s8.12.2.

A total of 688 prints by Tempesta (of a total oeuvre of about fifteen hundred)[1] are preserved in Spencer Albums 8 and 9. They are arranged according to one version of traditional subject-based order: religious prints come first, beginning with Old Testament subjects. Presumably these would be followed by New Testament and saintly subjects were any to be found, but one striking aspect of the Spencer Tempesta collection is that none of the artist's many etchings of scenes from the lives of Christ, martyrs, and saints is included; the only prints with Christian associations are many-figured scenes of contemporary processions of the church hierarchy and of diplomats to the Holy See.[2] In the albums, Old Testament scenes are succeeded by historical prints, with episodes, sites, and personalities from ancient history preceding those from modern history; it is at the end of the latter that the Christian cavalcades are found. All of these prints, which present a distinctly secular version of the actual history of the world, comprise the first volume.[3]

The second volume begins again with the creation of the world, but now as provided by mythology: it starts with Tempesta's lengthy set of illustrations to Ovid's *Metamorphoses* and continues through the Labors of Hercules, other ancient myths, the Four Ages of Man, the Seasons, and the Months. Gradually these shade into hunting scenes, blends of fanciful recreations of ancient, exotic, or entirely imaginary prey and pursuers and of contemporary practices so specific that one could construct traps, pits, and snares from their examples. The second volume closes with series of animals.[4]

The common thread uniting the prints is Tempesta's characteristic obsession with violence. A search of titles, for example, for the words "army," "soldier," "war," "battle," "combat," "attack," "defeat," "kill," and "death" finds about a fifth of the etchings in the albums, and this does not begin to account for the many hunt scenes in which the fate of the prey, and occasionally the hunters, is not explicit in the title. Tempesta's contemporary artistic sources, largely the works of

133

Quis clo\[…\]m illius noctis quis juncta dicat? ((CLADES SENACHRIB.)) Non hominū uires, hæc numinis edidit ira
Quot duce cum fædo millia cæsa cadant. Se sceleru ultorem præbuit ipse Deus.

his master Stradanus (Jan van der Straet), especially as interpreted in the prints of Goltzius and other Northern engravers, represent many of the same subjects,[5] but their compositions do not consistently convey the bloodlust so striking in Tempesta. Even in Christian subjects omitted from this collection he reveled in the tools and techniques of sadistic mutilation as applied to the flesh of hapless martyrs.

The immense number of Tempesta's etchings and their proliferation through many editions and copies testifies to a sympathetic audience, presumably the upper echelons of a European society riven by wars and feuds and intent upon defending the prerogatives of their class, notably hunting. A contemporary, appreciative Italian connoisseur, in categorizing the various forms of painting, singled out Tempesta's prints:

> The ninth method is to paint like . . . Antonio Tempesta, powerfully drawn scenes taken from life. Such scenes were in black and white, in copper engravings. In originality and good design, especially in the battles, hunts, and other scenes with people and animals in motion, they are generally very much esteemed, even though they did not attain that level in oil painting as their works bear witness.[6]

134

Likewise, Mariette acknowledged a taste for Tempesta's subjects that overcame the deficiencies of his artistic talents:

> As he had the ability to represent horses and all other sorts of animals very well, battles and hunts were those subjects in which he had the greatest success. . . . as there are connoisseurs who are more attracted by the *gout* [taste in the special French sense] of prints than by their particular quality, his [prints] have their admirers.[7]

Tempesta was greatly admired indeed in late seventeenth-century England, where issues of the reestablishment of monarchial perquisites after the Commonwealth and of the tensions among new and old peerage, landed gentry, and nouveaux riches commoners, all in the shadow of Continental wars, led to an appreciation for his military and, especially, hunting imagery.[8]

Ironically, modern biblical scholarship shows the truth of the matter to have been very different with reference to the particular Old Testament battle scene on exhibition, one of a set of twenty-five combats that feature surging masses of spearmen, frantic horses, and exotic encampments (even in the case of David slaying Goliath where a focus on the two protagonists would seem more appropriate).[9] Tempesta has illustrated the passage in the Book of Isaiah that describes the annihilation of the army of Sennacherib, the Assyrian king who had captured all of Judah except Jerusalem and who had laid siege to the holy city, which Jehovah had pledged would never be conquered by the enemies of the Jews:

> Then the angel of the Lord went forth, and smote in the camp of the Assyrians a hundred and fourscore and five thousand: and when they arose early in the morning, behold, they were all dead corpses. So Sennacherib king of Assyria departed, and went and returned, and dwelt at Nineveh.[10]

But Second Kings gives another version:

> Now in the fourteenth year of king Hezekiah did Sennacherib king of Assyria come up against all the fenced cities of Judah and took them. And Hezekiah king of Judah sent to the king of Assyria . . . saying, I have offended; return from me: that which thou puttest on me will I bear. And the king of Assyria appointed unto Hezekiah . . . three hundred talents of silver and thirty talents of gold. And Hezekiah gave him all the silver that was found in the house of the Lord, and in the treasures of the king's house. [He] cut off the gold from the doors of the temple of the Lord . . . and gave it to the king of Assyria.[11]

The account of submission and tribute (though not of subsequent palaver and plague found in II Kings 18:18–37, 19:1–36) is confirmed in the Annuals of Sennacherib, published only in the twentieth century:

> Hezekiah himself, whom the terror-inspiring splendor of my lordship had overwhelmed and whose irregular and elite troops which he brought into Jerusalem, his royal resi-

135

dence, in order to strengthen [it], had deserted him, did send me later, to Nineveh, my lordly city, together with 30 talents of gold, 800 talents of silver, precious stones, . . . elephant-hides, ebony-wood, box-wood [and] all kinds of valuable treasures, his [own] daughters, concubines, male and female musicians.[12]

Whether Sennacherib was driven off by Jehovah's angel or paid off by the Jewish king is, of course, irrelevant to the etching by Tempesta, who looked here, as elsewhere, simply for an opportunity to represent horses (which he, like Géricault, favored over men for their emotive force), armed hordes, and exotica. Note the details of the stalwart bull, a mobile symbol of royal Assyrian might, and of the cheetah-paw buskins on the soldier at the near right, once fleet of foot but now tumbled into a heap of corpses.

MBC

1. Bartsch lists 1,471 items; A. Calabi supplements this number in his essay on Tempesta in Thieme-Becker, vol. 32, p. 516; and *The Illustrated Bartsch* promises to add yet more in its commentary volumes (the picture atlases have been issued as TIB35–37). See also V. Birke, "Towards a Tempesta Catalogue," *Print Quarterly* 2, no. 3 (1985):205–18. The Fogg collection is supplemented by the holdings of books illustrated by Tempesta in the Houghton Library at Harvard, most notably by the *Roscius Emblemata sacra* of 1589 and the fowling manuals by Valli da Todi and Olina of 1601 and 1622 (TIB37.132–137.1248–1267 and TIB36.213–258.969–1014, respectively). Houghton also owns the funeral book for Margaret of Austria, which contains six Tempesta etchings (TIB35.358–363.628–33).

2. *Procession of the Pope upon His Inauguration to Saint John Lateran* (TIB36.152.860) and *Cavalcade for the Entry of an Ambassador into Rome* (TIB36.150.857).

3. With reference to the historical sequencing of the prints in the first Tempesta album, it should be noted that the compiler interrupted the set of twenty-five small Old Testament battles to insert at (almost) the appropriate chronological point the huge single-sheet plate of the battle of the Israelites and the Amalekites (TIB35.60.234). This print, a superb impression, is so large that it extends beyond the double-page spread of the open album and is folded at the right edge.

4. This is notably different from the order of arrangement of Tempesta prints given in the Mariette manuscript in the Bibliothèque Nationale (BNMS R069406–R069428) and also in the catalogue by Le Comte 1702, vol. 2, p. 335. In both of these eighteenth-century catalogues, mythological subjects precede historical subjects, with hunts at the very end. This is also the convention followed in the nineteenth century by Bartsch.

5. Note especially the 1578 series *Equus liber et incom-*

positus (*The royal stable of Don Juan of Austria*) (H.VIII. 113.334–348) and also H.VIII.36.161–170 and H.VIII.113. 329 among the works of Goltzius.

6. Enggass and Brown 1970, p. 18, quoting a letter from Vincenzo Giustiniani (1564–1637), who is described (p. 16) as the most cultivated and sophisticated of the small group of wealthy connoisseurs who were patrons of contemporary art in Rome at the turn of the century. Giustiniani listed all the forms of painting, which included drawing, copying, making portraits, etc., starting with the least important and progressing to the most.

7. Mariette 1851–1860, vol. 5, p. 282: "Comme il avoit le talent de très bien représenter les chevaux et toutes les autres espèces d'animaux, les batailles et les chasses sont les sujets où il a le mieux réussi. . . . tant qu'il y aura des connoisseurs qui seront plus touchés du goût que de la propreté dans les estampes, les siennes auront des admirateurs."

8. See Deuchar 1988, p. 37, for his description of paintings at Wilton of the fourth earl of Pembroke "amidst most unlikely views of crocodile-catching and monkey-baiting." These were copied by Edward Pierce the Elder (1598–1668) after Tempesta. See Ogden and Ogden 1955, pp. 72–73. The Ogdens found thirteen listings of works by Tempesta (p. 108). Kren 1978, pp. 129–30, provides a discussion of hunting lodge commissions for emperors, kings, and nobles in the sixteenth and seventeenth centuries, many for tapestry suites.

9. TIB35.61–85.235–259.

10. Isaiah 37:36–37.

11. II Kings 18:13–16.

12. James B. Pritchard, ed., *Ancient Near Eastern Texts, Relating to the Old Testament*, 2nd ed. (Princeton: Princeton University, 1955), p. 286. I am indebted to Cynthia Kane for her research on the historical background of this Old Testament episode.

ANTONIO TEMPESTA

Florence 1555 – 1660 Florence

23   *Hunters with Ladies Watching a Bird Trap Baited with an Owl,*
from *The First Book of Different Hunts*

etching

98 x 142 mm

inscribed in plate, lower left: *Ant. tempest. fioren.*

B.XVII.164.1069, TIB36.313.1069

Gift of Herrman L. Blumgart, by exchange, s9.83.3

Tempesta's *Hunters with Ladies Watching a Bird Trap* brings together in a single dense composition imagery of the hunt, of the labors of months, of landscape, and of pastoral poetry. The hunters hidden in the trees demonstrate a particular technique of fowling while enjoying one of the pleasures of country life; the half-concealed woman and the pair of lovers show that the delights of hunting can be shared by spectators. The background landscape suggests the context of a country estate; the farmer with his plow provides a contrast between leisure and productive activity.

The artist has provided the suggestion of a narrative. The attention of the two lovers appears to have been drawn away from each other to the bird-catching scene. The house on the distant hillside, given its modest proportions, must belong to the farmer. One can imagine a much larger villa from which the lovers have ventured for privacy, and the hunters for sport. The activities of the farmer indicate that it must be planting or harvest season, spring or fall. Aside from the farmer, the five visible figures are all observers. Their proximity to the picture plane invites us to join them in watching the sport.

The conceit by which the lovers occupy the same pictorial space as the hunters dates at least to medieval poetry, which abounded with associations between hunting and courting.[1] Petrarch elaborated and refined the conceit, giving it an emotional intensity and enriching it through mythological allusions to Diana and Actaeon. Fifteenth- and sixteenth-century pastoral poetry by Angelo Poliziano, Lorenzo de' Medici, Pietro Bembo, Andrea Navagero, and Jacopo Sannazaro perpetuated the metaphor and amplified the significance of the rural setting.[2] At the opening of Poliziano's *Stanze cominciate per la Giostra del Magnifico Giuliano de' Medici* of 1475, the main character Julio expresses his preference for hunting over love. He says that love "steals away your every / masculine thought" and "strips you of your proper valor."[3] He continues by singing the praises of hunting:

> How much sweeter, how much safer to hunt
> the fleeing beasts through ancient forests outside

of wall or moat, to discover their dens after long
tracking! To see the valleys, and hills, and the
purer air, the grass and flowers, the clear icy living
waters! To hear the birds unwinter themselves,
the cascades resounding, the sweet murmur
of branches in the wind![4]

Tempesta's print suggests that love does not have to exclude the pleasures of the hunt, and the couple he depicts enjoy not only love but also "the valleys, and hills, and the purer air." The chase, which usually forms the substance of the metaphoric conceit, is absent in Tempesta's print. A number of birds appear to have been caught already, and the lovers are in each other's arms. Rather than suggest the frustrations of the hunt, Tempesta portrays love realized and pastoral harmony achieved. While Poliziano's *Stanze*, in portraying Giuliano de' Medici as a hunter and referring to Lorenzo il Magnifico as a shepherd, suggest the proximity of men of the court and of the country, Tempesta's print, in clearly dividing the background space of the farmer from the foreground space of the hunters, emphasizes the distance separating the realm of work from the realm of leisure.

The pastoral tradition in poetry led to the development, fostered by sixteenth-century Venetian painters Giorgione, Lorenzo Lotto, and Titian, of the genre of pastoral landscape painting.[5] Tempesta, however, populates his landscape not with the classical gods, forest nymphs, and lute

138

players of these paintings but with the more realistic and active figures of farmers, hunters, and lovers. Whereas sixteenth-century pastoral painting described an idealized vision of the simple life of a shepherd, Tempesta's prints depict the leisure activities of gentlemen who, motivated in part by the idealization that accompanied the development of pastoral landscapes, had invested in rural properties.

Unlike many of the other hunting images within Tempesta's oeuvre that have mythological protagonists and are drenched with violence, the special character of this scene arises from its serenity of mood and from the inclusiveness of its imagery. It portrays the range of leisure activities to be enjoyed in the country against a background of fruitful labor. As a group, Tempesta's etchings in the Spencer Albums associate three activities of the aristocratic class: warfare, courtly love, and hunting.[6] European aristocratic culture seems to have been defined more by these pursuits than by national identities; the enthusiastic patronage his prints found in both Italy and England attests to the common aspects of country living. As the Englishman Robert Burton noted appreciatively in his *Anatomy of Melancholy*, first published in 1621, "The Italians have gardens fitted out for [fowling], with nets, bushes, glades, sparing no cost or industry, and are very much affected with the sport."[7]

Hunters with Ladies Watching a Bird Trap reflects a preference for generalized landscapes over precisely descriptive ones.[8] Tempesta devotes his attention to the depiction of the specific features of fowling technique rather than to trees or topography. He presents the landscape not as a beautiful object to be contemplated but as a site for hunting and for agricultural production, and his human figures are no more particularized than the scenery. Comparing his representation of people in this print to that of horses and dogs in other hunting scenes reveals the extent to which Tempesta's talent for portraiture was specific to animals.

Tempesta's prints emerged more directly from the tradition of illustrated hunting manuals than from that of pastoral poetry. They were intended not only to provide technical instruction but also to codify an art at which gentlemen ought to be accomplished.[9] Tempesta produced two sets of illustrations for manuals on singing birds, Antonio Valli's *Il canto degl'augelli* (1601) and Giovanni Pietro Olina's *Uccelliera, o vero discorso della natura, e proprieta di diversi uccelli* (1622), the texts of which describe the characteristics of the various species, the means of their capture, and how to feed and care for them. The illustrations provided by Tempesta include large-scale portraits of birds, schematic diagrams of methods of fowling, and more pictorial images of landscapes with hunters in action. Valli and Olina indicate their awareness of the antique precedents for hunting, referring to the tradition of Aristotle and Pliny, and imply the significance of this model for seventeenth-century hunters. The treatises, like the print on exhibition, describe hunting at its most refined. They demonstrate that hunting had achieved the status of an art form.

This print describes with precision an elaborate method of capturing small birds that had been widely used since the Middle Ages. The fowler concealed himself in a bush near an owl decoy. Because the owl is a predator, the decoy served to lure groups of small birds to mob the owl. When birds approached the owl, the fowler would use a device known as a clapstick, consisting of two sticks bound together with a rope, to catch them by their wings or feet. With the sticks in one hand and the rope in the other, the fowler would pull on the rope when a bird flew into his range, closing the sticks around his prey.[10]

Olina characterized fowling as "innocent pleasure, without difficulty, without disturbance . . ." According to medieval writers, the advantages of hunting were that it gave men activity (and kept them from the sin of idleness), that it prepared them for war, and that it provided an opportunity for fellowship among men.[11] Practiced for sport rather than out of necessity, hunting came to be associated with leisure and affluence.[12] And so Tempesta's print describes not merely a single country scene but an entire lifestyle. The farmer, the hunters, and the lovers are all part of a conception of country life fostered by the landed gentry in Italy and in England. While the etching cannot be taken as a literal representation of country life, it does suggest the appeal that the country held for city dwellers. Arising out of the Italian tradition of pastoral poetry, landscape paintings, and hunting manuals, *Hunters with Ladies Watching a Bird Trap* epitomizes the development of sporting imagery as a distinct genre.

CB

1. Cummins 1988, p. 8.

2. The Italian pastoral tradition had its British counterparts in the Petrarchan poetry of Thomas Wyatt, Philip Sidney, Edmund Spenser, and George Gascoigne. Gascoigne was also the author of an illustrated treatise on hunting, *The Noble Art of Venerie or Hunting* (1575).

3. Poliziano 1979, p. 9.

4. Poliziano 1979, p. 11.

5. Cafritz, "Introduction," in Robert C. Cafritz, *Lawrence Gowing*, and David Rosand, *Places of Delight: The Pastoral Landscape* (New York: Clarkson N. Potter, 1988), p. 17.

6. Gaston III, count of Foix, wrote in his *Livre de chasse*, "All my life I have taken special delight in three things: arms, love, and hunting" (quoted in Cummins 1988, p. 1). The omission of religious prints from the Tempesta Albums in order to concentrate on these three aristocratic occupations is also suggestive.

7. Robert Burton, *The Anatomy of Melancholy*. 3 vols. (London: Dent, 1932), vol. 2, p. 73 (pt. 2, sec. 2, mem. 4, in Burton's original subdivision of his text).

8. For a more general discussion of this issue in seventeenth-century art, see Deuchar 1988, p. 34.

9. Deuchar 1988, p. 34.

10. Cummins 1988, p. 243.

11. Cummins 1988, pp. 3–6.

12. Deuchar 1988, pp. 2–4.

JACQUES CALLOT

Nancy 1592 – 1635 Nancy

24   *Parterre of the Palace of Nancy*, 1625

etching

258 x 383 mm

inscribed in plate, upper center, in banderoles above and below the arms of the duchess of Lorraine: *PARTERRE DU PALAIS DE NANCI. / TAILLE EN EAU FORTE ET DEDIE A MADAME LA DUCHESSE DE LORRAINE / par Iacque Callot Son tres hu:serv et suject / le 15. doct.*

1625.; in left front flowerbed: *IC*; in right front flowerbed: *INF*; lower margin; *Ce dessein faconné des honneurs des printemps, / Eniolivé d'obiectz de divers passetemps; / C'est nostre aage, Madame où les douceurs encloses / Nous font autant de fleurs, ou Rosiers precieux / Qui pousseront sans fin des doux-flairantes roses / Dont l'odeur aggréra aux hommes et aux Cieux*; lower margin, right: *Iac. Callot excudit Nanceij*

L.566 i/ii

Gift of William Gray from the collection of Francis Calley Gray, by exchange, s3.67

Two of the Spencer Albums contain well over a thousand prints by, after, and of Jacques Callot. A native of Nancy, capital of the independent duchy of Lorraine, Callot was trained in Rome; he left in 1611 for Florence, where for a decade he enjoyed the patronage of Cosimo II de' Medici, grand duke of Tuscany. Callot's method and style, geared toward the rapid production of intricate etched compositions in imitation of the more prestigious but far slower technique of engraving, were his innovative response to Medici demand for visual records of weddings, funerals, royal entrances, theatrical productions, and other festivals.

The distorted vista, where perspective is manipulated to make room for an exquisitely lucid, densely populated spectacle, became the formal mainstay of Callot's repertoire of courtly themes. After 1621 when the death of his patron forced the artist to return to Nancy to seek his living at the Lorraine court, he maintained and developed this format in works such as the *Parterre of the Palace of Nancy*, dedicated in the banderoles surrounding the ducal arms to Nicole, duchess of Lorraine, and dated October 15, 1625.[1]

Despite its autumnal date, the etching, as explicitly stated in the inscription, celebrates the season of renewal in regulated manner, as befitting both the planting of formal gardens, that is, *parterres*, and the ascension of a new ruler (*façonner* meaning literally to work the soil as well as to fashion or model). For Nicole had succeeded her father only the previous year, there being no male heir. She would be deposed by her father-in-law exactly one month after Callot's dedicatory date; the artist could not have known that he was witnessing the fall and not the springtime of her reign.[2]

The *Parterre of the Palace of Nancy* follows a convention for the representation of spring, or one of the spring months, which by then was well established. A view from a high vantage of a formal garden in active cultivation, surrounded by fountains and pavilions and populated not only by gardeners of both sexes but also by their masters and mistresses—persons whose dress and idle occupations leave no doubt of their high social position—is seen in prints by Northern artists such as Adriaen Collaert (*April, May*; H.IV.207.562, 563) and Nicolaes de Bruyn (*Spring*, H.IV.23.190). Perhaps the most striking precedent in Italian etching is *April* (TIB37.177.1337) by Antonio Tempesta. Even specific details of the Tempesta print can be found in the Callot: the game of bocce, the deer—although the tame buck strolling with his doe as if they were members of the noble company in Tempesta's garden becomes a solitary stag hunted to the death in Callot's distant vista.

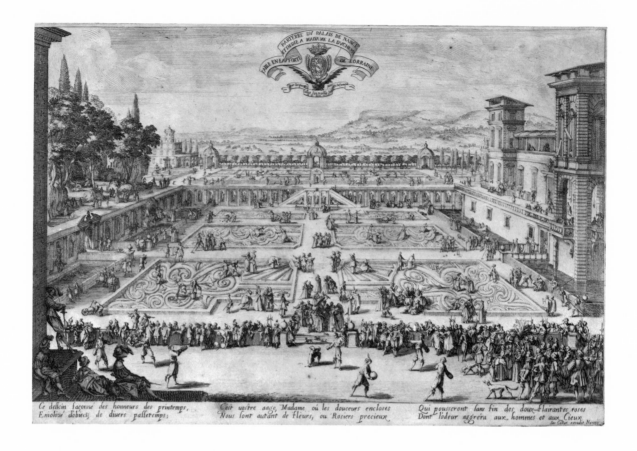

The difference between Callot's conception and those of his predecessors lies more in the formal presentation, particularly of the spatial system, than in subject or iconography. The *Parterre of Nancy* is among the most subtle and successful examples of his willful distortion of linear perspective, which he had mastered in his work with Italian designers for the stage.[3] More rudimentary, or at least single-minded, versions of this characteristic manipulation are Callot's early festival prints and his multiplate representations of military actions. The former class is well represented by the *Theater Erected in Florence . . .* (L.182) of 1616, in which a symmetrically scrolling formation of combatants in a "War of Beauty" is tipped up toward the vertical. In *The Siege of Breda* (L.593) of 1626, the foreground that extends before us is only gently rising, its figures, villages, and camps diminishing in correct perspective, with square troop formations represented as tapering lozenges. But then the midground in which militarily critical topography is described rears up before us through the device of delineating the fortresses and shorelines as if they were seen practically from above. A square encampment *is* a square. Once past various significant landmarks, the city, land, and sea settle back toward horizontality. That Callot was perfectly capable of putting warfare or anything else on a horizontal plane is shown by landscapes such as *The Battle* (L.1341) and *Scene of Pillage* (L.1345) from "The Large Miseries of War"

142

of 1633. Their easy recession makes the subtle pauses and dislocations of the *Parterre of Nancy* all the more extraordinary.

The most easily described distortion in the garden scene is in its scrolling floral designs. Callot has capitalized upon the mind's willingness to allow the chance for eccentric curves on the part of the landscape designer and not the etcher, and thus tolerate the eye's perception of the curves rising up as if on inclined planes rather than receding on the flat surface of the beds. This horizontality is indicated by the perspectivally correct orthogonals of their side boundaries (as well as guaranteed by the realities of seventeenth-century garden design). Callot has concocted this ambiguity, in which the beds pose a sequence of angled hurdles to our vision's quick exit into deep space, in order to ensure our appreciation of all the figural details of his composition. Most conspicuous is the group centered by the duchess herself, standing with the duke and their courtiers at the front entrance of the garden. The suggestion of rising toward the vertical imparted to the flower beds makes their scrolls and wedges compose into an ornamental frame about her person as well as extend beyond into her realm.[4] The falsely slanting beds are a softer stop than the horizontals of the composition. These too, however, are only pauses and not barriers for the eye. Although they span the sheet, they are so artfully broken by dark accents and highlights that they act more to control the undulation of the beds than the description of the larger space of the composition.[5]

Such subtleties operate only in very early impressions when delicate modeling lines, like those that shade the exquisitely spaced trees, are intact. This impression of the *Parterre of Nancy* is rich and fresh, although at the right edge it is dryly printed. Lieure notes that printing flaws are common in this print and fine, early impressions very rare, as if the plate, which is still preserved in the Musée Historique Lorrain at Nancy, sustained few such pressings. Indeed, among the 1,138 prints by Callot himself in the Spencer Albums, there are many impressions of early states that present an excellent effect, but few are of exceptional brilliance. This, then, is not only one of the most beautiful but is among the rarest.

MBC

1. See Russell 1975, p. 28, for a translation of the inscriptions on the print.

2. Shortly afterward, the father-in-law, François de Vaudémont, now François II of Lorraine, abdicated in favor of his son Nicole's husband (and first cousin), now Charles IV of Lorraine. She thus regained her throne but only as consort. For details of the complex political events within which Callot worked, see Brown/RISD 1970, chronology [n.p.]; and Russell 1975, pp. 10–12.

3. Perhaps it is also significant that the first three editions of the earliest published manual on linear perspective, Jean Pélerin's *De Artificiali Perspectiva*, were printed in Lorraine in 1505, 1508, and 1521, and so there could well have been a strong native tradition in which Callot was working.

4. Not incidentally, the upper edge of the first pair of flower beds, that is, that area most warped by Callot's spatial scheme, bears symmetric monograms which would be virtually invisible if the beds receded in conventional array: on the left, "IC" (Jacques Callot), and on the right "INF" ("INvenit et Fecit"). The monograms were noted by Lieure in his discussion of the print.

5. In the two large compositional drawings for the print, which survive in the collections of the Hermitage and the Musée Historique Lorrain, Callot has represented the scrolling flowerbeds in a slightly more (but not completely) normal linear perspective. The perspective of the general scheme of the composition is meticulously worked through in the Nancy drawing.

JUSEPE DE RIBERA

Játiva, Valencia 1591 – 1652 Naples

25   *Drunken Silenus*, 1628

etching

273 x 347 mm

watermark: fleur-de-lys on three mountains within an oval

inscribed in plate, lower center of design: *Al Molto Illre St Don Giuseppe Balsame Barone di Cattasi, Giorato dell Illmo / Senato della nobile Citta di Messina / Giovanni Orlandi Romano. D.D.*; lower right: *Joseph, a Ribera Hisps. Valenti / Setaben f. Parthenope / 1628*

inscribed, verso, in brown ink: *P. mariette 1672*

B.XX.84.13 ii/ii; TIB44.272.13; Brown 14

Richard Norton Fund, s6.53.2

This etching of 1628 reproduces a picture of the drunken Silenus that Ribera had painted two years earlier for a Flemish merchant resident in Naples, Gaspar Roomer.[1] In his characterization of Roomer's patronage of Ribera, Haskell has offered a particularly sordid reading of the image:

> . . . Roomer had a taste for the grotesque, the dark and the cruel which the painters of Naples were well able to satisfy. Over the years he collected a grim series of works by Ribera: *The Drunken Silenus*—a gross, dirty, fat-paunched, androgynous travesty of the god of wine lying obscenely across the picture attended by his goat-like fauns and a braying donkey, the very embodiment of harsh stupidity. . . .[2]

Yet a writer on Pieter van Laer, a Dutch artist resident in Rome, suggests another, more high-minded aspect of the attraction of Bacchic subjects to Netherlandish artists and patrons alike, one which relates

> . . . to the age-old view that poets create best when under the influence of wine. . . . Thus, it was possible for authors such as Horace and Ovid to refer to poets as being inspired by Bacchus, and for Hellenistic artists to express the idea visually by showing the god of wine and his drunken entourage [including Silenus] entering the house of an expectant bard.[3]

It should be noted that the distinction was not always maintained between personifications of Bacchus, the true god of wine, and Silenus, who according to classical lore was Bacchus's tutor in

both the intellectual and physical senses. Relevant to our consideration of this print, it should be noted that in the description of another impression in the Mariette manuscript catalogue of Prince Eugene's collection, "Bacchus" was written first, and then crossed out and "Silene" inserted.[4]

The intellectual implications of a representation of Silenus are further suggested by his frequent association, especially in Italian Renaissance and Baroque writings and representations, with the philosopher Socrates.[5] One can hardly know at this remove, however, what interpretation was intended by Ribera, although Brown in his catalogue of the artist's prints observes that among the changes from the painting to the etching is the elimination of symbolic apparatus. This change might incline one to view the print as Brown himself does, as the embodiment of "the joyful, mindless sensuality of the Bacchic orgy."[6]

More easily interpreted is the attitude of the compiler of the Spencer Albums, where Silenus occupies the lower portion of a folio, with Ribera's *Poet* (Brown 3) mounted above it. This arrangement enforces a constant contemplation of the orgy by the sober downward gaze of the classically garbed and wreathed figure. That the connection was not arbitrarily arrived at simply by the convenience of filling the page is suggested by the placement of *The Poet* among the Ribera etchings in Prince Eugene's album now at the Albertina. There *The Poet* gazes not at a man disfigured by drink but rather at Ribera's *Large Head with Grotesque Growths* (Brown 11), where a hideously blemished visage arouses comparable musings on the corrupted states to which human flesh is susceptible.

Such complexity of meaning is underscored by a comparison of the *Drunken Silenus* with its adaptation etched by Francesco Maria di Domenico Burani (TIB44.289.1). Burani's print is undated, but the artist's life dates (1600–1631) indicate that it must have been an immediate response to Ribera's work.[7] In it the somber suggestiveness of the Spaniard's etching is replaced by a transparent jollity.   MBC

1. *Drunken Silenus* (Museo e Gallerie Nazionali di Capodimonte, Naples, Pérez Sánchez and Spinosa, no. 28). An additional Silenus subject, a print that reproduces only fragments of the figures in Ribera's etching, has also been attributed to Ribera: " . . . a small etching at the S. Martino Museum in Naples (portfolio I, no. 17829) listed on the Museum's files as being by Stefano della Bella. The De Vesme-Massar catalogue [of the etchings of della Bella] does not even include it among those considered to be of doubtful origin. . . . The work is 122 mm high and 142 mm wide. The subject is an experiment in drawing [which] shows hands and arms [and] a detail of the right arm in the top centre of the print which bears a shell-shaped vessel into which a liquid is flowing from above. This arm is identical or at most very similar, even if in counterproof to the left arm of *Drunken Silenus* which in turn is holding a shell-shaped cup precisely the same as the one in this work and into which a liquid is flowing from above exactly in the same way" (Bellini 1975, pp. 19–20).

2. Haskell 1980, p. 205.

3. David A. Levine, "Pieter van Laer's *Artist's Tavern*: An Ironic Commentary on Art," pp. 169–91 in Bock 1987, p. 177.

4. BNMS R068640: "[Bacchus *crossed out*] Silene couché par terre . . . "

5. Goldstein 1988, pp. 202–3, n. 87. See also Caroline Houser, *Dionysos and His Circle* (Cambridge: Fogg Art Museum, 1979), p. xvi, for further definitions of Silenus, which stress both his intellectual attainments and his frailties. Kren 1978, pp. 196–98, offers a summary of the history of the braying donkey motif as a commentary on human foolishness.

6. Brown, p. 19.

7. Reggio Emilia, Dell' Ente Provinciale per il Turismo, *Mostra della incisione reggiana dal '400 all '800* (Reggio Emilia: dell' Ente Provinciale per il Turismo, 1961), pp. 31–32. This catalogue notes (p. 32) that Le Blanc, misinterpreting Malvasia, says that Burani could have done his version prior to Ribera, which would make it "extrèmement intéressante" (LEB.I.545).

MOYSES VAN WTENBROUCK
The Hague c. 1590 – 1646/7 The Hague

26 *Sleeping Silenus*, c. 1627 or later

engraving

123 x 95 mm

watermark: fragmentary

B.V.103.33, TIB6.88.33, TIB0605.77.033 S1/2

Gift of Melvin R. Seiden, s5.34.4

This print of Silenus reproduces in reverse the pose of a sleeping youth seen at the right in Wten-brouck's *Triumph of Bacchus*, a painting of 1627 now in the collection of the Herzog Anton Ulrich-Museum, Brunswick.[1] In the painting the central figure is also Silenus, older, grosser, but still conscious. He rides his ass directly toward the viewer, his legs spread around the animal's barrel-shaped body and his torso slumped back so that he assumes a slightly less exaggerated version of the pose of the sleeping youth. The exact duplication in the print of the pose of the youth and not Silenus superficially suggests that the print's traditional title is incorrect; yet in the engraving, in the shadow of the rock behind the unconscious figure, Silenus's raucous ass can be glimpsed (see also Cat. 25).

Thus the print represents the morning after a bacchanal, with Silenus still happily stupefied, his wreath of grape leaves being delicately adjusted by a solicitous satyr. In its celebration of Arcadian dissipation, the print perfectly illustrates an ode attributed to the Greek poet Anacreon:

When gay Bacchus fills my breast,
All my cares are lull'd to rest,

.   .   .   .

Ivy-wreaths my temples shade,
Ivy that will never fade:
Thus I sit in mid elate,
Laughing at the farce of state.
Some delight in fighting fields,
Nobler transports Bacchus yields:
Fill the bowl—I ever said
'Tis better to lie drunk than dead.[2]

Probably the print postdates the painting: it is executed entirely in engraving, considered a technical indicator of a later date among Wtenbrouck's prints; his plates that are dated earlier include etching. It represents deep shade, which according to Mariette is also a feature of his later work (see Cat. 37).

This particular impression is the best among the fifteen plates by Wtenbrouck that represent classical myths or more generic Arcadian subjects among the total of thirty-four prints by the artist in Spencer Album 5. In its unpretentious sweetness and in its subordination of the figures to their ambience, it is typical of his prints as a whole. Also typical is the diagonal emphasis, amounting almost to distortion, of the pose of the figure of Silenus. This does not derive entirely from the artist's incompetence in drawing foreshortened figures. Wtenbrouck seems often actively to seek out motifs requiring the representation of contorted, boneless, nude bodies. Perhaps his most astonishing conception of this sort is his painting *Io Changed into a Cow, with Her Father and Sisters* (Betty and David M. Koetser Foundation, on deposit, Kunsthaus, Zurich), in which the sisters, disporting in a waterfall, are tumbled by the cascade into the most outlandish poses. Even the clouds in that painting race overhead at a disconcerting angle. Nowhere in Wtenbrouck's work, however, is his predilection for the naked body seen askew more appropriate than in this sodden Silenus.

MBC

1. Reproduced in TIB0605.78. See this publication and other works cited in Cat. 37 for further information on the life and career of the artist.

2. *Anacreon Ode XXVI* (trans. Fawkes) in *The Works of the English Poets*, ed. Samuel Johnson (London: J. Johnson et al., 1810), vol. 20, p. 350. There is no reason to believe that Wtenbrouck knew this particular poem.

JAN GERRITSZ. VAN BRONCHORST

Utrecht c. 1603–1661 Amsterdam

27 *Juno or Venus Seated on the Clouds*, 1636, after Poelenburch

etching and drypoint

151 x 132 mm

watermark: I L

inscribed in plate, upper left: *C.P inu / J G Fecit*

B.IV.60.6, TIB5.78.6, H.III.229.13

Gift of Melvin R. Seiden, s5.43.1

Of the forty prints by Bronchorst listed by Hollstein (H.III.227–234), no fewer than twenty-five are after the works—paintings and drawings—of Cornelis van Poelenburch (c. 1594–1667), also a native of Utrecht and one of the first Dutch painters of the seventeenth century to work in Rome.[1] Poelenburch is documented there as early as 1617; he returned to Utrecht in 1625 or 1626 and after that time presumably began his close friendship and working relationship with Bronchorst, who had been trained as a glass painter and is not known to have traveled to Italy.[2] Bronchorst continued as a glass painter through the late 1640s, when he accepted important commissions for the Nieuwe Kerk in Amsterdam and resettled there, but by this time he had begun a second career as a painter of pictures. He had been recognized as a talented etcher since the late 1630s; Gerard van Honthorst (1590–1656), the preeminent Utrecht painter who had worked in Rome prior to Poelenburch and whose style, heavily influenced by Caravaggio, was an influence on that slightly younger artist, recommended Bronchorst as an etcher to the secretary of the prince of Orange in 1637,[3] the same year that Bronchorst produced a six-plate illustration of the siege of Breda.

Topographical representations of contemporary events were not, however, the forte either of Poelenburch or of Bronchorst. The two works by the etcher on exhibition (see also Cat. 33) together summarize the production of the painter, whose specialty was small, exquisitely finished landscapes that often incorporated both classical ruins and female nudes. Poelenburch had a particular predilection for full-bodied seated figures, and he managed to find subjects from every tradition—biblical, antique, and genre—which afforded the opportunity to demonstrate his specialty.[4] A drawing in the collection of the British Museum entitled *Female Nudes in a Landscape*,[5] which shows seven women (and a man and a baby), represents five of them nude from the back, with none being integrated with each other or with the somewhat incoherent topography that supports their various poses. This sort of sketch sheet is a revelation both of the free choice of the artist's imagination and of his consummate skill: the nudes are drawn with the tip of a brush, which admits neither hesitation nor correction.

In Rome, Poelenburch's acquaintance Joachim von Sandrart testified that the painter "exerted himself to the utmost to paint his figures in the manner of Raphael."[6] If one looks in Raphael's works for the prototype of Poelenburch's favored female form, one immediately locates her in the frescoes of the Villa Farnesina, which represent the story of Psyche. The spandrel figure of one of the Graces is a conspicuous example, and another is the most prominent single figure in the ceiling painting immediately above the spandrel, of the *Wedding of Cupid and Psyche*. Both are less fleshy and more muscular, in the High Renaissance mode, than Poelenburch's nudes, and neither represent Juno. Raphael's Juno of the Psyche frescoes is seen in *Psyche*

Received into Olympus, in much the same general pose as this print, but she is clothed and accompanied by her attribute, the peacock.

One of the striking aspects of the etching is, of course, the figure's nudity, which is exceptional in representations of Juno. She seems to be in active communication with someone unseen to the left, and there is another print by Bronchorst after Poelenburch of virtually identical format and dimensions that represents a proportionate Cupid standing on the clouds and responding in a somewhat crestfallen manner to someone equally unseen to the right (TIB5.78.7).[7] The prints have not been paired in the literature, and as the Cupid was catalogued after the Juno by Bartsch, inevitably they have been reproduced back-to-back rather than facing each other as the pendant pair they truly seem to be.

This raises the issue of exactly whom this etching represents.[8] Venus is the goddess usually paired with Cupid, as she is in another print by Bronchorst after Poelenburch (TIB5.76.4). Coupled with the nudity of the figure, the relatively unmatronly hairdo (which, with braid and loose locks, is like that of Poelenburch's Venus), and the lack of any other attributes that would identify the figure as the wife of Jupiter, Venus seems a more appropriate identification than that advanced by Bartsch: "This piece seems to represent Juno looking down at earth from heaven, to spy out some amorous intrigue of her husband. . . . Her gaze is fixed toward the ground, and the gesture of her hand seems menacing."[9] In fact, close inspection shows the figure's eye focused directly to the left and not downward. The traditional theme of Venus Chiding Cupid would seem likely, but given Poelenburch's ability to locate a beautiful, buxom woman with ample thighs, robust hips, and a sensuously dimpled back in every context, perhaps one should not worry too much about the identification and simply remember that the draftsman's nickname in the Schildersbent, the Dutch artists' association in Rome, was "Satyr."[10]

M B C

1. The prints by Bronchorst after Poelenburch are listed and discussed in Chong 1987, Appendix B, pp. 57–60.

2. Thieme-Becker, vol. 5, p. 57.

3. Thieme-Becker, vol. 5, p. 57.

4. For example, *Lot and His Daughters* (Private Collection, 16[3?]2, repro. Duparc and Graif 1990, no. 54), *The Bath of Diana* (Musée Nancy, Meurtre-et-Moselle), *Frightened Nymphs* (Rijksmuseum, Amsterdam), *Olympian Banquet* (Wadsworth Atheneum, Hartford), *Girls after a Bath* (Rijksmuseum, Amsterdam).

5. Gersheim photograph 32998.

6. Quoted in Washington 1980, p. 190. The essay in this catalogue by Albert Blankert, "Classicism in Dutch Painting, 1614–1670," pp. 182–90, is very valuable concerning Poelenburch, Bronchorst (including his later career as a painter), and the development of Dutch clas-

sicism from the Northern Caravaggists through the establishment of the style in its later aspects as a quasi-official state art.

7. The *Cupid* is dated in the plate 1636, which is the basis of the date I have assigned to this print.

8. Hollstein repeats Bartsch's identification of the figure as Juno, but Chong in his list of Bronchorst's prints after Poelenburch titles it *Venus Sitting on a Cloud*, without making explicit the association with *Cupid Standing on a Cloud* (Chong 1987, p. 58).

9. B.IV.60: "Ce morceau semble représenter Junon regardant du ciel en terre, pour épier quelqu'intrigue amoureuse de son mari. . . . Son regard est fixé vers le bas, et le geste de sa main élevée semble indiquer la menace."

10. Sutton 1987, p. 402.

PIETRO TESTA

Lucca 1612 – 1650 Rome

28   *Venus Giving Arms to Aeneas*, c. 1638

etching

373 x 405 mm

watermark: fleur-de-lys on three hills, within a circle surmounted by an M, identical to Heawood 1620 (Rome, 1647)

inscribed in brown ink, verso: *P. mariette 1676*

B.XX.221.24, TIB45.146.24, TIB4506.152.024 S1/2, Cropper 59

Arnold H. Knapp Fund, by exchange, S2.15

This lyrical landscape etching in which the subject—the gift of arms and armor to Aeneas by his mother Venus—hangs like a blossom among the trees was executed by Testa during a comparatively quiet period in his brief career. This "shy man who lived a solitary life of melancholy"—the characterization of Joachim von Sandrart, his close friend[1]—would drown in the Tiber, a probable suicide, a dozen years later. In the interim, his infrequent commissions as a painter from his native city Lucca and in Rome, where he resided, were poorly received and increasingly rare. His elaborately conceived, meticulously worked prints seemed to have become the compensation of an intellect and imagination increasingly thwarted in professional advancement by a suspicious, contrary personality. The toll that his neurotic anguish took is demonstrated by a comparison of the gracious print on exhibition with his morbid and horrific (but nonetheless magnificent) late etchings, such as *Achilles Dragging the Body of Hector Around the Walls of Troy* (Cropper 121) and *The Suicide of Cato* (Cropper 116).

By the late 1630s, the probable date of the etching of *Venus Giving Arms to Aeneas*, Testa had already executed several comparable prints that feature tender sentiments exchanged within bosky settings, the adult protagonists always wreathed by cherubs.[2] This particular subject may have been suggested to him by the commission given to his close acquaintance Nicolas Poussin by yet another artist, Jacques Stella. Poussin's painting of the same title, dating to the mid-1630s and documented to 1639 (Musée des Beaux-Arts, Rouen), did not, however, provide Testa with his composition. The print is clearly related to one of his most beautiful drawings, of *Echo and Narcissus* (Private Collection, Cropper 193), which has been dated to c. 1631–1637. The etching presents an elaboration and a tonal reversal of this sheet in which, appropriately, the figure of Echo, the prototype for Venus, was cast into shade and the ivy-girt, framing tree trunk to the left arching above her is light. The figure of Echo was drawn, however, as an addition over a rocky outcrop which, in the original pure landscape conception of the drawing, was a highlight set off by a burst of deeply shadowed shrubbery, the visual equivalent in location and value of the

baroque chariot in the print, which cradles Venus rather like a hovering, soft-bodied moth. The Narcissus of the drawing finds its parallel in the even more downcast river god (Tiber) at the right of the etching.

There is no match in the drawing for the figure of Aeneas, whose prototype has been identified by Cropper in works by Sodoma and the workshop of Raphael. These precedents and two explicit preliminary drawings for the etching as well as its close relationship with *The Sacrifice of Iphigenia* (Cropper 61), a print Testa is believed to have executed several years later, indicate that *Venus Giving Arms to Aeneas* can be completely analyzed only within a complex array of sources and sequences.[4]

While Testa's representation of *Venus Giving Arms to Aeneas* is obviously associated with his renditions of other antique subjects, it must not be understood merely as a generic scene in a sylvan classical mode. The artist has conscientiously interpreted an exact moment from Virgil's *Aeneid* when the goddess fulfills her promise to her mortal son and provides him with "arms divine" forged by Vulcan:

> Within a winding vale she finds her son,
> On the cool river's banks, retir'd alone.
> She shews her heav'nly form without disguise,
> . . . and, having first her son embrac'd,
> the radiant arms beneath an oak she plac'd,
> Proud of the gift, he roll'd his greedy sight
> Around the work, and gaz'd with vast delight.
> He lifts, he turns, he poises, and admires
> The crested helm, that vomits radiant fires:
> His hands the fatal sword and corslet hold,
> One keen with temper'd steel, one stiff with gold;
>
> . . . .
>
> He shakes the pointed spear, and longs to try
> The plated cuishes on his manly thigh;
> But most admires the shield's mysterious mold,
> And Roman triumphs rising on the gold . . .[5]

The sharp etched line typical of Testa is particularly successful in this print in its capacity to articulate the significant details of the decorated metalwork and also to render the tapestry of tree forms and foliage that envelops the figures. The line's precision conveys Testa's pleasure in such natural ornament as the strands of ivy, dark around the brightly illuminated tree trunk at the top left and light along the shadowed edge of the trunk to the right of the cuirass. It permits his impeccable regulation of density of tone so that the ivy on the dark foot of the trunk in the left foreground does not break up the bulk of the tree, which is otherwise shaded by parallel and crossed hatchings.

This characteristic sharpness of line may have been achieved by Testa through the use of an exceptionally hard ground. His plates are notoriously plagued by foul-biting; the fractured edges of a patch on this plate, in the tree trunk to the left of the cuirass, suggests both the cause of the etcher's technical problems and also the means of his achievement, in his use of a ground that permitted practically infinite elaboration of detail. This brittle ground, protective, receptive, and fragile all at the same time, may stand as a metaphor of his troubled personality—unyielding until it shattered, but in the interim conducive to ever-increasing complexities of form, thought, and sensibility.

Spencer Album 2 contains twenty etchings by Testa, including some of his largest plates, which take up the full double-page spread of the open album. Many impressions are of very high quality; they include a number of rare first states. Because of the protection offered by the album over the past 280 years or so, the prints are largely in superb condition, in contrast to the circumstances of Testa's etchings in other collections where they "are rarely found in good condition, and . . . are unmounted, tattered, and creased."[6] The album also enforces a sequential viewing of the prints, which is peculiarly sympathetic to Testa's etched oeuvre. A superficial cross-referencing of his reuse of poses and motifs is inhibited, and each plate can be read at length, with the light glancing off the swelling surface of the page enlivening the fine mesh of inked line.

MBC

1. Joachim von Sandrart, *Academie der Bau-, Bild- and Mahlery-Künste von 1675*, A. R. Pelzer, ed. (Munich, 1925), p. 289, translated in Cropper, p. xii. Cropper, pp. xi–xxxvi, provides the best interpretive summary of the artist's life and artistic career. See also the section on Testa by Paolo Bellini in TIB4506.133–189.

2. See, for example, *The Garden of Charity* in two versions (Cropper 9 and 11), *The Garden of Venus* (Cropper 13), *The Dream of Joseph* (Cropper 25), and *Venus and Adonis* (Cropper 16).

3. Reproduced in color in Cropper, frontispiece.

4. See Cropper, pp. 117–18, for a full analysis of the scene in terms of its representation of the subject and of its derivations from earlier works by Poussin, Sodoma, Primaticcio (by way of prints by Léon Davent), and Raphael's workshop.

5. Vergilius, *Aeneid* 8.809–830, trans. John Dryden.

6. Cropper, p. xxxii.

SIMONE CANTARINI

Pesaro 1612 – 1648 Verona

29 *Mercury and Argus*, c. 1639–1640

etching

262 x 308 mm

watermark: illegible device within a circle

B.XIX.142.31, TIB42.105.31, Bellini 37 i/ii

William M. Prichard Fund, S1.72.2

The story of Mercury and Argus was told by the Roman poet Ovid (Publius Ovidus Naso, 43 B.C.– A.D. 18) in the first book of his *Metamorphoses*, a mélange of tales of the vicissitudes of gods and men which largely involve physical love and bodily transformations. Briefly, in the story from which an episode is illustrated here, Jove falls in love with the maiden Io. His spouse Juno, ever jealous (for cause), transforms Io into a beautiful white heifer and puts her under the watchful care of the herdsman Argus, who, with one hundred eyes, never sleeps. Io is miserable, mooing and eating grass; Jove, pitying her, dispatches his messenger Mercury to her rescue. Let us take up the tale here in the words of Arthur Golding in his English translation of *Metamorphoses* of 1575:

    . . . downe to earth he flue

And there both Hat and wings also he lightly from him thrue,

Retayning nothing but his staffe . . .

    . . . and through the common field

Went plodding like some good plaine soule that had some flocke to feede,

And as he went he piped still upon an Oten Reede

Queene Junos Heird-man farre in love with this strange melodie,

Bespake him thus: Good fellow mine I pray thee heartily Come sit downe by me on this hill

. . . .

He played upon his merrie Pipe to cause his watching eyes

To fall a sleepe. Poore Argus did the best he could devise

To overcome the pleasant naps . . .

At this point Mercury tells Argus the tale of Pan and Syrinx, a soporific which overcomes even the last of the hundred eyes: " . . . behold his eyes had bid him all good night."[1] The tale concludes with Mercury slaying Argus, whose hundred eyes are immortalized by the outraged Juno in the peacock's tail; the bird becomes her emblem. The rescued Io, recovering her maidenly beauty, is prudently exiled by Jove to Egypt.

Even this abbreviated excerpt makes evident Cantarini's deviations from the text. Mercury is not fully disguised as a shepherd: his right foot is winged, and he retains his caduceus, which remains untransformed and conspicuous on the rock beside him. Moreover, Argus has only the normal human complement of two eyes. These iconographic discrepancies are virtually always observed in contemporary illustrations of Ovid, whether in independent prints such as this and etchings by Jan Lievens (H.XI.16.18) and Moyses Wtenbrouck (TIB6.77.22, TIB6.79.24, TIB6.80.25), or in book illustrations such as that on page 26 of *Metamorphoses d'Ovide en Rondeaux . . .* (Paris: Imprimerie royale, 1676) and in plate 16 of *Metamorphose . . .* (Zeeland: Crispin de Passe, 1602). Only in the plate by Antonio Tempesta (TIB36.14.647) does Argus have an abundance of eyes, so many that the artist, finding the head insufficient, sprinkled them down the herdsman's shoulders and arms, where they have the unfortunate appearance of carbuncles.

This disfigurement makes understandable the artistic appeal of the figure of Argus as he was usually conceived in the seventeenth century. Cantarini has modeled his herdsman after the colossal statues of recumbent river gods that were among the most admired classical relics disinterred in Renaissance Rome.[2] The tensed belly of his Argus also suggests the abdomen of the *Torso Belvedere*, the so-called "Hercules."[3] Aspiring to a conventional ancient masculine nobility of form that precluded the monstrosity of one hundred eyes, Cantarini had to retain the attributes of Mercury in order to differentiate his narrative subject from a generic pastorale.

Yet one must ask: how interested in the specifics of the text was this artist, or any of the others in the seventeenth century who illustrated it? Has he not seized upon it as a pretext for a classical idyll, with the nearly nude men, the sylvan pasturage, and the rustic music serving simply to evoke the Age of Gold? A musicologist has written,

> If we wish to focus on the symbolic connotation of the flute in the Italian Renaissance, we must deal with at least two different sources. One is [the intellectual and rational] impact of the ancient authors. . . . The other source is not humanist but human . . . the perennial underground stream of universal magic signs or symbols for elementary powers in human life. . . . It is the golden glow of nostalgia for an Arcady . . . the summer day of human existence, with the vibrating landscape and the sensuous flesh of the body all permeated by an inaudible music. And if this music is made visible by the representation of its tools, the musical instruments, these are organic elements of the magic substance conjured up by the master.[4]

Nothing could better characterize this etching than its description as "the summer day of human existence." Even if one knows the tale and realizes that the moment depicted is but a prelude to sleep and death, the brilliance of the light that pervades the scene only makes more poignant our yearning for a lost eternal summer.

Note especially the care that Cantarini took not to make any of his hatchings too dark. Particularly deft is the passage of light along the lower edge of the left calf of Argus, which keeps his form from resting too heavily on the ground. Cantarini has completely avoided the professional engraver's combination of line and stippling. He has added flicked touches to his lines, but as adjuncts beyond them, sometimes strung out in linear array. The dots and dashes practically never penetrate the hatching systems, and stipple is used only on flesh and fur (the dog's face) to model the major animate forms within the composition and to soften them a little. Other forms are much less developed as volumes in space, more drawn as scenic props and stage flats for his Arcady.

The vista in this lost paradise is closed with a straight horizon line. In the best impressions we recognize it as the ultimate limit of vision across a sparkling sea. Characteristically, the Italianate Dutch and Flemish etchers such as Swanevelt and Neve would close their views of Ovid's landscapes with a distant mountain range. It is as if they could epitomize their exotic locale—whether it was Italy or Arcady—only with that aspect of nature—mountains—which was completely foreign to their native, sea-girt Netherlands; whereas the Mediterranean Cantarini, at ease in his re-creation of Southern summer light by every means, welcomed the ocean's mirror below his blazing skies.

MBC

1. Ovid 1575, p. 12.
2. Bober and Rubinstein 1987, nos. 64–67.
3. Bober and Rubinstein 1987, no. 132.
4. Winternitz 1967, p. 52.

MONOGRAMMIST GpP
mid-17th c.

30   *The Death of Nessus*

etching

148 x 190 mm

watermark: six-pointed star

inscribed in plate, lower edge, center: *.GpP.*

inscribed in brown ink, verso: *P. mariette 1707*

B.XIX.185.4 (Monogrammist CpP), TIB42.161.4 (Monogrammist CpP), LEB.5 (Possenti)

Gift of Belinda L. Randall from the collection of John Witt Randall, by exchange, s2.55

The small oeuvre of seven prints which were catalogued by Bartsch under the name "Monogrammist CpP," whom he described as "de l'école de *Guide*,"[1] divides into two distinct parts. Two religious works, a *Crucifixion* (TIB42.158.1) and a *Saint Michael Vanquishing Lucifer* (TIB42.159.2) do not bear the artist's characteristic monogram, which is prominently inscribed on the five remaining plates. I differ from Bartsch in that I read this monogram clearly as GpP and not CpP. Nagler also read a G and not a C, but he considered the oeuvre of this etcher to date from the turn of the sixteenth century and attributed the etchings to Georg Peham (or Pecham) or another German artist of the period.[2]

John T. Spike, editor of *The Illustrated Bartsch* volume that contains the works of GpP, has raised the possibility that the artist was a Northerner in his introduction to Volume 42.[3] In a more recent personal communication, he has reaffirmed this opinion and has further made strong associations with the drawings of Pier Francesco Mola and the work of Salvator Rosa more generally, believing that "the only place where an artist could combine such an amalgam of styles was *Rome*."[4] In view of the hybrid style of GpP (or CpP, as Spike continues to call him) and the absence of references to him in the early sources, the possibility must be seriously considered that he was a Northern artist active in Italy, as Spike has conjectured.

The unsigned religious subjects share the taste shown in the five remaining prints, all of mythological subjects, for male nudes in vigorous, even agonized, poses. The musculature of these figures is distinctive, being represented by disconcertingly uniform patches of brief cross-hatching distributed over the torsos and limbs. It should be noted that the figures in the two religious subjects largely escape this mannerism; these two prints also exhibit a quite different compositional sense, with a willingness to crop forms dramatically by the edges of the plate so that the figures seem to ornament its surface. In the five mythological scenes, the tableaux are contained more conventionally within landscape settings.

The temptation to remove the two unsigned plates from the oeuvre of GpP, which arises from these differences in figure style and composition, is offset by the presence of two mannerisms common to both groups: a flourish of drapery, often a looping scarf, silhouetted against the sky, and a habitual pleasure in single strands of hair curling or streaming from the figures' heads (or tail, in the case of Nessus). And all of the prints share the same great freedom of touch, utterly oblivious to the conventions of engraving or niceties of etching technique. Still, the assimilation of the two religious prints into the oeuvre of GpP must be only provisional, and if they are accepted, they should be considered the products of a separate campaign of printmaking.[5]

The five mythological scenes provide a completely unified stylistic image; only their differing sizes inhibit one from considering them a set. Undoubtedly Bartsch identified the monogrammist with a follower of Reni with such etchings as Reni's *Saint Jerome* (TIB40.165.15) and even his *Holy Family* (Cat. 12) in mind, in which the modeling is also achieved with small patches of uninflected cross-hatching. This device is seen in other prints of the Bolognese school, in works by Cantarini (e.g., Cat. 29) and Flaminio Torri (e.g., TIB42.196.7), for example.

Giovan Pietro Possenti, an artist with the appropriate initials, was considered and rejected by Nagler as the creator of these etchings, on the grounds of style[6] and also the fact that his life dates were too late for prints which Nagler believed were created around 1600. Possenti was born in Bologna in 1618 and was the student of his father Benedetto, who had been a pupil of Lodovico Carracci; thus an affiliation with the works of Reni, while not direct, is certainly reasonable.[7] Le Blanc accepted the identification of GpP with Possenti,[8] and a print by GpP, *Vulcan's Forge* (*Mars Abducting Venus*) (TIB42.164.7), is catalogued as Possenti at the Pinacoteca Nazionale, Bologna.[9] Spike, however, rejects this attribution on the basis of comparison of these prints with the one documented painting by Giovan Pietro Possenti of his knowledge, the *Miracle of Saint Egidio* (Duomo, Mantua), which he considers not by the same hand as the etchings if only because the draftsmanship of the painting seems "too competent" (letter of 25 August 1991)—certainly a correct appraisal by inference of the skills of GpP. Spike cites also the lack of reference to Possenti as an etcher by Malvasia, who was well informed on Bolognese prints.[10]

The table of contents of Spencer Album 2 suggests that its eighteenth-century compilers thought GpP was Possenti. *The Death of Nessus* is described as follows: "Nessus percé d'une fleche par Hercules du Pocetti," which translates in comparatively inflexible English as "Nessus pierced by an arrow by Hercules by Pocetti." In French the "ce" of Pocetti would be sibilant, approximating the "se" sound of the Italian.[11] "Pocetti", of course, lacks the "n" and doubles the "t" of "Possenti," but the orthography of the albums' tables of contents has lapses on other occasions that can probably be attributed to the error of a calligrapher attempting to transcribe an unfamiliar foreign name from handwritten copy. Curiously, another instance of a misspelling occurs with yet another Italian seventeenth-century monogrammist, PBC, the etcher of a large *Madonna and Child with Saints Anthony and Catherine* (TIB40.249.2), whom the table of contents of Spencer Album 1 identifies as "Le Golbo." Although Bartsch catalogued the print as a Cavedone,[12] modern scholars attribute it to Pietro Paolo Bonzi of Cortona, who was traditionally known as "Il Gobbo de' Carracci."[13]

The only remaining puzzle, if the compilers of the Spencer Albums believed *The Death of Nessus* was by Possenti, is why it was mounted in Album 2 rather than Album 1, which is devoted to the Carracci and their school. Album 2 contains what can best be described as "mixed" Italians (as well as French artists). The most notable series of etchings in the volume is by Pietro Testa, from Lucca, who worked mostly in Rome (see Cat. 28). Curiously, Testa is not identified by name at all in the table of contents. Other Italian artists in Album 2 include Schiaminossi and Galestruzzi, who were both born in Florence and worked in Rome and elsewhere (see Cat. 54); Battista Angolo del Moro, who worked in Venice (see Cat. 1); and Giovanni Francesco Grimaldi, who *was* Bolognese and strongly influenced by the Carracci although he worked largely in Rome and Paris (see Cat. 31, 32).

Many of the prints in this album are of landscapes, with long sequences by Grimaldi, Bourdon, and Claude, and it may be this aspect of the print by the Monogrammist GpP which attracted the compilers. While the composition is certainly a subject piece, the figures are so poorly articulated by the negligible stress on chiaroscuro or silhouette that they seem absorbed into the landscape, as if they were stumps or rocks or, at the most, crumbling ancient statuary.

MBC

1. B.XIX.183.

2. Nagler 1858–1879, vol. 2, no. 565; vol. 3, nos. 249 and especially 276. Peham was born in Augsburg and worked in Munich; he died in 1604 (Thieme-Becker, vol. 26, p. 333). Doubtless Nagler was responding to the distinctive pose of Christ in the *Crucifixion*, where the corpus, its head downcast, drags from the straining arms in a pose reminiscent of earlier German works. The graphism of Peham drawings, as represented in the Gersheim Corpus (nos. 20705, 57133–4, 58777, 59627–8, 83903), looks nothing like the prints. In rejecting the attribution to Possenti, Nagler gave the artist's first name as Giacomo.

3. TIB42.[9].

4. Letter of 25 August 1991.

5. Nagler definitively separated the two religious prints from the rest of the artist's (Peham's) oeuvre (vol. 3, no. 276). Spike continues to include them in the rest of the oeuvre (letter of 25 August 1991).

6. ". . . es sind aber darin so wenig Anklänge an die Carracci'sche Schule, dass man auch damit nicht übereinstimmen kann" (vol. 3, no. 276).

7. Possenti died in 1659 in Padua, killed by a rival painter. See the very short entry on Possenti in Thieme-Becker, vol. 27, p. 296. The one drawing in a public collection which has ever been attributed to him is in its most recent publication assigned to his father Benedetto; see Annamaria Petrioli Tofani, *Inventario 2. Di-*

segni esposti. Gabinetto disegni e stampe degli Uffizi (Florence: Leo S. Olschki, 1987), no. 928 E. It has nothing in common with the etchings. In this catalogue the first name of the son is given as Giovan.

8. LEB.II.239. He, like Nagler, gives a very poor drawn rendition of the monogram as it appears on the prints.

9. My thanks to Shelley R. Langdale for this information.

10. Possenti is briefly mentioned in Malvasia 1841, vol. 1, pp. 391, 410; vol. 2, p. 85.

11. Many of the foreign names in the albums' tables of contents are rendered into French, e.g. "*Carrache*" and "*Labelle*," and presumably all were pronounced according to French phonetics. There is no reason to identify the "Pocetti" of the table of contents with the Florentine artist Bernardino Pocceti, an artist familiar to Mariette, whose draftsmanship in any case is very different from that seen in the works of GpP.

12. B.XVIII.333.2.

13. Nagler 1858–1879, vol. 1, no. 2299, followed by Thieme-Becker, vol. 4, pp. 330–31.

GIOVANNI FRANCESCO GRIMALDI
Bologna c. 1606 – 1680 Rome

31   *Landscape with a Bird Perched on a Tree Stump*

etching

270 x 382 mm

watermark: three mountains surmounted by a fleur-de-lys, a letter on each side, S and ?

inscribed in brown ink, lower left corner: *8* [sideways]

B.XIX.106.40 i/ii, TIB42.47.40 S1/2[1]

Gift of Philip Hofer, by exchange, s2.31

Best known in his day as an architect and decorator, today Giovanni Francesco Grimaldi is more commonly recognized as one of the more popular exponents of Carraccesque landscape in the mid-seventeenth century. In the circles of modern drawing connoisseurs his name is now often used as a substitute for "Anonymous Bolognese Artist" with reference to second- or third-rate landscape drawings that cannot be ascribed to the Carracci or Domenichino.

Born in Bologna in 1606, Grimaldi probably came to Rome in 1627.[2] His large-scale painted work in Rome is fairly well documented,[3] and a substantial corpus of prints has been convincingly attributed to him.[4] His drawings reveal him to have been a competent, albeit slightly stiff and uninventive, follower of the Carracci. His prints and drawings show that he was greatly influenced by the Venetian landscapes of Titian and Campagnola, a taste certainly in keeping with the Carraccesque style. Although he most probably did not know any of the Carracci personally, it is fairly certain from his involvement in the Academy of Saint Luke in Rome[5] that he was acquainted with other artists working in the Carracci tradition, such as Domenichino and Albani.

Many of his oil paintings are, in fact, closely related to, or in some cases dependent upon, Domenichino compositions, and he would have been able to study Carracci drawings in the Roman collection of Francesco Angeloni.

Grimaldi was very popular among several of the more important patrons of his day. In Rome he worked for the Pamfili family, at the Pamfili Villa near Porta San Pancrazio, and in the palace of Cardinal Antonio Santacroce, the Quirinal Palace, and the Gallery of the Palazzo Borghese, and in Paris from 1649 to 1652 for Cardinal Mazarin, the Jesuits, and the king.[6] Both his style and his patrons place him among the more important artists who benefited after 1630 from the renewed interest in classical landscape painting.[7] Clovis Whitfield has suggested that,

> . . . a generation after Annibale's death there was a moment when a kind of reassessment took place. It consisted of an intellectual realization that his teaching about painting was of enduring value. . . . On the one hand this laid the foundation for the academic tradition; on the other it gave rise, at home and abroad, to enthusiastic collecting and copying of Carraccesque originals.[8]

Artists such as Claude, Domenichino, Dughet, and Grimaldi received major landscape commissions from these patrons, and, as Richard Spear has noted, they "could place the genre on the level of history painting by equating order in nature with human values."[9]

Although Italian theorists never gave their wholehearted approval to the notion of landscape as a proper subject for painting, contemporary taste was quite taken with these ordered and carefully constructed panoramic landscapes, with low horizons and interesting trees, populated by small figure groups. It was only later in France that the genre would receive academic approval. Roger de Piles discussed the merits of the pastoral landscape in his *Cours de peinture par principles*,[10] and Pierre-Jean Mariette greatly praised Grimaldi: "This skilled artist had an excellent manner of drawing landscape. There are few masters who have engraved with ease and this is the best model one can choose for those who wish to draw *de bon gout*."[11]

Mariette's taste for Grimaldi is evident in the compilation of the Spencer Albums. There are twenty-eight different prints and one duplicate. In Album 6, five of Grimaldi's prints after Titian compositions represent most of the work of that Venetian master in the albums (also see Cat. 1). The remaining twenty-four prints, in Album 2, present a clear picture of Grimaldi himself as a printmaker. His plates are tightly constructed and carefully executed. The lines are not particularly freely etched, although one would never confuse them with engraved lines. Although he does not really exploit the capacity of the medium for loose and dashing strokes, as we see in Carpioni, for example (Cat. 15), his prints do seem to have the ease noted by Mariette.

Grimaldi used somewhat calligraphic lines to create the rounded presence of clouds; large numbers of organized and rationally disposed short strokes evoke both the fullness of the trees and the effects of light falling across them throughout the expansive vista. Although the atmospheric quality we see in Claude's etching (Cat. 35) is missing from these landscapes, it is obvious that Grimaldi studied nature and took great pains to make convincing scenes that mirror its physical appearances. His landscapes often concentrate upon one feature such as a tree or rock or river, and are constructed out of connecting, intersecting planes by means of rivers and roads, which lead the viewer through space by these devices as well as by repoussoir motifs.

The *Landscape with a Bird Perched on a Tree Stump* is inspired by both Venetian and Carraccesque precedents. The print seems to have no other subject than the landscape itself. The two figures sitting under the trees at the center are part of the scene; their backs are to the viewer and their activity is uncertain. The only other figures in the print are the pair walking up the hill to the town in the distance. Both groups have been integrated into the landscape by means of Grimaldi's etching technique. The figures in the foreground do not stand out from the central tree mass but rather have been etched with the same networks of cross-hatching as the trees under which they sit, so as to form part of the shade cast by the foliage. The figures walking up the hill are etched as lightly as the trees and shadows in that part of the composition.

The intertwined trees and stump at the center are the focus of the print. The motif, enframed by hills and trees at the left and right, comes right down to the front of the picture plane and, at its base, is so round as to create both a ground and a space at the front of the print, separating one plane from the next. These trees function in very much the same way as the central tree in Swanevelt's *Third View of the Zugro* (Cat. 34).

This print is one of the very few cases in the nine Spencer Albums in which there are duplicate impressions. This impression, s2.31, is a rich, well-preserved first state in black ink on white paper. The medium and support, therefore, allow for a wide range of light and shadow and help create the effect of a scene bathed in bright light. The other impression, s2.24, equally well preserved, is in a warm brownish ink on off-white paper of a cool tone.[12] The gradations of that impression are much more subtle, and its muted light effects might lead one to believe that this impression is inferior to s2.31. Careful examination of the prints reveals that this assessment is incorrect. It seems, from plate scratches, line quality, and our judgment that both are first states,[13] that the two impressions must have come from the same period in the life of the plate. Grimaldi or the printer must have chosen the different inks and papers to achieve the different tonalities, supporting the widely held notion that Grimaldi was particularly interested in these kinds of problems.[14]

ACB

1. The print is trimmed within the platemark; however, sufficient space remains in the lower margin so that the capital letters of the inscription "An. Carrac." added in the second state would be visible if present. Thus this is almost certainly a first-state impression.

2. Montagu 1985, vol. 1, p. 30.

3. Salerno 1977–1978, vol. 2, pp. 578–79; see also Montagu 1985.

4. Bartsch attributes fifty-five landscape prints to Grimaldi; Paolo Bellini, "Giovanni Francesco Grimaldi: a complete catalogue of his graphic work," *Print Collector* 10 (1974):6–27, ascribes fifty-seven landscapes to him.

5. Salerno 1977–1978, vol. 2, p. 578. Grimaldi was made a member of the Academy in 1634, an appraiser in 1639, and president in 1666.

6. Salerno 1977–1978, vol. 2, p. 578. See also M. Laurain-Portemer, "Le Palais Mazarin à Paris et l'offensive baroque de 1645, d'après Pietro da Cortona et Grimaldi," *Gazette des beaux-arts* ser. 6, 8 (1973):151–68. Mariette 1851–1860, vol. 2, p. 333, tells us that ". . . l'attachement, qu'il avoit au cardinal Mazarin, lui faisant craindre d'estre enveloppé dans sa disgrâce, lui fit prendre le party de se retirer chez les Jésuites . . . et ce fut alors qu'il peignit dans cette église une magnifique décoration . . . laquelle . . . fut tellement au goût de S. M. [Louis

XIV] . . . qu'il lui en ordonna une pour la chapelle de son Palais . . . "

7. Whitfield 1984.

8. Whitfield 1984, p. 85.

9. Richard Spear, *Domenichino* (New Haven: Yale University Press, 1982), p. 84.

10. Piles 1766, pp. 159–60. The entire section on landscape, pp. 157–204, is of interest in relation to many of the prints in the Spencer Albums.

11. Mariette 1851–1860, vol. 2, pp. 333–34: "Cet habile artiste s'esoit fait une excellent manière de dessiner le paysage. Il y a peu de maistres qui l'ayent gravé avec de légèreté, et c'est le meilleur model que puissent choisir ceux qui veulent dessiner de bon goût."

12. This impression is squared for transfer in graphite. It is unlikely that this was done by the artist himself. It was common practice for artists to copy each other's work from prints, and the print was probably squared by one of its owners between the 1660s and the time when it came into the Mariettes' possession. It is worth noting that a related landscape print in the exhibition, by Battista Angolo del Moro (Cat. 1), was also used for transfer, as witnessed by the red-chalk tracing on its reverse.

13. See n. 1.

14. Reed and Wallace 1989, p. 179.

GIOVANNI FRANCESCO GRIMALDI

Bologna c. 1606 – 1680 Rome

32   *The Colossal Bust*

etching

197 x 196 mm

inscribed in plate, lower left: *Gio fran.^{co} Grimaldi Bolognese inv. et fec.*

B.XIX.86.1, TIB42.11.1

Gift of Philip Hofer, by exchange, s2.27.1

This print is one of a series of round etchings depicting fictive landscapes in and around Rome; eight of the set are in Spencer Album 2. The series represents a wide range of subjects, from this monumental bust taken from classical antiquity, to an Italian medieval town (TIB42.15.5), to a rude contemporary thatched hut (TIB42.14.4). Both Mariette and Bartsch seem to have considered *The Colossal Bust* to be the first plate in the series.[1] It is the only one that does not have landscape or architecture within landscape as its principal subject. Everything in the print is dwarfed by the sculpture.

The colossal busts are those of the emperor Constantine, known in Grimaldi's time in both bronze and marble and situated in Rome in the Palazzo dei Conservatori.[2] Although the Parmigianesque figure on the right points to the fallen statue, the print does not seem to have a moralizing message, given the presence of an identical intact bust and within the context of the series. The figure is consistent with others in the etchings who point and gesture within the compositions, either to each other or to the viewer, and the position of the two busts probably simply reflects the state in which they could be seen in Rome at the time.[3]

The Colossal Bust is one of two prints in the series that depict a recognizable Roman monument, the other—mounted on the same album folio as *The Colossal Bust*—shows the Pyramid of Cestius (TIB42.12.2). Both this print and the *Pyramid* represent ancient monuments removed from the immediate topographical context in which they would be found. Sixteenth-century artists working in Rome such as Cock and Heemskerk recorded monuments exactly as they found them or trumped them up to look as if they were in the past. This antiquarian interest began to diminish for some artists of the seventeenth century. Grimaldi, Bronchorst (see Cat. 33), and others began to use and distort recognizable structures and sites to achieve artistic ends, to add character and interest to purely fictional scenes and create a place that *could* exist. In *The Colossal Bust* the two statues provide vertical and horizontal axes for the composition, as well as an opportunity for the artist to copy after the antique and make extravagant juxtapositions of scale.[4]

Gio fran.co Grimaldi Bolognese inu et fe.

Grimaldi's interest in classical remains in landscape can also be seen in a drawing now in the Kunstmuseum, Dusseldorf. Here he has taken a colossal bust like the one in the print, and also bas-relief medallions, and placed them in an evocative fashion, confounding the distinction between living flesh and stone, in a seventeenth-century landscape that contains not an ancient but rather a Gothic structure in the background.[5]

The etching style of *The Colossal Bust*, as well as the type of landscape, is typical of Grimaldi. As in his *Landscape with a Bird Perched on a Tree Stump* (Cat. 31), he uses the full range of tones from dark, for example under the statue and on the left side of the pedestal, to the white of the paper, as on the fallen statue's chest, to create a sense of volume as well as the fall of light. This print is a fine example of Grimaldi's interest in the effects of light and shade.

ACB

1. Bartsch lists the print as the first in the series, and Mariette, in the unpublished manuscript in the Bibliothèque Nationale (BNMS R069901), identifies the series by describing this print: "Une Suitte de huit paysages en rond, dont il y en a un où sont représentés deux bustes de statues colossales, l'un posé sur un piedestal, & l'autre renversé par terre."

2. Bober and Rubinstein 1987, no. 183.

3. See Bober and Rubinstein 1987, fig. 183a, which reproduces a drawing by Francesco de Hollanda showing both busts, one of which is upright and the other not.

4. Bober and Rubinstein 1987, p. 217, point out that throughout the Renaissance and into the seventeenth century, these statues and others "provided . . . artists with outstanding examples of monumental scale."

5. Gernsheim photograph 79683.

JAN GERRITSZ. VAN BRONCHORST

Utrecht c. 1603 – 1661 Amsterdam

33 *The Trophies of Marius*, plate 2 of *The Ruins of Ancient Rome*, after Poelenburch

etching

202 x 262 mm

watermark: blossoming plant above a grotesque mask (?)

inscribed in plate, lower right: *C. V. Poelenburch Inventor. / I. G. Bronchorst Schulptor.*

B.IV.63.13, TIB5.85.13, H.232.23

Gift of Melvin R. Seiden, s5.46.2

The subject of this etching has usually been identified as the Trophies of Marius, the traditional name of an actual ruined structure of the third century of the Christian era which still stands in the Piazza Vittorio Emanuele in southeastern Rome. Much about this identification is confused or suspect, however.

The print does not show the trophies themselves, which are marble sculptures of armor and weapons and are not in fact the trophies of Marius known from Plutarch. It is now believed that they were trophies of a Germanic war from the time of the emperor Domitian, who ruled A.D. 81–93.[1] They were remounted in the third century to decorate the structure seen in the etching, where they were placed in two arches that flanked a central vaulted niche. The building, con-

structed by the emperor Alexander Severus, is represented on coins of his reign which have been
dated to 226.[2] In 1590 the trophies were removed from the ruin and reinstalled on the Campo-
doglio, flanking the newly restored statues of the Dioscuri.[3]

The structure itself was not simply a frame for the trophies. It was a nymphaeum, a Roman
building type ornamented by and associated with water. This, the Nymphaeum of Alexander
Severus, was the urban endpoint of an aqueduct, now believed to have been the Aqua Anio
Novus, which began in artificial lakes near Subiaco and brought water of the highest quality over
eighty kilometers to Rome.[4] The trophies would have overlooked a cascade and fountain, an
amenity and essential service for the neighborhood; extensive underground vaulted chambers
indicate elaborate storage and distribution systems.[5]

At the time of the trophies' removal in 1590 the right arch was intact, but the the left arch of
the framing pair was already broken at its top, and the pier at the left that had supported it stood
isolated, a dramatic vertical accent at the periphery of the ruin.[6] When Poelenburch made his

drawing, the ruin would have appeared much as it does in a surviving drawing by Stefano della Bella, where the empty flanking arch and pier make a picturesque effect against the sky.[7]

The etching by Bronchorst shows no such thing, of course. The artist has shifted his vantage point so that the interior silhouettes of both pier and arch meld with the mass of the central niche. Indeed, the crumbling edges of the various elements of the architectural form are so artfully mingled with the foliage of shrubs growing from every point of the ruin that the ground-plan of the tripartite structure is indecipherable.[8] The ruin looks like a single great hulk of decayed brickwork overwhelming the lone pedestrian,[9] who seems to have come across this isolated survival of an ancient kingdom in an otherwise vast, unpopulated countryside rather than in the heart of a major European capital. If della Bella has chosen the picturesque viewpoint, Poelenburch has chosen the sublime, to continue the use of anachronistic classifications of landscape views.

The choice of the least revealing view, architecturally speaking, is entirely characteristic of the series from which this etching is taken. An even more astonishing example is plate 4, an etching of the Arch of Constantine (TIB5.87.15), which has been drawn from the side so that no arch whatsoever is visible. Like the nymphaeum, it too has been rendered as a rural monolith, towering in this case over a herd of cattle. When one compares these prints by Bronchorst after Poelenburch and also some other seventeenth-century views of Roman sights with prints from the previous century, a change in attitude is evident. Earlier sets of views of Roman ruins, such as one by G. B. Cavaleriis after Dosio published in 1569, which includes this subject, and a set drawn and etched by Hieronymus Cock published in 1551 (H.IV.182–183.22–47), concerned themselves with details of ancient architectural style and form, even to the point of articulating the classical orders of columns. Seventeenth-century views, such as the set by Bronchorst, another series of ruins of Rome by his countryman Breenbergh (TIB5.173–178.1–12), the *Diverse Views in and near Rome* by Swanevelt (TIB2.257–269.53–65, see Cat. 34), and the many Roman views by Giovanni Battista Mercati (TIB44.376–425.12–63), evince a new subjective appreciation of the poignancy of effect of the shattered remains of antiquity.[10]

The particular form of the ruin in this etching on exhibition became a favorite pictorial device in the pictures of Poelenburch and also those of Bronchorst after he took up easel painting.[11] It may be characterized as a towering, two-story ruin with the upper level invariably crowned by shrubbery and the boundary between the two levels also overgrown with plants. The structure itself is like a broken molar, still held fast by roots sunk deep into the earth. The ruin is usually placed to the side of a composition, with small figures below and beside it, oblivious to its presence. It became such a formal cliché that it could not be dispensed with even when the subject of the painting required a wilderness. Thus in Poelenburch's *Apollo and Diana*,[12] where the god is pursuing the chaste huntress, a nearby cliff stands in the ruin's stead; it too is crowned with tufts of foliage and has a pronounced horizontal division.

Bronchorst's transformation of a very real and substantial pile of bricks into a symbol of vanished empire is enhanced in this early impression of his etching by a gray tone which, although it probably results from an accident in biting, was apparently appreciated and exploited by the artist. The surface of the plate reveals a blotchiness that has been removed, probably by burnishing, from the areas of clear sky and distant topography. It remains in other areas of the sky, however, and in the ruin itself, to further veil the scene with a haze of time.

MBC

1. Bober and Rubinstein 1987, no. 174.

2. Thomas 1935, p. 298.

3. Bober and Rubinstein 1987, no. 174.

4. Thomas 1935, pp. 253–98. The nymphaeum was traditionally thought to be the endpoint of the Aqua Iulia, and the issue may not be completely settled.

5. Thomas 1935, pp. 297–98; Rome 1985, vol. 2, pp. 287–507, where the section on the ruin is by Doriana Cattalini.

6. See the print by Giovanni Battista Cavaleriis after Giovanantonio Dosio, 1569, reproduced in Bober and Rubinstein 1987, fig. 174a.

7. The drawing is in the collection of the Uffizi, Florence (inv. no. 4681), and is reproduced in Rome 1985, vol. 2, p. 289, fig. 2. It must date to the mid-seventeenth century, somewhat after Poelenburch's departure from Italy. By 1753 when Piranesi etched the ruin as *Del Castello dell'aqua Giulia*, the right arch had disappeared, but the left pier continued to stand, as it does, heavily restored, to this day. For a reproduction of the Piranesi, see Rome 1985, vol. 2, p. 289, fig. 3.

8. Alan Chong, in his listing of prints by Bronchorst after drawings by Poelenburch, discounts the traditional identification of this etching as the *Trophies of Marius* (Chong 1987, p. 58). While I continue to believe that the ruins are represented in this print, the disguising viewpoint chosen by the artist makes Chong's opinion understandable. A drawing by Poelenburch of the ruins viewed from the opposite side, also from an oblique angle, in which the arches are slightly more legible, is reproduced in Chong 1987, pl. 20.

9. It should be noted that the figure gives the correct scale for the ruin, which is about twenty meters high.

10. See Reed and Wallace 1989, pp. 160–62, for a discussion of this change in attitude as expressed in Mercatti's work.

11. See his *Italian Landscape*, Museum Boymans-van Beuningen, Rotterdam.

12. Collection of Lord Lothian, Melbourne Hall, Derby.

HERMAN VAN SWANEVELT

Woerden c. 1600 – 1655 Paris

34   *Third View of the Zugro*, 1630–1633

etching and engraving

116 x 185 mm

inscribed in plate, lower right: *HS. fe. et. ex. Cum pr Re*; lower center: *Altro vedutin dal Zugro.*

B.II.281.64, TIB2.268.64, H.XXIX.80.61 i/iii

William M. Prichard Fund, by exchange, s5.85.1

Herman van Swanevelt was probably born in Woerden, near Utrecht, around the turn of the seventeenth century. It has been suggested that his earliest artistic training would have been with

some of the minor masters active in Utrecht in the 1610s.[1] We know that by 1623 he had left the Netherlands and gone to Paris, since there are two signed and dated drawings now in the Herzog Anton Ulrich-Museum in Braunschweig that situate him in the French capital by this date.[2] By 1624 he was living in Rome, and it has been suggested that he was living in the same house with Claude Lorrain in 1627. In 1629 he is recorded as living with the artists Michelangelo Cerquozzi and Charles Audran.[3] He is known to have continued his friendship with Claude, and he made the acquaintance of Pieter van Laer and Joachim von Sandrart, with whom he went sketching in the Roman Campagna.[4] He departed Rome for Paris in 1641.[5] Although Swanevelt died in Paris in 1655, he returned to the Netherlands at least three times, in 1643, 1649, and 1650.[6]

Swanevelt was a prolific printmaker. Bartsch attributed 116 prints to him, and 118 are given in Hollstein. The Spencer Albums contain thirty-eight of the choicest examples of his work, in which every aspect and phase of the artist's career are represented. Although many of Swanevelt's prints are signed, unfortunately none is dated. One of his three series of views in and around Rome—the one to which this print belongs—bears the date of its publication in Paris: 1653. It is evident, however, that these works and many others were in fact executed in Rome years earlier. This can be inferred because many of the prints, as well as being signed, are inscribed "Fe. Rom." or some variation of this inscription. It is most likely that Swanevelt took the plates he had etched in Rome with him to Paris, where he must have found a publisher.

By comparing the prints with works by contemporary artists, we can discern a rough chronology. In an analogy to the development of his painting style convincingly demonstrated by Malcolm Waddington,[7] Swanevelt's prints seem to emerge from the milieu of the Northern artists working in Rome and steadily take on a more independent character. His earliest etchings appear to be a series of four Old Testament scenes (H.XXIX.50–51.1–4). In their technical similarity to engraving and in the description of nature by means of recognizable and often repeated motifs, they are related stylistically to the work of Northern Italianate artists such as Bril, Poelenburch, Breenbergh, and to a lesser extent Elsheimer (as known through prints by Goudt).[8] Then in the late 1620s and into the early '30s, Swanevelt's style seems to develop in a parallel course with Claude's. This can be seen in the prints in his series of twelve *Diverse Views in and around Rome* (H.XXIX.74–80.50–62), especially in the *Third View of the Zugro*. When we compare this print with Claude's *Flight into Egypt* (Cat. 35) we see that both artists exhibit a marked interest in the atmospheric depiction of the sky. Figures merge into the background, and the narrative (where there is one) is subsumed into the landscape by treating the figures in exactly the same loose etching manner as the rest of the scene. Throughout the late 1620s and into the '30s, Swanevelt shows a growing interest in landscape itself. This can been seen when comparing his *Hagar and the Angel* from the Old Testament series (H.XXIX.50.2), which I would place in the late 1620s and which must be somewhat dependent on Goudt's *Small Tobias and the Angel* after Elsheimer (H.XXIX.151.1), and the *Third View of Zugro* of around 1630–1633.

In the later 1630s and into the 1640s and beyond, people and stories once again grow in prominence. The landscape becomes less naturalistic and more dramatic, taking on an almost sublime character, which can be seen most clearly in his post-Roman work, exemplified by the Venus and Adonis series (H.XXIX.59–62.18–23) in such prints as *The Death of Adonis* (Cat. 58). Here the landscape begins to assume a life of its own. Specific details such as tree stumps and foliage are made prominent and executed in an especially expressive manner. It was around this time that Swanevelt is known to have come into contact with Salvator Rosa, when in 1640 the duke of Modena commissioned them to paint a pair of landscapes.[9] Rosa's landscapes are much more creations of fancy and drama than Swanevelt's previous work. Renewed contact with the North after his arrival in Paris may also have made Swanevelt think more about the dramatic possibilities of landscape.

The *Third View of Zugro* depicts a specific location outside of Rome and provided Swanevelt with an opportunity to create a pure landscape. Its principal subjects are the sky and the tree to the left of center; this lone tree is the centerpiece of the composition. Pictorial emphasis has been moved away from the sides, and recession is suggested by the winding path in the foreground. Swanevelt's earliest known use of a centrally located tree as the focus of a composition is his painting *Jacob's Departure* (Bredius Museum, The Hague). The tree in the etching is the kind one finds in the drawings of Annibale Carracci. Unlike Annibale, however, Swanevelt has drawn the tree using vertical strokes rather than curved hatching. In other prints in the series, such as the central tree in the *First View of Zugro* (H.XXIX.79.59) and the trees at the upper left of the *View of the Acqua Acetosa* (H.XXIX.76.53), Swanevelt etches in a more Carraccesque manner.

In the *Third View* the clouds have a puffy plasticity not found in other prints. The etcher has not been afraid to use the white of the paper as a contrast to the dark sky around it. This device allows the cloud to seem as if it were closer to the front of the picture plane. By contrast, the figures are almost completely absorbed within the landscape. The travelers along the path have no substantiality and are difficult to distinguish from their shadows.

ACB

AUTHOR'S NOTE: Many of the ideas in this entry were originally presented to a seminar on Dutch prints at Harvard University, Fall 1990. I am grateful to Prof. Seymour Slive for his comments and suggestions.

1. Waddingham 1960, pp. 37–38.
2. Alan Chong in Sutton 1987, p. 489; Waddingham 1960, p. 37. Both authors refer to these sheets without citing an inventory number or other reference. There seems to be no photograph of either drawing in the Gernsheim Corpus, and neither drawing is illustrated in Eduard Flechsig, *Zeichnungen alter Meister im Landesmuseum zu Braunschweig*, 3 vols. (Frankfurt-am-Main, 1920–1925).

3. Eckhart Knab, "Die Anfänge des Claude Lorrain," *Jahrbuch der Kuntshistorischen Sammlungen in Wien* 56 (n.f.20) (1960):63–164, p. 81.
4. Waddingham 1960, p. 43.
5. Waddingham 1960, p. 38.
6. Alan Chong in Sutton 1987, p. 489.
7. Waddingham 1960.
8. See Salerno 1977–1978, vol. 2, pp. 64–65, where he suggests that "he certainly studied Bril and the Carraccesque tradition, but only occasionally did his work echo that of Elsheimer."
9. Sutton 1987, p. 498.

CLAUDE GELLEE (called LE LORRAIN)

near Chamagne, Lorraine 1600 – 1682 Rome

35 *The Flight into Egypt*, c. 1630–1633

etching

105 x 173 mm

inscribed in plate, lower right: *CLAU*

R.-D.I.7.1, Russell 9 i/iii, Mannocci 9 i/iv

Gift of Belinda L. Randall from the collection of John Witt Randall, by exchange, s2.107.2

Orphaned at twelve, Claude left Lorraine for Rome in 1613, purportedly in search of employment as a pastry cook, a trade requiring considerable artistic talent.[1] He found work as a servant in the house of the painter Agostino Tassi, and it was here that he learned the painter's trade. Eventually he established himself as an independent artist in Rome, which he apparently left

only twice: he spent two years in Naples, c. 1618–1620,[2] and traveled to Lorraine (via Venice and Bavaria) where he assisted Claude Deruet with frescoes in the Carmelite Church in Nancy in 1625. Claude returned to Rome in 1627, where, spurred by the commission of two paintings from Cardinal Guido Bentivoglio several years later, he launched his highly successful career, with life-long affiliations with some of the most important patrons of his time.

It is not precisely known when or why Claude took up etching, though it has been suggested that he might have been encouraged by his colleague and outdoor sketching companion the German painter Joachim von Sandrart, who came to Rome in 1628.[3] He may also have been stimulated by the thriving print trade in Rome at the time.[4] Although he had become technically proficient by the end of the 1630s, his interest in the medium waned, possibly because of pressure to fulfill prestigious commissions, which had greatly increased by the early '40s, or perhaps etching seemed less challenging once he had mastered the technique.[5] He returned to etching in 1651 for equally uncertain reasons.

Claude has long been viewed as the greatest landscape painter of the seventeenth century, and by some as the greatest of all time. He made only landscapes, producing nearly three hundred paintings, twelve hundred drawings and forty-four etchings.[6] He was particularly admired in England, where his paintings were so avidly collected that by the mid-nineteenth century almost two-thirds of Claude's *Liber Veritatis* pictures were in British collections.[7]

While the admiration for Claude's paintings has rarely wavered, the popularity of his etchings has been less consistent. It is difficult to assess the response of Claude's contemporaries. His

175

prints did not receive the same level of acclaim as his paintings, and although there was mounting interest in the medium in Italy and throughout Europe at the time, the etchings were probably considered merely a by-product of his production as a painter. Claude's great reputation as an etcher developed later, mainly in France and England and to some extent in Germany. Mariette praised Claude for his ability to put atmosphere and freshness into his landscapes and noted that "the same intelligence prevails in everything he has etched."[8] Paradoxically, however, there was distaste for the etchings in England in the eighteenth century, reflected in the writings of Jonathan Richardson and Reverend William Gilpin during the same period when the popularity of Claude's paintings was at its peak. Only after the publication of the first catalogue of Claude's prints in 1835 did the etchings experience a marked increase in popularity and monetary value.[9] Although the cataloguer Robert-Dumesnil praised Claude for his technique and the picturesque qualities of light in the prints, in his opinion only fourteen of the forty-two plates he described were exemplary of Claude's achievement; *The Flight into Egypt* was among this group.[10]

Originally, eighteen Claude etchings were mounted on the last pages of Spencer Album 2. Ten were cut out and sold in 1919;[11] they were undoubtedly selected for removal because of their monetary value. Of the eight that remain, *The Flight into Egypt* is the finest impression. However, this print is of interest in subject as well, both in relation to the numerous depictions of the Flight by other artists in the album (see Cat. 51, 61) and as a recurring theme in Claude's work.

First, it is noteworthy that this print is not specifically listed in the album's table of contents, as the *View of the Campo Vaccino*, *The Rape of Europa*, and others are, but is lumped under the heading of landscapes to be found on folios 104–107. The Flight into Egypt enjoyed tremendous popularity in the seventeenth century since the subject's potential for elaborate outdoor settings was well suited to the growing interest in the landscape genre (which was, however, still classed among the lower categories in the hierarchy of subject types). The artist could use the religious theme to elevate the importance of what was essentially a marvelous scene. The extent to which pure landscape subjects were not only accepted as worthy but particularly cherished by the early eighteenth century is indicated by the designation in the table of contents.

Claude executed more drawings and paintings of the Flight into Egypt or the Rest on the Flight than any other subject. Paintings of the theme occur throughout his career, and he frequently made drawings, several of which appear to be independent works unconnected to any painting.[12] In addition to the attraction of the landscape setting, the Flight is the quintessential journey in the history of Christian mankind, and journeying is a prime subject of Claude's art in mythological and genre subjects as well. This is somewhat surprising, since he apparently did not travel after 1627, but a more personal reason may elude us.

Claude's two earliest painted versions of the Flight are small, executed on copper (MRP 234 and 241), the latter dated 1631, around the same time of the etching. There does not seem to be a painting related to the composition of the etching, but the group of figures appears in reverse in a drawing (MRD 347, c. 1635–1640), in quite different surroundings. Although stylistically the drawing dates to the mid- to late 1630s, Roethlisberger notes that the etching appears more "firmly constructed" than similar asymmetrical compositions of this period (*Liber Veritatis* 3, 7, and 12). He proposes that the print could have been executed after the drawing, which nonetheless is not close enough to be considered a study.

The lack of refinement in technique clearly suggests an early date, although hints of Claude's talent as an etcher are also evident. The plate has been meticulously worked; the resulting image is rather dense in areas, particularly the group of figures that is difficult to distinguish from the background, a problem he overcame in later prints. Claude also seems to have had difficulty with the sky, which shows evidence of burnishing and accidental scratches. But despite the technical complications, a closer look reveals a marvelous effect of fresh air in the freely etched lines of the wind-tussled palm and an unequaled ability to describe effects of sunlight through sensitive manipulation of gradations of tone. Claude went on to perfect these luminous effects in his later prints through the eventual mastery of an energetic, vibrant quality of line, graded biting, burnishing, and selective wiping of the plate.

SRL

1. According to Joachim von Sandrart, *Der Teutschen Academie Zweyter Theil* (Nuremberg, 1675), as summarized in Mannocci 1988, p. 3. Filippo Baldinucci's account in *Notizie de'professori del disegno da Cimabue in qua* (Florence, 1728), vol. 4, is less dramatic, suggesting that after learning to draw from his brother (who made wood-intarsia), Claude was sent to Rome with a relative where he sought further artistic training with financial support from the family. Current scholarship supposes that some combination of these possibilities is most probable. See Roethlisberger 1961, vol. 1, p. 5, and Mannocci 1988, p. 3.

2. Although Claude may have reached Rome as early as 1613, he is not documented there until 1623. See Harris 1985, p. 126, n. 2.

3. Emilia Frances [Strong], Lady Dilke, *Claude Lorrain, sa vie et ses oeuvres, d'après des documents inédits, par Mme Mark Pattison . . .* (Paris: J. Rouam, 1884), p. 165, as noted in Mannocci 1988, p. 7, n. 1.

4. A printing press was listed in the inventory of Claude's possessions at his death, published by Ferdinand Boyer, "Les inventaires après décès de Nicolas Poussin et de Claude Lorrain," *Bulletin de la Société de l'Histoire de l'Art Français* (1929):143–62.

5. Mannocci 1988, p. 9. Mannocci also suggests (pp. 20–22) that Claude's abandonment of etching may be related to a failed attempt to publish a set of his etchings in the 1630s.

6. The most recent publication on Claude's oeuvre (in all media) is Russell 1975, where fifty-one etchings

are given to him. Mannocci 1988 attributes forty-four etchings to him, rejecting six copies after Callot. Hereafter, the catalogue numbers that follow the title of Claude's etchings will refer to Mannocci's text and will be abbreviated as M. and the corresponding numeral.

7. Claude's *Liber Veritatis* sketchbook, now in the collection of the British Museum, London, records the composition of 195 pictures painted between 1635 and 1682.

8. Mariette 1851–1860, vol. 1, p. 290.

9. R.-D.I.3–38. Claude is the first printmaker listed in this multivolume compendium. For a more complete discussion of the cataloguing and criticism of Claude's prints see Mannocci 1988, pp. 10–16. For commentaries on Claude's art in general, see the appendix in Russell 1975, pp. 417–33, compiled by Larry J. Feinberg.

10. R.-D.I.3, his nos. 1, 5, 6, 8, 10–13, 15, 18, 20–23.

11. Christie 1919, lots 35–41. There are ten rectangles cut out of the Claude section of Album 2, and there were ten Claude prints listed in this sale; see the Checklist. Two were listed in the album's table of contents by title; the remaining eight fall under the general heading of "*Quatorze Tempestes, Ports de Mer & Paysages.*" Six prints of this category remain in the album.

12. These works are dated variously between 1631 and 1663. For examples see MRD 347, 492, 518, 612–14, 639, 744, 747–48, 884–88, 1129, MRP 88, 229, and 242. MRD refers to Roethlisberger 1968; MRP refers to Roethlisberger 1961.

JEAN MORIN
Paris c. 1590 – 1650 Paris

36 *Ruins of an Aqueduct*, after Claude Lorrain, c. 1648?

etching

147 x 212 mm

inscribed in plate, lower margin, left: *Cl. le Lorrain pinxit*; center: *Auec priuilege du Roy*;
right: *Morin sculp. et excud.*

R.-D.II.75.102, LEB.III.57.108

Gift of Melvin R. Seiden. s5.48.1

Though he began as a painter, Jean Morin devoted most of his career to printmaking. Best known for portrait etchings after the paintings of his teacher Philippe de Champaigne, he has been greatly admired for the roughness of his etching technique. It imbues the sitters with a certain immediacy and sense of personality, especially in comparison with the polished restraint and discretion of the engraved portraits of Robert Nanteuil (1623–1678). Clearly it was this aspect of Morin's tactile, painterly etched style that Pierre-Jean Mariette appreciated. In his discussion of Philippe de Champaigne, he singled out Morin as deserving special mention among the master's students and praised his graphic technique for its pictorial style, achieved without sacrificing a sense of finish. He noted the capacity of this technique to convey the subtleties of a range of tonal values, as well as the fact that this approach was widely admired.[1] It is significant that the characteristics of Morin's style that Mariette identified are particularly effective in rendering the atmosphere and varied textures of landscape.

Of the approximately 112 images that comprise Morin's etched oeuvre, only twenty or so are landscapes, the majority after Jacques Fouquières, six after his own designs, three after Cornelis van Poelenburch, and this one after Claude Lorrain.[2] At first it might be surprising to find Morin represented in the Spencer Albums by landscapes rather than portraits and to discover this landscape after Claude in the album devoted to Dutch and Flemish works rather than in the album of French and Italian prints, which included Claude's own landscape etchings. Even within Album 5, this impression was not mounted together with other Morin landscapes or prints by Platte-Montagne that were published by Morin.

Conceding that albums of portraits may have been lost from the Spencer collection and admitting that Album 5 is atypical among the volumes that have come down to us in its lack of a title page and table of contents, one can surmise that this print was placed on the basis of its content among other Italianate Dutch landscape prints featuring ruins and genre subjects. This arrangement is not typical of the albums in general, including Album 5, which mostly are organized into sections according to painter-printmaker or sometimes by artist, as in the case of

Cl. le Lorrain pinxit.   Auec priuilege du Roy   Morin sculp. et excud.

prints after Teniers and Titian. According to the Mariette manuscript that describes the contents of another volume of prints containing Morin etchings, an impression of this print was mounted along with three others after Poelenburch (as it is also in Spencer Album 5), among folios mounted with etchings by Platte-Montagne. That volume presented the works of Philippe de Champaigne and his students.[3]

Perhaps Mariette's particular admiration for Morin's talent compelled him to find a place for this print even among Dutch etchings in the album we now know as Spencer Album 5. Compositions similar to Claude's painting recur in numerous works of Dutch and Flemish artists who were working in Rome in the 1620s and '30s with him, such as Bartholomaeus Breenbergh, Herman van Swanevelt (see Cat. 34), and Poelenburch (see Cat. 33).[4] In any case, there could be no better example of the printmaker's "*pittoresque*" qualities than this fine impression after the master painter of the Roman landscape. Morin has skillfully captured Claude's almost palpable shadows rendered in rich cross-hatching in the foreground, the penetrating light of the setting sun as it dissolves the forms of delicately etched foliage in the background, and the luminous interiors of the massive stone archways in the middleground. The print seems at home here among the Italianate scenes on the preceding and following pages, more, perhaps, than it would have among Claude's own etchings in Album 2, which were executed in a much freer manner (see Cat. 35).

The two landscape etchings by Morin and others by Platte-Montagne that appear later in Album 5 are of Netherlandish woodlands and waters (see Cat. 45).

The Claude painting reproduced by this etching has only recently been identified, and its attribution is largely based on its likeness to the print. Marcel Roethlisberger has dated the painting to the early years of Claude's career in Italy, c. 1625–1630, by comparison with other paintings and drawings from this period.[5] Unfortunately, little is known about Morin himself. Although his birth was recorded in Paris and he is known to have studied there, there is no indication that he ever traveled to Italy. An illustration in the *Icones Biblicae* of 1679 that bears a remarkable resemblance in reverse to Morin's *Aqueduct* in its cropping of forms, lighting, and details of foliage suggests that either the painting or the etching were known outside Italy or Paris by the last quarter of the century.[6] The most likely scenario would have Morin learning of Claude's picture through one of the expatriate painter's French patrons or through Giovanni Francesco Grimaldi (see Cat. 31), who has been credited with bringing the influence of Claude to Paris in the 1640s,[7] or through Herman van Swanevelt (see Cat. 34, 58), who arrived in Paris in 1646 and had lived in Claude's house in Rome for several years.[8] Nicolas Poussin's brief sojourn in Paris in 1640–1642, the return of a number of artists, including Jacques Stella and Remy Vuibert (both friends of Poussin), from their studies in Rome, and the presence of Grimaldi and Swanevelt in the French capital in the 1640s led to an increased taste for the depiction of the pastoral Italian landscape and antique ruins. Thus the execution of Morin's print falls logically toward the end of this decade.

SRL

1. Mariette 1851–1860 vol. 1, p. 352: "Jean Morin mérite ussy d'etre distingue parmy les élèves de Champaigne . . . il devint graveur; la nouvelle mainière de graver qu'il imagina avant esté bien reçeue. Elle est pittoresque, sans manquer de costé du fini, très propre à exprimer les différens dégres de teintes et de tous les tons de la couleur . . ."

2. Roethlisberger 1972, p. 25. Le Blanc also lists a landscape print after Corneille LEB III.57.112).

3. BNMS RO65902: "f.51–52. Quatre auttres Paysages representans des Veues de ruines de Rome, gravé à l'eau forte par le mesme, les trois premiers d'après des tableaux de Corneille van Polembourg & le quatrieme d'apres Claude le Lorrain." RO65908: "Pour les Titres [*instructions to the calligrapher*] Oeuvres de Philippe de Champagne / de Bruxelles Peintre Recteur de l'Academie Royale de peinture / . . . Jean Morin de Paris . . . / Mattieu de Platte-Montagne d'Anvers / peintre de Marines & Nicolas de Platte- / Montagne son files de

Paris . . . / Tous peintres & graveurs sortis de L'ecole de / Champagne ou qui imité sa maniere."

4. For example, Poelenburch's drawing *Ruins with Arched Gateway* (Pierpont Morgan Library, inv. no. 1 116) and Breenbergh's etching *Ruins of the Colosseum* (H.III.207.10).

5. Roethlisberger 1979, p. 24. In this article Roethlisberger identifies a source for the Morin etching that is in reverse of the print and discounts the painting he had suggested in the *Paragone* article cited above in n. 2.

6. Melchior Kuesel, *Icones Bibliae* (Augsburg, 1679), cited in Roethlisberger 1972, p. 25, and no. 4, fig. 12b. A prophet and a lion were added to correlate the scene with the biblical text. Other illustrations were derived from works by Raphael, Rubens, Rembrandt, and Lucas van Leyden.

7. Bellini 1974, pp. 6–27.

8. Waddingham 1960, p. 43. See also Cat. 34, n.3.

MOYSES VAN WTENBROUCK

The Hague c. 1590 – 1646/7 The Hague

37a *Horses and Other Animals beside a Wall,* c. 1625 or later

etching and engraving

147 x 141 mm

watermark: fleur-de-lys within a shield, surmounted by a crown, similar to Heawood 1663–1666 (Amsterdam, 1646)

B.V.107.42, TIB6.96.42, TIB0605.81.042 s1/5

Gift of Melvin R. Seiden, s5.38.1

37b *Donkeys and Other Animals beside a Wall,* c. 1627 or later

etching and engraving

147 x 142 mm

watermark: fleur-de-lys within a shield, surmounted by a crown, similar to Heawood 1663–1666 (Amsterdam, 1646)

B.V.108.44, TIB6.98.44, TIB0605.82.044 s1/5

Gift of Melvin R. Seiden, s5.38.4

Adam Bartsch's early nineteenth-century catalogue of the prints of Wtenbrouck (whose name he spelled Uytenbrouck, alternatively Vytenbroeck; it is also frequently seen as Uyttenbroeck or Wttenbrouck) has not been superseded. That print scholar considered these two images of domesticated animals clustered before ruined fortifications to be part of a set of four. All are of approximately the same dimensions and format, the other two (TIB6.95.41 and TIB.6.97.43) having cows and goats as their primary subjects. However, on folio 38 of Spencer Album 5—the page from which these two prints have been removed for exhibition—the four prints mounted as a set omit the plate with goats and include a fifth print, again of approximately the same size and format, with assorted animals silhouetted against the sky and a vista, and with fortifications looming up in the middle distance. But this print, *A Woman Surprised at Her Bath,* has humans as its focus; Bartsch tacitly recognized its close affiliation with the four animal prints by cataloguing it immediately before them (TIB6.94.40). The nude woman, strategically draped by an amorphous cloth, is evidently the rustic shepherdess of the flock beside her on the riverbank. She has been surprised by an exceptionally unkempt shepherd who looks as startled as she. The two appear hardly higher on the evolutionary scale than the creatures they guard, and there seems no reason not to assume that the artist intended a set of five.[1]

An obelisk appears in the one print of the five not found in the album, as well as in other paintings and prints by Wtenbrouck, including his etched self-portrait (TIB6.60.1). This architectural feature, as well as the artist's affinity for antique mythological subjects (see Cat. 26) and Arcadian themes more generally, has led scholars to posit a trip to Italy, which is undocumented.[2] Yet even prints whose principal subject is domestic animals, a motif accepted as quintessentially Dutch, may be speculatively adduced as suggestive of travel south. If one scans the illustrations to Bartsch's first volume, which features Northern animal prints, and to Hollstein's multivolume, ongoing catalogue of prints of Netherlandish artists of the sixteenth and seventeenth centuries (which does not yet include Wtenbrouck, at the end of the alphabet), eigh-

teen printmakers can be identified whose oeuvre includes such subjects. The birthdates of these artists range from c. 1592 (Laer) to 1650 (Verkolje). Dividing this period at 1625, the birthdate of Paulus Potter, who is generally regarded as the paradigmatic Dutch cow painter, we discover that of the fifteen printmakers born before this date, nine are known to have gone to Italy; of the twelve including Potter born during the period 1625–1650, only three went to Italy.[3] Thus, statistically a trip south of the Alps by Wtenbrouck, born c. 1590, is likely (though, to reiterate, undocumented). At the least, one can say that an interest in the representation of animals was very strong in the first generation of Dutch seventeenth-century etchers who did travel south.

The effect of the paintings of Adam Elsheimer, a German artist resident in Rome, has also been discerned in works by Wtenbrouck, who would presumably have known Elsheimer through the latter's works as reproduced in engravings by Goudt. The Elsheimer/Goudt influence is, however, reflected more in figural compositions and their landscape settings and not in Wtenbrouck's animal subjects. Another German artist whose works are more clearly associated with the animal prints is Johann Heinrich Roos (1631–1685). Roos's own etchings of sheep, cattle, and goats (which are dramatically larger than Wtenbrouck's more delicate representations) also show livestock as their primary subject. The animals are posed in the foreground and are associated with ruined classical architecture rather than integrated into a larger landscape. Neither Roos nor Wtenbrouck, nor Laer nor Swanevelt, for that matter, isolated their animals as if they were specimens, either of exotica or especially prized breeding stock. Thus they do not seem to demonstrate inspiration from the obvious Italian prototype, the series of animal representations such as *Horses from Different Lands* by Antonio Tempesta, who otherwise in his many etchings of hunts and animal combats shows none of the affection for domestic species so obvious in these prints by Wtenbrouck and his compatriots.

The Spencer Albums now at Harvard contain full runs of the Tempesta animal series and also the set of animals by Swanevelt, as well as the three Wtenbrouck animal prints; and the Spencer library at Althorp once held another album of prints, now in the collection of the John Rylands Library, Manchester, in which a very large number of prints of livestock are mounted, including eleven plates by Roos and more than thirty by Karel Dujardin.[4] Presumably all of these would have been greatly enjoyed by John Charles, third Earl Spencer (1782–1816), one of the leading Whig politicians of his day. "The one extravagance he permitted himself was his herd of prize cattle . . . his addition to the magnificent collection of pictures at Althorp consisted of a series of portraits of his prize bulls."[5]

The technique of Wtenbrouck's set of animal subjects deserves some mention, as it has been variously described. To quote his most recent cataloguer,

> Uyttenbroeck's prints frequently combine etching and engraving. Mariette initially divided his oeuvre by media, and Bartsch discerns three methods: etching, engraving, and a combination of the two. The earliest works are usually etched, often with drypoint, whereas the later work prints reveal more burin work [sic].[6]

What Mariette said was,

> With regard to printmaking, he had two sorts, a first, that of 1620 [when the artist executed many of his prints], is less concerned with chiaroscuro; the basis of the process is etching, but they are so heavily retouched with the graver's burin that this is difficult to perceive.[7]

In fact this exactly describes the plates of the animals, which are so little concerned with chiaroscuro as to be blond in their effect. Close inspection reveals that in these, etching was used to provide only minimal outlines of the main forms of the motif and also to hatch in more heavily the foreground vegetation. Then the artist reworked the entire plate with the burin, filling in the coats of the animals and adding all of the farther landscape details and the skies. Bartsch characterized this added work as drypoint; the distinction is moot in the lightest lines, where the sharp tip of any tool could have produced the hair-fine scratches, but in the heavier flicks the distinctly triangular cut of the burin can be identified.

The animal plates have been dated c. 1627 on the basis of their relationship to animals included in Wtenbrouck's painting of that date of *The Triumph of Bacchus*.[8] The figure of a bather in the plate we have associated with the four animal prints is seen in reverse in a painting of 1625.[9] Wtenbrouck could have used the paintings themselves as a mine of motifs for prints of isolated elements, or, conversely, he could have assembled figures which he had first used in small prints into larger painted compositions. His career is still too poorly known to decide between these options or upon a certain chronology. Mariette's technical observation would tend to place the animal prints and the etching of the startled bather, which is identical in its combination of skeletal etching and fully fleshed engraving, at a relatively early point, yet their general conception is inconceivable without the assimilation of the examples of Cornelis van Poelenburch (see Cat. 33) and Bartholomaeus Breenberg, Wtenbrouck's close contemporaries who were both leaders of the first generation of Italianate Dutch artists.

MBC

1. A later state of this print was published by Joannes Day. Later states of the plates whose primary motifs are horses (B.42), goats (B.43), and donkeys (B.44) were published by Evert van Swynen. No impression is known of the cows bearing any publisher's credit after that of the artist's son Matheus, whose inscription ("Ma. V. Wytenbrouck ex.") is found on the second state of all five prints. The impression of B.40 in the album is a worn impression of the second state, in contrast to the impressions of B.41, B.42, and B.44, which are excellent impressions of the first state.

2. See Weisner 1964, p. 191. A biography of the artist and bibliography of the brief literature on Wtenbrouck may be derived from the notes in TIB0605.55–108. See also Sutton 1987, pp. 30–31, 535–36, for an intelligent analysis of the artist's painted oeuvre; Sutton strongly doubts the likelihood of a trip to Italy.

3. The list in full, with those who traveled to Italy given in italics: *Laer, Pieter van (c. 1592–1642); Swanevelt, Herman van (c. 1600–1655)*; H[illegaert], P[aulus] v[an], (c. 1595–1640); Vlieger, Simon de (c. 1600–1653); Stoop, Dirk (1610–1686); Verbeeck, Pieter (c. 1610–1654); *Fyt, Jan (1611–1661)*; Aken, Jan van (1614–1661); Wouwermans, Philips (1619–1668); *Berchem, Nicolas (1620–1683)*; Hecke, Jan van den (1620–1689); *Weenix, Jan (1621–1660)*;

Dujardin, Karel (1622–1678); Does, Jacob van der (1623–1673); Ossenbeeck, Jan (c. 1624–1674); Potter, Paulus (1625–1654); *Ducq, Johanne le (c. 1629–c. 1676); Borssom, Anthony van (1630–1677); Jonckheer, Jacob de (b. c. 1630? act. 1659–1696); Roos, Johann Heinrich (1631–1685)*; Moeyaert, Claes (1632–1696); *Velde, Adriaen van de (1636–1672); Begeijn, Abraham (1637–1697)*; Bije, Marcus de (1639–c. 1690); Toorenvliet, Jacob (c. 1641–1719); Verkolje, Jan (1650–1693); *Meer, Jan van der (1656–1705)*.

4. This album now in the collection of the John Rylands Library of the University of Manchester is numbered 8055 inside its front cover in the same hand as the numbering in Harvard's Spencer Albums. The album also includes landscapes by Lucas van Uden, Lodewyk de Vadder, and Simon de Vlieger. It is worth noting that the Vliegers duplicate prints found in Spencer Album 5, from which these Wtenbroucks and all other Netherlandish prints in this exhibition are taken, and that the Vlieger impressions in the Rylands Library album are far superior. See the Introduction for a further description of this album.

5. Battiscombe 1984, p. 142.

6. TIB0605.55.

7. Mariette 1851–1860, vol. 2, p. 15: "A l'égard de la

graveure il a eu deux manières, la première, qui est celle de 1620, est moins recherchée pour le clair obscur; le fond de la gravure est à l'eau forte, mais elles sont tellement retouchées au burin qu'on l'aperçoit difficilement." Mariette noted that "généralement tout ce qu'il a gravé est très estimé" (p. 14). See also B.V.82–83.

8. Weisner 1964, no. 15, repro. p. 198, fig. 4. The painting, from the Herzog Anton Ulrich-Museum, Brunswick, is also reproduced in TIB0605.78.

9. Formerly collection of Dr. E. Shapiro, London; see Weisner 1964, no. 34.

JAN MIEL

Beveren-Waes, near Antwerp 1599 – 1664 Turin

38   *A Shepherd with a Bagpipe*, c. 1640

etching

137 x 124 mm

watermark: fragmentary

inscribed in plate, lower left: *G^{no} Miele fecit et inv*

B.I.339.1, H.XIV.34.11

Gift of Melvin R. Seiden, s5.28.2

This etching is one of a suite of three, which comprises Jan Miel's representation in the Spencer Album devoted to Dutch and Flemish prints. By the later seventeenth century, the copper plates for the suite had become the property of Giovanni Giacomo de Rossi, the most important print publisher in Rome. Their listing in his 1677 catalogue (where we note that this plate of a bagpiper, more fully signed than the other two, is considered the first of the series) provides us with basic descriptions:

> A seated shepherd, who plays the bagpipe, with some goats: invented, and engraved in etching by Gio[vanni] Miele...
> A rustic, who draws a thorn from his foot...
> An old woman, who delouses the head of a little boy, with a donkey nearby...[1]

All three subjects resonate with iconographic implications beyond these transparently plain descriptions, especially if one is familiar with current interpretations of genre paintings by Miel's Netherlandish contemporaries who had remained north of the Alps. These usually hold that the shepherd playing the bagpipe had been a stock representation of ignorant folly and lust since the early sixteenth century.[2] The woman grooming her child is now read as a Dutch metaphor for the need to cleanse one's moral self; to quote a seventeenth-century aphorism: "Comb, comb again and again, and not only the hair but also what lies hidden inside." Thus the concept repre-

sented here would be not only the care for body and soul but also the responsibility of parenting.[3] The peasant lad removing a thorn from his foot holds the exact pose of the *Spinario*, a bronze statue which among "all the antiques visible in Rome, none was more copied" by Renaissance and Baroque artists, including the many Dutch and Flemish painters resident in Rome.[4] By the seventeenth century, this figure had received a standard interpretation as "a conscientious shepherd boy named Martius . . . who delivered a message to the Roman Senate before removing a thorn from his foot."[5]

Whether in fact the Miel etchings and in particular the bagpiper should bear burdens of moralizing implications is questionable, as Miel's career in Rome took an increasingly divergent path away from his Northern compatriots. Miel and his sometime Italian collaborator Michelangelo Cerquozzi[6] were among the most important followers of Pieter van Laer, the originator in Rome of an Italianate version of Northern lowlife painting which as a genre took the name *bambocciate* and which, according to contemporary commentators and modern analysts alike, seems to bear less of a moralizing import than that now attributed to art produced in the Netherlands in the seventeenth century.[7]

The term *bambocciate* apparently derived from van Laer's nickname "Bamboccio"—rag doll—which may have reflected his own physical deformity and, as well, referred back to his favored subject matter: peasants, soldiers, peddlers, and other ill-clothed representatives of the lower classes.[8] Miel had his own nickname—"Bieco," menacing. These names were not acquired casually; Dutch and Flemish artists working in Rome in the seventeenth century were initially excluded from the local artists' association, the Accademia di San Luca, with important consequences for patronage and taxation. In response they formed their own association, the Schildersbent; collectively they were Bentvueghels—birds of a feather—and individually they were dubbed with monikers, now often cryptic, as a part of the society's notoriously bacchic initiation rites.

Miel, who had arrived in Rome as early as 1633, took an increasingly formal role in the Schildersbent and then, beginning in the early 1640s when he joined the studio of Andrea Sacchi, gradually began an unprecedented transformation from a painter of *bambocciate*, which were scorned by Italian artists and critics (though not patrons), to a history painter working in that most prestigious of traditional Italian techniques, fresco. In 1648 he became the first among the Bamboccianti to join the Accademia di San Luca; his first fresco commission is recorded one year later.[9]

Miel's etched oeuvre reflects this shift: apart from the series of three genre figures, which are, it should be noted, specifically Italian in costume and accessories;[10] it also includes six holy virgins in various guises, one etching of God the Father, one of Venus and Cupid, and another of the Rape of Ganymede—all standard subjects of seventeenth-century Italian etchers but virtually nonexistent among other Bamboccianti. Of these etchings, three have been attributed by some cataloguers to the Italian etchers Biscaino and Cantarini because of their affiliation with purely Italian iconography and style.

It can only be assumed that *A Shepherd with a Bagpipe* and his two companion plates were etched relatively early in Miel's Roman career,[11] and that their commercial potential encouraged him to disseminate through etchings his successful practice of a kind of art that he would disclaim by his new allegiance to history painting. The graphic representation of the animals in the three genre etchings in particular are closely tied to prints by other members of the Schildersbent, notably Pieter van Laer's 1636 series of domestic animals (H.X.4.1–8) and Herman van Swanevelt's undated landscapes with animals (H.XXIX.97–99.110–116), which were published in later states in Paris but which may well antedate the artist's departure from Rome c. 1641. Certainly, the continued printing of Miel's plates into the eighteenth century testifies to their enduring popularity.

Our bagpiper in particular would have remained a commercially attractive image because of the unprecedented popularity of the instrument itself, which in the seventeenth and early eighteenth century throughout Europe became, in an adapted form called the musette, the precious musical toy of wealthier classes who sought to ape rustic pleasures. Playing the musette was a musical equivalent of composing pastoral poetry for the sophisticated amateur, even including the king of France. Whenever this vogue is cited today, it is visually epitomized by the reproduction of portraits of François Langlois that make "the connection between the musette and the pastorale . . . absolutely clear, since Langlois is dressed up as the shepherd Celadon . . . His musette is actually a *surdelina*, an Italian version of the instrument."[12] François Langlois, called Ciartres, a Parisian print publisher, was the first husband of the wife of Pierre Mariette II. A reproductive engraving of his portrait as a shepherd playing the bagpipe was published by Mariette, and its image must have been a constant presence in the household of the compiler of the Spencer Albums, who chose to include in them this more humble shepherd with his pipes by Miel.

MBC

1. Rossi 1677, p. 55: "Un Pastore sedente, che suona la piua, con alcune capre: inventione, & intaglio all'acqua forte di *Gio. Miele* . . . Un Rustico, che su caresa una spina dal piede . . . Una Vecchia, che pulisce la testa di un fanciullo in sero, con un asino appresso . . ." The prints continue to appear in later editions of Rossi's stock list.

2. For early precedents, see engravings by Lucas van Leyden, *The Beggars* (B.VII.423.159), identified by Lawrence Silver as an illustration for Sebastian Brant's *Ship of Fools* (see Ellen S. Jacobowitz and Stephanie Loeb Stepanek, *The Prints of Lucas van Leyden & His Contemporaries* [Washington: National Gallery of Art, 1983], p. 206), and Jacopo de' Barbari, *Two Fauns, One Drinking from a Wineskin, the Other Playing the Bagpipes* (B.VII.522.14). A pair of roundels by Joachim Uytewael (Fogg Art Museum, loan of Vermeer Associates, 3, 4.1985) of a bagpipe-playing shepherd and his coy shepherdess make the typical lusty seventeenth-century representation explicit.

3. Jacob Cats, quoted in Philadelphia 1984, pp. 143, 158, which reproduce and discuss paintings on this theme by Gerard Terborch and Quirijn van Brekelenkam.

4. Bober and Rubinstein 1987, p. 235.

5. Bober and Rubinstein 1987, p. 236.

6. Most notably in the second volume of *De Bello Belgico* (1647) by Famiano Strada on the Spanish campaign in Flanders, for which Miel etched illustrations after drawings by Cerquozzi and others (H.XIV.36.16–18).

7. See the thoughtful discussion of these issues in Briganti et al. 1983, Introduction. On p. 102 the seventeenth-century Italian writer Baldinucci is quoted on Miel: "He had . . . a talent that we can almost say was uniquely his, and this was to depict from life brigades of slovenly idlers, urchins, beggars, and others absolutely just as they look, with appropriate physiognomies, gestures, ways of dressing, and implements, along with their rest-takings and revels in the countryside."

8. Kren 1978, pp. 50–51, discusses van Laer's painting of *Resting Shepherds* (1636), which incorporates a quotation of the *Spinario*, in terms of the artist looking "beyond his circle of Dutch friends in Rome to the classical aspects of the local tradition."

9. On Miel's career in Italy and his critical reception, see Kren 1978; Briganti et al. 1983, pp. 13, 110; Philadelphia 1984, pp. 254–55.

10. The bagpipe is an accurate rendering of the South Italian *zampogna a paro*. See Febo Guzzi and Roberto Leydi, *Le Zampogne in Italia* (Milan: Ricordi, 1985), p. 225. Note that this crude bagpipe is made from the whole skin of a goat-sized animal, with the legs tied off and the pipes inserted into other orifices. One wonders whether Miel intended the sly humor implied by the presence beside the bagpiper of living goats, whose fate is presaged in his instrument.

11. The first documented existence of the plates is in Giovanni Giacomo de Rossi's 1677 index. However, Francesca Consagra (letter of 1 August 1990) has kindly informed me that the 1653 manuscript inventory of the shop of Giovanni de Rossi, which was acquired by his brother Giovanni Giacomo at that date, includes "Quatro pezzi di rame, quarti fogli de Bambocci," a description that corresponds to the three plates of this series and a fourth by Miel of a shepherd milking his sheep (H.XIV.33.10) also owned by de Rossi in 1677.

12. Leppert 1978, pp. 36, 71, pl. 32; Winternitz 1967, pl. 27b. Langlois was painted by Antony van Dyck and Claude Vignon. A particularly lush color reproduction of the original Vignon portrait (Anonymous Loan to the Wellesley College Museum) is in Rosenberg 1982, p. 187. An old copy which for centuries was thought to be the original has been at Althorp at least since the early eighteenth century, descending to the Earls Spencer through the Sunderland collection (Garlick 1976, p. 87, no. 673; Rosenberg 1982, pp. 332–33, no. 113).

JAN BOTH

Utrecht c. 1618 – 1652 Utrecht

39a *Sight*, c. 1641–1643, from the series *The Five Senses* after Andries Both

etching

225 x 176 mm

inscribed in the plate, upper left of design area: *t'GESICHT*; lower left of design area: *ABoth f*; superimposed over signature: *1*; lower margin: *Anderies.Both.Inventor. Ian slodder met syn mars. Coopman van Cramer en / Veylt besje klonter pels een Cristal ne Bril / Doch Slodder. en Vrou Slomps. en kunnen niet bed en / Wat baet de Bril indien men niet toe sien en wil / Ian.Both.Fecit. / Fratres.*[1]

B.V.211.11, TIB7.17.11, H.III.162.11 ii/iv

Gift of Melvin R. Seiden, s5.52.1

39b *Touch*, c. 1641–1643, from the series *The Five Senses* after Andries Both

etching

225 x 176 mm

inscribed in the plate, upper right of design area: *t'GEVOEL*; lower right of design area: *5*; lower margin: *Both.Inven. Wat drommel doeje met dit Yser in mÿn tanden / Hou Miester Ieurian, hou op je. doet me sier. / Help Iutje lieue wÿf, och Fop. ick wringh mÿn handen / Iut Iutick swym. loop heen hael Doctor Lubbert hier. / Both.Fecit.*[2]

B.V.213.15, TIB7.21.15, H.III.162.15 ii/iv

Gift of Melvin R. Seiden, s5.53.2

All five plates in the series—*Sight, Hearing, Smell, Taste, and Touch*—purport to be by Jan Both after compositions by his older brother Andries. The latter traveled from their birthplace in Utrecht, where he had studied painting with Abraham Bloemaert, through France to Italy; he was living in Rome by 1635. His younger brother joined him by 1638 at the latest, when he was admitted to the Roman painters' association.[3] Commentators from Joachim von Sandrart in 1675 to the present have discussed the collaboration of the two brothers in paintings, with Italianate landscapes by Jan populated by genre figures by Andries.

Ten etchings are attributed to Andries himself (TIB7.22–28.1–10). Given the dates of his mature career, they were probably executed in Italy, and five are Catholic in their subjects, being representations of saints, anchorites, and mendicants, with rosaries and crucifixes on prominent display. Among the others are several genre scenes, with one, *Drunkards* (TIB7.28.10), being close in composition to those of *The Five Senses*. It too features a group of peasants backed at one side by a blocky architectural element fringed with foliage. The leaves offer a brief transition to a vista that opens into the distance at the other side of the main figure cluster.

Sight is distinctly different from the other four plates in the series etched by Jan Both. Not only does it actually bear Andries's signature in the design area, it also reveals a different system of biting: the figures and foreground shading are homogeneously related to hatchings that describe the masonry which forms the backdrop. In the other four plates, including *Touch* on exhibition here, architecture is etched in a much more delicate tracery of lines, apparently the result of a separate biting, so that the figures form a frieze detached from the structural elements.

This tempts one to attribute *Sight*, at least in an unknown preliminary state, to Andries, with his brother picking up the plate after Andries's unexpected death as the two were traveling through Venice toward the Netherlands. Back in Utrecht, Jan would have coordinated the composition with an additional four etchings developed from Andries's designs. Against this hypothesis stands the figure style seen in Andries's own ten etchings, where the personages—not incidentally, all adults—are more elongated than those seen in *The Five Senses*.[4] Also, in all of Andries's genre etchings where figures are seen full length, at least one is barefoot, suggestive of a warm Italian locale; yet every character in *The Five Senses* is by contrast heavily shod, usually in Dutch wooden shoes. Finally, although the signature form in *Sight* is exactly that of Andries's own etchings, in none of the latter did he feel obliged to add "f."—*fecit*, made it. Yet in *Sight*, on the same plate we read "ABoth f." and "Ian.Both. Fecit." Perhaps we should indeed take these signatures at face value.

The Both brothers have here represented a favorite subject of the seventeenth-century Netherlands,[5] where scientists and artists were revolutionizing the design, manufacture, and uses of optical devices. Dutch moralists, including those who painted and etched, were quick to point out the irony of putting the new tools of extended vision before the eyes of those such as Bessie Clod Fur who were too ignorant to use them. From the representation of folly and potential deceptiveness of sight it was an easy extension to mock the other four senses as barriers to intellectual understanding or aesthetic pleasure. In Both's *Hearing*, Jochum Yawner and a friend bellow a duet about "marvelous things," apparently communicating fabulous news to the unlettered. In *Smell*, a woman wipes her baby's stinking bottom while two boys take turns defecating into a pot which the legend below locates "by the hearth or at the table." In *Taste* a crowd gathers around a woman cooking pancakes; that these cakes, commonly available from outdoor vendors, were not regarded as treats by any but the lowest classes is suggested by the contemporary saying, "When rich people are sick or poor folk cook pancakes, they can be smelled from afar."[6]

Touch emphasizes the quackery of medical and dental care available to the poor, not only by the legend (the Doctor Lubbert sought by our distraught patient bore a stock name "for characters of uncommon stupidity" in contemporary Dutch literature[7]) but also by the figure of the pilgrim at the left, who was customarily considered a fraud in pious disguise, and the pretentious certificate and vials of medicine hanging on the wall behind the scene. This print together with

t'GESICHT

Anderies. Both. Inventor.

Ian slodder met syn mars. Coopman van Cramerÿen Ian. Both. Fecit.
Veylt besje klonter pels een Cristalÿne Bril. Fratres.
Doch Slodder. en Vrou Slomps. en kunnen niet bedÿen
Wat baet de Bril indien men niet toe sien en wil   la Tour Torner

t' GEVOEL

Both. Inven.

Wat drommel doeje met dit Iser in mijn tanden
Hou Miester Ieurian, hou op je doet me fier.
Help Iutje lieue wijf, och Fop. ick wringh mijn handen
Iut Iutick fwym. loop heen hael Doctor Lubbert hier.

Both. Fecit.

Latoudjornen

the other four in the series was copied several times in mezzotint; in a version by Pieter Schenk (H.xxv.83.387) in which Both's figures are closely imitated, the vials are replaced by a poster of a man defecating exceptionally long turds. Beside it sits an owl, a symbol of filth and ignorance in Dutch seventeenth-century art, which is appropriately posed by Both on the hovel wall in *Smell*.

That children figure prominently in these gross versions of the senses, themes which had been elegantly celebrated in earlier Netherlandish prints such as those by Saenredam after Goltzius and Cort after Floris,[8] is not unexpected in mid-seventeenth-century Dutch art. It reflects a growing general preoccupation in contemporary culture with the role of children and the obligations of adults toward them, which has been broadly interpreted by Simon Schama. He has founded his extended analyses on paintings and prints as well as literature:

> That many of these pictures come loaded with messages about the follies of the world … does not alter in the least the important fact that the *stock* of images of childhood from which such morals could be represented had changed in the most dramatic way. So the replacement of the putto by the little perisher is a moment of high significance not just in the history of art but in that of Western culture's view of its children.[9]

None of Jan Both's later etchings (which were of his own invention) represents children, crudities, or morals. They portray the benign Italianizing landscapes which he painted and which were collected throughout seventeenth-century Europe. With such a picture he became the only Dutch artist represented in the collection of Cardinal Mazarin, a gift from the king.[10] The Mariette firm acquired his ten plates of landscape etchings; well-printed impressions bearing its publication line complete the suite of fifteen Both etchings in the Spencer Albums.

MBC

1. "SIGHT / John Slop the peddler with his pack / Sells Bessie Clod Fur a pair of crystal glasses. / But neither Slop nor Mrs. Slut can help her: / What use are glasses, if one doesn't want to see?" I am indebted to Walter Simons for this and the following translation. All five prints in the series, including these two, bear ink inscriptions at the lower edge that are apparently titles in French; in each case the complete spelling is illegible.

2. "TOUCH / What the hell are you doing with that iron in my teeth? / Stop, Master Jordan, stop, it hurts me so! / Help me, Jut, my dear wife— Oh Fop, I wring my hands. / Jut, Jut, I am fainting— run and bring Doctor Lubbert here!"

3. A firm chronology for both Boths is difficult to establish as documentary evidence conflicts. For biographical information pertaining to the dating of these prints, see Waddingham 1964, pp. 13–18, 27; Burke 1976, p. 288; Sutton 1987, p. 276.

4. Burke 1976, p. 86, considers this elongation to be characteristic of figures in Andries's paintings as compared to those by Jan, especially in work of Andries's last years.

5. Including Andries himself in 1631: *Peasant Scene*, a panel painting bearing this date, in the F. C. Bûtot Coll., Amsterdam, is described by Waddington 1964, p. 39, n. 11, as being virtually identical to *Sight* in the personages represented.

6. Philadelphia 1984, p. 163, where the pancake seller is discussed in relation to a painting by Adriaen Brouwer.

7. Kren 1978, p. 193.

8. Their versions of *Touch* are reproduced in Brown 1984, p. 38. See this publication, pp. 67–70, 99, for many other seventeenth-century Dutch representations of crude quack-dentists, or *kiezentrekkers*. Whether all of these are symbolic of the sense of touch is moot.

9. Schama 1987, p. 484.

10. Burke 1976, p. 4.

ADRIAEN VAN OSTADE

Haarlem 1610 – 1685 Haarlem

40   *The Dance beneath the Trellis,* c. 1647–1652

etching

128 x 175 mm

inscribed in the plate, lower right: *Av Ostade*

B.I.379.47; H.XV.62.47; Godefroy 47 iii/vii

Gift of Melvin R. Seiden, s5.20.8

Adriaen van Ostade was primarily a painter and etcher of peasant genre scenes, producing several hundred paintings and about fifty etchings. Spencer Album 5 contains impressions of all but one of his etchings,[1] in addition to several reproductive prints after his paintings. Most are of good quality, although generally not in very early states. The completeness of the collection allows the viewer to gain a sense of the range of Ostade's achievement as a printmaker, while a consideration of the selection and arrangement of the impressions reveals the aims of this particular eighteenth-century collection. The reproductive prints after Ostade (see Cat. 41), as well as two anonymous prints in his style and a single print by one of his pupils (see Cat. 44a), are not segregated from Ostade's etchings, but rather are interspersed throughout the sixteen folios.

Ostade spent virtually his entire career in his native Haarlem, which in the first half of the seventeenth century was perhaps the most significant center of artistic activity in the Northern Netherlands and home to some of the leading figures of the golden age of Dutch art, such as Hendrick Goltzius, Frans Hals, and Jacob van Ruisdael.[2] The reasons behind this explosion of artistic creativity in such a small city still recovering from the throes of war with Spain[3] are impossible to pinpoint, although one influence was certainly the arrival of Flemish emigré craftsmen and artists fleeing Spanish Catholic domination in the Southern Netherlands. During this period Haarlem's primary industries were brewing and the bleaching and weaving of linen, an activity preserved in Ruisdael's majestic landscapes of the bleaching fields outside the city. Ostade was the son of a weaver.

The tradition of representing peasant and lowlife scenes began well before the seventeenth century, notably in the influential work of the sixteenth-century Flemish artist Pieter Brueghel the Elder; but these kinds of subjects were taken to new levels of achievement in the seventeenth century, beginning with the work of Adriaen Brouwer, a Flemish artist active in Haarlem and Amsterdam c. 1625/26–1631/32.[4] Houbraken, in his *De Groote Schouburgh der Nederlantsche Konstschilders en Schilderessen* of 1718–1722, claimed that both Brouwer and Ostade were pupils of Hals, the great Haarlem portraitist and painter of genre figures, although this is undocumented. Nevertheless, Ostade surely came in contact with Brouwer's work, as evidenced by stylistic affini-

ties, as well as the fact that Ostade was completing his training at the same time that Brouwer was active in Haarlem. Brouwer's innovation has been characterized as lying in "the brutal power of [his] peasants. Any gloss of rustic charm or cute bumptiousness is eliminated, leaving only the unapologetic fact of the underclass and its appetites and passions."[5] Ostade never achieves the harsh reality found in Brouwer's work, but his peasants have a vitality all their own.

The subject of this particular print, an exterior scene of peasants dancing outside of an inn, has a lengthy tradition in Netherlandish art, tracing itself back to representations of kermises, fairs on the occasion of religious holidays in which social hierarchies and behavioral restrictions were broken down for a sanctioned period. By the mid–1640s, Ostade's treatment of his lower–class subjects had shifted from scenes of violence and debauchery clearly inspired by Brouwer to scenes characterized by an almost middle-class decorum,[6] and this aspect of Ostade's development is clearly present in this mature etching, which has been dated to 1647–1652.[7]

The focus of the composition is the dance taking place in front of the large thatched-roof cottage that occupies the left half of the scene. The smaller cottages strung out along the road extending back into the distance, as well as the small groups of working figures that can be picked out along the road, provide further visual interest and lead our eyes to the pale outlines of a church steeple. The delicate sketchiness of the background scenes in contrast to the richness of the foreground etching creates an extremely convincing atmospheric effect.

The central group of figures is arranged with an eye toward clarity and visual unity. Only one couple dances, not clasped together, but separating and swinging out towards the spectators, who are fairly static, the adults seated on logs and casks and the children standing. The musician, providing accompaniment with pipe and drum, rises above the semicircle, creating a balancing vertical. References to the less civilized activities that usually accompanied these celebrations are either indirect or hidden in shadow, and the exaggerated humorous and moralizing potential of these details found in more conventional representations of the subject is subdued. Overturned jugs and casks and the man seated to the left who turns away from the group and hunches over as if in a stupor are the only clear allusions to the consumption of alcohol, while a pig and a defecating man, both seen from behind along the right edge of the composition, are kept in fairly heavily hatched shadow. The viewer notices them only after observing the central, more decorous activity.

Facial features are not individualized, and with the exception of the few figures who perform the significant physical actions, the majority combine to create masses within the composition. The visual conventions of the subject matter, i.e., the standing musician, the dancing couple, the overturned basins, casks and jugs, as well as the animals and defecating figure, are all harmonized into a unified composition. Ostade's primary interest seems to be the creation of a convincing recession into space and a sense of the light and atmosphere surrounding the figures, rather than particular activities.[8]

This is surely one of Ostade's finest, most sophisticated etched compositions, and the quality of this impression allows the viewer to appreciate his masterful handling of the technique. The shift from the rich description of texture and form in the foreground (observe the treatment of the foliage of the trees and on the trellis contrasted with the thatched roof) to the delicate suggestiveness of the far distance is wonderfully evocative. Mariette's assertion that Ostade sought to imitate the etching style of Rembrandt is well supported by the quality of a work such as this.[9]

The print is a fine impression of the third state and is thus, comparatively, one of the earliest states of the Ostade prints contained in the album. Many represent the last state prior to that of the edition of Ostade prints issued by Bernard Picart, a Parisian publisher and printmaker in his own right who purchased Ostade's etched plates in 1710. After carefully reworking only those which had worn, he published the set as a collected edition, grouped by subject or format. The quality of the Picart edition was high and frequently the portfolios were cut apart and sold as single prints, passing as impressions of high quality to amateur collectors.[10] In fact, interspersed throughout the Spencer Ostades are several impressions in Picart states.[11]

In the case of *The Dance beneath the Trellis*, Godefroy identifies the sixth state as the Picart edition state, although he noted that it was missing from the one intact printing he had examined.[12] In Spencer Album 5, *The Dance beneath the Trellis* is mounted on folio 20 as the centerpiece of the third and lowest row of prints.[13] There is no apparent thematic explanation for the selection or arrangement of images mounted on this folio, or on any of the others in fact; rather, the arrangement seems intended to create a pleasing visual pattern. The three largest prints occupy the center position in each of the three rows, with two horizontal compositions, *The Anglers* and *The Dance beneath the Trellis*, placed at the top and bottom respectively, framing the vertical *Pater Familias*. The six smaller prints are either vertical or square and are again paired symmetrically on either side of the center column. Nor is there a consistent chronological system; the prints found on this one folio range in date from the 1630s to the 1680s. One intriguing note: the three prints of standing men (G.20, 21, 22), though wide-ranging in date, also appear on the same page in the Picart edition of Ostade's prints. Conversely, the two prints that appear in their Picart states mounted on this folio (G.4, G.25) did not appear together or with any of the other prints on the folio in the Picart edition.

It is also of interest to compare these aspects of the Spencer Ostade folios to those in Prince Eugene of Savoy's print collection now at the Albertina.[14] The character of the folios of this collection, whose catalogue was completed by Pierre-Jean Mariette in 1717–1719, reflects a very different, more scholarly aim. The Ostade prints are mounted on thirty-one folios of volume 70 and also include all but one of Ostade's original prints in addition to several apocryphal prints and copies after originals. The most significant difference of this collection from the Spencer collection is that it brings together impressions of different states of many of the prints. The arrangement of the folios themselves reflects this more scholarly interest, mounting the multiple impressions together in simple, symmetric patterns. In contrast to the more decorative arrangement of the Spencer folios, the larger compositions such as the *Dance beneath the Trellis* are mounted individually, following folios mounted with smaller prints, while the apocryphal prints and copies are mounted together on four folios at the end of the entire Ostade section.

Of additional interest is the fact that many of the pairings that are found in the Picart edition are also found in the Albertina volume, although in earlier states. Since there is no apparent iconographic or chronological sequence determining the arrangement, it presents us with a tantalizing link between Picart and the Mariettes. Apparently there was a warm relationship between them, as evidenced by a letter from Pierre-Jean to Jean Mariette from Amsterdam, 8 September 1717: "So far I have seen only Mr. Picart who received me very well indeed, & Mr. Pool . . . both of them have instructed me to make their compliments to you."[15] In 1717 Picart had already published his edition of Ostade, while neither the Spencer Albums nor Prince Eugene's albums had yet been completed. It is interesting to note as well that the "Mr. Pool" referred to is surely Matthys Pool, a printmaker resident in Amsterdam who had earlier lived for many years in Paris. Even before Pierre-Jean Mariette's known involvement with producing facsimile prints after drawings, Pool had etched a series after twelve Rembrandt drawings. One of these drawings which survives bears the signature of Claude Augustin Mariette.[16]

KHN

198

1. Missing from the album is *Bust of a Laughing Peasant* (Godefroy 1 [hereafter abbreviated as G.]); based on the arrangement of the folios, it was never included. In addition, two prints, *The Empty Jug* (G.15) and *The Hunchbacked Fiddler* (G.44), mounted on folio 12, also appear as duplicate impressions mounted on folio 16.

2. See Hofrichter 1983.

3. In 1622 the population was approximately forty thousand, double what it had been in 1572 during the Spanish Siege of the city (J. J. Temminck, "Haarlem: Its Social/Political History," pp. 17–18, in Hofrichter 1983).

4. See Philadelphia 1984, pp. xxxiv–xxxv.

5. Philadelphia 1984, p. xxxv.

6. Philadelphia 1984, p. 284.

7. While Godefroy tentatively dated it to 1652, both Schnackenburg and Ackley have placed it slightly earlier (Schnackenburg to 1647–1652 and Ackley to 1648–1652) on the basis of preliminary drawings and the tonal qualities of the image (Ackley 1981, p. 168). There is a pen and wash preparatory drawing in reverse in the Lugt collection of the Institut Néerlandais, Paris (inv. no. 3523). Evidence supporting the earlier dating surfaced with the appearance of an impression with the watermark "Ecu au Boeuf couronné" (Godefroy 7), an extremely rare watermark which appears on excellent impressions of the first states of Ostade's etchings from around 1645; it is probably the oldest of the identified watermarks in his printed work. There is a known third state of this print with this watermark as well. See C. G. Boerner, Inc., *Von Altdorfer bis Tiepolo: Druckgraphik aus Drei Jahrhunderten* (June 25, 1990), no. 34.

8. Ackley 1981, p. 168.

9. Mariette 1851–1860, vol. 4, p. 65: "... c'estoit un fort mauvais dessinateur et un génie peu élevé, mais il avoit beaucoup d'intelligence de clair obscur et un très-beau pinceau. Il a gravé luy-même à l'eau forte plusieurs pieces de son invention . . . il semble qu'il ait eu en veue en les gravant d'imiter la manière de graver de Rembrandt."

10. Godefroy, p. 20.

11. Included in the Picart state are *Man Leaning on Doorway* (G.9), *The Cobbler* (G.27), *The Smoker* (G.6), *Slaughtering the Pig* (G.41), *The Smoker* (G.5), *Bust of a Laughing Peasant* (G.4), *Woman Winding upon a Reel* (G.25), *The Barn* (G.23), *The Schoolmaster* (G.17), and *Bust of a Woman* (G.2).

12. Godefroy, p. 151.

13. Mounted on the same page, reading from left to right and top to bottom, are the *Bust of a Laughing Peasant* (G.4), *The Anglers* (G.26), *Man with a Crooked Back* (G.20), *Man with His Hand in his Cloak* (G.22), *The Pater Familias* (G.33), *Man with His Hands behind His Back* (G.21), *The Knife Grinder* (G.36), and *Woman Winding upon a Reel* (G.25).

14. My warm thanks to the staff at the Albertina for providing me with information about the contents and arrangement of the Ostade folios.

15. MLMS BS/B9/L2: "Je n'y ay encor vu que Mr. Picart qui m'a fort bien recu, & Mr. Pool . . . l'un & l'autre m'ont charge de vous faire leurs compliments."

16. Information on Matthys Pool was kindly provided by William W. Robinson.

JAN DE VISSCHER

Haarlem or Amsterdam 1636 – after 1692

41 *Dance outside an Inn*, after Ostade

etching

261 x 362 mm

watermark: Strasbourg Lily, similar to Heawood 1721a (Schieland, 1614)

inscribed in plate, lower margin: *Nu is't de reghte tydt om Pleuntjen koeck te kopen, / Dan siet die bolle Meyt so soet als Bakke-vis. / Wie sou om sulk een vreught geen ses myl komen lopen? / 'Tis al te sleghten Dorp daer 't noyt geen kermis is. Joan de Visscher fecit. Ad. van Ostade pinxit. Nicolaus Visscher excudit.*

Dutuit vi.530 (3) ii/ii

Gift of Melvin R. Seiden, s5.24.2

Jan de Visscher, younger brother of Cornelis and Lambert de Visscher, was a painter and print-maker, reproducing in prints paintings by Brouwer, Ostade, and others.[1] Interspersed among the Ostade etchings in Spencer Album 5 are several reproductive prints after Ostade's paintings: four by Johannes Suyderhoef and five by Visscher. While Suyderhoef's reproductive engravings (all of peasants in interiors) are mounted together with Ostade's etchings, the five Visschers (of both interior and exterior subjects) are mounted together on three folios, in between folios of Ostades.

The subject matter and composition of this etching are very similar to Ostade's *Dance beneath the Trellis* (Cat. 40). We again see a semicircular arrangement of figures around a dancing couple. The figures' physiognomy appears coarse but not grotesque, and there are no figures taking part in any obviously indecorous activity. Missing is the effect of light and atmosphere Ostade achieved through his sophisticated use of the possibilities of the etched line as well as the white of the paper, and the visual characteristics of Visscher's print certainly reflect its status as a reproductive print after an as yet unidentified painting. The lines throughout the print are basically regular and uniform in thickness, preventing the kinds of tonal gradations or sense of atmosphere found in Ostade's etching. Whereas Ostade in his etchings tends to leave his sky empty, here it is filled with clouds and the smoke from the chimney, conveyed by an overall pattern of etched lines. Yet even though the general effect is somewhat more mechanical, the technique is highly skilled, and this is a particularly fresh impression. The plate was deeply bitten and cleanly wiped with the exception of the small pennants in the center of the composition. Here a residue of ink remains to the left of the etched lines; although probably unintentional, it creates a very successful effect of rich shadow.

In addition to the technical differences between the two prints, it is also possible to discern a slightly different tone or emphasis in the treatment of the subject. In the Visscher, the main group of figures is contained within the space created by the inn on the left and the solid, shadowed mass of foliage to the right. There is no great recession into the far distance, nor are there secondary figures to distract the viewer's attention. Noticeably absent is the ever-present church steeple on the horizon. Also of interest is the greater attention paid to still-life details. Most prominent are the dead stump and overturned wagon wheel in the lower right corner; this image of death and decay conventionally inspires thoughts on the transience of life. The scattered pipes on the ground beneath the dancers' feet indicate at least one source for their happy mood, in addition to possibly reiterating the vanitas message as well as the social upheaval of the kermis.[2] Also noticeable are the doves flying into the dovecote at the upper left of center of the composition, conventionally a reference to love and sexual relationships. In this context the inscription

200

Nu is 't de reghte trdt om Pleuntjen koeck te kopen,
Wie sou om sulk een vreught geen ses myl komen lopen?
Dan siet die bolle Mert so soet als Backke-vis.
'T is al te sleghten Dorp daer 't noyt geen kermis is.

Joan de Visscher fecit. Ad. van Ostade pinxit. Nicolaw Visscher excudit.

that accompanies the print and seems to refer to the older woman, the partner in the central dancing couple, reinforces some of these references:

> Now it's high time for "Pleuntjen" to buy a cake,
> Then that plump maid will look as sweet as a frying-fish.
> Who wouldn't walk six miles to come see such a delight?
> It's a wretched village which never has a kermis.[3]

"Pleuntjen" would be the nickname for the woman, while the description of her appearance "as sweet as a frying-fish" is a colloquial reference to a teenage girl. The tone is clearly satirical, ridiculing this older woman for her girlish sexual urges. Nevertheless, the potentially critical tone of the inscription is not strongly emphasized visually in that the figures themselves are not made obviously ridiculous. The inscription was probably attached to the design after the fact, since inscriptions were not generally part of a painting, and this may explain its somewhat ambivalent relationship to the image.

Visscher reproduced a number of Ostade's paintings in etchings with attached inscriptions,

201

which reveal a number of different contemporary attitudes towards peasants and their lifestyle.[4] Prints like this one rely upon a set of stock associations regarding peasants and their social behavior, particularly in the kermis setting with its accompanying freedom from social taboos. In fact, this scene does not explicitly represent a kermis, but rather a group of peasants entertaining themselves.

Based upon the regularity and order of the composition as well as the attention paid to each individual figure, the painting this print reproduces belongs to Ostade's work after 1645. In his mature work, we see the old themes and motifs continuing to appear, but the peasants' activities are no longer perceived as potentially evil; instead, peasants eat, drink, and dance, enjoying their pleasures without ever crossing over into boorishness.[5] In fact, contained within the humorous tone of many of the pictures and the inscriptions that accompany them is an implicit assumption of basic goodness in the peasant, in some cases even a kind of idealization of the simplicity of their lives and values. In any case, Ostade does not explicitly satirize or condemn his peasants' conduct, presenting them as individuals endowed with a kind of rustic dignity.[6] These qualities are certainly also to be found in the original prints by Ostade included in the exhibition.

KHN

1. Wessely.
2. See Gaskell 1987 and Cat. 43 and 44a–b.
3. Translation by Rodney Nevitt.

4. See Schnackenburg 1981, particularly pp. 55–59.
5. Schnackenburg 1981, p. 58.
6. Philadelphia 1984, p. 284.

MATTHIEU PLATTE-MONTAGNE
Antwerp c. 1608 – 1660 Paris

42 *The Village in a Wood*, c. 1650

etching

215 x 315 mm

watermark: illegible design within an oval

inscribed in plate, lower margin, at left: *M [athieu burnished out] Montagne scul.*; at right: *Morin ex. Cum Pri. Re.*

R.-D.V.123.26 i/ii, H.XVII.132.26 i/ii

Lessing J. Rosenwald Fund, by exchange, s5.107.2

Although Spencer Album 5 contains only five of the twenty-eight etchings attributed to Platte-Montagne by Hollstein,[1] we have chosen to include as many as three in this exhibition because they are such exceptionally beautiful impressions and because the artist is so little known. There

is no doubt that his prints were very much to the taste of early eighteenth-century French connoisseurs and of Pierre-Jean Mariette in particular, who comments sympathetically on Platte-Montagne's technique and provides a brief description of his career and associations:[2]

> . . . Mathieu Van Plattenberg of Antwerp, . . . upon settling in France, changed his name to Platte-Montagne, having established his reputation there. He painted landscape very well, and especially seascapes. In imitation of Morin, his brother-in-law, he also took up etching. Many of his landscapes will be found in this collection, among them in particular one after Fouquière of winter [see Cat. 45b] . . . . It was also the example of Morin which determined J. Alix . . . to make etchings . . . . All of the works of these various masters are gathered together [in the section on Philippe de Champaigne because] they lose their value completely when separated one from another.[3]
>
> [Platte-Montagne] married a sister of Jean Morin [see Cat. 36] . . . . The two brothers-in-law, finding they shared many of the same inclinations and even the same serious-mindedness, became very close. They chose to live together, and would share their time together in painting and printmaking.[4]

And, indeed, it is in the Spencer Album otherwise devoted to Dutch and Flemish prints that we find etchings by Morin, who was born and trained in France. Morin's teacher was Philippe de Champaigne, himself a Flemish emigré; and Morin's work and the work of Platte-Montagne (all of which was published by Morin) serve to introduce the whole subject of Flemish influence, even dominance, in French landscape painting up to the period in the second half of the seventeenth century when the work of Poussin and Claude began to have a countervalent effect. As Mariette correctly insisted within his entry on Champaigne, the Flemish-associated landscapists were all of a piece.

These sentiments are implicit also in the consideration of landscape as a genre of painting by the French late-seventeenth-century theoretician Roger de Piles. De Piles divided landscape into the heroic and the pastoral, or rural. Poussin was preeminent as the painter of heroic landscape; the pastoral, or rural, was embodied at the highest level in the works of Rubens, but de Piles was also appreciative of the work of Fouquières, who so often provided a model for Platte-Montagne:

> The Rural style is a representation of countries (*campagnes*) rather abandoned to the caprice of nature than cultivated. We there see nature simple, without ornament and without artifice; but with all those graces with which she adorns herself much more when left to herself than when constrained by art. In this style, situations bear all sorts of varieties. Sometimes they are very extensive and open, to contain the flocks of the shepherds; at others, very wild, for the retreat of solitary persons and a cover for wild beasts.[5]

This description fits exactly the prints by Platte-Montagne, especially this one, comprising as it does every variety of terrain and degree of cultivation (or wilderness). Its composition is close to paintings of the same subject by other Netherlandish artists, by Jacques d'Artois (with figures by Daniel Teniers the Younger)[6] or Jan Griffier,[7] which also feature serene vistas into a larger world.

It is, in fact, the expansiveness of the Platte-Montagne etching accentuated by the high horizon, unexpected in a woodlands subject, that betrays its ancestry in the earlier Flemish "Weltlandschaft" tradition initiated by Joachim Patinir and perfected by Pieter Brueghel the Elder. The most telling comparison among earlier Northern landscapes is with the first, and greatest, German landscape etching, *The Cannon* by Albrecht Dürer (Hollstein VII.87.96), dated 1518. Platte-Montagne has reversed Dürer's basic composition and eliminated the prominent foreground subject, but otherwise the elements and even some details are the same. Particularly effective in both prints are the repoussoir tree, the habitations embedded within wooded terrain, the expression of space in open fields by means of trees complete with tiny trunks and cast shadows, and, dominating the distance, a mountain massif bright against a shaded sky.

Platte-Montagne's luminous rendition in black and white of such a sky, where sparse clouds catch the first (or last?) rays of a low sun, make one wonder about his paintings, especially the marines, which although praised by Mariette—"He painted landscape very well, and especially seascapes"—were criticized by Wurzbach as "heavy in tone and tending to be dark."[8]

Even beyond the influence of the Flemish landscape tradition was the huge role played in the larger seventeenth-century Paris print world by emigrés from the war-ravaged South Netherlands, with Gérard Edelinck, born in Antwerp in 1640, *graveur ordinaire* to Louis XIV and a knight of the Order of St. Michael, taking the lead.[9] As Préaud has noted in his discussion of this phenomenon, even once in Paris, the Flemings often married within their own community, thus retarding their acculturation in France.[10] Platte-Montagne's marriage to the sister of Jean Morin and his close working relationship with his brother-in-law are, rather, an indication of a pattern that was widespread throughout Europe but especially striking in France and the Lowlands, of marriages among families within a single trade. Often, as in the case of the wedding of the widow of François Langlois to Pierre Mariette II (see the Introduction and Cat. 38, 55a), this would result in the merging of assets (in this case engraving plates and presses) and the transmission of a business through the generations.

MBC

1. H.XVII.125–134.1–28. Hollstein listed the artist under Mathijs van Plattenburg, with the alternate names Van Platten and Platte-Montagne also given (H.XVII.125). Mariette noted that the artist changed his name twice after moving to France, so that it would be more easily pronounced, first to Matthieu Platte-Montagne and then to Matthieu Montagne. Robert-Dumesnil (R.-D.V.108) concluded that the artist's first name was not Matthieu but Michel, but his opinion has not prevailed.

2. See also Michiels 1874, pp. 298–301, for a somewhat breathless account of Platte-Montagne.

3. Mariette 1851–1860, vol. 1, pp. 352–53: "Mathieu Van Plattenberg d'Anvers, qui, en s'établissant en France, se fit appeler de Platte-Montagne, y avoit acquis de la réputation. Il peignoit parfaitement bien le paysage, et surtout des marines. A l'imitation de Morin, son beau-frère, il se mit aussi à graver. L'on trouvera de lui, dans ce recueil, plusieurs paysages, dont il y en a surtout un d'après Fouquière, représentant un hyver, qui est fait avec une merveilleuse intelligence. Ce fut aussi l'exemple de Morin qui détermina J. Alix . . . à graver . . . L'on a joint ensemble tous les ouvrages de ces différens maistres; ils auroient infiniment perdu de leur prix en les séparant l'un de l'autre."

4. Mariette 1851–1860, vol. 4, p. 186: "Il avoit épousé une soeur de Jean Morin. . . . Les deux beau-frères, se trouvent les mêmes inclinations et une même pente vers la sagesse, se lièrent étroitement. Ils ne voulurent avoit qu'une même habitation, et tous deux s'occupèrent à graver et à peindre en même temps." Presumably Mariette alludes to the particularly sober "Port-Royal" strain of Catholicism which allied many of the artists associated with Philippe de Champaigne. See the Introduction by Marc Fumaroli in Rosenberg 1982, pp. 12–14. Marolles commented upon Morin's pious attitude toward his work: "Jean Morin, acquitant son devoir à l'eau-forte, / A donne cent portraits, et des pieces encor / Sur des sujets divers, comme un pieux trésor. / Car il estoit dévot, et vesquit de la sorte" (Marolles 1855, p. 30). Morin was the teacher of Platte-Montagne's son Nicolas.

5. Quoted in Wintermute 1990, p. 15. See pp. 14–15 of this work for a discussion of the attitude of de Piles toward Dutch and Flemish landscape.

6. Reproduced in Davidson 1979, pl. 38.

7. Reproduced in Sutton 1987, pl. 122.

8. Wurzbach 1910, vol. 2, p. 333.

9. Linnig identified twenty-five Flemish engravers, publishers, print dealers, etc., in Paris from the end of the sixteenth until the end of the seventeenth centuries (Linnig 1911, pp. 36–37), and his list was greatly expanded and corrected by Weigert (Weigert 1969, pp. 445–56). A brief discussion of Platte-Montagne, including the indication that he began as a designer for embroideries and patterns, is found on p. 452 of the latter publication.

10. Préaud 1984, p. 81. Weigert 1969 goes into the question of marriages in great detail.

QUIRIN BOEL

Antwerp 1620 – 1668 Brussels

43 *The Smoker*, after David Teniers the Younger

etching

194 x 243 mm

watermark: illegible

inscribed in plate, lower left: *D Teniers inuet* [*excud* burnished but visible] *cum priuilegio.*; lower right: *Coryn Boel.f.*

inscribed, lower right, brown ink: *C. Augustin Mariette*

LEB.I.403.40, H.III.11.36 ii/ii

Gift of Melvin R. Seiden, S5.9.1

This is the only print in all of the nine Spencer Albums that bears the signature of Claude-Augustin Mariette (1652–after March 1701).[1] The younger half-brother of Pierre Mariette II, whose signature is found frequently throughout the albums, Claude-Augustin was also commercially involved with prints. In 1678 a settlement after a divorce forced divestment of his one-eighth interest in the family publishing house at the sign of *St. Jacques à l'Esperance*, and he seems to have been more active as a print dealer; presumably he signed this impression in that capacity.

The compiler of the Spencer Albums, whom we identify as Claude-Augustin's nephew Jean (together with the latter's son Pierre-Jean), shared his taste for reproductive prints after lowlife scenes by David Teniers the Younger (1610–1690). Spencer Album 5, entitled on the spine "OEUVRE DE TENIER OSTADE ET AUTRE FLAMAND," opens with a group of twenty-eight etchings by several artists after Teniers, dominated by twelve by Quirin Boel and including a complete set, with title page, of his *Het apenspel en de wereld* (*Monkeyshines in the World*, H.III.13.43–48), six plates in which monkeys ape human frivolity and dissipations, including pipe smoking.

The exclusive choice of lowlife subjects after Teniers is significant, for it implies a rejection of the print publication venture for which Teniers was best known and in which Boel was an important participant. Teniers—curator, court painter, and *ayuda de camera* to Archduke Leopold William of Austria, governor of the Southern Netherlands for King Philip IV of Spain—made reduced painted copies of Italian masterpieces in the archduke's collection as models for printmakers. The etched reproductions were published in 1658 as a collection, the *Theatrum Pictorum*, the first European initiative to reproduce a significant number of artworks (apart from portraits) within a conceptual framework, in this case not only that of a particular collection but also that of a specific regional school, for it excluded the many paintings in the archduke's famous cabinet that were not Italian.[2]

In the Spencer Albums, however, the Mariettes caused Italian painters to characterize them-

selves by presenting in orderly sequence the etched works of their own hands. Analogously, they presented Teniers not as a copyist but, in etchings after his works, as a leading painter in the Netherlandish lowlife art tradition. It should be noted that among all eighteenth-century biographers of Teniers, only Pierre-Jean gave the correct death date, indicating family expertise in the study of this artist.[3]

The Mariettes' appreciation of the lowlife genre is slyly suggested by the page placement within the Spencer Album of this print, *The Smoker* (which equally warrants the title *The Drinker*). Whoever arranged folio 9 took note of the man urinating against the wall in *The Smoker* and mounted directly below this etching Boel's rendition of Teniers's *The Urine Doctor*. In *The Urine Doctor*, even larger and more complex in composition and accessories than *The Smoker*, a man whose learned status is indicated by huge books open at a table before him is holding a flask of urine to the light. *The Urine Doctor* is one in a long line, stretching back to the sixteenth century, of Dutch and Flemish representations of *piskijkers*, "diagnosticians who claimed to be able to read ailments in the patient's urine."[4] More usually the urine doctor is discovering

207

the pregnancy of a swooning young woman, who must be unmarried judging by the distress of the old woman who is the customary witness. In the Boel print, however, the old woman, who has evidently brought the specimen to the doctor, is presumably the worried wife of some sick boor who had been drinking and smoking to excess: pasted up on the doctor's wall is a print of a toper raising a glass to his lips. The print's presence in a laboratory otherwise bare of art is explicable only as a gloss on the diagnostic drama.

Smoking was introduced to the Netherlands by seamen, and initially, at the beginning of the seventeenth century, local regulations classed it with alcohol.[5] There is no doubt that Teniers himself made the association: his *Smoker*, who has many brothers among his compositions, is joined by his several versions of *The Temptation of Saint Anthony* in which the holy hermit recoils from figures holding pipes and wine glasses.[6] Although tobacco gradually lost its evil reputation in the Netherlands through the seventeenth century,[7] its lowlife representation remained a cliché in later enthusiastic appreciation of Teniers and etchers like Quirin Boel who reproduced his work in prints.

MBC

1. For biographical information on Claude-Augustin Mariette see Préaud 1987, p. 228.

2. Filipczak 1987, p. 153; Davidson 1979, pp. 30, 66. The title page implies the purpose of the publication, to educate artists and connoisseurs about Italian art: "*Theatrum Pictorium*, David Teniers, Antwerp, Paintings of the most Serene Prince Leopold William, Archduke of Austria, and Joanne of Austria, Governors of Belgium for Philip IV of Spain, in which is exhibited delineated by my hands and carefully incised on copper, Pictures of original Italians which the most Serene Archduke himself has collected in his cabinet at Brussels. A very useful work of all the artistic paintings" (Balsiger 1970, pp. 592, n. 25.).

3. Davidson 1979, p. 1.

4. Brown 1984, p. 229; see also pp. 95–97 for reproductions of paintings by Hoogstraten, Steen, and Metsu, which show the doctor visiting a young and languid patient who is evidently being diagnosed as pregnant.

5. Gaskell 1987, p. 121. See also Cat. 44.

6. Davidson 1979, p. 38.

7. Gaskell 1987, p. 154, and Philadelphia 1984, p. 197, describe how this disapproving attitude was gradually modified; later representations of the subject often represent genteel smokers.

CORNELIS BEGA

Haarlem 1631/32 – 1664 Haarlem

ADRIAEN VAN OSTADE

Haarlem 1610 – 1685 Haarlem

44a   *The Group at the Fireplace*

> etching
>
> 78 x 59 mm
>
> H.I.217.23 i/ii
>
> Gift of Melvin R. Seiden, s5.17.1

44b   *The Smoker and the Drinker,*
       c. 1675–1680

> etching
>
> 79 x 63 mm
>
> inscribed in the plate, upper right, on plaque: *A. Ostade*
>
> H.XV.29.24a ii/v, Godefroy 24a ii/v
>
> Gift of Melvin R. Seiden, s5.17.9

Like his teacher Ostade, Cornelis Bega spent the bulk of his career in Haarlem, although he did travel through Germany and Switzerland in the early 1650s and may have made a trip to Italy.[1] He produced approximately thirty-five etchings, which, like his paintings and drawings, are primarily concerned with scenes of peasants. Most of the etchings are on this small scale, focusing upon single figures or small groups in nonspecific interiors.[2] The ten or so prints on a larger scale fit a similar description, although they are generally more carefully finished and detailed. Peasant types frequently have exaggerated features, producing a comical effect. Although clearly influenced by Ostade, it is apparent that Bega's handling of scenes like these has a strength and coarseness all its own.

These two small etchings are mounted on folio 17 of Spencer Album 5, the Bega in the upper left-hand corner and the Ostade in the lower right. The arrangement of the page is similar to that of folio 20 (see Cat. 40), with three symmetric rows of larger prints flanked by smaller ones. There is again no clear thematic or chronological pattern to the arrangement, although four of the small Ostade etchings on folio 17 also appeared on the same folio of the Picart edition published after 1710: *The Smoker and the Drinker* (G.133), *Three Grotesque Figures* (G.28), *The Couple Walking* (G.24), and *The Smoker and the Drinker* (G.24a). As for possible explanations for the inclusion of this Bega among the Ostades, it is interesting to note that in addition to the identification of Bega as one of Ostade's pupils (his first and best pupil according to Houbraken[4]), there is also the fact that Bernard Picart acquired Bega's plates as well as Ostade's in 1710 and published an edition of Bega's complete works during the same period. The placement of the Bega etching on this particular folio would seem to have as much to do with its comparable format as with its related subject matter. A second etching by Bega is actually mounted after the prints by Jan Miel that follow the section devoted to Ostade in the album.

A comparison between the two prints on exhibition reveals very different conceptions of the rendering of figures in an interior. While Bega relies on a silhouetting effect of white forms

against a dark, coarsely hatched background, Ostade's figures derive their solidity from their outlines and carefully placed internal modeling. An interest in light and space is a key characteristic of Ostade's work over the course of his career. In this late etching, darkness and shadow have disappeared, as have finely described details, replaced by simple contours and more monumental figures. In addition, Bega's figures appear comparatively rougher and more stereotypically peasantlike in their lack of individualization, as well as in the exaggerated expression and pose of the figure on the left. Furthermore, despite the contrast of light and dark that defines them, the figures seem to merge with their undefined surroundings. The roughness of these figures seems to refer back to the unapologetic characterization of peasants in the work of Brouwer and early Ostade, as well as to the standard comical associations of peasant appearances and activities. In contrast, Ostade's figures, while clearly drawing upon a vocabulary of peasant types, appear much more individualized and are separate from the space they inhabit.

A similar contrast can be made between the two etchings in terms of the specific activities that are taking place. Bega's three figures seem actively engaged with each other, conversing as the beer is poured out by the standing figure. The visual emphasis, however, is clearly not on the jug or the act of pouring. These details blend into the background in the same way the figures do, the individual lines not so clearly delineated one from another. Of greater interest is the general atmosphere of the scene, the coarseness of the figures, and the understood associations of their activity. The use of alcohol by the lower classes as a source of pleasure and ultimately as a cause of antisocial behavior such as fighting or vomiting was a well-established theme for Dutch artists. Bega's peasants, however, appear civilized in their actions, if not in their appearance.

Similarly, the two figures portrayed by Ostade appear restrained in their activity, which is here much more clearly established. The figure on the left stands holding a glass, his head tilted down so only his nose and mouth are visible. He is not drinking, and it is not clear that he is drunk, although the obscuring of his features may create that impression. His companion sits on an overturned washbasin, concentrating on the long-stemmed pipe he holds over a bowl on the table before him. Seen in profile, his features are more carefully described.

The narcotic effect of tobacco was perceived in the sixteenth and seventeenth centuries to be similar to that of alcohol, and was in fact treated in local regulations like alcohol. Furthermore, the language used to discuss tobacco use even used the same vocabulary: in seventeenth-century Dutch, tobacco is sipped or drunk.[5] Tobacco was believed to have medicinal value, in particular as a prophylactic against the plague, but its recreational use was a cause of great concern. Although it was by no means restricted to the lower classes, "the fact that these groups had adopted the substance for their own distinct, sub-cultural use prompted anxieties regarding propriety on the part of those sections of society which might be termed respectable."[6] In the pictorial language of festive comedy, smoking becomes an essential component, and pipes and smoke become symbolic of the world turned upside down. But Ostade's etching does not seem concerned with taking either an explicitly critical or a satirical tone. The isolation of the figures in their solitary pursuits seems almost antisocial, but with no obvious negative results for any other figures. In this context, Bega's etching appears even more positive, describing the more convivial aspects of drinking.

KHN

1. A drawing tentatively attributed to Bega, *The Dentist* (Schlossmuseum, Weimar, inv. no. 4763), is inscribed "Bega Romae" (Philadelphia 1984, p. 132).

2. See Pearce 1977.

3. The catalogue numbers for cited Ostade prints refer to Godefroy.

4. Philadelphia 1984, p. 132.

5. See Gaskell 1987, pp. 117–38.

6. Gaskell 1987, p. 122.

MATTHIEU PLATTE-MONTAGNE
Antwerp c. 1608 – 1660 Paris

45a   *The Skaters*

etching

149 x 142 mm

watermark: illegible

inscribed in plate, lower left: *Montaigne fecit*; lower right: *Morin Ex. Cum Priuil. Re.*

R.-D.V.112.6 i/iii, H.XVII.126.6 i/iii

Gift of Mrs. William Simes, by exchange, 85.106.4

45b *Winter Landscape,* after Fouquières

etching

260 x 312 mm

inscribed in plate, lower margin, left: *I. Fouquiere Pin. M*[*athieu* burnished out] *Montagne Scul.*; right: *Morin ex. Cum Priuil. Re.*

R.-D.V.122.25, H.XVII.132.25

Lessing J. Rosenwald Fund, by exchange, s5.108.2

These two winter landscapes by Platte-Montagne demonstrate by their common subject and their completely different interpretations of it the enormous range that was covered by the general landscape classification "winter piece," or, as Pierre-Jean Mariette called this etching that represents a village in a forest "un hyver."[1] The genre was so popular in the seventeenth century that winter pieces form the single most numerous category in the Ogdens' census of landscape paintings sold at auction in England in the period 1689–1692, outnumbering other "season pieces" five to one and also outnumbering every other strictly defined genre.[2]

The winter piece had a long history, beginning with representations of the months in medieval books of hours, and in prints it was frequently represented in series of the months and the seasons.[3] In easel painting its career was fairly launched by Pieter Brueghel the Elder's *Winter Landscape with Skaters and a Bird Trap* of 1565 (Brussels, Dr. F. Delporte Collection), which introduces the theme of skaters that became so popular in seventeenth-century Dutch winter scenes.[4] The painting shares an unusual feature with the small etching on exhibition: none of the many skaters has fallen, either on his rump or through the ice. Such falls—with attendant amused onlookers or rescuers, depending upon the seriousness of the situation—were part and parcel of the moralizing intent of skating scenes, which was often made explicit in prints by attached mottoes: "How lightly ventures man, carefree, On ice, not thinking deeper! And so he is an inch or three Ahead of the Big Reaper."[5]

The omission of the fallen skater in the Brueghel painting bears in context the same meaning; the foreground shows a bird trap which has not yet slammed shut on its prey, who are as unwitting of impending death as the skaters in the background. The print by Platte-Montagne, however, bears witness simply to a loss of moralizing content. The artist has moved from the context of the Lowlands to France, and his print was conceived as only one of a series of six decorative roundels, variations on marine views, with harbors or tempests or the ocean in moonlight being represented among the others (R.-D.V.110–112.1–6, H.XVII.126.1–6). And to an early-eighteenth-century French connoisseur, their common subject was simply one aspect of landscape at large; the compiler of the Spencer Album in which this print and one other from the set of six was included used them to make up the second page of the two folios on which a set of six prints by Jean Morin was mounted, four to a page (R.-D.II.70–71.1–6). None of the Morins is of a marine

Montaigne fecit   Morin Ex. Cum Priuil. Re.

subject, but all are identical in size and format. Morin published all twelve roundels, and given the intimacy between the two artists (see Cat. 36), it is safe to assume that the twelve prints, now usually thought of as two separate sets because they are by two artists of different nationalities, form a single series or at least a complementary pair of sets.[6]

In turning to the other "*hyver*" by Platte-Montagne on exhibition, we see a composition which comes closer to a moralizing scene, for all of its figures, man and beast, are bent to their labors, and one empathizes with the rigors of their life. Despite its frigid subject, the skating scene is frivolous and, with its bright sky, epitomizes even in black and white the "best and most pleasing kind of Landscape" favored by one seventeenth-century advocate of landscape painting: "For

213

a rising or setting sun affoard such varietie and beauty of colours, by reason of those Blushing reflexions upon the nearer clouds. . . . For cloudy skies and melancholly weather take up as much time as the other, yet are nothing soe pleasant."[7]

By contrast, the weather in Platte-Montagne's print after Fouquières is indeed melancholy. To represent it the etcher has tempered the sharp, linear contrasts of the skating scene and produced a range of the softest grays enhanced by the nicety of his choice of hatching structures. Note the virtually imperceptible passage from stippling to linework in the clouded sky and the orderly yet never mechanical superposition of horizontal, vertical, and two sets of diagonal strokes to form the opaque surface of the river. To quote Mariette, this is "a winter which is done with marvelous intelligence."[8]

Precedents in Flemish painting for this scene are found in several collaborative works by Joos de Momper and Jan Brueghel the Elder,[9] who were, not coincidentally, the teachers of Jacob

214

Foucquier before he emigrated to France in 1621 (perhaps in the company of Rubens, with whom he had worked in Antwerp) and changed his name to Jacques Fouquières.[10] His landscape style was greatly appreciated in Paris, and he was commissioned by Louis XIII to decorate the Long Gallery at the Louvre with views of the towns of France. Fouquières' lack of progress resulted in the hiring of Poussin in 1641; the collaboration was unfortunate for both artists, who were artistically and temperamentally irreconcilable, and the project was never accomplished. Fouquières died in poverty in 1659. His burial was paid for by his longtime willing collaborator Matthieu Platte-Montagne.[11]

MBC

1. BNMS R065910.

2. The breakdown of subject categories is fascinating; although there must be some overlap among the definitions, who would have expected winter pieces to have outnumbered prospects or hunting pieces in England! The census: 522 prospects, 605 winter pieces, 121 other season pieces, 316 ruin pieces, 171 moonlight scenes, 389 cattle pieces, 451 hunting pieces, and 302 battle pieces (Ogden and Ogden 1955, p. 90).

3. See Stechow 1966, pp. 82–88, for a discussion of the history of the theme in Netherlandish art.

4. The Skaters (H.III.47.22) by Hans Bol (1534–1593) is the prototypical round skating scene in printmaking. One is tempted to speculate that the round format of so many skating scenes, painted and printed, alludes to the topsy-turvy potential of the sport, but in fact landscape roundels of every subject were common in sixteenth- and seventeenth-century Netherlandish art. See Sutton 1987, p. 119, for a discussion of the format.

5. From an emblem book on the theme of the Dance of Death, Het Schouw-Toneel des Doods . . . (1707), cited in Dixon 1987, p. 23. See this source for many reproductions of seventeenth-century Dutch skating scenes and for a discussion of the history and significance of the subject.

6. Changes in state, which include the effacing of the inscriptions and the addition of shaded borders and combinations of letters and numbers, occur through the lifetimes of the plates by both Morin and Platte-Montagne, and indicate that the plates were published together until the later eighteenth century.

7. Ogden and Ogden 1955, p. 12, quoting from the 1649 edition of Edward Norgate's Miniatura.

8. BNMS R065910: " . . . un hyver qui est fait avec une merveilleuse intelligence."

9. See Klaus Ertz, Jan Breughel der ältere, 1568–1625 (Cologne: DuMont, 1979), nos. 398, 404, 420.

10. On Fouquières, see Wurzbach 1910, vol. 1, p. 547; Wintermute 1990, pp. 11, 27; and especially Wolfgang Stechow, "Drawings and Etchings by Jacques Fouquier," Gazette des beaux-arts ser. 6, 34 (1948):419–34.

11. Wurzbach 1910, vol. 1, p. 547.

CLAUDE GELLEE (called LE LORRAIN)

near Chamagne, Lorrain 1600–1682 Rome

46 The Shipwreck, c. 1638–1641

etching

129 x 182 mm

inscribed in plate, lower left side margin: 3

R.-D.I.12.7, Russell 44 iv/vi, Mannocci 35 iii(c)/v

Gift of Belinda L. Randall from the collection of John Witt Randall, by exchange, s2.104.1

This etching follows a long tradition of stormy seascapes depicted by Northern European artists in the sixteenth and seventeenth centuries. Claude's awareness of the tradition was probably extensive, given the influx of foreigners and circulation of Northern prints in his adopted city Rome. His interest was undoubtedly stimulated by the work of his teacher Agostino Tassi and colleague Filippo Napoletano. Tassi, strongly influenced by the Northern artist Paul Bril (1554–1626), produced a number of seaport and coastal subjects, as did Napoletano, whose experiences sketching from nature in the seaport of Naples led to the production of numerous drawings and several frescoes as well as canvases of marine themes.

Diane Russell traces the image of the storm-tossed ship and rock topped by a building in Claude's etching to a drawing by Matthew Bril that relates to Paul Bril's fresco in the Church of the Scala Santa, Rome, and Pieter van Laer's painting in the Galleria Spada, also in Rome.[1] Claude would certainly have been familiar with the Brils' work, so admired by Tassi, and was probably especially drawn to the later work of Paul, which shows a development away from the more decorative surface patterns of the Flemish "maniera" toward a simpler, less artificial style, in response to the increased naturalism of landscape painting of Annibale Carracci and his circle. However, with Filippo Napoletano, Claude shares a kinship in approach to light and nature that far surpasses natural effects merely suggested by Bril. Indeed, one particular canvas by Napoletano, *Ships in a Storm near a Lighthouse* (1620, Villa del Poggio Imperiale, Florence), bears striking affinities with the etching, although the composition of the print is much simplified.[2]

Not much is known of Napoletano's early career, save a document of 1613 relating to a Neapolitan commission of paintings and his apparent participation in the frescoed frieze with *Scene from the Life of Saint Paul* in the Quirinal Palace in Rome, c. 1616–1617 (until recently attributed to Agostino Tassi).[3] Allegedly in Rome in 1614 until his move to Florence in 1617, it is probable that Napoletano, like many other young artists interested in landscape painting at the time, would have worked with or for Tassi or at the very least associated with him. Claude therefore could have come into contact with Napoletano either during this period, shortly after his own arrival in Rome in 1613, or when Napoletano returned to Rome in 1621, while Claude was working for Tassi.

Even in the Quirinal frescoes, Napoletano demonstrated a richness of color and vivid effects of light and atmosphere not found in the work of Tassi, who remained under the influence of Paul Bril. Napoletano's style seems to have developed more directly from Adam Elsheimer's exploration of the fall of natural light and the *repoussoir* effect of trees silhouetted against the sky, but he then uses the light to convey a strong sense of atmosphere and recession into space— devices Claude was to develop more fully, yet using a strikingly similar method. In Florence, Napoletano's experience of the unfamiliar Tuscan countryside seems to have stimulated his observation of reality, resulting in numerous drawings and paintings of remarkable objectivity.[4] He also developed his studies of natural phenomena as evident in the fury of the wind-swept waves and flashes of lighting in the *Ships in a Storm Near a Lighthouse*, the very elements emphasized by Claude in *The Shipwreck*,[5] and executed a number of studies from life of ships tossed about in waves at this time. He took up the theme again slightly later, on his return to Rome and Naples, in drawings and a fresco in the Rospigliosi-Pallavicini Palace.[6]

Although no documentation survives of a link between Claude and Napoletano, the first sheet from the so-called Wildenstein Album of drawings by Claude is pertinent. This drawing of a shipyard is apparently very close to the series of drawings of ship studies by Napoletano in the Louvre.[7] Roethlisberger attributes the drawing to Claude, though he acknowledges a correspondence between the drawing and a painting belonging to the circle of Tassi, citing Filippo Napoletano as the most likely candidate.[8] Roethlisberger also acknowledges that this painstakingly precise sheet, partially executed with a ruler, is quite different from other known studies of ships by Claude,[9] but he sees the tiny Mannerist figures as precursors to those which appear in his drawings of the 1630s. Chiarini, however, has attributed the drawing to Napoletano based on its stylistic similarity to an unquestioned drawing by him in the Gabinetto Nazionale delle Stampe, Rome (F.C. no. 128323).[10]

Glued to the back of the sheet from the Wildenstein album was a gray chalk drawing of a lady on horseback with hounds, which is a copy after a detail of a painting, c. 1638–41, by Claude Deruet, whose assistant Claude had been in Nancy during 1625–1627. The technique reveals that it is not in Deruet's hand, and Roethlisberger hypothesizes that it could have been sent to Claude from Deruet's studio, or it could be his own copy. Regardless, if we accept Chiarini's attribution to Napoletano, the two sheets are highly significant as records of Claude's artistic beginnings, especially since their provenance indicates that they were among the drawings he saved until his death.[11]

The sense of an observed reality and preciseness that characterizes Napoletano's work from the beginning gives way to a more atmospheric and pictorial quality after his return from Florence, which accounts for the misattribution of some of his drawings to Claude.[12] The subjects of these drawings would have been important for Claude as a young artist trying to establish himself on his own, in the period following his return from Nancy and Lorraine in 1626–1627. The early phase of Claude's paintings included a number of lively seaport views.[13]

A *Storm off the Seacoast* (*Liber Veritatis* 33), a Claude pen and wash drawing closely related to this plate, is executed in the same direction as the etching except for the ship, which faces left instead of right.[14] According to the inscription on the verso of the drawing, Claude painted this picture (now lost) around 1638–1639 for Paolo Giordano Orsini, duke of Bracciano, whose motto was "contra ventos et undas" (against wind and waves). Roethlisberger has suggested that the etching might have also been done as an illustration of the motto and probably preceded the painting and the drawing.

Further evidence to support a date of 1638–1641 for the etching can be found in the documentation of Claude's trip to Naples in 1636, indicated by a signature on a copy of a lost painting (*Liber Veritatis* 6). Roethlisberger conjectures that this trip may have triggered many harbor scenes, which he started to paint immediately on his return to Rome.[15] Stylistically, this dating makes sense since the etching shows technical maturity in the simplification of forms and economic use of line resulting in a clearer image than the somewhat muddied images of Claude's earlier prints, such as *The Herdsman and the Shepherdess* (Mannocci 3) or *The Tempest* (Mannocci 6), both c. 1630.

In addition to the interpretation of the etching as an illustration for the duke's personal motto, one might also read the print as the popular seventeenth-century metaphor for "the sea of life" in which the dangers of life are seen as parallel to the dangers of the sea.[16] The motto and metaphor are sufficiently related in meaning that both interpretations could have been intended, or at least foreseen. Mariette's reference to "*Tempestes*" in the table of contents of Spencer Album 2 may suggest his awareness of the broader interpretation.

SRL

1. Russell 1982, pp. 391–93. For a detailed discussion of Bril's use of traditional Flemish motifs rendered in more naturalistic terms, see Harris 1985, pp. 94–103, no. 14.

2. For an illustration of the painting see Chiarini 1984, p. 15, fig. 3.

3. Chiarini 1984, p. 13. This article should be referred to for information regarding Napoletano's life discussed below, unless noted otherwise.

4. Chiarini 1984, pp. 16–17. Chiarini cites further examples and comparisons between works by Napoletano and early works by Claude.

5. According to his biographer Baldinucci, Claude himself had experienced violent storms while at sea on

his return to Rome from Lorraine in 1627 (see Roethlisberger 1961, p. 55).

6. See Chiarini 1984, figs. 4, 7–9.

7. Chiarini 1984, n. 46.

8. Roethlisberger 1971, p. 13, pl. 1. Refer to this text for Roethlisberger's opinions about this drawing discussed below.

9. See Russell 1982, nos. D23 and D24, which appear considerably looser in handling and less linear and detailed than the Wildenstein Album sheet.

10. Chiarini 1984, n. 46.

11. Roethlisberger, 1971, pp. 5–8.

12. See note 5.

13. For example see *Genoa, from the Sea*, c. 1627–1629 (Russell P4), *Coast Scene with Setting Sun*, c. 1630–35 (Russell P10), and *Coast Scene with Europa and the Bull*, c. 1634 (Russell P15).

14. Roethlisberger 1968, no. 196.

15. Roethlisberger 1979, p. 23.

16. Russell 1982, p. 392.

SALVATOR ROSA

Naples 1615 – 1673 Rome

47   *Jason and the Dragon*, c. 1664

etching and drypoint

338 x 217 mm

watermark: fleur-de-lys (?) within a circle

inscribed in plate, lower left: ROSA

B.XX.275.18, TIB45.259.18, TIB4512.019, Wallace 118

Richard Norton Fund, s6.64

Richard Wallace, the modern cataloguer of Rosa's prints, has described *Jason and the Dragon* as Rosa's "latest as well as his most successful etching."[1] His dating places it at a slack period in the artist's tumultuous career as a history and landscape painter in Naples, Florence, and Rome. Defining Rosa merely as an artist, however, hardly renders justice to a man whose principal creation must at times have seemed to his contemporaries to be his own notorious personality, which he expressed in virulent poetic satires and by rejection of the conventional patronage system, both aggressions against a society he courted for material support and, more importantly, fame.

In 1666 Rosa wrote to one of Europe's most active painting collectors, Don Antonio Ruffo (who commissioned Rembrandt's *Aristotle Contemplating the Bust of Homer* now in the Metropolitan Museum of Art, New York), that he could not be bound by any patron's schedule; and in 1664 he told one of his best friends, "To painters of my condition and extravagant genius it is necessary to leave everything after the measurements free. . . . "[2] Rosa compensated for his intractable refusal to accept dictated commissions by strategies that have since become routine: he

opened his studio to prospective buyers and he consigned to public exhibition paintings he had created according to his own inspiration and intention.

That Rosa did not refuse commissions per se, however, is indicated by his letter of 1664, the probable year of this etching, wherein he regrets their lack: "As for commissions, for the last year there's been absolutely nothing—even from a dog! . . . I might as well go and plant my paint brushes in the garden."[3] Opportunities for artists in Rome had been limited ever since the death of the Barbarini pope Urban VIII twenty years earlier, and one can surmise that Rosa had taken up etching because he found little else to do.

But by 1669 Rosa would report, "Every day I have to turn down commissions (and important ones at that) from all over Europe";[4] and it is only at about this time that he seems to have produced paintings of the same subject and approximate composition as his print of *Jason and the Dragon*.[5] This reverses the usual sequence, in which an artist would reproduce his painting by means of a print. Typically, in the three centuries before the institution of public galleries and the invention of photography, a completed easel painting would in effect disappear into the collection of its purchaser; and the artist, in order to capitalize upon his now-invisible achievement, would through printmaking circulate its image to a wider public. Not the least of his motives would be to encourage patronage for future work by this advertisement of his accomplishments. The ambitious Rosa, whose insistence upon the independence of his own genius proscribed conventional patronage, took the next logical step and sought to stimulate commissions of paintings whose subjects, compositions, and style he had chosen for himself and whose merits he had already demonstrated through their realization in etching.

That this intention is not simply a latter-day deduction from an imposed chronology among prints and paintings that are in fact undated is proved by Rosa's own words in letters of 1666 and 1663 in reference to two of his largest prints, *The Fall of the Giants* (TIB45.262.21) and *The Rescue of the Infant Oedipus* (TIB45.247.8). Both plates are inscribed "Pinx.," that is, "painted"; but the artist admitted that they were not yet painted three years after he had worked on the etchings, and that he hoped to initiate commissions of the subjects by his inscriptions.[6] Wallace has proposed that all of Rosa's prints except for his very earliest plates (which exist only in one or two impressions) were undertaken as self-advertisements, for they are all figural compositions, and it was as a figure painter, that is, as a painter of historical compositions, that Rosa wished to be known.

An international reputation as a landscape painter, which conferred status only in a lesser genre, had accrued from Rosa's earliest years in response to talent and originality that far exceeded his capacity as a figural artist. Despite the wide circulation of his etchings—or even because of them, because they were felt to embody the spirit of his emotionally charged landscape paintings—Rosa's renown as a landscape artist only increased after his death. It flourished especially in England, where in the eighteenth century it would set the tone for a developing native tradition of romantic landscape painting.[7] Not surprisingly, in a country where noble connoisseurs competed to amass collections of Continental paintings as evidence of both their wealth and their sensibility, the Spencers brought Rosas to Althorp. Of the six that remain there, three were acquired prior to the mid-eighteenth century;[8] the other three, among the most important Rosa paintings in England, were purchased by the first Earl Spencer in the 1760s.[9]

The pristine condition of the pages of Spencer Album 6 suggests that the six Rosa etchings in the volume were not so well known to the lords of Althorp as the six paintings. Two of the canvases, *Cincinnatus Called from the Farm* and *Alexander Visiting Diogenes*, a pair, are 93″ high by 102″ wide and could hardly have been missed even by the third Earl Spencer, who preferred paintings of his prize cattle. But to the print connoisseur, the Spencer Rosa etchings are equally memorable. They are all early printings, including two first states,[10] and they are in a remarkable state of preservation. This impression of *Jason and the Dragon* is wiped with delicate plate tone, with a residue of gray left on the rocks at the upper left. Without this tone and without the pristine white of the paper, we should not appreciate the blaze of light penetrating the dragon's lair, where Jason has come to pour the soporific potion into the monstrous guardian's eyes. Likewise, it is only in a fresh impression such as this that the curling ornament in the dragon's webbed wings and the drypoint toning of its scaly tail can be enjoyed. Yet linear detail, printing niceties, and even the faint ludicrousness of the dragon itself are in such an impression whirled into a vortex that coalesces beast, hero, cape, tree, rock, and cloud. Neither figure nor landscape dominate but rather catalyze each other into a new genre of art. The originality and accomplishment of Rosa lie here.

MBC

1. Reed and Wallace 1989, p. 194.

2. Wallace 1979, p. 83. To Ruffo, Rosa wrote, "I do not paint to enrich myself but purely for my own satisfaction. I must allow myself to be carried away by the transports of enthusiasm and use my brushes only when I feel myself rapt." One wonders if Rosa was aspiring to the status of the highly successful Poussin, his rival; already by the 1650s Poussin had arrived at somewhat the same relationship with patrons. See, briefly, Albert Châtelet and Jacques Thuillier, *French Painting from Fouquet to Poussin* (Geneva: Editions d'Art Albert Skira, 1963), p. 215.

3. Haskell 1980, p. 48.

4. Haskell 1980, p. 49.

5. Museum of Fine Arts, Montreal, and Collection of the Earl of Harrowby, England. See Wallace 1979, pp. 105, 312.

6. Wallace 1979, p. 93.

7. For Rosa's English reputation, see Ogden and Ogden 1955, p. 108; Hayes 1965–1966, p. 188; Wallace 1979, pp. 107–20; and J. Sunderland, "The Legend and Influence of Salvator Rosa in England in the Eighteenth Century," *Burlington Magazine* 115 (1973):785–89. Pierre-Jean Mariette wrote concerning the eighteenth-century British passion for collecting paintings "de mode" at any price: "Il ne faut pas d'ailleurs être surpris des prix exhorbitans que les Anglois donnent de certains tableaux. Il suffit qu'ils soient de mode chez eux, et en Angleterre, peut-être encore plus qu'ailleurs, il est des maîtres pour lesquels on se passionne; les Salvator Rosa, les Claude Lorrain, les Gaspres [*Dughet*], etc., bons ou mauvais, ils se les arrachent et les couvrent d'or" (Mariette 1851–1860, vol. 5, p. 368).

8. Garlick 1976, nos. 561, 562, 563.

9. Garlick 1976, nos. 564, 565, 566.

10. *Ceres and Phylatus* (TIB45.260.19) and *Saint William of Maleval* (TIB45.240.1). It should be noted that only unique impressions of the first state exist of the two prints which are second states (of three) in Spencer Album 6, and that the other two Spencer Rosas exist only in single states.

GIOVANNI BENEDETTO CASTIGLIONE

Genoa 1609 – 1664 Mantua

48 *Young Herdsman on Horseback*, 1638

etching

181 x 249 mm

watermark: anchor (?) within a circle

inscribed in plate, lower right: *GIO. BENEDETO 16[?] / CASTILIONVS GENO. FEC.*

B.XXI.25.28, TIB46.41.28, TIB4402.42.28 S2, Percy E 4

Richard Norton Fund, S6.78.1

Although this print, which probably dates from 1638,[1] was etched prior to another by Castiglione already discussed (Cat. 14), we make no pretense to strict chronological order, and it seems more interesting to consider this subject together with the two later seventeenth-century French prints that follow, which reproduce designs by Castiglione. All three represent a person herding animals, the mixed flocks so beloved of Castiglione and also, it must be added, of many other seventeenth-century etchers. One needs only to look at the two prints of animals by Wtenbrouck also in this exhibition (Cat. 37a–b) to be reminded of the pleasure that artists inclined toward the representation of domestic animals took in characterizing each species not only by its physical attributes but by its physiognomy. In Castiglione's etching, his alert mutt, slow cow, and silly, splay-footed sheep convey the essence of canine, bovine, and ovine personality.

But unlike Dutch Bambocciati such as van Laer and Miel (see Cat. 38), whose prints Castiglione could have seen during his first stint in Rome, 1632–c. 1641, when this plate was etched, the Italian etcher's herdsmen were not necessarily contemporary figures. Although in this plate there is no indication through costume or narrative allusions that an ancient scene is intended, there is also no intimation of modern, that is, seventeenth-century, daily life, such as that which one easily recognizes in Miel's etching of the goatherd playing his bagpipes. Instead the scene is suffused with a serenity that implies that the passage of time is stilled. The ancient lineage of the shepherd as the human link between primitive hunter and civilized farmer is somehow revived by the young man's rough, indeterminate clothing and his herd's and dog's motley appearance. (Yet the late twentieth-century viewer, inured by modern husbandry to homogeneous flocks, one species per pasture, must resist reading too much into the commingling of so many different animals.) Even to his Roman contemporaries, Castiglione was characterized by his pastoral subjects and, more specifically in his pictures, which as full-scale paintings required a more definite historical subject, by his representations of the wanderings of the fathers of Israel—"li viaggi di Giacobbe," in the words of testimony in a 1635 lawsuit involving Castiglione.[2]

Our sense that an earlier time is suggested in this print was also shared by the compiler of the Spencer Albums. The prints were mounted in a rough approximation of what would become the traditional cataloguing order for old-master prints, codified in the early nineteenth century by Adam Bartsch, which begins with the Old Testament, continues to the New Testament, then to saints and other images of Christian history, then to ancient history, and eventually to genre scenes. Applying this system strictly, as Bartsch did, the Castiglione *Young Herdsman* falls in Bartsch order after several classical allegorical figure pieces and, together with two other etchings of flocks, before the series of large and small heads. But in the Spencer Albums, our herdsman is mounted at the very beginning of the Castiglione etchings together with the comparable subject *A Flock of Sheep Surrounding a Laden Donkey* (TIB46.42.29). This is not, however, the first Castiglione subject in the album; it is preceded by "a suite of eight prints of religious subjects . . . after drawings by Benedetto," to quote the album's table of contents.[3] All of these are of incidents in the Old Testament, and most feature people and their flocks on the march—*Abraham and Sarah Voyaging to Egypt*, *The Angel Commands Noah to Enter the Animals into the Ark*, *Rachel's Journey to Her Husband Jacob*, and so forth.

We know that for Pierre-Jean Mariette these subjects conveyed the essence of Castiglione's art: at his death his drawing collection, sold at auction, contained three Castiglione drawings:

> A herd of various animals, led by three shepherds ... ruins and landscape ornament this charming drawing ...
>
> A herd of animals on the march, with various persons who guide them. As an angel flies above them and indicates the way, it would seem that the author of this fine drawing wished to represent Abraham with his family. ...
>
> The adoration of the shepherds ... [4]

Much like the oeuvre of Claude, Castiglione's subject pieces, whatever their ostensible story (or lack of same), celebrate a pastoral age when all of man's affairs were imbedded in a landscape in which vegetation always encroaches upon architecture, and light, or shadow, always overwhelms form. The human and animal dramatis personae are absorbed within this shimmering, harmonious ambience, so that sheep's fleece, trees' bark, and ruins' mosses seem to participate in a coruscating memory of antiquity.

Some accident in the biting of the plate of the *Young Herdsman* resulted in spotted, dark streaks cascading over the main subject of the print, which the artist attempted to remedy by burnishing. The resultant smudging causes this print in particular, among all of Castiglione's etchings, to bear a startling resemblance to Claude's etchings, where the surfaces also often show signs of extensive burnishing and reworking. Closer study suggests that the resemblance to Claude is not merely fortuitous. The finely detailed foliage of the trees and the attempt to evoke luminous atmosphere through tone are also characteristic of Claude's prints of the 1630s, most notably the large *Landscape with Country Dance* (Mannocci 20). Castiglione's association in Rome with Nicolas Poussin and Pietro Testa—himself in his early years a lyrical etcher of groves and copses—has been suggested in the literature;[5] a sympathetic appreciation of the early prints of Claude is also indicated.

MBC

1. The lines of the first part of the inscription including the "*16*" were reinforced by the etcher and are easily read. The two numerals that follow were not, and they are difficult to differentiate from the squiggles that shade the ground area. See Percy 1971, p. 136.

2. Percy 1971, p. 25. Pages 26–28, figs. 8, 10–13 of this publication reproduce six characteristic paintings of patriarchal journeys.

3. "Une suite de huit pieces de Sujets tirées de l'histoire Sainte gravées ... Sur des desseins de Benediitte."

4. Blanc 1857–1858, pp. 276–67 (in Mariette sale, 1775): "Un Troupeau de divers animaux, conduit par trois bergers, descendant dans un vallon au pied d'une haute montagne; des ruines et du paysage ornent ce charmant dessin, fait à la plume et au bistre ... Un Troupeau d'animaux en marche, avec diverses figures qui les conduisent. Comme on y remarque en l'air un ange qui leur indique la route, il faut croire que l'auteur de ce dessin supérieur a voulu représenter Abraham avec sa famille ... il est fait au pinceau at à l'huile, sur papier ... L'Adoration des Bergers, ... la première pensée du fameux tableau de ce maître, connu dans l'église de Saint-Luc, à Gênes ..."

5. See Percy 1971, pp. 25–28. The foreword of this book, pp. 17–60, provides an excellent overview of the artist's career.

LOUIS BERNARD

Paris? c. 1650? – after 1717 The Hague?[1]

49 *A Shepherdess on Horseback with a Flock of Sheep and Cattle,* c. 1692[2]

mezzotint

336 x 248 mm, watermark: B C (?) separated by a heart, within a cartouche

inscribed in plate, lower left: *Bernard f;* lower right: *6*

Andresen I.113.3 i/ii, Meyer III.634.10 i/ii

Gift of Belinda L. Randall from the collection of John Witt Randall, by exchange, s6.100

This is the only mezzotint among the thousands of prints in the nine Spencer Albums. That this unique example of the technique falls among the compositions by and after Castiglione is not surprising in that he is a featured artist within the albums that contain mixtures of painters and schools, and there are proportionately more reproductive prints after this painter than after the many others represented in the albums. Curiously, none of the later cataloguers of the mezzotint attribute the composition to Castiglione, but there was no doubt in the mind of the compiler of Spencer Album 6: in the table of contents it is described as being after a painting by the Genoese master. That a painting and not a drawing is specified is interesting in that the table of contents describes the preceding prints by Macé as being after drawings or, more generically, compositions ("*desseins*"), implying that the compiler was familiar with the original from which this mezzotint was taken.

From its invention in the middle of the seventeenth century, mezzotint was considered to be peculiarly adapted to the reproduction of paintings because it simulated the painting process in working up the lights of a composition from a dark field. In the introduction to two volumes of "prints engraved in mezzotint, in England as well as in France and the Low Countries," the Mariette manuscript in the Bibliothèque Nationale contains a particularly enthusiastic report of the invention of the technique specifically as it served painting:

> This new manner of engraving was only discovered towards the middle of the last century. We are indebted to Robert Count Palatine of the Rhine Duke of Cumberland and Vice-Admiral of England. The prince has not only the taste for painting, he practiced it himself; he loved it, no other proof is necessary than his having enriched it in imagining this new sort of engraving, entirely different in its working method than all those which till then had been in use: For instead of merely marking the outline on the copper with the needle or burin of whatever one intends to [print *crossed out*] represent, on the contrary it is necessary in this other method to efface in order to express what one wishes.[3]

226

Bernard f.

6

This introduction to mezzotint continues with an accurate description of the tools and method of the technique, noting its susceptibility to wear compared to ordinary engraving. It includes as marginalia delightful sketches of mezzotint rockers at rest and in use, held by a hand cuffed with a very eighteenth-century ruffle (which would seem an impediment to laying an even ground). The introduction concludes with an appreciation of mezzotint's appropriate use to reproduce portraits, remarking that Smith in England had recently "pushed this [kind of] engraving to the highest point of perfection that it could attain."[4]

Yet the compositions included in the two volumes of mezzotints described in the manuscript listing of their contents are practically all of historical subjects. On the ninety-six folios of volume 1, for example, portraits are found only on folios 89 through 96. In the albums of prints assembled by the Mariettes for Prince Eugene of Savoy, now in the Albertina, several mezzotint reproductions, including an impression of Bernard's after Castiglione, are mounted with the prints of the artists whose compositions they represent. Thus in the Albertina Ribera volume, a mezzotint by Francis Meheux (1644–c. 1690) reproduces one of the Spanish painter's many *Saint Jerome*s,[5] and the Corneille volume includes a mezzotint by Isaac Sarrabat (c. 1680–?) after Michel Corneille the Elder published by Jean Mariette.[6] Despite the warm appreciation for English mezzotinters, the Mariettes selected French mezzotinters for these albums.

In the manuscript instructions for the preparation of the table of contents of the Albertina album of Castiglione prints, the print by Bernard was initially attributed to yet another French mezzotinter:

> f.32. A woman on horseback in the midst of a herd of cattle and sheep, engraved in mezzotint by [A. Bouys *crossed out*]. Bernard related to Bouys the same who has engraved [*illegible*] after Rembrandt.[7]

This original misattribution is mysterious considering the legible signature of Bernard, which appears even on the first state of the print, that state included in the Albertina album on folio 32.[8]

The print is entirely characteristic of the artist in its distinctive emphasis on the personification of the animals in the herd. All of Bernard's mezzotints that reproduce portraits of humans show their sitters with alert stares, and his *Virgin and Child* features in the foreground a rabbit who casts a humorously wry look to the spectator. That Bernard's expressive animals were not always appreciated is indicated by the obliteration of the toothy grins of the sheep in the print on exhibition when the plate was republished in a second state.[9] MBC

1. Thieme-Becker, vol. 3, p. 431. The very speculative birth date is based upon Bernard's having been a page to Louis XIV.

2. This dating is based only upon the handwritten dates on two proofs of Bernard portraits, of Louis XIV and the grand dauphin, in the Bibliothèque Nationale, Paris.

3. BNMS R069883: "Table du recueil des estampes gravées au maniere noire, tant en Angleterre qu'en France & aux Pays-Bas / Tome Premiere / Cette nouvelle manière de graver ne fut trouvée que vers le milieu du dernier siecle. Nous en sommes redevables à Robert Comte Palatin du Rhin Duc de Cumberland & Vice-admiral d'Angleterre. Le prince avoit non seulement du goût pour le peinture, il l'exercoit luy meme; il l'aimoit, il n'en faut d'autre preuve que de avoir enrichie en imaginant cette nouvelle espèce de gravure, fort differente pour la conduitte du travail de toutes celles qui avoient

jusques alors eté en usage: Car aulieu que n'est guère marquant des trait sur le cuivre avec la pointe ou le burin, que l'on y fait paroistre ce que l'on a dessein d'y [imprimer *crossed out*] representer il faut aucontraire dans cet autre genre efface pour y exprimer ce que l'on desir."

4. BNMS R069883–069884: "Smith en a gravé un grand nombre de cette sorte en Angleterre dans ce dernier temps & l'on peut dire qu'il a poussé cette gravure au plus haut point de perfection on elle pouvoit arriver."

5. The print, mounted on fol. 43, is signed by Meheux, who is identified by Nagler 1835–1852, p. 189, and other older cataloguers as Jacques Maheux. Thieme-Becker, vol. 24, p. 337, corrects this identification to Francis Meheux, describing him as an engraver and not a mezzotinter but citing the mezzotint after Ribera among his works.

6. Jean Mariette assumed his place in the family trade in 1691, setting up shop at "rue St-Jacques aux colonnes d'Hercules," the address inscribed on the mezzotint (Préaud 1987, p. 230).

7. BNMS R065895: "Une femme à cheval au milieu d'un troupeau de boeufs & de moutons, gravé en maniere noire par [A. Bouys *crossed out*]. Bernard parent de Bouys c'est le même qui a gravé une [?] d'après Rimbrand." "Bouys" was André Bouys (1656–1740), a French portrait painter and mezzotinter whom Mariette complimented only as a printmaker (Mariette 1851–1860, vol. 1, p. 166). The illegible word presumably specifies the *Adoration* by Bernard after Rembrandt.

8. The eighteenth-century print cataloguer Heinecken attributed the print to Samuel Bernard, presumably Jacques-Samuel Bernard (1615–1687), one of the founding members of the French Academy, whom he takes pains to differentiate from three other artists with the same surname, *not* including Louis (Heinecken 1778–1790, vol. 2, p. 558). A print by Samuel Bernard is included in Spencer Album 7. What would seem to be the most detailed account of Louis Bernard's life and oeuvre is found in Meyer, vol. 3, p. 634; but there is no doubt that the artist, whose works are rare, remains very obscure.

9. The second state was published by "la veuve Chéreau." In fact, there were two women, the widows of François Chéreau I and II, who were active print publishers after 1729 (Préaud 1987, pp. 80–82). Other alterations of the plate in the second state include the reworking of the light sky at the upper left, so that two-thirds of the area is covered with an amorphous patch that looks rather like a funnel cloud. Some of the highlights on the woman and horse are burnished; others are darkened. Speaking generally, the rework is extremely coarse. An impression of this state is in the Stauffer Collection, New York Public Library. Inspection of the Spencer Album impression, which is excellent, indicates that the mezzotint ground was probably not laid by a mezzotint rocker or a file. It is possible that the plate was grounded by stippling individual dots without a specialized tool.

CHARLES MACE AND CHARLES SIMONNEAU?

Paris 1631 – after 1665 Paris?   Orléans 1645 – 1728 Paris

50   *Jacob Returning from Mesopotamia Sends Messengers to His Brother Esau*, after Castiglione, c. 1665?

etching

319 x 462 mm

inscribed in plate, in design area, lower left: *Gio Benedetto Castiglione Genouese in.*; in lower margin, left: *G. Chasteau, ex cum priuilegio Regis / A Paris Rue St Iacques a l'Ange Gardien*; center: *Jacob ex Mesopotamia redux, nuncios et munera ad fratrem suum Esau mittit. Gen. 32.*

R.-D.VI.281.118 ii/ii, LEB.II.583.8 and LEB.II.618.7, TIB4602.115.45

Richard Norton Fund, s6.76

Jacob ex Mesopotamia redux, nuncios et munera ad fratrem suum Esau mittit. Gen. 32.

This plate is in fact not signed, but every cataloguer has attributed the entire set of twelve prints of Old and New Testament subjects after compositions by Castiglione to which this plate belongs to Charles Macé (or Massé).[1] The compiler of the Spencer Albums began the Castiglione section of the table of contents of Album 6 thus:

> Works invented & engraved by Giovanni Benedetto Castiglione,
>> A Set of eight works of Subjects drawn from sacred history, engraved by Macé & fin-
> ished by Charles Simonneau from drawings by Benedetto,
>> To wit . . .[2]

It is here and not in any subsequent published catalogues that we find a reference to Simonneau. His role in this print would have been very minor, in that this plate was etched in a single bite; also, there are no apparent differences in the handling of figures versus landscape. There are brief passages of engraving in the sky, but these additions would hardly be sufficient to call for the attribution of a second hand. Robert-Dumesnil indicates, however, that several of the other plates in the set were substantially reworked,[3] and inspection of impressions in Spencer Album 6 proves that the revisions were executed entirely with the burin. This reengraving was, presumably, Simonneau's contribution.

Given Simonneau's collaboration in the production of plates for the *Cabinet Crozat* edited by Pierre-Jean Mariette,[4] there seems no reason to doubt the authority of the table of contents, and Simonneau certainly would have had access to the plates. He was a pupil of Guillaume Chasteau (1635–1683) and of Chasteau's brother-in-law Noël Coypel (?–1707), whose names appear as publisher on later states of the Old Testament plates.[5] (No *excudit* appears on first states, which were presumably issued by Macé himself.)

In any case, the set, published and republished over a number of years, indicates the continuing popularity of Castiglione's drawings in early-eighteenth-century Paris.[6] Their subject and mood, especially the gentle and sometimes humorous evocation of ancient pastorales, provided a more approachable model than the austerity of Poussin or the remote nostalgia of Claude. And compared to seventeenth-century Dutch landscape and genre representations, which were increasingly favored by a faction of Parisian connoisseurs, Castiglione's mastery of the academic rhetoric of pose and expression could provide a more comprehensible example to French painters with comparable training.

The particular Castiglione composition used by Macé for *Jacob Returning from Mesopotamia* is known in several versions, all of which feature the youth and the bulging slat-work bird cage carried on horseback. In her catalogue of Castiglione drawings, Percy discusses an example from Windsor, cites another in the collection of the Metropolitan Museum of Art (which she describes as the model for an engraving by Chasteau, mistakenly referring to the publisher whose name is the only one which appears on this print), and mentions others as well. She classifies them all as "variant studio versions"; her summation: "No doubt they all record a lost original."[7]

MBC

1. Le Blanc catalogued the print (and the others in the artist's oeuvre) under both Macé and Massé, assigning a different order to the plates in each listing. See LeB.II.583, 618. Robert-Dumesnil catalogued the print under Massé, and prefaced his listing with a discussion of the spelling of the artist's name, justifying his preference by its spelling in the *Receuil Jabach*, a reproductive print project published in 1754 in which Massé, or Macé, participated. See R.-D.VI.254–255. As the name is spelled Macé on the plates after Castiglione and in the Spencer Album's table of contents, I have preferred this spelling.

2. "Pieces inventées & gravées par Jean Benoist Castiglione, Une Suitte de huit pieces de Sujets tirés de l'histoire Sainte, gravées par Macé & terminées par Charles Simonneau Sur des desseins de Beneditte, Scavoir . . . " The other four plates of the full series of twelve are also included in the album, falling at a later point in the series of works by and after Castiglione.

3. R.-D.VI.280.114, 115; R.-D.VI.282–283.120–123.

4. See the entries on Simonneau in LeB.III.523–525; Thieme-Becker, vol. 31, p. 76; and Paris 1967, p. 175, no. 300.

5. Noël Coypel was for a brief period in the 1680s a print publisher. Two plates bearing a Coypel *excudit* can be ascribed by inference to him; the first, a second edition of a *Visitation* first published in 1681, is inscribed: "A. Coypel junior invenit, Coypel ex." A. Coypel *junior* was Antoine Coypel, a son of Noël born in 1661; both his young age and the distinction made between *invenit* and *ex* point to Noël as the publisher, a commercial role of substantial responsibility. The same distinction, *in* versus *ex* (although without the indication of *junior*), is made in the inscriptions on a print published in 1685, *Christ Healing the Blind Man*. See Garnier 1989, pp. 94, 97. The first print is of more relevance in the context of this print by Macé and Simonneau, because its first edition of 1681 was printed by Chasteau, implying that at Chasteau's death in 1683 his brother-in-law took over his print publishing business, however briefly. The sequences of states given by Robert-Dumesnil for impressions of the set of twelve biblical subjects after Castiglione give Chasteau as its first publisher and Coypel as the second for seven of the twelve plates, not entirely in-

cluding the six that were reworked, presumably by Simonneau. Chasteau's name appears only on second states of the prints and Coypel's only on third states.

6. A set of twelve copies (in reverse and much prettified) of the Macé series by Cajetan Zampini was published in 1786. In the Albertina Castiglione album, which

contains on fol. 11 the print by Macé under discussion here, fol. 75 bears the equivalent print by Zampini, which is inscribed on the rock at the far right: "G. Bened. Castiglionus Genevensis 1758 caz."

7. Percy 1971, p. 64, n. 4.

SEBASTIEN BOURDON

Montpellier 1616 – 1671 Paris

51   *Flight into Egypt*, c. 1650

etching

185 x 236 mm

watermark: illegible

inscribed in plate, lower left: *S. Bourdon, in. et s. cum priuil,*; lower right: *P. Mariette excud.*

R.-D.I.146.25 ii/ii

Gift of Belinda L. Randall from the collection of John Witt Randall, by exchange, s2.73.2

In his manuscript notes Mariette acknowledged the fecundity of Bourdon's powers of pictorial invention, which impelled the seventeenth-century French painter and etcher to create repeated variations of the same subjects; Mariette also commented on Bourdon's "astonishing rapidity" of execution.[1] These artistic attributes are particularly evident in a suite of prints on the theme of the Flight into Egypt, etched in Bourdon's cursory "sketch" style and published in its second state by Pierre Mariette II. The set included in Spencer Album 2 is from this edition, each of the six plates being inscribed "P. Mariette excud." or some variation thereof.

By the seventeenth century, the story of the Flight into Egypt, barely mentioned by only one of the Evangelists,[2] had been elaborated into a lengthy and picturesque narrative and had become a favorite of artists throughout Europe. As in this series by Bourdon, the briefest of biblical descriptions, for example of the angel appearing to Joseph in a dream to instruct him to flee with his family, would be broken into individual images suitable for illustration much like the frames of a movie. The angel appears to the sleeping Joseph *and* the angel instructs Joseph, now awakened. These separate events are represented in plates 1 and 2 of the Bourdon set, which continues, showing the Holy Family on the road (3), embarking on a boat to cross a river (4, this plate), passing a pagan idol which shatters in their presence (5), and returning from Egypt (6). Strangely, in the Spencer Album the two images that refer to the initiating dream of Joseph are mounted *after* two other scenes from the later narrative, and they are separated in the sequence by yet a third.

S. Bourdon, jri.et f.cum priuil.   P. Mariette excud.

The compiler of the album did recognize the suite as such, mounting the six impressions on three successive folios (s2.71–73) and so describing them in the table of contents. Curiously, the standard catalogue of Bourdon's prints published more than two centuries later does not acknowledge that they form a set and simply lists them individually among Bourdon's Holy Family images that are wider than they are high, with one "*Fuite en Egypte*" followed by an "*Autre Fuite en Egypte*" (this print).[3] That the compiler of the Spencer Album did not observe the correct order is an uncharacteristic lapse considering the same compiler's perceptiveness in his arrangement of the four Bourdon landscapes that comprise the far less evident narrative of the parable of the Good Samaritan (see Cat. 60).

Although the etched suite of the Flight into Egypt does not receive nearly the elaboration of scenery or tonal complexity that Bourdon lavished upon the far larger Acts of Mercy and landscape plates, its compositions are nonetheless systematically organized, with attention to every plane and level, as is usual with Bourdon. This rigor of overall organization is masked by the rapid and informal graphic style and a certain calculated casualness; note, for example, the off-center placement of the ovoid form on the pedestal, an antique boundary marker commonly incorporated into Flights into Egypt by classicizing artists such as Poussin and Bourdon for the perfection of its geometry.

The seemingly casual draftsmanship in the suite is matched by a studied informality of pictorial device. In this river landscape, the boatman backing his punt toward the rude wharf plants his pole *outside* the picture frame, and the hindquarters of the ass are just cut off by the plate's edge on the opposite side. These apparent miscalculations of allotted space cause the action to span the entire sheet, exactly parallel to the picture's plane and parallel, too, to the cascade, building façades, and cliffs stacked behind, to form yet another paradigm of Bourdon's characteristic system of spatial recession through accumulation.

The specific episode of the Holy Family crossing a river was represented in Italian art by the end of the sixteenth century; it was not introduced to France until the seventeenth, perhaps by Nicolas Poussin.[4] Presumably this etching, and the entire set of six, date from sometime after Poussin's influence becomes increasingly evident in the art of Bourdon, in the early 1640s. Bourdon retains in this series a love of genre detail, however, which was marked in his earlier career in Rome, when he was strongly indebted to the art of Pieter van Laer and other Bambloccianti.[5]

MBC

1. Mariette 1851–1860, vol. 1, p. 170: "... plein de feu et de facilité, il inventoit et executoit avec une étonnante rapidité; il produsoit aisement une infinité de compositions differentes sur un mesme sujet."

2. Matthew 2:13–15.

3. R.-D.I.144–147. The catalogue does, however, list them in correct iconographic sequence, and they thus implicitly form a set, as these six are the only horizontal Flights into Egypt within Bourdon's printed oeuvre.

4. According to Réau 1955–1959, p. 283. A French artist, François Perrier, made a print of the same subject, which Clark dates to c. 1640, when Perrier was resident in Rome (Clark 1987, pp. 43–44). Perrier returned to Paris only in 1645; the plate was issued by a French publisher.

5. See Briganti et al. 1983, pp. 238–47.

JACQUES CALLOT

Nancy 1592 – 1635 Nancy

52a   *Frontispiece, Balli di Sfessania*, c. 1622

etching

71 x 93 mm

inscribed in plate, below background figures: *Benemia Cucurucu*; below foreground figures: *lucia mia Bernoialla Che buona mi sa*; in lower margin: *BALLI DI SFESSANIA / di Jacomo Callot / Jac. Callot In. fe.*

L.379 i/iii

Gray Collection of Engravings Fund, by exchange, s4.27.1

52b *Capitano Esgangarato and Capitano Cocodrillo,*
from *Balli di Sfessania,* c. 1622

etching

71 x 93 mm

inscribed in plate, below figures: *Cap.º Esgangarato. Cap.º Cocodrillo*

L.392 i/ii

Gray Collection of Engravings Fund, by exchange, s4.27.3

52c *Capitano Babeo and Cucuba,* from *Balli di Sfessania,* c. 1622

etching

72 x 91 mm

inscribed in plate, below figures: *Cap. Babeo Cucuba.*

L.394 i/ii

Gray Collection of Engravings Fund, by exchange, s4.28.1

52d *Razullo and Cucurucu,* from *Balli di Sfessania,* c. 1622

etching

72 x 93 mm

inscribed in plate, below figures: *Razullo. Cucurucu.*

L.397 i/ii

Gray Collection of Engravings Fund, by exchange, s4.29.2

Throughout his career, both in Florence and in Nancy, Callot frequently etched representations of theatrical events and characters. The set of twenty-four plates titled *Balli di Sfessania* is generally agreed to present his powers in this genre at their height, shortly after his return to his homeland in 1621. Presumably the *Balli* was inspired by his memories of Italian comedians whose fantastic costumes and performances would have been very much to the taste of the court of Lorraine—"luxury-loving, extravagant and given to masques and balls"[1]—which he hoped to impress. The care with which he prepared the plates from drawings and counterproofs, exceptional for him in its technical thoroughness, is indicative of his concern for the series's success.[2]

And succeed it did. Among Callot's many series, the *Balli de Sfessania* has remained one of the most popular. The plates, which still survive in the Musée Historique Lorrain, were printed until only the deepest lines of the foreground figures remained, with the distant background scenes

utterly worn away; and they were copied repeatedly, with some of the pirated versions being remarkably accurate.[3]

One of the consequences of their wide diffusion was that within the larger context of latter-day study of seventeenth-century culture, the *Balli* came to be identified with the commedia dell'arte, that form of dramatic presentation which, from its origins in the sixteenth century and continuing through the eighteenth, retains its hold on the imagination even now, when the names Punch, Harlequin, and Scaramouche still evoke their characters' stereotypical roles. The strength of the popular association of Callot's plates with the commedia dell'arte is the despair of modern scholars whose histories of the theatrical form dwell upon its consummate achievement in developing sustained, complex characterizations through ever self-renewing verbal improvisation.[4] Neapolitan actors have been regarded as a contaminating influence on its fragile balance,[5] and there is general agreement that the bizarre musicians and sinewy acrobats of the *Balli* represent in fact characters from the world of the carnival to whom Callot somewhat haphazardly assigned the names and costumes of both Neapolitan and Tuscan commedia dell'arte actors.[6]

A conventional, albeit rudimentary, commedia dell'arte production is seen in the background of *Razullo and Cucurucu*. A *zanni* (servant) and *capitano* on each side of an elegantly garbed and gracefully posed lady stand before a backdrop painted with noble architecture complete with a statue in a niche, all arranged on a portable stage. Their audience ignores the flamboyantly ithyphallic musician and dancer in the near ground of the print. Obscenities of costume are only one aspect of Callot's ribaldry: in *Capitano Babeo and Cucuba*, Cucuba's well-padded posterior suggests the slam-bang comedy routine for which he is prepared; and the lewd gesture of Babeo with his sword is amplified in a mid-ground episode in which bellows wielded by a patch-clad Harlequin pump into the anus of a donkey, whose tail is held up by another *zanni* mounted backwards upon the beast. On the back of that *zanni* a basket contains two cats (or dogs?) who, one suspects, are also about to be subjected to ridiculous tortures.

The name *Balli di Sfessania* "appears as the name of a popular dance in a description of carnival festivities of 1588 in Naples,"[7] and in the Neapolitan dialect the root word *sfessà* means to break, beat up, reduce to a rough and ugly condition. Together these suggest the peculiar and local aspects of commedia dell'arte Callot has represented.

Nothing, of course, could be less rough or ugly than Callot etchings, and their appeal to the highest society and the most refined connoisseurs is no more remarkable than the modern-day success enjoyed by Leonard Bernstein's *West Side Story*, his version of *Romeo and Juliet* embedded in the culture, musical and otherwise, of New York's Puerto Rican ghetto. The reception today of break dancing and rap, veering between "dangerous depravity" and "elegant expressionism," is no different from earlier responses to the commedia dell'arte troupes whose acrobatics in the flesh appalled and enchanted depending upon the relative quotient of obscenity and prudery among players and public at any given performance.[8] Finally, one might extend the parallel to a consideration of the undeniable reflection of the late works of Michelangelo in these etchings by Callot.[9] Does the reduction of sublime works of art, such as those by Michelangelo or Shakespeare, provide a frisson of recognition which, along with eroticism and the appropriation of vital ethnic art forms, is essential for the stimulus of taste in "luxury-loving, extravagant," and perhaps jaded societies?

MBC

1. Wright 1985, pp. 15–16.

2. Russell 1975, p. 77, nos. 80–88.

3. Russell 1975, nos. 101–103.

4. See for example Nicoll 1963, pp. 61, 74–75, and Taviani and Schino 1984, pp. 56, 129. Russell 1975, pp. 74–75, gives a summary of the scholarly history of the *Balli* specifically as it relates to the larger study of the history of theater. The section relating to Callot and the theater in this source was written by Jeffrey Blanchard.

5. Nicoll 1963, p. 61.

6. Callot is not known to have visited Naples, but one of the most important commedia dell'arte troupes played in Florence under the patronage of his Medici patron during his sojourn there.

7. Russell 1975, p. 76.

8. Two entertainingly ambivalent eighteenth-century reactions to commedia dell'arte performances in England are recorded in the diaries of Mrs. Delany and Count von Uffenbach (Delany 1861–1862, vol. 1, p. 127; Uffenbach 1934, p. 31).

9. My thanks to Alvin L. Clark, Jr., for his provocative suggestion of the derivation of Callot's muscular figures from the late style of Michelangelo and the Mannerist art that derived from it.

GIOVANNI BENEDETTO CASTIGLIONE

Genoa 1609 – 1664 Milan

53 *Man Wearing a Cap with a Large Plume (so-called Self-Portrait)*, c. 1648

etching

189 x 137 mm

watermark: three mountains surmounted by an illegible device, perhaps a fleur-de-lys within a circle, perhaps similar to Heawood 1617 (Rome?, c. 1630)

inscribed in plate, upper left: *GB. CASTILIONVS / GENOVESE. FE.*; at left below faint sketch of a head: *.CASTILIONVUS*

B.XXI.27.31 and B.XXI.56.53, TIB46.44.31, TIB4602.47.031 s1, Percy E 19

Gift of Belinda L. Randall from the collection of John Witt Randall, by exchange. s6.94.5

Castiglione etched twenty-two heads of exotic and ornamental character (TIB46.44–56.31–53).[1] They are called, generally, Oriental heads, although the title of their republication by Basan, *Diverses testes du Benedet [Various Heads by Benedetto]* is more accurate if specifics of costume and facial type are examined. Yet the catch-all "Oriental" is not entirely misplaced, for in costume, features, and expression all except the virtually classical profile of a young man facing right (TIB46.50.47) fall within the long tradition of the Magi, wise men from the East who do not participate in Western conventions of beauty and garb. This fascination with the Oriental as the type of the exotic had long since extended to figures who represent the "other," whether actual Orientals such as Suleyman II as engraved by Melchior Lorch in 1559 (Hollstein XXII.209.34, Hollstein.XXII.211.35) or the ragged band of scowling mercenaries engraved by Albrecht Dürer as early as 1495 (Hollstein VII.76.81), whose turban and plumes are as fantastic as any Baroque headgear. In Castiglione's scenes of Old Testament patriarchs and pagan herdsmen, there too the prominent head coverings are wrapped and slung, not formed and poised, and the features, old or young, are apt to be pudgy or gaunt, pouting or distorted into a grimace.

Yet there are many distinctions to be made among the twenty-two etched heads. The most obvious one is size: six, including this one, are relatively large, and the rest are relatively small. Within the two classes, dimensions are approximately the same; but in this case even a small difference is significant: the plate of this head is four millimeters higher than its closest comparison, the other large head facing forward (TIB46.55.52). Unlike the head on exhibition, which is delicately etched, that large head is richly textured like the remaining four, all older men (TIB46.51–54.48–51); and the unity of these five as a subset of large heads, suggested by their virtually uniform size, is confirmed by the survival of two proof sheets which demonstrate that

Bartsch 52 and 51 and Bartsch 50 and 49 were originally etched as pairs on two plates, later cut in half.[2] This head of a young man, then, stands apart, in size and in lightness of touch and complexity of expression.

Among the smaller heads, the distinction is not so much size as technique. A number of them, too, were originally etched on a single plate (B.34, 38, 39, 42, 46, 47).[3] These six are in what Röhn has called Castiglione's "*Kritzeltechnik*,"[4] or scribble technique, an apt description of lines formed as if by a directed nervous tremor so loosely controlled that their clusters only gradually take on the characteristics of a specific substance or surface. This scribbled line and the soft, flickering shadow masses it forms in these six heads, in the five large heads that seem to be closely associated, and in some of Castiglione's mysterious etched nocturnal scenes (see Cat. 14) have led all of the Italian artist's admirers to compare him to Rembrandt; and the heads themselves have traditionally provided the obvious link, for virtually identical conceptions were etched in the 1630s by Jan Lievens, Rembrandt, and Salomon Konick.[5]

Rembrandt's influence on Castiglione has been discerned in his prints as early as the late 1630s, when the Italian artist was working in Rome.[6] The heads are conventionally dated to the late 1640s, after his return to Rome c. 1647 following a stay of several years in his native Genoa and before his departure for Mantua in 1651, with the *post quem* of 1647 determined by the logical inconsistency of an artist still living in Genoa feeling obliged to identify himself as "Genovese" on each plate, as Castiglione did.[7]

Why the heads cannot be later than 1651 has never been so sensibly derived. If, however, the small heads that did not once form a single plate and are not in the scribble technique—that is, all ten others—are examined, it will be seen that they are in quite another graphic style, one which Bellini in another context has associated with the influence of the great etcher from Lucca, Pietro Testa, as early as 1635–1640.[8]

While we do not propose to move these heads to such an early date, the "sharp rendering of line," to quote Bellini's apt characterization, does seem to be favored by Castiglione as late as his *Genius of Castiglione* (TIB46.36.23), generally agreed to have been etched in Genoa but printed in Rome and thus datable to c. 1647.[9] Not incidentally, this etching features two of the artist's most elaborate inventions of headcoverings, and the small heads that are not in the scribble technique can be associated with this composition in that they too tend to be more generically ornamental and less specifically Oriental in their headgear.

Thus one can imagine that the artist etched the first ten as a set in 1648. Then, caught up by a new graphic style, perhaps seen in prints by Rembrandt and other Dutch artists newly available to him in Rome in his association with its large colony of resident Lowlanders,[10] he essayed the large heads in direct imitation of Dutch prototypes and also scribbled six additional small heads, using a single plate to guarantee uniformity of bite.

Why am I so preoccupied with differentiating among the various heads by Castiglione when only one is the ostensible subject of this entry? Because the three pages of the Spencer Album on which all twenty-two are mounted are among the most impressive ensembles in all of the albums, and, more importantly, the compiler of the album over 250 years ago recognized all of the distinctions I am making today. All six small scribbled heads are among the eight which frame the dark larger head seen full face, with these eight carefully arranged so that their gazes wreathe the somber glare of the central image. This magnificently Baroque array is followed by a page holding the four remaining dark large heads. All are in rich impressions. Two pages later we are confronted by the head that is our primary subject. Much paler, veiled in a brownish plate tone rather than intensely black and white, it is surrounded by the remaining eight small sharp-style heads, their gazes nodding and bobbing around the focal visage.

This face does not seem to confront us, however, so much as to look within itself; and it is for this reason, as well as its obvious derivation from Rembrandt's etched self-portraits of the 1630s, that it has been considered Castiglione's self-portrait.[11] It derives its strength from the same traditional associations that make Rembrandt's self-portraits, painted and etched, in which he has dressed in exotic and ornamental costume, so compelling. The tradition of the Oriental, or "other," has become absorbed into the self so that it is within one's own body and soul that a strange and unaccustomed world is to be sought.

Although the earliest print catalogue to identify this head as a portrait of Castiglione was not published until 1800,[12] Mariette implied that he understood it to be such when he arranged the Castigliones in Prince Eugene of Savoy's album, now at the Albertina.[13] The prince's collection features many portraits of artists as the appropriate first image in the compilations of their works, and this large head begins the set of Castiglione compositions, which then continues in traditional iconographical order with subjects from the Old Testament. The rest of the etched heads are inserted much later in the sequence.   MBC

1. B.XXI.56.53 as described by Bartsch seems to be a first state of this print, with the sketched head and secondary signature at the lower left absent. No impression of this state or of another print answering the same description is known, and it is presumed that Bartsch was mistaken. See the discussion by Paolo Bellini in TIB4602.47.31.

2. Although B.XXI.32.48 is slightly larger than the other four large heads with which it is usually associated, it is identical in hatching technique with B.XXI.33.49–51. See TIB4602.58–60, for reproductions of the undivided plates. In all cases the individual heads were fully signed by the artist before the division of the plates, indicating that they were always intended to be divided.

3. See TIB4602.49, for reproductions of the undivided plates, which also contained brief landscape and figure sketches catalogued after their separation as B.XXI.8. 63–66.

4. Röhn 1932, p. 2.

5. For references to these plates, see Ackley 1981, pp. 140–41.

6. Percy 1971, pp. 27, 136.

7. This author must confess to the suspicion that any printmaker hopeful for the wide distribution of his works might cite his native city even if he remained there. But the chronology proposed by Percy, Bellini, and others is still credible.

8. TIB4602.16, in connection with Castiglione's *Laban Searching for Idols* (TIB46.18.4).

9. Reed and Wallace 1989, p. 267.

10. *The Genius of Castiglione* is dedicated to a Dutch art patron resident in Rome; see the previous note.

11. See TIB4602.46–47, where this identification and also one as a portrait of the sculptor Gianlorenzo Bernini are discussed and reproductions of other portraits of Castiglione and Bernini are given.

12. Huber 1797–1804, p. 30, no. 25. He also saw a self-portrait among the smaller heads. In his earlier print manual, Huber titled the heads *Têtes de caracteres* (Huber 1787, p. 429).

13. The sequence of Castigliones in Prince Eugene's album is given in BNMS R065889. This print is mounted on fol. 1.

GIOVANNI BATTISTA GALESTRUZZI

Florence 1618 – after 1669 Rome

54a *Bust of a Woman in a Niche between Two Vases,* c. 1656–1660, after Polidoro da Caravaggio

etching

118 x 169 mm

inscribed in plate, lower left: *POLIDORO INVEN.*; lower right: *3 / Gio. Batta. Galestruzzi fece*

B.XXI.64.49, TIB46.106.49

Gift of Belinda L. Randall from the collection of John Witt Randall, by exchange, s2.51.2

54b *Coat of Mail with a Bandolier between Two Vases,* c. 1656–1660, after Polidoro da Caravaggio

etching

119 x 157 mm

inscribed in plate, lower left: *POLIDORO INVEN*; lower right: *4 / Gio. BaT Galestruzzi f*

B.XXI.64.50, TIB46.107.50

Gift of Belinda L. Randall from the collection of John Witt Randall, by exchange, s2.51.5

These two etchings reproduce elements from the frescoed façade of a Roman palace, the Palazzo Milesi in the Via della Maschera d'Oro. The paintings, now worn by the elements and essentially destroyed,[1] presented an assortment of mythological and ancient Roman figures and subjects together with ornamental devices derived from antique sources. These were simulated in strong chiaroscuro, imitating the effect of statues and bas-relief friezes not by means of simple grisaille but rather in a colored imitation of marbles and bronze.[2] The Palazzo Milesi paintings, dated to c. 1527, were the masterpiece of Polidoro da Caravaggio (c. 1600–1643), an artist who was the pre-eminent specialist of his time in the decoration of building exteriors.

The painting of façades had by the early 1500s a long history in Europe, with religious, heraldic, and purely ornamental motifs predominating. There was also a late medieval figurative tradition in Italy, which lasted into the sixteenth century, of the civic dishonoring of enemies by hanging their painted representation on city buildings.[3] Façade painting offered, of course, a less expensive alternative to the building or rebuilding of a structure with architectural or sculptural elements to conform to prevailing fashion.

The works of Polidoro marked the introduction into façade painting of a greater figurative element, with an emphasis upon the ancient legends, histories, and heroes. Ornament was not neglected, but it was increasingly dominated by schemes derived from antiquity, usually with the intention of organizing the components of a façade that might in itself, like that of the Palazzo Milesi, be architecturally undistinguished, into a larger ensemble reflecting the antiquarian ideals of the Renaissance.[4] Polidoro's scheme for the Palazzo Milesi, which was apparently completed just before the sack of Rome in 1527 when the artist left the city, was acknowledged as the masterpiece of the new style. Famous through the following centuries, its motifs were repeatedly copied in prints and drawings and were widely influential. Galestruzzi's plates continued to be published long after they had lost the freshness that characterizes the Spencer Album impressions.

Galestruzzi divided the elements of the façade decoration into homogeneous groups of like motifs, which he issued in five separate sets. Three of these (*Story of Niobe* [TIB46.87–89.16–20], *Antique War Trophies* [TIB46.100–103.41–46], and *Statues of Three Ancient Romans* [TIB46.109.52, a single print that reproduces two separate façade elements]) are dated 1656, 1658, and 1660 respectively; one can only assume that the two undated sets (*Subjects from Roman History* [TIB46.78–80.3–8] and *Trophies of Arms and Vases* [TIB46.104–108.47–51]) were published during the same approximate period. With regard to size, the five sets are not perfectly uniform within themselves, nor do their relative dimensions exactly reproduce the relationships among the various façade elements. Still, however, an interested purchaser in 1660 could have cut and pasted his print acquisitions to assemble significant portions of the entire façade. (Interestingly, the compiler of Spencer Album 2, which contains three of the five sets, made no attempt to do this on the album folios.)

Our putative seventeenth-century purchaser would have the entire frieze above the ground floor of the Palazzo Milesi (*Story of Niobe*). He would have the painted statues (*Statues of Three Ancient Romans*) that filled the spaces between the first and second, and second and third windows of the first story; and he would have the complete frieze, of alternated narrative scenes (*Subjects from Roman History*) and decorative elements (*Trophies of Arms and Vases*), which ran above these windows. Finally, he would have the trophies (*Antique War Trophies*) that formed decorative pediments for the five windows on the second story. He would lack, however, another five[5] single and paired standing statues that completed the first floor decorations and the leftmost decoration on the second story; three large narrative scenes featuring representations of important classical monuments, which filled in the spaces between the windows on the second story;[6] and five[7] smaller figural groups that ornamented the third story.[8]

One can only speculate whether Galestruzzi intended to complete his reproduction of the palazzo with these additional subjects. The existence of only one plate of the statues of ancient Romans, which is the only case of an incomplete representation of a single type within the façade decoration as a whole and which bears the latest date of the three dated sets, implies that an ongoing project was interrupted and never resumed before the etcher's death a decade or so later.

243

These sparkling impressions betray Galestruzzi's debt to Stefano della Bella, his virtual contemporary who had also been born in Florence and who at the time of these etchings was also working in Rome. Della Bella, too, made many etchings with antique motifs, and even copied an "antique bas-relief" painted on a house façade by Polidoro.[9] He also executed a series of prints of antique vases alike in type to the four seen on these two plates by Galestruzzi, but della Bella's were free inventions, caprices which even included spritely blossoms and tufts of foliage ornamenting the ornaments (DEV.-M.1045–1050). By comparison, Galestruzzi's vases and his bust and shirt of mail are serious productions. Although they are copies of Polidoro and not of antiquities, they betray Galestruzzi's own more literal approach to the archaeological recoveries so sought after and emulated in sixteenth- and seventeenth-century Rome. He was the etcher commissioned to illustrate a scholarly publication of ancient carved gems; the 274 plates (TIB46.117–256.59–335) that he produced for *Le gemme antiche figurale* (1657) make up the largest portion of his oeuvre.

This is not to minimize, however, Galestruzzi's lively touch with the needle. Although his plates should be characterized as reproductive, nowhere does he lapse into the conventions of

244

the engraver. The designs were first completely realized, with a substantial amount of shading included, in a single bite; and then a second, heavier set of lines was added overall. Like many seventeenth-century Italian etchers, Galestruzzi did not resort to expedients particular to etching, such as the use of stop-out varnish or burnishing, but depended upon his draftsmanship to make faithful reproductions and vivid representations.

MBC

1. The palazzo façade as it appeared in 1969 is seen in Marabottini 1969, vol. 2, pl. 146. Plate 147 reproduces a late nineteenth-century engraving by E. Maccari, which shows the decorations to have been largely intact, or at least legible, at that time. Marabottini 1969, vol. 1, pp. 108, 126–29, 366–69, provides a full discussion of the work and its importance within the oeuvre of Polidoro da Caravaggio.

2. Marabottini 1969, vol. 1, p. 127.

3. See Samuel Y. Edgerton, *Pictures and Punishment: Art and Criminal Prosecution during the Florentine Renaissance* (Ithaca: Cornell University Press, [1985]).

4. See Marabottini 1969 and also Brown/RISD 1980 concerning these developments. Gunther and Christel Thiem, *Toskanische Fassaden-Dekoration in Sgraffito und Fresko, 14. bis 17. Jahrhundert* (Munich: F. Bruck-

mann, 1964), and Cecilia Pericoli Ridolfini, *Le casa romane con facciate graffiti e dipinti* (Rome, 1960), offer overviews of central Italian façade painting.

5. Or seven? These figures are derived from the representation of the façade in the engraving by Maccari, in which the right edge of the structure at the levels of the windows on the first, second, and third floors is shown as undecorated. The left edge at these levels is decorated, and the asymmetry represented by the engraving is highly improbable.

6. Marabottini 1969, p. 367.

7. Or six; see n. 5 relative to the standing statues.

8. Marabottini 1969, vol. 1, p. 367, suggests that a print by Cherubino Alberti (TIB34.287.158) that represents putti supporting garlands could reproduce ornamental elements of the façade's painted decoration, which had been lost by the time of the Maccari engraving. One of the putti holds a mask, perhaps referring to the Via della Maschera d'Oro, the location of the palazzo.

9. *Phalaris and Perillus* (DEV.-M.41); an impression is included in Spencer Album 7 (s7.138.2).

STEFANO DELLA BELLA
Florence 1610 – 1664 Florence

55a   *Title Page*, plate 1 of *New Inventions for Cartouches*, 1647

etching

124 x 91 mm

inscribed in plate, in cartouche: *Nouuelles inventions de / Cartouches designes et graues / a leau forte par E de la belle / florentin. / A PARIS / chez la Vefue F.Langlois dict / Chartres, rue S. Iacques, / aux collonnes d'Hercules, / auec priuilege du Roy / 1647*; lower right: *1*

DEV.-M.1015 ii/ii

Gray Collection of Engravings Fund, by exchange, s7.182.1

55b   *Cartouche, Its Field Formed by Drapery over an Ionic Monument Held by Two Skeletons Lying on the Entablature*, plate 10 of *New Inventions for Cartouches*, 1647

etching

123 x 89 mm

inscribed in plate, lower left: *S. Della Bella fecit cum Priuil Regis*; lower right: *10*

DEV.-M.1024 ii/ii

Gray Collection of Engravings Fund, by exchange, s7.183.4

55c *Cartouche with Five Ducks and Four Dogs*, plate 3
of *New Inventions for Cartouches*, 1647

etching

121 x 97 mm

watermark: fragmentary

inscribed in plate, lower left: *S. Della Bella fecit cum Priuil Regis*; lower right: *3*

DEV.-M.1017 ii/ii

Gray Collection of Engravings Fund, by exchange, s7.182.3

55d *Cartouche, Its Field Formed by a Tiger Skin Held by Two
Centaurs*, plate 4 of *New Inventions for Cartouches*, 1647

etching

123 x 91 mm

inscribed in plate, lower left: *S. Della Bella fecit cum Priuil Regis*; lower right: *4*

DEV.-M.1018 ii/ii

Gray Collection of Engravings Fund, by exchange, s7.182.4

Ornament prints have been in circulation since the fifteenth century as direct models for artisans in many trades, as demonstrations of technical virtuosity, and as inventions engraved for the pure pleasure of their creator and others. Della Bella was a prolific and endlessly inventive source of ornament designs, utilizing earlier forms and adapting them to his own practical and fanciful purposes. It should be recalled that he was first apprenticed to a Florentine goldsmith, where he undoubtedly was exposed to such design work.

The more practical designs for embroidery, architectural decoration, metalwork, or even calligraphy were literally used to death in workshops and homes throughout Europe, and consequently their survival rate has been lower than their more impractical fantastic counterparts. While definitely leaning toward the more surreal, many of Stefano's ornamental prints actually were quite influential in later Baroque and Rococo decorative arts.[1] In addition to this series of cartouches, della Bella etched series of ornamental designs for vases, friezes, grotesques, and book titles—nearly one hundred separate plates. The Spencer Albums contain virtually all of his ornament prints and a few engraved by other printmakers after his designs.[2] Few print rooms have such extensive runs of ornament prints, and the della Bella sets complement others in the Spencer Albums, such as those by Galestruzzi and Fialetti also in the exhibition (Cat. 54a–b, 19a–b).

Stefano etched two series of cartouches, loosely defined; this set of twelve designs and a sec-

Nouuelles inuentions de
Cartouches designes et graues
a leau forte par E. de la belle
florantin.

A PARIS
chez la Vefue F. Langlois dict
Chartres, rue S. Iacques,
aux collonnes d'Hercules,
auec priuilege du Roy
1647

S. Della Bella fecit cum Priuil. Regis

S. Della Bella fecit cum Priuil. Regis

S. Della Bella fecit cum Priuil. Regis

ond one of eighteen larger, more formal designs executed the year before and entitled *Raccolta di varii capriccii et nove inventioni di cartelle et ornamenti* (*Collection of various caprices and new inventions of inscriptions and ornaments*, DEV.-M.1027–44). The set exhibited here was etched in Paris and published by the widow of one of the most important publishers in that city, François Langlois (1588–1647), who had spent time in Rome and cultivated relationships with many printmakers there. Madeleine de Collemont Langlois (d. 1664) ran the print publishing firm after her husband's death and merged the Langlois holdings with the Mariette family business in 1655 through her marriage to Pierre Mariette II (see the Introduction and Cat. 38).[3]

By this time, the term *cartouche* had already traveled far from its original meaning of an ornamental tablet "simulating a scroll of cut parchment usually framing an inscription or shield."[4] Della Bella certainly applied the term loosely to his framing devices, which include cavorting humans, satyrs, ducks, dragons, putti, and skeletons. Certain of the blank "shields" at the center of these designs are formed of animal skins or draped cloths. Massar has read a scribbled inscription by della Bella on a touched first-state proof of the title to the series (DEV.-M.1015) as representing cartouches or coats of arms ("scudi d'armes"), but the more inclusive title did not make it to the engraved title inscription.[5] Certainly, della Bella regarded the term as merely a stepping-off point for his "new inventions." Through the myriads of ornament designs and forms that have come down through history, styles and terms often become inextricably mixed and at times fruitless to trace.

The earliest, more specific cartouche ornament prints would seem to have arisen in Northern Europe in the sixteenth century, including those by Hans Sebald Beham in Germany and Cornelis Bos and Hans Vredeman de Vries in the Netherlands, in some cases derived from the innovative decorations of the Palace of Fontainebleau by Rosso Fiorentino from the 1530s.[6] An influential new style of cartouche was inaugurated by Federico Zuccaro in Italy about 1600 and further developed by Agostino Mitelli in the 1630s.[7] These ever more elaborate cartouches have been seen by Berliner as an important element in the emerging style of Baroque ornament, and they were utilized on many architectural façades in the seventeenth century.[8]

Several of the designs in della Bella's *New Inventions for Cartouches* (though none of the four exhibited) employ the common expedient of showing asymmetrical variants of the same design on either side of the shield, i.e., splitting the design elements along the vertical axis. For instance, plate 7 (DEV.-M.1021) has a knight's helmet on the left half of the design and a cardinal's hat on the right. Several assume an insubstantial, floating quality on the sheet, anticipating the eighteenth-century love of the vignette for book illustrations. For instance, plate 3 (DEV.-M.1017) has several ducks paddling about in the water in the foreground and flapping their wings in the reeds around the central shield, all attempting to escape four eager dogs. Plates 5 and 6 (DEV.-M.1019, 1020) excerpt the Ovidian myths of Pan and Syrinx and Apollo and Daphne. Plates 9 and 10 (DEV.-M.1023, 1024) reveal della Bella's constant preoccupation with the theme of death, expressed most notably in his own version of the traditional Dance of Death (DEV.-M.87–92) and his panoramic view *Death on a Battlefield* (DEV.-M.93).

Six preparatory studies for these cartouches are in the Kunstbibliothek, Berlin; they are free and fairly finished ideas for the final prints, executed in della Bella's characteristic medium of pen and brown ink over preliminary graphite sketches.[9] In addition, three sheets in the Louvre[10] contain several studies probably made from life for the ducks in plate 3.

DPB

1. See, for instance, several late eighteenth-century Wedgwood vases based on Stefano's *Raccolta di vasi diversi* (DEV.-M. 1045–50), cited by Timothy Clifford, "Some English Ceramic Vases and their Sources, Part One," *English Ceramic Circle Transactions* 10, no. 3 (1978), pp. 166–67, repr. pls. 76–77.

2. The primary sets of ornament plates are DEV.-M.980–1050; these do not include his many theatrical designs, title pages, initials, etc.

3. See Préaud 1987, p. 193.

4. Harold Osborne, ed., *The Oxford Companion of Art* (Oxford: Clarendon Press, 1970), p. 210. The term, taken from the French, ultimately derives from the Latin word for paper (*charta*). See also the discussion of the term in Ward-Jackson 1967, pp. 131–34.

5. In the Metropolitan Museum of Art, New York; see DEV.-M.1015 addenda.

6. See Ward-Jackson 1967, p. 131, and Berliner and Egger 1981, cat. 113, 643–644, and 687–690, respectively.

7. Zuccaro's designs were engraved in 1628 by H. Picart; they are reproduced in Berliner and Egger 1981, cat. 731–734; Mitelli's are reproduced in cat. 755, 756. See also another printed series designed by Bernardino Radi, engraved in Florence in 1636 (Berliner and Egger 1981, cat. 754).

8. For some uses of the cartouche on architectural façades, see Rudolf Wittkower, *Art and Architecture in Italy 1600 to 1750* (Harmondsworth: Penguin Books, 1980), p. 240, fig. 145 (Pietro da Cortona), or p. 204, fig. 119 (Francesco Borromini).

9. They are catalogued, and four are reproduced, in Ekhart Berckenhagen, *Die französischen Zeichnungen der Kunstbibliothek Berlin* (Berlin: Bruno Hessling, 1970), p. 82.

10. Viatte 1974, p. 119, nos. 168–70, repr. p. 117.

STEFANO DELLA BELLA

Florence 1610 – 1664 Florence

56   *Saint Prosper Relieving the City of Reggio*, c. 1652

etching

238 x 350 mm

watermark: radiant sun within a circle; countermark: illegible

inscribed in plate, lower margin, left: *PRECATIO / Salua plebem presentem tibi commissam S. Prosper, pie Pastor, / neqi sinas perdere greges, quos hic reliquisti orphanos, sed semper / tuere munimine tuo, quos habes representandos omnipotenti Deo / V. Ora pro nobis Beate Prosper. / R. Vt digni efficiamur promissionibus christi.*; right: *OREMVS / Propitiare quesumus Domine, nobis Famulis tuis per gloriosa S. prosperi / Confessoris, atq. Pontificis merita, ut eius pia intercessione ab omnibus / Semper, et ubique muniamur, et protegamur aduerssis. Per. Xpm. Dnm. Nom. A / V. Exaudiat nos Dominus. / R. Et custodiat nos semper.*; lower right corner: *SDBella I. & F.*

DEV.-M.28 i/ii

Gray Collection of Engravings Fund, by exchange, s7.6.3

The subject of this print would seem to be conclusively established by the prayers to Saint Prosper inscribed in the margin, prayers that are still said in the basilica dedicated to that saint in Reggio, near Modena. The evidence is yet more definitive in the second state of this plate, in which a dedication with appropriate armorial bearings to Count Francesco Calcagno, who was named provost of the basilica of Saint Prosper in 1647, fills in the blank center of the margin. But in fact no such incident, in which a besieging army is routed by the heavenly apparition of a warrior bishop, is recorded in the life of Saint Prosper or in the annals of Reggio, nor does Reggio look like the fortified city lying in a broad plain seen in the midground of the etching.

We do read, however, in the life of Saint Andrea Corsini, bishop of Fiesole (d. 1373), of his intercession against the Florentines in the battle of Anghiari, fought in 1440. An ingenious print connoisseur of the early nineteenth century, Fr. Pietro Zani, has suggested that the Florentines, della Bella's compatriots, would have been offended by his portrayal of several among the fleeing soldiers in Turkish costume, as if the Florentines had hired infidel mercenaries; and so the artist, seeking a more compliant patron for the etching, added the incongruous prayers and dedication to Saint Prosper.[1]

Certainly this was a print destined for public presentation. It is etched in a style that comes closest among Stefano della Bella's many hundred prints and several styles to the accepted graphic ideal for prints of significant historical subjects, for which engraving rather than etching was the technique of choice in the seventeenth century. Orderly sequences of bitings establish etched equivalents to engraving's typical swelling and tapering burin strokes, and all of the forms are neatly outlined. Nowhere does the artist lapse into his characteristic clouds of jiggled shadings, which in his sketch plates accumulate to form contours without rigid definition and textures of color rather than mass. The designs for cartouches also included in this exhibition (Cat. 55a–d) provide a useful contrast; compare especially the orderly cross-hatching in the clouds supporting the bishop and his celestial entourage to the sketched feathers and foliage in plate 3 of the cartouches.

The plunging horsemen in antique and Oriental attire in the foreground of *Saint Prosper,* however, draw upon many of della Bella's less formal etchings. These sketch plates, gathered together in collections entitled (after the fact, one suspects) *Agreable diversité de figures* or *Diversi capricci* or *Varii capricci militari* or *Livre pour apprendre à dessiner,* were doubtless sold as model books, to provide staffage for painters and graphic artists. In prints such as *Saint Prosper,* della Bella shows himself to have been his own best customer.

The della Bella Spencer Album contains hundreds of these small sketch plates, most in relatively poor impressions. It is only in the most important compositions or in relatively coherent suites that the album's compilers seem to have sought out early states and excellent printings. Comparative examples of the very highest quality would, however, have been available to the Mariettes, whom we posit as the compilers of the album in the early eighteenth century. François Langlois, who may have known the artist in the 1630s in Italy, welcomed him into his household in Paris in 1640;[2] and Pierre Mariette II, who married Langlois's widow, printed many of his plates, a tradition that continued through generations of Mariettes. Many of the impressions in the Spencer Albums bear the *excudit* of their publishing house.[3]

Pierre-Jean Mariette's special pride was the family collection of the complete oeuvre of della Bella prints, which he had inherited.[4] In the Mariette manuscript now in the collection of the Bibliothèque Nationale, the entry on della Bella breathes the self-satisfied chauvinism of this family of Parisian print connoisseurs, which had such influence in the success of the Italian etcher in France:

> Nothing contributes more to the flowering of the Fine Arts than to favor them, and one would not perhaps have seen born in France so many illustrious artists in these past centuries if there were not also there persons who loved and protected them. The honors and rewards liberally distributed . . . attracted talented foreigners from abroad. . . . Among them, there was scarcely anyone of higher reputation than Stefano della Bella, nor any who, by the great number and the beauty of those works that he made in France, better deserves to be ranked among the French.[5]

The impression of *Saint Prosper* included in the mammoth Spencer Album 7 is one among 889 prints by and after Stefano della Bella mounted on 189 numbered folios;[6] there are many blank pages as well. In fact, this is the only one of the nine surviving Spencer Albums that seems to have been assembled with a view toward its eventual owner adding more prints. Subject groups are separated by blank, unnumbered folios, and corresponding gaps are left in the table of contents, as if to invite new accessions. Even within the pages containing prints, one sees evidence of prints being removed and shifted to another location, and the prints on one page, fol. 151 bis, a suite of "Persian" heads, are self-evidently —because of the "bis"—later additions. Yet all of these are listed in their present arrangement in the same French hand in the table of contents,[7] and there is no sign that the owners of the della Bella album ever, over the centuries, added to it or otherwise altered its original format. Given its immense size—it weighs in at thirty pounds (13.5 kilos)—it may not have been lifted frequently from its shelf at Althorp.[8]

MBC

1. All of the above information is drawn from the standard catalogue of della Bella prints, DEV.-M.I.50–51.28. The print is identified as of Saint Prosper in the Spencer Album table of contents and in French eighteenth-century auction and catalogue references.

2. Mariette 1851–1860, vol. 1, p. 73.

3. Weigert 1953, p. 171.

4. Pierre-Jean Mariette described the collection as having been begun by Langlois (Mariette 1851–1860, vol. 1, pp. 74–75) and, in another source, by his grandfather Pierre Mariette II (Dumesnil 1973, pp. 303–4). Probably it is a case of the collection having been begun by Langlois and perfected by Pierre II. In addition, the oeuvre of della Bella as published by the Medici grand duke of Tuscany was given to Jean Mariette by Prince Eugene of Savoy (Dumesnil 1973, p. 45). This combined inheritance, or its residue as refined by Pierre-Jean, was described in the 1775 sale catalogue of Pierre-Jean's collection: "Et. La Belle. Son Œuvre, composé de plus de quinze cent quarante pièces de la plus parfaite conservation et beauté d'épreuvres . . . le tout contenu dans trois volumes in-folio, reliés en maroquin . . . " (quoted in Blanc 1857–1858, p. 297). A less attractive side of Pierre-Jean's character was revealed by his adamant refusal to show his della Bella collection to the rival Parisian print publisher and connoisseur Claude-Antoine Jombert, who was writing the catalogue of della Bella's oeuvre eventually published in 1772. See Ris 1877, p. 325, and Joly 1988, p. 54.

5. BNMS R065076: "Rien ne contribue davantage à faire fleurir les Beaux Arts, que de les favoriser, & l'on

n'auroit peut-être pas veu naitre en France, tant d'illustres artistes dans ces derniers siecles, s'il ne s'y etoit pas trouvé en même temps des personnes qui les aimoient & qui les protegeoient. Les honneurs & les recompenses distribuiees abondamment . . . y ameneront aussy au dehors d'habile etranges dans toutes sortes de genres . . . Parmy eux, il n'y en a guerres qui ait acquis plus de réputation qu'Etienne della Bella, ny qui, par rapport à la multitude, & à la beauté des ouvrages qu'il a fait en France, mérite mieux d'estre rangé parmy les François."

6. There are 830 prints by della Bella in Album 7.

7. Interestingly, the table of contents is tipped into the binding rather than bound in, as if a new table was drawn up after the volume was bound. The watermarks are the same as for the rest of the volume, however, and a number of the tables of contents of the other volumes have been cut out and are simply laid loosely into the backs of the appropriate volumes, presumably for ease of consultation while looking at the prints. Perhaps the della Bella table pages were likewise cut out at a later date and then tipped in still later, to preserve them. Probably not coincidentally, the della Bella album is the only one whose binding appears to have been repaired.

8. This album would not have been a novelty in eighteenth-century England, where even in the seventeenth century, "Stefano della Bella was very well known. . . . Six entries in the auction catalogues, one of them containing 183 pictures, list prints by him. . . . Apparently della Bella enjoyed a greater vogue than any other Italian etcher of landscapes" (Ogden and Ogden 1955, p. 108).

STEFANO DELLA BELLA

Florence 1610 – 1664 Florence

57 *Scene from* Mirame *(II, iv)*, 1641

etching

on two sheets, 295 x 416 mm ("frame" plate); 182 x 272 mm ("scene" plate)

watermark on framing sheet: ring and bunch of grapes

DEV.-M.938

Gray Collection of Engravings Fund, s7.62

Della Bella arrived in Paris in October of 1639 in the entourage of the Medici ambassador to the French court, Alessandro del Nero. He stayed there for just over a decade, quickly finding patrons and publishers ready to issue his prolific designs. Building on his Florentine training and his experience executing commissions for the Medici commemorating their festivals and achievements, Stefano continued in Paris to document military campaigns, ceremonies, funerals, and theatrical performances, in addition to creating a stream of smaller ornamental designs, sketches, figure studies, and landscapes (see Cat. 55a–d).

One of della Bella's first patrons in Paris was Cardinal Richelieu (1585–1642), Louis XIII's prime minister and an enormously powerful figure for two decades before his death.[1] He actively promoted the arts, particularly literature, virtually creating the Académie Française in 1634. He also employed a number of writers and dramatists to create works under his direction, among whom was Jean Desmarets de Saint-Sorlin (1595–1676), the author of the play illustrated here by della Bella.

Desmarets was a versatile writer noted today for being the first chancellor of the Académie Française and the initiator of the battle during the latter half of the seventeenth century on behalf of the new French writers against the traditions of the "ancients." He was also appointed to various lucrative official positions thanks to Richelieu's patronage. First achieving success with his prose work *Ariane* in 1632, Desmarets wrote a play a year for Richelieu from 1637 until the latter's death in 1642. One of these, *Les Visionnaires* (1637), is credited with being a source for Molière's comedy style. In later decades, Desmarets wrote two epic poems, *Clovis, ou la France chrestienne* (1657) and *Les délices de l'esprit* (1658), both emphasizing the religious basis of his opposition to the pagan ancient writers.[2]

Several of Desmarets's published works were illustrated by contemporary printmakers in addition to della Bella, including François Chauveau and Abraham Bosse. In addition to *Mirame*, della Bella provided a frontispiece to Desmarets's *Oeuvres poétiques* of 1641 (DEV.-M.942) and etched four sets of playing cards devised by the writer for the amusement and educa-

tion of the young Louis XIV (DEV.-M.489–687) and a "trial" plate to illustrate his *Clovis* (DEV.-M.211); these are all included in Spencer Album 7.[3]

Della Bella brought with him to Paris a long practice of depicting theatrical performances, developed in Florence under the tutelage of Jacques Callot (see Cat. 24, 52) and others. His skills and his influential Italian connections made him an ideal choice to represent various scenes from a play that was a pompous and expensive vanity production to humor the influential cardinal (who was forced to import his own claque to performances). The "tragicomedy" *Mirame* was commissioned by him to be the first production in a brand-new theater he built for the occasion in his own newly constructed Palais-Cardinal (now the Palais Royal).[4] While Desmarets receives credit on the title page for the authorship of *Mirame*, most authorities believe it to be more or less a collaboration with Richelieu himself. The inaugural performance was given on January 14, 1641, in front of an audience that included the king and queen.[5]

In addition to della Bella's prints, this production of *Mirame* was notable for the technical innovations of the new theater and its set designs, both of which followed developments in Italy. The theater itself was the first in Paris to feature a raised stage and formal proscenium, and the set designer, Georges Buffequin (active 1607–1641), took advantage of the facility to utilize parallel painted scenery flats, which could be quickly changed to evoke different effects in turn, such as full daylight, nighttime darkness, or, as shown here, the light of a full moon. The deep perspective of the scene, a garden setting looking out to sea, also follows Italian precedent.[6]

Della Bella provided five illustrations of scenes from *Mirame*, in addition to a title/frontispiece (DEV.-M. 936–41; the frontispiece is not included in Album 7). They are straightforward representations of the staged performance of each scene, complete with a "frame" around each scene showing the actual proscenium of Richelieu's private theater. The five prints are each composed of a smaller "scene" impression laid over the blank center area of the larger "frame" impression. (The printing plate for the frame had a hole in the center corresponding to the inner proscenium arch.) In the impression exhibited, it can be seen that the trimmed paper of the scene covers the projecting cornice at the sides of the stage.

The frame plate is identical for all the scenes, and features the arms of Cardinal Richelieu at the top center of the proscenium arch. A scene of a Roman sacrifice appears in the spandrel at the upper left and that of a victor being crowned with a laurel wreath at the upper right. The Spencer impressions of the *Mirame* plates are extremely fresh and bright; indeed, the publisher's address and date, which appear on the top of the first step below the stage in later impressions, are not present, indicating that these are proof impressions before publication. Further shading on the stairs and pilaster bases was also added in the published state. Neither della Bella's own name nor monogram appear on these plates, even in the published state. A folio edition of the text of the play was issued by Henry LeGras in 1641 with the etchings bound in; he published unillustrated quarto and duodecimo editions the same year.[7]

The particular scene exhibited is from act 2, scene 4, where Mirame, the Princess of Bithynia, is being wooed in the moonlight by Arimant, a young favorite of her father's current enemy, the King of Colchos. By the end of the scene the characters remark on the approaching daylight, implying some of the theatrical lighting effects. While these plates are somewhat ponderously dominated by the grand architectural and stage setting, the grace and movement of della Bella's carefully observed figures can be appreciated. He also successfully strove to reproduce within an unvarying setting the subtle stage lighting shown in the sky, here depicting a somewhat stolid full moon.

One preliminary drawing for *Mirame* is in the Edmond de Rothschild Collection in the Cabinet des Dessins of the Louvre. It is a study for the third act, and is in reverse to the final print (DEV.-M.939).[8] Interestingly, while it shows the rusticated columns on one side as they appear in the prints, there is a grand fountain with fantastic sea creatures on the other side. Della Bella made many drawn studies throughout his career of theatrical figures in numerous poses, testifying to his practice and powers of translating them into the believable etched miniatures seen here, but none of these has been directly connected to his illustrations for *Mirame*.[9]

DPB

1. Della Bella was commissioned by Richelieu to etch the large *Siege of Arras* (DEV.-M.880), completed in 1641. Further, Blunt attributed a large allegorical portrait of Richelieu to Stefano (see Anthony Blunt, "Stefano della Bella, Jean Valdor, and Cardinal Richelieu," *Master Drawings* 16, no. 2 [1978]:156–62).

2. A fairly extensive biography of Desmarets can be found in *Dictionnaire de biographie française* (Paris: Letouzey et Ané, 1933ff), vol. 10, cols. 1449–51.

3. The drawing for the print is at Windsor Castle and is reproduced in Blunt 1954, cat. 15, pl. 5. The final design used in the published edition of Clovis is by François Chauveau. See Alvin L. Clark, Jr., "A New Drawing by François Chauveau," *Master Drawings* 28, no. 1 (1990): 74–79, and also the letter by Phyllis D. Massar, *Master Drawings* 29, no. 2 (1991), p. 208.

4. Begun in 1633, the palace was designed by Jacques Lemercier; a contemporary view of it is reproduced in a collaborative print by Israel Silvestre and della Bella (DEV.-M.863), which is also in Album 7 (S7.79.1)

5. Its history and a synopsis of the plot are included in Henry Carrington Lancaster, *A History of French Dramatic Literature in the Seventeenth Century, Part II: The Period of Corneille 1635–51* (Baltimore: Johns Hopkins Press, 1932), vol. 2, pp. 375–79. *The Oxford Companion to French Literature*, Sir Paul Harvey and J. E. Heseltine, comps. (Oxford: Clarendon Press, 1959), p. 619, lists *Mirame* as a work by Richelieu and describes it succinctly as "a play of no merit."

6. For Buffequin, see Robin Thurlow Lacy, *A Biographical Dictionary of Scenographers 500 B.C. to 1900 A.D.* (New York and Westport [CT]: Greenwood Press, 1990), p. 92. Further on the 1641 production of *Mirame*, see Nicole Decugis and Suzanne Reymond, *Le décor de théatre en France* (Paris: Compagnie Française des Arts Graphiques, 1953), pp. 56–59.

7. Jacques-Charles Brunet, *Manuel du libraire et de l'amateur de livres* (Paris: Firmin Didot, 1861), vol. 2, pt. 1, cols. 632–33, describes the folio edition as "more sumptuous than truly beautiful." A copy of this rare edition (no copies listed in the NUC) is described in *Catalogue général des livres imprimés de la Bibliothèque Nationale* (Paris: Imprimerie Nationale, 1897–1981), vol. 39, col. 587.

8. Viatte 1974, cat. 576, repr.

9. See, for instance, several sketches in the Gabinetto Nazionale, Rome (Rome, Villa della Farnesina alla Lungara, *Disegni di Stefano della Bella* [Rome: De Luca, 1976], cat. 48–59, repr.), or a group in Munich (one repr. in Anna Forlani Tempesti, "Miscellaneous Album by Stefano della Bella at Munich," *Master Drawings* 14, no. 3 [1976], pl. 21b). A larger costume study at Windsor which bears a striking resemblance to the figures in *Mirame* is reproduced in Blunt 1954, cat. 23, pl. 6.

HERMAN VAN SWANEVELT

Woerden c. 1600 – 1655 Paris

58   *The Death of Adonis*, plate 5 from *The Story of Adonis*, 1654

etching and engraving, 233 x 332 mm (lower margin trimmed)

watermark: elaborate coat-of-arms within a beaded circle, identical to that on an impression of the first state of *The Birth of Adonis* (pl. 1 in the series), Fogg Art Museum, loan from Robert M. Light (inv. no. 264.1990)

B.II.311.105; TIB2.309.105; H.XXIX.61.22 i/iii

William M. Prichard Fund, by exchange, S5.90.1

The story of Venus and Adonis is found in the tenth book of Ovid's *Metamorphoses*. The maiden Myrrha, impregnated by her own father, is so wretched that she wishes neither to live nor to die. Pitying her, the gods turn her into a tree. In due time the tree splits to give birth to Adonis, who

is raised by forest nymphs and becomes passionate about hunting. Venus sees the beautiful youth and lures him from his tutelage under the chaste Diana to sport with her, but Venus can teach him only about love. Recognizing the allure that the chase still holds for her beloved, she warns him not to hunt dangerous animals.

Swanevelt's fourth plate in the six-piece series, the scene prior to this etching, represents Adonis heeding the warning and, with Venus, coursing hares. Although hunters and prey alike run in sunlight on a grassy hillock, they are plunging toward a dark trench, from which the tips of one hare's ears barely extend. The trench, which forms the dividing diagonal typical in mid-seventeenth-century Dutch landscapes as a device to organize space and recession, here assumes an iconographical role, for on the other side stands an ominously shadowed forest, with some of its ancient trees already dead. A black, shattered trunk offers a bridge to the unwitting Adonis.

To continue the story, Adonis's hounds lead him to a wild boar hidden in the thickets. Adonis spears the boar, which turns on the hunter and gores him in the groin. Mortally struck, he bleeds to death from the wound suffered in the seat of love. Arthur Golding, the first English translator of *Metamorphoses*, draws the moral from the tale: ". . . Adonis' death doth shew that manhood strives / Against forewarning though man see the peeril of their lives."[1]

This is indeed the moral that seventeenth- and early eighteenth-century Dutch advocates for Ovid as a source for painters found in the story of Adonis.[2] It is echoed in the engraved inscription on *The Death of Adonis* (which has been trimmed from the impression on exhibition): "Adonis meets the wild boar and is killed because / he had not mastered his vocation. / Thus the first adversity overthrows the ignorant, / without hope of their ever being able to recover themselves."[3] But somber morals presented in inscriptions and literature are often belied by the fleshly beauties of Venus and Adonis as represented by Italianate Dutch and Flemish seventeenth-century painters. By the implication of their repeated choice of the Adonis story, artists and patrons indicated that they too shared an obvious enthusiasm for love and the chase.

Subjects from *Metamorphoses* and especially the story of Adonis became favored themes in mid-seventeenth-century Paris as well, the city where Swanevelt, who left Rome c. 1641, took up residence by 1644, when he was appointed *peintre ordinaire* to Louis XIII. Haskell has described the vogue in Paris in the 1640s for Italian landscape style and Ovidian themes, led by the king's first minister, the Italian Cardinal Mazarin, who took advantage of changes in patronage in Rome following the death of Pope Urban VIII to lure Italian painters to the French capital:

> . . . by June [1646, Francesco] Romanelli was already at work painting the newly built upper gallery of Mazarin's palace. . . . The artist proposed a series of Roman Histories. But the Cardinal "showed that he preferred the *Metamorphoses* of Ovid as being gayer and conforming more to the taste of the country". . . . Then in 1648, soon after the departure of Romanelli, the Bolognese painter Giovanni Francesco Grimaldi came to complete the decoration of the Cardinal's gallery, by painting landscapes. . . . [4]

Swanevelt's most important Parisian painting commission was in the Hotel Lambert, as Mariette admiringly reported:

> [He] painted very beautiful landscapes in the panelling of the Chamber of Love in the residence of President Lambert, and on one of these paintings he put his name and the date 1640 or 1646 [it would have been 1646, according to our knowledge of Swanevelt's residence in Rome until 1641]. . . . In these landscapes one sees that he sought to imitate in his choice of scenes the manner of [Jan] Both of Italy and in the effects of light that of Claude Lorraine.[5]

Yet Mariette does Swanevelt a disservice in assuming priority for Both and Claude. The three had earlier worked together in Rome on landscapes commissioned for "Buen Retiro," the country house of Philip IV of Spain, and in paintings of their shared Roman years the question of influence has been decided in Swanevelt's favor by some modern scholars.[6] Thus he is seen as a seminal figure in the development of the classical landscape style of seventeenth-century European painting.

For despite Mariette's acknowledgment that the artist's "talent in painting the figure [developed because] he frequented with the same assiduity the academy [to work from] the live model [as he worked before nature in the Roman landscape],"[7] it is as landscape art that Swanevelt's paintings, his prints in particular, and specifically this etching, figures and all, should be evaluated. Mariette himself recognized this by his placement of all of Swanevelt's prints, whether topographical, ideal, or historiated, within volumes specifically devoted to "*paysages*" and "*marines*."[8]

In *The Death of Adonis*, the artist has found pathetic expression of the death of a beautiful youth by lighting his features lividly from below. The etched extension of the boar's shadow to form the stain of gore spreading beyond Adonis's delicately raised tunic is a touch of brilliant subtlety. Yet despite these attentive details in the figures, the principal protagonists of this etching remain the riven stump and rotted trunk that embrace the hunter slain by his prey. The branch cut short in the massive, split bole is a metaphor for the brief life of the son of Myrrha.

MBC

1. Ovid 1575, n.p., from the Epistle to the Reader.

2. Sluijter 1986, pp. 146, 225–42, 582–84; and his essay "Depiction of Mythological Themes," pp. 55–64, in Washington 1980. See also in the same publication Albert Blankert, "Classicism in Dutch Painting, 1614–1670," pp. 182–90.

3. "Adonis Rencontre le Sanglier et fut tue a cause / quil Nauoit pas bien apris son Mestier / Aussy les Ignorens la premiere Aduersitte les Renuerse / Sans Esperence de Jamais plus se Releuel"

4. Haskell 1980, pp. 181–82.

5. Mariette 1851–1860, vol. 6, p. 10: "[Il] a peint de très beaux paysages dans les lambris du cabinet de l'Amour, à l'hotel du président Lambert, et sur l'un de ces tableaux il a mis son nom et la date 1640 ou 1646. . . . Dans ces paysages on voit qu'il cherche à imitier, pour les sites, la maniere de Both d'Italie, et pour les effets de lumière celle de Claude le Lorrain." Other artists employed in the same project were the Italianate Dutch painter Pieter Asselijn (c. 1615–1652) and the French painters Pierre Pastel (d. 1676) and Eustache le Sueur (1617–1655) (Sutton 1987, pp. 113–14, 246).

6. Sutton 1980, p. 489; Blankert 1978, pp. 20–21.

7. BNMS R069937: ". . . talent de peindre la figure il frequentoit avec la même assiduité l'academie du modele."

8. See BNMS R069924, his description of vol. 3 of the specialized landscape volumes containing the work of artists of various nationalities, which included all of Swanevelt's prints whether they are landscapes or not and in which fol. 86–90 hold "La Fable d'Adonis representée en une suitte de six paysages inventés & gravés en 1654." See also R069937, "Tables des Oeuvres / des Maistres François / Qui ont peint, dessiné, & gravé des Paysages / ou des Marines / ** / Tome Second / ** / Paysages dessinés & gravés par Herman van Swanevelt."

FRANCISCO DE NEVE, THE YOUNGER

Antwerp or Rome? c. 1635? – after 1691 Antwerp?

59   *Diana and Endymion,* c. 1665 or later

etching

194 x 260 mm

inscribed in plate, in margin, lower left: *Fran. de Neue In. e fecit*; lower right: *Si Stampano in Roma da Gio: Iacomo de Rossi alla Pace.*

B.IV.119.1, TIB5.138.1, H.XIV.147.1

William M. Prichard Fund, by exchange. s5.94.2

This etching and thirteen other plates representing classical or pastoral landscapes in an Italianate style which are signed "Franciscus [or some contraction thereof] de Neue" are conventionally attributed to an artist named Franciscus, Francisco, or Frans de Neve. Born in Antwerp in 1606, Neve was enrolled as a master in the Antwerp painters' guild in 1629, married there on May 13 of the following year, and may have died in Brussels in 1681. He was in Rome by the end of 1630, where he was enrolled in the Schildersbent, the Netherlandish artists' association, and given the nickname "Blaserke" or "Bloosaerken," meaning "Little Blower."[1]

By all accounts, Neve had a son of the same name, also a painter. One source indicates, probably erroneously, that the younger Neve was enrolled into the Antwerp guild in 1643–1644, entering as the son of a master.[2] He is recorded as having been in Rome from 1660 until 1666 and in Antwerp in 1690–1691.[3] The son is even more obscure than the father in that no works whatsoever are specifically attributed to him; he is reputed to have been a landscape painter. A few paintings of religious and mythological subjects, painted portraits, and one landscape drawing supposed to be by the father are recorded in the literature, as well as the fourteen etchings.

Adolphe Siret anticipates me in his suggestion that "the biographers have undoubtedly confused the works of the father with those of the son, who could well, in our opinion, have been the landscapist."[4] He gives no justification for this idea nor does he specify the etchings as works of the son. A consideration of the prints themselves, however, leads quickly to the realization that they could not have been created by an artist who was an independent master as early as 1629, for the etchings show every characteristic of the third phase of Netherlandish artists working in the late seventeenth century in an Italianate style.

This phase, first defined by Stechow[5] and further described and analyzed in many recent publications and exhibitions,[6] is strongly associated with the art of the French landscape painters in Rome—Nicolas Poussin, Claude Gellée, and especially Gaspard Dughet (1615–1675), who was French by descent but a native of Rome and the pupil of his eventual brother-in-law

Poussin. It was Dughet's "unique ability to reconcile classicism with the depiction of nature as a vibrant living force that made his vision so remarkable."[7] Particularly influential were his paintings for the Roman palazzo of Lorenzo Onofrio, grand constable of the Kingdom of Naples and husband of Maria Mancini, the niece of Cardinal Mazarin who had been raised as the royal favorite in the court of Louis XIV. This well-connected patron's "striking preference for landscape decoration . . . helped to launch, or at least to confirm, a fashion which did not meet with general critical approval."[8] The French association of both artist and patron is symptomatic of the trend toward a version of Italianate landscape that became dominant in the second half of the century in works painted for Dutch patrons as well.[9]

Dughet's influence is strongly seen in the painted and etched works of three other Antwerp natives, Abraham Genoels II (1640–1723), Jan Frans van Bloemen (1662–1749), and Hendrik Frans van Lint (1684–1763), as well as many North Netherlanders.[10] It should be noted that most of these men were somewhat younger than Neve the Younger, whose conjectural birthdate c. 1635 is derived from the known wedding date of his father and the dates of the son's known period of residence in Rome in the early 1660s. The association in subject, format, and style of Neve's prints with the paintings and prints of the third generation of Italianate landscapists is un-mistakable, however, as is made immediately obvious by a scan of the section devoted to the Northern followers of Rosa and Dughet in Salerno's invaluable compendium of landscape paint-ing in seventeenth-century Rome (in which neither Neve is mentioned).[11]

As is evident from the reproductions selected by Salerno, late seventeenth-century Dutch painters of ideal landscape adhered to the approach to landscape eventually formalized by Gerard de Lairesse, the head of the Amsterdam Academy and the leading classicist of the North Netherlands (who could legitimately assume this role despite the fact that he had never traveled to Italy, so widespread had the style become). His teachings, published in Dutch in 1707, defined the most "perfect" mode of landscape, the "Antique," in terms which exactly describe Neve's prints:

> Nature is modern, that is, imperfect, [but] in her objects she appears the same as she was a thousand years ago; woods, fields, mountains, and water are always the same. . . . But she is Antique and perfect, when we judiciously adorn her with uncommon and magnifi-cent buildings, tombs and other remains of antiquity . . . including classical staffage, such as wood nymphs, river-gods, shepherds, and bacchanals. . . . [12]

Classical ruins imbedded in vistas of the Roman Campagna are prominent in the set of eight Neve etchings (TIB5.142–149.5–12) in which the proportion of landscape and figural elements is weighted heavily toward the former; the remaining six prints (TIB5.138–141.1–4, TIB5.150–151.13–14) feature the human figure, whether specifically mythological or generically Arcadian. That these etchings may have helped form the style for Dutch Italianate painters rather than de-rive from it is suggested by their relatively early date within the third phase as it has been defined. The set of six appeared in Giovanni Giacomo de Rossi's catalogue of 1677,[13] and Neve's works are listed as early as 1689 in a precocious English compendium of landscape prints.[14]

Linkages among the six Neve etchings included in Spencer Album 5, which are the six pub-lished as a set by Rossi, offer complexities of subject, format, and rendering more appropriate to suites of painted decoration for grand domestic interiors in the 1650s and later. The six divide into two symmetric and complementary groups of three, each featuring a single larger composi-tion flanked by two smaller ones, a conventional arrangement within an architectural setting but exceptional among print series, in which images are typically the same size. In one group, com-prising *The Trained Dog* (TIB5.140.3), *Shepherdess Playing a Tambourine* (TIB5.150.13), and *Seated Shepherd* (TIB5.141.4) (reading from left to right), Arcadian shepherds and shepherdesses rest among their flocks in rocky groves in foregrounds immediately accessible to the viewer, with vis-tas of open woods and still waters opening to mountains gleaming under cloudless skies. In the second group, comprising *Diana and Endymion* (TIB5.138.1), *Narcissus* (TIB5.151.14), and *Venus and Cupid at the Water* (TIB5.139.2), the skies are clouded, and although distant mountains are visible, in each case dense foliage in the middle distance effectively separates the figures from this larger world. They are isolated from the viewer by water, which lies as a barrier in the immediate foreground. The figures appear as tableaux and in fact each print presents or at least implies a narrative deriving from Ovid's *Metamorphoses*, that compendium of erotic tales so favored by seventeenth-century artists. Indeed, they perfectly illustrate a modern historian's characterization of Dutch paintings of Ovidian subjects; they

> ... convey the impression of an idyllic situation in scenic surroundings, and are invariably concerned with love and eroticism. Problems of beauty, chastity, virginity, and desire, seduction and deception, are the main elements of the depicted stories. Although the idyll is often on the brink of disaster, violent actions and emotions, even when required by the story, are usually minimized.[15]

The most surprising quality of these six landscape prints is the competence of their figure drawing. The body of Endymion, whose physical beauty is the essence of his attraction, is so well realized that study from the live model must be presumed; and it is possible that its attitude was generally derived, entirely appropriately, from a Hellenistic marble in the Vatican Museum which represents a shepherd sleeping among his flock.[16]

The thorough-going classicism of the image is not, however, to be located in a specific allusion to an antique subject or model. Rather it is found in the tableau's decorum, all the more intensely understood once it is observed that Endymion's leg and draped cloak are raised sufficiently to reveal his genitals. Likewise, in this etching's companion prints, Narcissus lifts his mantle to display in the mirroring pond his entire naked body and Venus allows her hand to drop across her thigh beyond her genitals rather than cover them coyly. The frank yet proportionate representation of each figure's sex evokes an unaffected sensuality, as if Christianity had never occurred.

MBC

1. Wurzbach 1910, vol. 1, p. 231; Hoogewerff 1952, p. 140. My thanks to Jeroen Giltay for the translation. See also Rombouts and van Lerius, vol. 2, p. 1, where Neve is recorded in guild archives of the year 1629–1630.

2. Siret 1876, p. 584. This date is not confirmed in Rombouts and van Lerius, but they do record (vol. 2, p. 548) Francisco de Neve II as a master in 1690–1691. His admission at this date may signal his return from a protracted stay abroad. Rombouts and van Lerius's list for 1643–1644 contains a Ph. de Neve; this may be the mistaken source of Siret's information.

3. See previous note.

4. Siret 1876, p. 584: "Les biographes ont, sans doute, confondu les travaux du père avec ceux du fils, qui pourrait bien, selons nous, avoir été le paysagiste."

5. Stechow 1966, p. 148.

6. Zwollo 1973, p. 223; Blankert 1978 p. 35; Sutton 1987, p. 55; Duparc and Graif 1990, p. 42.

7. Wintermute 1990, p. 72. See Rosenberg 1982, pp. 161–62, 243–45, for a brief summary of the French landscapists apart from Poussin who were working in Rome in the mid-seventeenth century.

8. Haskell 1980, p. 155.

9. Blankert 1978, p. 42. In prints this tendency is beautifully represented by etchings by Isaac de Moucheron (1667–1744), especially his eight plates of the *Zaal-Stucken in 't Huis van de Hr. B. B. Mezquita* (H.XIV.94.2–9).

10. Such as Adriaen van der Kabel (c. 1630–1705), Albert Meyeringh (1645–1714), Johannes Glauber (1646–1726), and Isaac de Moucheron (1667–1744), among others.

11. Salerno 1977–1978, vol. 2, ch. 12, pp. 807–909. See also vol. 2, ch. 11, pp. 691–805.

12. Sutton 1987, p. 56, quoting Lairesse's *The Art of Painting*, the first English translation of his treatise, which was published in London in 1738.

13. Rossi 1677, p. 55: "Vedute diverse de' Paesis inventione, & intaglio all'acqua forte di *Francesco di Neve*, libro in 6. foli, et mezzi fogli reali per traveso." Their inscriptions indicate that all fourteen Neve etchings were published in Rome, presumably between the years 1660 and 1666, the period of Neve the Younger's known stay. Of course, he may have stayed longer than his documented period of residence.

14. Ogden and Ogden 1955, p. 96. See Sutton 1987, p. 304, for a more general discussion of early English patronage of landscape artists such as Dughet and his imitators.

15. Sluijter 1986, p. 580. See Le Comte 1944 for discussion of the Renaissance and Baroque interpretation of the story of Diana (or Selene, another personification of the moon goddess) and Endymion. His translation, pp. 8–9, of a passage from Lucian's *Dialogue of the Gods* is particularly apposite to the print by Neve:

"*Aphrodite*: Whenever you are in Caria you halt your chariot to gaze down on the huntsman Endymion asleep in the open air. Sometimes they say, you even dismount to him in the midst of your course [an embodiment of the cosmic catastrophe of the moon leaving its orbit].... But tell me, is Endymion handsome? For that would be a very great consolation.

"*Selene*: To me he seems utterly beautiful, Aphrodite, especially when, having made a bed of his cloak on the rocks, he lies sleeping with his javelins just slipping from his left hand, while the right, bent upwards to the head, frames his becoming face. Relaxed in slumber, he exhales an ambrosial breath. Noiselessly, then, I descend, stepping on tip-toe so that on awakening he would not be startled. You understand, need I say more, except that I am dying of love?"

16. *Musées et galeries pontificans, I. Guide du musée de sculpture du Vatican* (Vatican City: Vatican Museum and Galeries, 1933), p. 51, no. 153, repro. p. 52. No earlier provenance is indicated for the statue.

SEBASTIEN BOURDON

Montpellier 1616 – 1671 Paris

60 *Landscape with the Priest and the Levite Shunning the Wounded Traveler*, after 1664

etching

296 x 436 mm

watermark: bunch of grapes; countermark: A B V, the letters separated by hearts, within a cartouche

inscribed in the plate, lower left, design area: *S. Bourdon pinx et sc. C. P. R.*; lower right, margin: *P. Mariette excud.*

R.-D.I.151.35 ii/iii, Ponsonailhe 36 ii/iii

Gift of Belinda L. Randall from the collection of John Witt Randall, by exchange, s2.83

The French painter Sébastien Bourdon is well represented in Spencer Album 2, which contains forty-three[1] of the forty-five etchings usually attributed to him plus the *Virgin Seated on a Vault*, traditionally assigned to Bourdon but reattributed by Robert-Dumesnil to "Mariette"—presumably Pierre Mariette II.[2] The album's table of contents, however, explicitly describes that print as being by Bourdon; and as we posit the compilers of the Spencer Albums to have been the Mariettes, this would seem authoritative.

Indeed, it is seven of the Bourdon etchings in Album 2 that provide conclusive evidence of the Mariettes' responsibility for the albums: the impressions of the Seven Acts of Mercy (R.-D.I.134–137.2–8 ii/ii, s2.59–.65), which according to their engraved inscriptions were published by Pierre Mariette, are so large that they are bound directly into the volume rather than being mounted on blank pages like the vast majority of the prints. The watermark on these impressions is identical to one of the two marks that is consistently found on all nine albums' blank pages. Taken together with the fact that another etching in Album 2, an impression of a plate by Corneille also published by Mariette,[3] bears the other of the two watermarks consistently found in all nine albums, the evidence is clear.

Among the forty-four Bourdon etchings in Album 2, thirty-three were published by the Mariettes, a fact which unfortunately guarantees that most of his prints in the Spencer Album are later impressions. They are well printed but, as is seen in this landscape whose somber aspect is in part generated by the film of plate tone added across the central rocks and trees, they do not have the metallic clarity notable in early impressions published by the artist himself.

Pierre-Jean Mariette was a great admirer of Bourdon, as witnessed by his manuscript dictionary of artists, which specifically praises Bourdon's landscapes and etchings: "It is above all in his landscapes that one sees the fecundity of his genius, these are enchanted lands . . . he has re-

266

produced many [of his own compositions] in etching with great success. . . . "[4] The plates of the Seven Acts of Mercy figured in the sale of Mariette's commercial goods in 1768, and a drawing by Bourdon of the Flight into Egypt was included in the sale of his collection in 1775.[5] Bourdon was also admired in England as early as the late seventeenth century, when his landscape prints appeared in an auction catalogue;[6] and he is known to have been favored by the first Earl Spencer, whose drawing collection when sold in 1811 included seven sheets attributed to him, including three classical landscapes.[7]

This landscape is one of twelve unnumbered and untitled plates that have always been grouped together. Robert-Dumesnil ordered the twelve in an approximation of traditional iconographical sequence, with what he believed were Old Testament subjects preceding New Testament subjects; he placed a pastoral scene with no apparent biblical reference at the beginning of the set and three others in which civilization appears to be in a somewhat more advanced state at its end. As he misidentified two of the subjects, including this etching, the twelve should be reordered, and the table of contents of Spencer Album 2 offers a valuable guide.

Here the landscapes are sorted into three groups of four. The first set presents scenes from the life of Christ.[8] Four landscapes with rural staffage comprise the third set. The second set, whose second plate is the subject of this catalogue entry, is described as representing the parable of the Prodigal Son. This is manifestly a misidentification as none of the apparatus of that story—luxurious revels, swine, a parental embrace—are seen. Robert-Dumesnil is closer to the mark in identifying the last two of these four prints (R.-D.I.152–153.37–38) as episodes from the parable of the Good Samaritan, but he misinterprets the other two, describing the first generically as brigands assaulting a traveler (R.-D.I.152.36) and the second, this print, as a representation of the Judaic law that deals with the purification ritual obligatory upon the discovery of an unknown murder victim (R.-D.I.151–152.35).[9]

In fact, all four scenes present the essential episodes, mounted in correct narrative order, of the parable of the Good Samaritan (S2.82–85). In the first we see the traveler who "fell among thieves, which stripped him of his raiment, and wounded him, and departed, leaving him half dead."[10] The second, this print, shows a priest and a Levite who have happened upon the apparently lifeless victim and shun him: "And by chance there came down a certain priest that way: and when he saw him, he passed by on the other side. And likewise a Levite, when he was at the place, came and looked on him, and passed by on the other side."[11] The third and fourth plates portray the kindness of the Samaritan, next to discover the victim, who binds his wounds and carries him to a hostel.[12] Presumably the scribe of the table of contents, recognizing all four etchings as episodes of a single parable, inadvertently wrote "*l'Enfans prodigue*" for "*le bon Samaritain.*"

The moral of the parable of the Good Samaritan—"Which now of these three, thinkest thou, was neighbor unto him that fell among the thieves? . . . He that showed mercy on him . . . Go, and do thou likewise"[13]—is an extension of the themes of Bourdon's great cycle of the Seven Acts of Mercy, all illustrated by episodes from the Old Testament.[14] The artist filled those scenes with many figures; in the landscapes, however, the figures are fewer, and smaller in proportion to the ordered expanse of rocks, trees, waters, structures, and sky. Yet Bourdon does not neglect the potential of staffage to further his message. In this print, an intense light is focused on the naked breast and outflung arm of the traveler, who is isolated in an otherwise shadowed foreground. By the pose of an inert hand and its illumination, the comatose victim begs for succor. In contrast, the arms of two men who have discovered him are tightly folded across their chests, signifying their heartlessness, and their hands, which could have reached out, are concealed within their priestly robes.

These landscape prints, like the Seven Acts of Mercy, show the strong influence of Nicolas Poussin, whom Bourdon may have encountered during his stay in Rome, 1634–1637, but whom he is generally agreed not to have emulated until after Poussin's brief sojourn in Paris, 1640–1642. From this time on, Bourdon's art became increasingly less influenced by the Bamboccianti and Venetian painting. As a founder of the Académie Royale de Peinture et Sculpture in 1648, he was a leader of the developing "Atticism," a classicizing mode that dominated painting in the French capital in the later seventeenth century and resonated in the Netherlands, Italy, and England.[15] He painted his Seven Acts of Mercy, profoundly influenced by the art of the mature Poussin, around 1655 and presumably etched them soon after.[16]

Bourdon could have acquired his formidable command of the etching technique in Rome or from his association with Abraham Bosse (1602–1676),[17] the Parisian printmaker and publisher whose treatise on etching published in 1645 remained the standard manual for centuries. The series of twelve landscapes could date from any point subsequent to the appointment of Colbert as *surintendent des batimens* to Louis XIV, a position he assumed in 1664; this title is given in the plates' dedication to Colbert.[18] Perhaps the landscapes were executed about 1668, given their association with landscape etchings after Bourdon by Jacques Prou, who was Bourdon's student at that time (see Cat. 61).

MBC

1. *The Virgin at the Curtain* (S2.70.1, R.-D.I.139.13) was removed from the album at some earlier date.

2. R.-D.I.131–157. The print (S2.75.2), which Robert-Dumesnil attributes to "Mariette" (no first name), is no. 3 among his "pièces faussement attribuées à Bourdon" (p. 157). "P." Mariette is mentioned earlier as the print's publisher, and so one infers that Pierre II is intended. However, it was Jean Mariette who was the family printmaker.

3. *Christ and the Virgin Appearing to Saint Francis* (S.2.101, R.D.VI.301.24 iii/iii). See Cat. 62.

4. Mariette 1851–1860, vol. 1, p. 170: "C'est surtout dans ses paysages que l'on remarque la fécondité de son génie, ce sont des pays enchantés. . . . Une bonne partie des ouvrages de Bourdon a eté gravée par d'excellens graveurs au burin & luy mesme il en a gravé plusieurs à l'eauforte avec beaucoup de succés. . . . "

5. Blanc 1857–1858, vol. 1, pp. 151, 291.

6. Ogden and Ogden 1955, p. 110.

7. Philipe 1811, pp. 10–11. Two of these drawings are reproduced in Goldfarb 1989, nos. 91 and 93.

8. Including a scene here described as Jesus instructing his apostles, which Robert-Dumesnil identified as Joseph and his entourage governing Egypt (R.-D.I.151.34).

9. Deuteronomy 21:1–9.

10. Luke 10:30. I should like to thank Rev. Richard Brenneman for pointing me toward this parable in a consideration of the typology of Deuteronomy 21:1–9.

11. Luke 10:31–32.

12. Luke 30:33–35.

13. Luke 10:36–37.

14. Geraldine E. Fowle has discussed the thematic significance of the parallelism of Old and New Testament subjects in the work of Bourdon, a devout Protestant ("Two Pendants by Sébastien Bourdon: A Study in Iconography and Style," *Boston Museum Bulletin* 71, no. 364 [1973]:75–91).

15. See Thuillier and Châtelet 1964, pp. 63–89.

16. For published synopses of the milieu, career, and influence of Bourdon, see Rosenberg 1982, pp. 103–4, 226–31; Clark 1987, pp. 53–56, 62; Goldfarb 1989, pp. 181–85.

17. Ponsonailhe, pp. 81–82. This is the most recent monograph on Bourdon.

18. Fowle 1970, vol. 1, p. 151, n. 155. See vol. 1, pp. 106–8, concerning the series of twelve landscapes.

JACQUES PROU

Blois c. 1639 – after 1727 Paris?

61   *Landscape with the Flight into Egypt*, after Bourdon, c. 1668

etching

365 x 466 mm

watermark: bunch of grapes; countermark: A R, the letters separated by a heart and followed by illegible letters, in a cartouche

inscribed in plate, lower margin, left: *S. Bourdon, Pinxit, cum priuil*; lower margin, right: *S. Prou, sculp.*; lower edge of margin, left: *A Paris chez Pierre Mariette rue St Jacques a l'Esperance avec privilege du Roi.*

LEB.III.257.4 (one of 6)

Gift of Belinda L. Randall from the collection of John Witt Randall, by exchange. s2.90

Although standard dictionaries and catalogues give an indefinite late seventeenth-century date of death for Jacques Prou, Pierre-Jean Mariette reported that he knew him in Paris in 1727, "dans un âge fort avancé."[1] Mariette provides us with one other firm date and circumstance in the artistic life of this very obscure French painter and etcher when he refers to Prou's recollection of yet another artist whom he had known "à Paris en 1668 chez Bourdon."[2] Mariette recorded that Prou had been a student of Bourdon, and lacking any other indication I shall assign that approximate date to this print by Prou after Bourdon.

Other scanty references to Prou are found in the records of the French Académie de Peinture et Sculpture, whose fourth prize for drawing he won in 1672, one year after the death of his master.[3] Prou subsequently entered the Académie de France in Rome, where in 1676 its director Charles Errard took a dim view of his talents and prospects, reporting that despite a certain popularity among his fellow students, he "has little talent or ability, and there is no indication of any potential for great achievement, in view of his advanced age and minimal skill."[4]

Errard himself was an etcher and Prou did etch views in Rome "d'après nature" (again in the

words of Mariette).[5] Prou would probably have learned the technique under Bourdon, however, a far more accomplished printmaker. Bourdon's compositions provided Prou with landscape models on a grand scale, as this *Flight into Egypt* attests.

The role assigned to water in the print is especially distinctive, and is characteristic of Bourdon's ideal landscape conceptions. This aspect of his art was singled out by Roger de Piles in his recommendations to painters: "Consult the works of *Bourdon*, or at least his prints, he is one of those who have given more spirit to waters, and treated them with more genius."[6] Unlike contemporary Dutch landscape etchings, where harbors, ponds, and rivers are introduced to provide a locale or ambience, here water becomes a structural element as amenable to formal manipulation as geological formations, vegetation, or architecture. Indeed, water proves the ideal medium for the construction of an ordered landscape made up more by the articulation of volumes than space, a concept derived by Bourdon from the paintings of the mature Poussin. Water is ideal because of our visceral understanding of its dependence for formal definition upon the force of gravity: if water is contained it lies in a horizontal plane; if water is released it falls in a vertical stream. The forms of rocks or trees are not so unequivocally subject to gravity, and the lines of architecture will be only if man contrives them so (as they usually are in Bourdon's compositions).

Thus in order to capitalize upon the structural potential of water, in all of the landscapes by Bourdon and those by Prou after him, it is never left to lie or run in an uncomplicated, natural hollow. It is always distributed through the composition on many discrete levels which are usually articulated by artificial troughs, channels, dams, cascades, and sluices, whose surfaces and outlets all emphasize the horizontal and the vertical status of the liquid. Running water is rarely permitted to be seen on a diagonal; streams and falls viewed frontally or from the side collaborate compositionally with standing water's insistent planarity enforced by gravity.

As is evident in this *Flight into Egypt* in comparison with Bourdon's episode from the parable of the Good Samaritan (Cat. 60), Prou exceeds his master in an interest in the textural characterizations of substances, whether liquid or solid. A waterfall by Bourdon is a pale, striated version of a rock cliff, whereas Prou elaborates every possible wavelet. Likewise, the foliage of Prou's leafy trees does not meld with the stony surfaces of outcrops or structures, and his cloud-hung skies are differentiated from the distant mountains below them. Attractive as the final effect is, in fact these careful descriptions of the varying substantiality of the elements of landscape detract from the absolutism of an ideal world, the achievement of Bourdon's etchings. Bourdon pushes a theoretical construction to its most concrete realization; Prou dissipates his model's rigor with his own pleasure in the surfaces of things. It is not surprising that his etchings are for many the more congenial view.

MBC

1. Mariette 1851–1860, vol. 4, p. 222.

2. Mariette 1851–1860, vol. 4, p. 45. Alvin L. Clark, Jr., has kindly provided a reference to Prou as "Menuisier du Roy," as he was referred to by the abbé de Marolles in the seventeenth century (Marolles 1855, p. 93). If Prou did begin his career as a cabinetmaker, this would explain his late start as a painter and etcher.

3. Anatole de Montaiglon, *Procès-verbaux de l'Académie Royale de Peinture et de Sculpture. I. 1648–1672* (Paris: J. Baur, 1875), p. 388.

4. Anatole de Montaiglon, *Correspondance des directeurs de l'Académie de France à Rome. I. 1666–1694* (Paris: Charavay frères, 1887), p. 62. The passage on Prou in its entirety, dated 2 December 1676: "Le nommé Prou, Peintre, est un garson de trente-scinq à trente-six ans, lequel a bonne opinion de luy, chef de party, lequel par ses discours se donne du crédict parmy ses camarades, choze peu avantageuze dans une sosiété; a peu de génie et de capacité, et il n'y a pas aparance qu'il face grande réheusite, veu son âge avancé et qu'il l'est peu dans son art."

5. Mariette 1851–1860, vol. 4, p. 222.

6. Piles 1766, pp. 175–76: "Voyez les ouvrages de *Bourdon* du-moins en estampes, c'est un de ceux qui a donné plus d'ame aux eaux, & qui les a traitées avec plus de génie."

MICHEL-ANGE CORNEILLE

Paris 1642 – 1708 Paris

62 *Saint Francis of Assisi*

etching and engraving

290 x 155 mm

inscribed in the plate, lower margin: *S.ᵗ Francois d'Assise.*

R.-D.VI.300.22 ii/ii

George R. Nutter Fund, by exchange, s2.100.2

This representation of Saint Francis of Assisi is one of a pair of prints by Corneille; the other, of Saint Anthony of Padua (R.-D.VI.299.21), was mounted on the same page of Spencer Album 2, although in reverse of the order implied by the prints' complete inscriptions in their first states. These inscriptions, altered in the second states and in any case trimmed from this impression, read from left to right, that is, from *Saint Francis* to *Saint Anthony*: "Peint et gravé par M. de Corneille avec privilege du Roy / Se vend chez l'autheur à l'hôtel Royal des Manufacture des Goblins."[1]

As suggested by the inscription, Corneille was a member of the inner circle of painters patronized by the royal court. A pupil of Charles Le Brun, he was received in 1663 into the Academy, of which his father, Michel Corneille, had been a founding member.[2] Michel-Ange's brother Jean-Baptiste also became a painter and in addition the brother-in-law of Jean Mariette by virtue of marrying Mariette's sister. As a youth Jean Mariette, too, aspired to be a painter, and we read in the Mariette manuscript in the Bibliothèque Nationale, "In his studies, he examined prints [with pleasure *inserted*]. He set himself to learn about them, [he even tried to draw them *inserted*]. . . . He put himself under the guidance of Jean Baptiste Corneille his brother-in-law. . . . "[3] It was to this first training as well as to the family collection that his son Pierre-Jean attributed Jean Mariette's superlative abilities as a connoisseur of prints.

In fact, Jean was soon discouraged in his ambition to become a painter and learned printmaking instead, as well as the family trade of print publishing, selling, and buying.[4] Among the 860 plates he created during his very long life are a number after the two younger Corneilles, whose plates he also acquired and published. The inscription trimmed away from this impression of *Saint Francis* stated that it was published by Jean Mariette, and all of the other Corneille impressions included in Spencer Album 2 bear the Mariette *excudit*. Although perforce this insures that they are later states, the plates appear to have remained in good condition, and they were meticulously printed in the Mariette shop.

On at least one of these, Mariette imposed more than his publication line. The Bibliothèque

St François d'Assise.

Nationale manuscript describes Michel-Ange Corneille's *Saint Andrew Adoring the Cross of His Martyrdom* (R.-D.20) as being retouched throughout with the burin by Jean Mariette. An impression of the print in this state, together with an earlier state with pen retouchings and a later state with inscriptions (the state included in the Spencer Album, s2.99), was among the Corneilles in the collection the Mariettes assembled for Prince Eugene of Savoy, now in the Albertina.[5]

And it is two other Corneille impressions in the Spencer Album, the large plates of *The Flight into Egypt* (R.-D.VI.296.15, S2.98) and *Christ and the Virgin Appearing to Saint Francis* (R.-D.VI.301.24, S2.101), which directly implicate the Mariettes in the Spencer Albums' production as a set. The plates, both so large that the impressions are bound at their left edges directly into the volume rather than being tipped onto blank folios, were printed on paper with the watermark of a dovecote and matching countermark of P and G separated by a heart, which is identical to one of the two papers exclusively used for the folios of all of the Spencer Albums. It is only logical that the printer and the album maker in the same firm would draw from the same stock of paper; it would be a coincidence beyond reckoning if two different firms in the print trade in Paris had access to the same lot.

The image of Saint Francis presented by the Corneille print is in striking contrast to the many portrayals of the saint found throughout the Italian prints contained within Spencer Albums 1, 2, and 6. Those by Procaccini, Faccini, and Annibale Carracci on exhibition here (Cat. 5, 4, 3) are excellent examples of the post-Tridentine emphasis on mystical revelation. Corneille's saint is but a barefoot monk, barely distinguished by a modest halo and understated stigmata. The usual attributes of skull or crucifix, with their morbid connotations, are absent, and the saint's stocky thigh and broad hips do not suggest ascetic isolation. His face, turned upward in prayer, is actually cast into shadow rather than illuminated by the blaze of revelation. Behind the figure, fair-weather clouds part only to show a deeply toned zenith, doubtless a clear and classical blue: if ever the heavens were represented as earthly, it is in this picture.

The distinctive colorism of the print was realized by engraving. Although the saint and the tree to the left were worked up in etching, these areas were finished and the architecture and sky largely created with the burin. Robert-Dumesnil noted as Corneille's most attractive talent this facility in the combination of etching and engraving:

> He executed etchings sometimes with a broad and firm point, sometimes in a very gentle manner, but always with infinite taste. He was expert in handling the burin so as to give harmony and color to work which he had laid out in etching.[6]

MBC

274

1. The prints were also mounted in this order on fol. 43 of the album described in BNMS R066174, in which they are described as having been "gravées à l'eau forte par Michel Corneille d'après deux de ses tableaux," that is, after paintings. The prints were catalogued by Robert-Dumesnil with Saint Francis being described as the pendant of Saint Anthony (R.-D.VI.299–300).

2. See Wright 1985, p. 168, and R.-D.VI.285–287 for brief discussions of the artist.

3. BNMS R067508: "En faisant ses etudes il regardoit d'y a [avec plaisir *inserted*] des estampes, il s'appliquoit a les connoitre, [il le hazardoit même a dessiner *inserted*] . . . Il se mit sous le conduitte de Jean Baptiste Corneille son beau frere . . . " Despite the familial relationship, the Mariette manuscript evinces more interest in Michel-Ange than Jean-Baptiste. Michel-Ange's passion for drawing, specifically for copying and recopying "desseins de grands maitres" is especially remarked upon (R066169): "Jamais peintre n'est peutetre plus d'amour pour son art, et ne mengea moins sa peine & son travail il ne luy coutoit rien de repasser plusieurs fois sur un même ouvrage toujours mécontent de luy même lorsque les autres eu paroissoient la plus satisfaits."

According to a recent study, he is suspected of having done more than copy old-master drawings: Corneille has been tentatively identified as the artist who defaced a number of works formerly in the Jabach Collection and now in the Louvre, by heavily retouching them in white (C. Monbeig Goguel, "Taste and Trade: The Retouched Drawings in the Everard Jabach Collection at the Louvre," *Burlington Magazine* 130, no. 1028 [1988]: 821–35).

4. Dumesnil 1973, pp. 2–3.

5. The prints are described in the draft of the contents pages for Prince Eugene's albums in the Mariette manuscript in the Bibliothèque Nationale (R066159); the prints are on fol. 29–31 of the album containing Corneille's works in the Albertina. Prints by Jean Mariette after compositions by Michel-Ange Corneille are on fol. 14 of this album.

6. R.-D.VI.286: "Il a gravé à l'eau-forte, tantôt d'une pointe large et ferme, et parfois d'une manière trés-moelleuse, mais toujours avec infinnement de goût. Il savait assez manier le burin pour donner l'accord et la couleur aux travaux qu'il avait établis à la pointe."

BIBLIOGRAPHY

THIS BIBLIOGRAPHY contains works cited frequently and in abbreviated fashion in the notes. Works cited only once in a note that have more general reference to this publication are also included, but those that refer only to a specific point are fully cited in the note and not in this Bibliography.

Citations in the notes are ordinarily abbreviated to the author(s)'s last name and the date of publication. There are major exceptions, however. Multivolume, multiartist dictionaries and print catalogues are abbreviated by name or initial(s), with the volume, page, and entry numbers separated by periods. Thus a reference to a print catalogued by Bartsch on page 84 of volume 20 as number 13 of a particular artist's oeuvre will read "B.XX.84.13." If the text relating to that print is quoted, it will be cited as "B.XX.84." In citations of this form, roman numerals indicate volume numbers except for citations to *The Illustrated Bartsch*, where that publication's arabic numbering system for volumes and sections is maintained. In the case of multivolume, single-artist catalogues or multiartist, single-volume catalogues, only the author(s)'s name or initial and the catalogue number are given in the citation, with volume and page number omitted. This system is also used for watermark and collector's mark dictionaries.

Manuscript sources are referred to by abbreviations of the repository followed by "MS"; thus, for example, documents in the British Library are cited by the abbreviation "BLMS" followed by the inventory number of the actual document. The manuscript sources are cited in full in this Bibliography.

Ackley 1981: Ackley, Clifford S. *Printmaking in the Age of Rembrandt.* Boston: Museum of Fine Arts, 1981.

Albertina 1988: Albertina. *Guido Reni und der Reproduktionsstich.* Vienna: Albertina, 1988.

Amornpichetkul 1984: Amornpichetkul, Chittima. "Seventeenth-Century Italian Drawing Books: Their Origin and Development." In Brown University, *Children of Mercury: the Education of Artists in the Sixteenth and Seventeenth Centuries.* Providence: Department of Art, Brown University, 1984, pp. 108–18.

Andresen: Andresen, Andreas. *Handbuch für Kupferstichsammler oder Lexicon der Kupferstecher, Maler-Radirer und Formschneider aller Länder und Schulen.* 2 vols. Leipzig: T. O. Weigel, 1870, 1873.

Askew 1969: Askew, Pamela. "The Angelic Consolation of St. Francis of Assisi in Post-Tridentine Italian Painting." *Journal of the Warburg and Courtauld Institutes* 32 (1969):280–306.

Balsiger 1970: Balsiger, Barbara Jeanne. *The Kunst- und Wunderkammern: a Catalogue Raisonné of Collecting in Germany, France and England, 1565–1750.* Ph.D. diss., University of Pittsburgh, 1970.

B.: Bartsch, Adam. *Le peintre graveur.* 21 vols. Vienna: J. V. Degen/Pierre Mechetti, 1803–1821.

Battiscombe 1984: Battiscombe, Georgina. *The Spencers of Althorp.* London: Constable, 1984.

Bellini: Bellini, Paolo. *L'opera incisa di Simone Cantarini.* Milan, 1980.

Bellini 1974: Bellini, Paolo. "Giovanni Francesco Grimaldi." *Print Collector* 10 (1974):6–27.

Bellini 1975: Bellini, Paolo. "New Attributions to Ribera." *Print Collector* 11 (1975):18–21, 50–55.

Bellini 1982: Bellini, Paolo. *L'opera incisa di Giovanni Benedetto Castiglione.* Milan, 1982.

Bellori 1968: Bellori, Giovanni Pietro. *The Lives of Annibale and Agostino Carracci.* Translated by Catherine Enggass. University Park: Pennsylvania State University Press, 1968.

Berliner 1926: Berliner, Rudolf. *Ornamentale Vorlage-Blätter des 15. bis 18. Jahrhunderts.* 3 vols. Leipzig: Klinkhardt & Biermann, 1926.

Berliner and Egger 1981: Berliner, Rudolf, and Gerhart Egger. *Ornamentale Vorlageblatter des 15. bis 19. Jahrhunderts.* Munich: Klinkhardt & Biermann, 1981.

Blanc 1857–1858: Blanc, *Charles. Le trésor de la curiosité.* 2 vols. Paris: Vᵉ J. Renouard, 1857–1858.

Blankert 1978: Blankert, Albert. *Nederlandse 17e Eeuwse Italianiserende Landschapschilders.* Soest-Holland: Editions Davaco, 1978.

Blunt 1954: Blunt, Anthony. *The Drawings of G. B. Castiglione & Stefano della Bella in the Collection of Her Majesty the Queen at Windsor Castle.* London: Phaidon, 1954.

BLMS: London. British Library. *Blenheim Papers from the British Library.* The archives of the Spencer and Churchill families, from Blenheim Palace and Althorp (on microfilm).

BNMS: Paris. Bibliothèque Nationale. Ya. 24/pet. fol. Pierre-Jean Mariette. *Abécédario.* 10 vols. plus vol. 11, *Table* . . . by Jean Adhémar. All page references in citations are not to the folios of this manuscript, which are often difficult to identify, but to the frame numbers of the microfilm of the manuscript. Each frame number begins with R.

Bober and Rubinstein 1987: Bober, Phyllis Pray, and Ruth Rubinstein. *Renaissance Artists & Antique Sculpture.* Rev. ed. London: Harvey Miller, 1987.

Bock 1987: Bock, Henning, and Thomas W. Gaehtgens, eds. *Holländeishe Genremalerei im 17.Jahrhundert. Symposium Berlin 1984. Jahrbuch Prussicher Kulturbesitz, Sondernad 4.* Berlin: Mann Verlag, 1987.

Bohlin: Bohlin, Diane De Grazia. *Prints and Related Drawings by the Carracci Family, a Catalogue Raisonné.* Washington: National Gallery of Art, 1979.

Bolten 1985: Bolten, Jaap. *Method and Practice: Dutch and Flemish Drawing Books.* Landau: Pfälzische Verlagsamstalt, 1985.

Braubach 1965: Braubach, Max. *Prinz Eugen von Savoyen. 5. Mensch und Schicksal.* Munich: Oldenbourg, 1965.

Briganti et al. 1983: Briganti, Giuliano, Ludovica Trezzani, and Laura Laureati. *The Bamboccianti.* Translated by Robert Erich Wolf. Rome: Ugo Bozzi, 1983.

Brown: Brown, Jonathan. *Jusepe de Ribera: Prints and Drawings.* Princeton: Princeton University Press, 1973.

Brown 1984: Brown, Christopher. *Scenes of Everyday Life: Dutch Genre Painting of the Seventeenth Century.* London: Faber & Faber, 1984.

Brown/RISD 1970: Brown University/Rhode Island School of Design. *Jacques Callot, 1592–1635.* Providence: Brown University, 1970.

Brown/RISD 1980: Brown University, Department of Art, and Rhode Island School of Design, Bell Gallery. *Ornament and Architecture: Renaissance Drawings, Prints and Books.* Providence: Brown University, 1980.

Burke 1976: Burke, James D. *Jan Both: Paintings, Drawings and Prints.* New York: Garland Publishing, 1976.

Calabi 1924: Calabi, Augusto. "The Etchings of Giulio Carpioni." *Print Collector's Quarterly* 11, no. 2 (1924):133–61.

Chiari 1982: Chiari, Maria Agnese. *Incisiori da Tiziano: Catalogo del fondo grafico a stampa del Museo Correr.* Venice: Museo Correr, 1982.

Chiari Moretto Weil 1989: Chiari Moretto Weil, Maria Agnese. *Tiziano: corpus dei disegni autografi.* Milan: Berenice, [1989].

Chiarini 1984: Chiarini, Marco. "The Importance of Filippo Napoletano for Claude's Early Formation." In *Claude Lorrain 1600–1682: A Symposium (Studies in the History of Art, Vol. 14),* edited by Pamela Askew. Washington: National Gallery of Art, 1984.

Chong 1987: Chong, Alan. "The Drawings of Cornelis van Poelenburch." *Master Drawings* 25 (Spring 1987):3–62.

Christie 1919: Christie, Manson & Woods. *Important Etchings by Old Masters Removed from Althorp, the property of the Rt. Honourable Earl Spencer, K.G.* London, 25 June 1919.

Churchill: Churchill, William Algernon. *Watermarks in Paper in Holland, England, France, etc., in the XVII and XVIII Centuries and Their Interconnection.* Amsterdam: Menno Herzberger, 1935.

Churchill 1938: Churchill, Winston S. *Marlborough, His Life and Times.* 6 vols. New York: Charles Scribner's Sons, 1938.

Clark 1987: Clark, Alvin L., Jr. *From Mannerism to Classicism: Printmaking in France, 1600–1660.* New Haven: Yale University Art Gallery, 1987.

Cowles 1983: Cowles, Virginia. *The Great Marlborough and His Duchess.* New York: Macmillan, 1983.

Cropper: Cropper, Elizabeth. *Pietro Testa, 1612–1650: Prints and Drawings.* Philadelphia: Philadelphia Museum of Art, 1988.

Cummins 1988: Cummins, John. *The Hound and the Hawk: The Art of Medieval Hunting.* London: Weidenfeld & Nicholson, 1988.

Davidson 1979: Davidson, Jane P. *David Teniers the Younger.* Boulder: Westview Press, 1979.

De Grazia 1984: De Grazia, Diane. *Correggio and His Legacy.* Washington: National Gallery of Art, 1984.

Delany 1861–1862: Delany, Mary Granville. *The Autobiography and Correspondence of Mary Granville, Mrs. Delany.* Edited by Lady Landover. 6 vols. London: Richard Bentley, 1861–1862.

Dempsey 1977: Dempsey, Charles. *Annibale Carracci and the Beginnings of Baroque Style.* Gluckstadt: Augustin, 1977.

Denvir 1983: Denvir, Bernard. *The Eighteenth Century: Art, Design and Society, 1689–1789.* London: Longman, 1983.

Deuchar 1988: Deuchar, Stephen. *Sporting Art in Eighteenth-Century England: A Social and Political History.* New Haven: Paul Mellon Centre for Studies in British Art, 1988.

DeV.-M.: De Vesme, Alexandre, with Introduction and Additions by Phyllis Dearborn Massar. *Stefano Della Bella, Catalogue Raisonné.* 2 vols. New York: Collectors Editions, 1971.

Devauchelle 1959–1961: Devauchelle, Roger. *La reliure en France, de ses origines à nos jours.* 3 vols. Paris: J. Rousseau-Girard, 1959–1961.

Dixon 1987: Dixon, Laurinda S. *Skating in the Arts of 17th Century Holland.* Cincinnati: Taft Museum, 1987.

Dumesnil 1973: Dumesnil, J.-G. *Histoire des plus célèbres amateurs français, I. Pierre-Jean Mariette, 1694–1774.* Geneva: Minkoff, 1973.

Duncan 1975: Duncan, David C. *English Scholars, 1660–1730.* Westport: Greenwood Press, 1975.

Duparc and Graif 1990: Duparc, Frederik J., and Linda L. Graif. *Italian Recollections: Dutch Painters of the Golden Age.* Montreal: Montreal Museum of Fine Arts, 1990.

Elsum 1704: Elsum, John. *The Art of Painting after the Italian Manner.* London: D. Brown et al., 1704.

Enggass and Brown 1970: Enggass, Robert, and Jonathan Brown. *Italy and Spain, 1600–1750: Sources and Documents.* Englewood Cliffs: Prentice-Hall, 1970.

Ewald 1978: Ewald, William Bragg, Jr. *Rogues, Royalty and Reporters.* Westport: Greenwood Press, 1978.

Ferrara 1985: Ferrara. Castello Estense, Casa Romei. *Torquato Tasso tra letteratura, musica, teatro, e arti figurative.* Ferrara: Castello Estense, Casa Romei, 1985.

Ferrari and Scavizzi 1966: Ferrari, Oreste, and Giuseppe Scavizzi. *Luca Giordano.* Naples: Edizioni Scientifiche Italiane, 1966.

Filipczak 1987: Filipczak, Zirka Zaremba. *Picturing Art in Antwerp, 1550–1700.* Princeton: Princeton University Press, 1987.

Finch 1968: Finch College Museum of Art. *Drawings of Lucas Cambiaso.* New York: Finch College Museum of Art, 1968.

Fletcher 1895: Fletcher, William Younger. *Bookbinding in France.* London: Seeley & Co., 1895.

Foss 1971: Foss, Michael. *The Age of Patronage: the Arts in England, 1660–1750.* Ithaca: Cornell University Press, 1971.

Fowle 1970: Fowle, Geraldine Elizabeth. *The Biblical Paintings of Sébastien Bourdon.* 2 vols. Ph.D. diss., University of Michigan at Ann Arbor, 1970.

Freedberg 1980: Freedberg, David. *Dutch Landscape Prints of the Seventeenth Century.* London: Colonnade Books, 1980.

Garlick 1976: Garlick, K. J., comp. "A Catalogue of Pictures at Althorp." *Walpole Society* 44 (1974–1976).

Garnier 1989: Garnier, Nicole. *Antoine Coypel.* Paris: Arthena, 1989.

Gaskell 1987: Gaskell, Ivan. "Tobacco, Social Deviance and Dutch Art in the Seventeenth Century." In *Holländeishe Genremalerei im 17. Jahrhundert. Symposium Berlin 1984. Jahrbuch Prussicher Kulturbesitz, Sondernad 4.* Edited by Henning Bock and Thomas W. Gaehtgens. Berlin: Mann Verlag, 1987:117–37.

Gernsheim: *Gernsheim Corpus of Old-Master Drawings* (photographs consulted at the Fine Arts Library, Harvard University).

Girouard 1978: Girouard, Mark. *Life in the English Country House: A Social and Architectural History.* New Haven: Yale University Press, 1978.

Godefroy: Godefroy, Louis. *The Complete Etchings of Adriaen van Ostade.* Translated by Susan Fargo Gilchrist. San Francisco: Alan Wofsy Fine Arts, 1990.

Goldfarb 1989: Goldfarb, Hilliard T. *From Fontainebleau to the Louvre: French Drawings from the Seventeenth Century.* Cleveland: Cleveland Museum of Art, 1989.

Goldstein 1988: Goldstein, Carl. *Visual Fact Over Verbal Fiction.* Cambridge: Cambridge University Press, 1988.

Gordon 1986: Gordon, Peter, ed. *The Red Earl: The Papers of the Fifth Earl Spencer, 1835–1910.* 2 vols. Northampton: Northampton Record Society, 1986.

Griffiths 1989: Griffiths, Antony. "Early Mezzotint Publishing in England - I. John Smith, 1652–1743." *Print Quarterly* 6, no. 3 (1989):243–57.

Grummond 1972: Grummond, Nancy de. "Giorgione's 'Tempest': The Legend of St. Theodore." *L'Arte* 5, no. 18–19/20 (1972):5–53.

H.: Hollstein, F. W. H. *Dutch and Flemish Etchings, Engravings, and Woodcuts, ca. 1450–1700.* Amsterdam: Menno Hertzberger, 1949–.

Hale 1954: Hale, J. R. *England and the Italian Renaissance.* London: Faber & Faber, 1954.

Harris 1985: Harris, Ann Sutherland. *Landscape Painting in Rome: 1595–1675.* New York: Richard L. Feigen & Co., 1985.

Haskell 1980: Haskell, Francis. *Patrons and Painters.* Rev. ed. New Haven: Yale University Press, 1980.

Haskell 1988: Haskell, Francis. *The Painful Birth of the Art Book.* New York: Thames & Hudson, 1988.

Hayes 1965–1966: Hayes, John. "British Patrons and Landscape Painting: I. The Seventeenth Century; II. The Eighteenth Century." *Apollo* 82, no. 41 (1965):38–45; 83, no. 49 (1966):188–97.

Heawood: Heawood, Edward. *Watermarks, Mainly of the 17th and 18th Centuries.* Hilversum: Paper Publications Society, 1950.

Heinecken 1771: Heinecken, Carl Heinrich von. *Idée générale d'une collection complette d'estampes.* Leipzig and Paris: Jean Paul Kraus, 1771.

Heinecken 1778–1790: Heinecken, Karl Heinrich von. *Dictionaire des artistes, dont nous avons des estampes* ... 4 vols. Leipzig: J. G. I. Breitkopf, 1778–1790.

Henderson 1964: Henderson, Nicholas. *Prince Eugen of Savoy.* London: Weidenfeld & Nicolson, 1964.

Herrmann 1972: Herrmann, Frank. *The English as Collectors: A Documentary Chrestomathy.* London: Chatto & Windus: 1972.

Hofrichter 1983: Hofrichter, Frima Fox. *Haarlem: The Seventeenth Century.* New Brunswick: Jane Voorhees Zimmerli Art Museum, Rutgers, The State University of New Jersey, 1983.

Hollstein: Hollstein, F. W. H. *German Engravings, Etchings, and Woodcuts, ca. 1400–1700.* Amsterdam: Menno Hertzberger, 1954–.

Holmes 1986: Holmes, Geoffrey. *Politics, Religion and Society in England, 1679–1742.* London: The Hambledon Press, 1986.

Hoogewerff 1952: Hoogewerff, G. J. *De Bentvueghels.* The Hague: Martinus Nijhoff, 1952.

Huber 1787: Huber, M[ichel]. *Notices générales des graveurs* ... Dresden and Leipzig: J. G. I. Breitkopf, 1787.

Huber 1797–1804: Huber, M[ichel]. *Manuel des curieux et des amateurs de l'art* ... 8 vols. Zurich: Fuesslin, 1797–1804.

Hughes 1988: Hughes, Diane Owen. "Representing the Family: Portraits and Purposes in Early Modern Italy," pp. 7–38. In *Art and History: Images and Their Meaning.* Edited by Robert I. Rotberg and Theodore K. Rabb. Cambridge: Cambridge University Press, 1988.

James et al. 1991: James, Carlo, Caroline Corrigan,

Marie Christine Enshaian, and Marie Rose Greca. *Manuale per la conservazione e il restauro di disegni e stampe antichi.* Translated by Maria Letizio Strocchi. Florence: Leo S. Olschki, 1991.

Joly 1988: Joly, Hugues-Adrien. *Lettres à Karl-Heinrich von Heinecken, 1772–1789.* Edited by W. McAllister Johnson. Paris: Bibliothèque Nationale, 1988.

Johnson 1982: Johnson, W. McAllister. *French Royal Academy of Paintings and Sculpture, Engraved Reception Pieces: 1672–1789.* Kingston: Agnes Etherington Art Centre, Queen's University, 1982.

Karpinski 1989: Caroline Karpinski. "The Print in Thrall to Its Original: A Historiographic Perspective." *Retaining the Original: Multiple Originals, Copies, and Reproductions. Center for Advanced Study in the Visual Arts, Symposium Papers VII. Studies in the History of Art* 29 (Washington: National Gallery of Art, 1989):101–9.

Kren 1978: Kren, Thomas. *Jan Miel (1599–1664), a Flemish Painter in Rome.* 3 vols. Ph.D. diss., Yale University, 1978.

L.: Lieure, J. *Jacques Callot.* 8 vols. New York: Collectors Editions Limited, 1969.

Lambert 1987: Lambert, Susan. *The Image Multiplied.* London: Trefoil Publications, 1987.

LeB.: Le Blanc, Charles. *Manuel de l'amateur d'estampes.* 4 vols. Paris: Emile Bouillon, 1856–1888.

Le Comte 1944: Le Comte, Edward S. *Endymion in England.* New York: King's Crown Press, 1944.

Le Comte 1702: Le Comte, Florent. *Cabinet des singularitez d'architecture, peinture, sculpture et gravure . . .* 2nd ed. 3 vols. Brussels: Lambert Marchant, 1702.

Leppert 1978: Leppert, Richard D. *Arcadia at Versailles.* Amsterdam: Swets & Zeitlinger, 1978.

Linnig 1911: Linnig, Benjamin. *La gravure en Belgique.* Anvers: Janssens Frères, 1911.

Lipking 1970: Lipking, Lawrence. *The Ordering of the Arts in Eighteenth-Century England.* Princeton: Princeton University, 1970.

Lippincott 1983: Lippincott, Louise. *Selling Art in Georgian London: the Rise of Arthur Pond.* New Haven: Paul Mellon Centre for Studies in British Art, 1983.

Los Angeles 1988: Los Angeles County Museum of Art. *Guido Reni, 1575–1642.* Los Angeles: Los Angeles County Museum of Art, 1988.

Lugt: Lugt, Frits. *Les marques de collections de dessins & d'estampes.* Amsterdam: Vereenigde Drukkerijen, 1921. *Supplément.* The Hague: Martinus Nijhoff, 1956.

Mâle 1932: Mâle, Emile. *L'art religieux après le Concile de Trente.* Paris: Librarie Armand Colin, 1932.

Malvasia 1841: Malvasia, Carlo Cesare. *Felsina Pittrice.* Edited by G. Zanetti. 2 vols. Bologna: Tip Guidi all'Ancora, [1678] 1841.

Manchester 1864: Manchester [William Drogo Montagu], 7th Duke of. *Court and Society from Elizabeth to Anne.* 2 vols. London: Hurst & Blackett, 1864.

Mandroux-França 1986: Mandroux-França, Marie Thérèse. "La collection d'estampes du Roi Jean V de Portugal: une relecture des Notes Manuscrites de Pierre-Jean Mariette." *Revue de l'art* 73, no. 3 (1986):49–54.

Mannocci 1988: Mannocci, Lino. *The Etchings of Claude Lorrain.* New Haven: Yale University Press, 1988.

Marabottini 1969: Marabottini, Alessandro. *Polidoro da Caravaggio.* 3 vols. Rome: Edizioni dell'Elefante, 1969.

Mariette 1851–1860: Chennevières, Ph[ilippe] de, and A[natole] de Montaiglon. *Abécédario de P. J. Mariette.* 6 vols. Paris: J.-B. Dumoulin, 1851–1860.

Marolles 1855: Marolles, Michel de. *Le livre des peintres et graveurs.* Edited by Georges Duplessis. Paris: P. Jannet, 1855.

Marzocchi 1983: Marzocchi, Lea. *Scritti originali del Conte Carlo Cesare Malvasia spettanti alla sua "Felsina Pittrice."* Bologna: Alfa, [1983].

Meder 1978: Meder, Josef. *The Mastery of Drawing.* Translated by Winslow Ames. 2 vols. New York: Abaris, 1978.

Meyer: Meyer, Julius, Hermann Lücke, and Hugo von Tschudi. *Allgemeines Künster-Lexicon.* 3 vols. Leipzig: Wilhelm Engelmann, 1885.

Michiels 1874: Michiels, Alfred. *Histoire de la peinture flamande.* 2nd ed. vol. 9. Paris: Lacroix, 1874.

MLMS: Paris. Musée du Louvre, Département des Arts Graphiques. BS/b9 (letters of Pierre-Jean Mariette); BS/b10 (letters of Jean Mariette). The individual letters are numbered in chronological order with each number preceded by an L.

Montagu 1985: Montagu, Jennifer. *Alessandro Algardi.* 2 vols. New Haven: Yale University Press, 1985.

Muller 1989: Muller, Jeffrey M. "Measures of Authenticity: the Detection of Copies in the Early Literature on Connoisseurship." *Retaining the Original: Multiple Originals, Copies, and Reproductions. Center for Advanced Study in the Visual Arts, Symposium Papers VII. Studies in the History of Art* 29 (Washington: National Gallery of Art, 1989):141–49.

Nagler 1835–1852: Nagler, Georg Kaspar. *Neues allgemeines Kunstler-Lexicon.* 22 vols. Munich: E. A. Fleischman, 1835–1852.

Nagler 1858–1879: Nagler, Georg Kaspar. *Die Monogrammisten.* 5 vols. Munich: Georg Franz, 1858–1879.

Nicoll 1963: Nicoll, Allardyce. *The World of Harlequin, a Critical Study of the Commedia dell'Arte.* Cambridge: Cambridge University Press, 1963.

Nielson 1979: Nielson, Nancy Ward. *Camillo Procaccini Paintings and Drawings.* London, 1979.

Ogden and Ogden 1955: Ogden, Henry V. S., and Margaret S. Ogden. *English Taste in Landscape in the Seventeenth Century.* Ann Arbor: The University of Michigan Press, 1955.

Ovid 1575: Ovidus. *The XV. Bookes of P. Ovidius Naso, Entitules, METAMORPHOSIS.* Translated by Arthur Golding. London: Willyam Seres, 1575.

Paris 1967: Paris. Musée du Louvre. *Le cabinet d'un grand amateur, P.-J. Mariette, 1694–1774.* Paris: Musée du Louvre, 1967.

Pearce 1977: Pearce, Barry. *Cornelis Bega Etchings.* Adelaide: Art Gallery of South Australia, 1977.

Pears 1982: Pears, Iain. "Patronage and Learning in the Virtuoso Republic: John Talman in Italy, 1709–1712." *Oxford Art Journal* 5, no. 1 (1982):24–30.

Pears 1988: Pears, Iain. *The Discovery of Painting: the Growth of Interest in the Arts in England, 1680–1768.* New Haven: Yale University Press, 1988.

Pepper 1984: Pepper, D. Stephen. *Guido Reni.* Oxford: Phaidon, 1984.

Percy 1971: Percy, Ann. *Giovanni Benedetto Castiglione, Master Draughtsman of the Italian Baroque.* Philadelphia: Philadelphia Museum of Art, 1971.

Pérez Sánchez and Spinosa 1978: Pérez Sánchez, Alfonso E., and Nicola Spinosa. *L'opera completa del Ribera.* Milan: Rizzoli, 1978.

Philadelphia 1984: Philadelphia Museum of Art. *Masters of Seventeenth-Century Dutch Genre Painting.* Philadelphia: Philadelphia Museum of Art, 1984.

Philipe 1811: Philipe, T. *Catalogue of a Superb Cabinet of Drawings; the Entire Collection of a Nobleman: Formed with Taste and Judgment, about the Middle of the Last Century, and Abounding in Choice Specimens of the Great Masters of all the Schools, Particularly the Italian.* London, 10–18 June 1811.

Piles 1766: Piles, Roger de. *Cours de peinture par principes.* Paris: Charles-Antoine Jombert, 1766.

Pilo 1961: Pilo, Giuseppe Maria. *Carpioni.* Venice: Edizioni Alfieri, 1961.

Poliziano 1979: Poliziano, Angelo. *The Stanze of Angelo Poliziano.* Translated by David Quint. Amherst: University of Massachusetts Press, 1979.

Pomian 1982: Pomian, Krzysztof. "La culture de la curiosité." *Le temps de la réflexion* 3 (1982):337–59.

Ponsonaihle: Ponsonaihle, Charles. *Sébastien Bourdon, sa vie et son oeuvre.* Paris: Jules Rouam, 1886.

Préaud 1984: Préaud, Maxime. "Jacques van Merle, a Flemish Dealer in Paris." *Print Quarterly* 1, no. 2 (1984):80–95.

Préaud 1987: Préaud, Maxime, et al. *Dictionnaire des éditeurs d'estampes à Paris sous l'Ancien Régime.* Paris: Promodis, 1987.

Réau 1955–1959: Réau, Louis. *L'iconographie de l'art chrétien.* 3 vols. Paris: Presses Universitaires de France, 1955–1959.

Reed and Wallace 1989: Reed, Sue Welsh, and Richard Wallace. *Italian Etchers of the Renaissance & Baroque.* Boston: Museum of Fine Arts, 1989.

Richardson 1792: Richardson, Jonathan. *The Works of Jonathan Richardson.* "A new edition . . . with the Additions of an Essay on the Knowledge of Prints, and Cautions to Collectors." London: T. and J. Egerton, 1792.

Ris 1877: Ris, L. Clément de. *Les amateurs d'autrefois.* Paris: E. Plon, 1877.

R.-D.: Robert-Dumesnil, A. P. F. *Le peintre-graveur français.* 17 vols. Paris: Allouard, 1835–1844.

Röhn 1932: Röhn, F. *Die Graphik des Giovanni Benedetto Castiglione.* Charlottenburg, 1932.

Roethlisberger 1961: Roethlisberger, Marcel. *Claude*

Lorrain: The Paintings. 2 vols. New Haven: Yale University Press, 1961.

Roethlisberger 1968: Roethlisberger, Marcel. *Claude Lorrain: The Drawings.* Berkeley and Los Angeles: University of California Press, 1968.

Roethlisberger 1971: Roethlisberger, Marcel. *The Claude Lorrain Album in the Norton Simon, Inc., Museum of Art.* Los Angeles: Los Angeles County Museum of Art, 1971.

Roethlisberger 1972: Roethlisberger, Marcel. "Nuovi aspetti di Claude Lorrain." *Paragone* 23, no. 273 (1972):24–36.

Roethlisberger 1979: Roethlisberger, Marcel. "Additional Works by Goffredo Wals and Claude Lorrain." *Burlington Magazine* 121, no. 910 (1979):20–29.

Rombouts and van Lerius: Rombouts, Ph., and Th. van Lerius. *De Liggeren en andere historische Archieven der Antwerpsche Sint Lucasgilde.* 2 vols. The Hague: Martinus Nijhoff, n.d.

Rome 1985: Rome. Soprintendenza archeologica di Roma. *Roma. Archeologia nel centro.* 2 vols. Rome: De Luca Editore, 1985.

Rosenberg 1982: Rosenberg, Pierre. *France in the Golden Age.* New York: Metropolitan Museum of Art, 1982.

Rossi 1677: Rossi, Gio[vanni] Giacomo de. *Indice delle stampe intagliate in rame, al bulino, & all'acquaforte. Esistenti nella Stamperia di Gio. Giacomo de Rossi in Roma alla Pace.* 1677, 1696, 1700 eds. (The 1677 edition is that referred to unless otherwise indicated; 1700 ed. with addition of Domenico de Rossi.)

Rostenberg 1963: Rostenberg, Leona. *English Publishers in the Graphic Arts, 1599–1700.* New York: Burt Franklin, 1963.

Rowse 1958: Rowse, A. L. *The Later Churchills.* London: Macmillan, 1958.

Russell 1975: Russell, H. Diane. *Jacques Callot: Prints & Related Drawings.* Washington: National Gallery of Art, 1975.

Russell 1982: Russell, H. Diane. *Claude Lorrain, 1600–1682.* Washington: National Gallery of Art, 1982.

Russell 1990: Russell, H. Diane. *Eve/Ave: Women in Renaissance and Baroque Prints.* Washington: National Gallery of Art, 1990.

Salerno 1977–1978: Salerno, Luigi. *Landscape Painters of the Seventeenth Century in Rome.* Translated by Clovis Whitfield and Catherine Enggass. 3 vols. Rome: Ugo Bozzi, 1977–1978.

Schama 1987: Schama, Simon. *The Embarrassment of Riches.* New York: Alfred A. Knopf, 1987.

Schnackenburg 1981: Schnackenburg, Bernhard. *Adriaen van Ostade, Isack van Ostade. Zeichnungen und Aquarelle.* 2 vols. Hamburg: Hauswedell, 1981.

Siret 1876: Siret, A[dolphe]. "Neve, Franciscus de." vol. 5, p. 584. In Belgium, L'Académie royale des sciences, des lettres et des beaux-arts, *Biographie nationale.* Brussels: Bruylant-Christophe, 1876.

Sluijter 1986: Sluijter, Eric Jan. *De 'Heydensche Fabulen' in de Noordnederlandse Schilderkunst circa 1590–1670.* Leiden: Rijksuniversiteit, 1986.

Snyder 1975: Snyder, Henry L. *The Marlborough-Godolphin Correspondence.* 3 vols. Oxford: Clarendon Press, 1975.

Sopher 1978: Sopher, Marcus S., with the assistance of Claudia Lazzaro-Bruno. *Seventeenth-Century Italian Prints.* Stanford: Stanford Art Gallery, 1978.

Stechow 1966: Stechow, Wolfgang. *Dutch Landscape Painting of the Seventeenth Century.* London: Phaidon, 1966.

Stone 1989: Stone, David M. *Theory and Practice in Seicento Art: the Example of Guercino.* Ph.D. diss., Harvard University, 1989.

Stone 1991: Stone, David M. *Guercino, Master Draftsman.* Cambridge: Harvard University Art Museums, 1991.

Sutton 1981: Sutton, Denis. "Aspects of British Collecting, Part I." *Apollo* 114 (1981):282–339.

Sutton 1987: Sutton, Peter C. *Masters of 17th-Century Dutch Landscape Painting.* Boston: Museum of Fine Arts, 1987.

Taviani and Schino 1984: Taviani, Ferdinando, and Mirella Schino. *Le secret de la commedia dell'arte.* Translated by Yves Liebert. Florence: La Casa Usher, 1984.

Thieme-Becker: Thieme, Ulrich, and Felix Becker. *Allgemeines Lexikon des bildenden Künstler.* 37 vols. Leipzig: Wilhelm Engelmann/E. A. Seemann, 1907–1950.

Thomas 1935: Thomas, Ashley. *The Aqueducts of An-*

cient Rome. Edited by I. A. Richmond. Oxford: Clarendon Press, 1935.

Thuillier and Châtelet 1964: Thuillier, Jacques, and Albert Châtelet. *French Painting, from Le Nain to Fragonard.* Translated by James Emmons. Geneva: Editions d'Art Albert Skira, 1964.

TIB: *The Illustrated Bartsch.* Gen. ed. Walter L. Strauss. 50+ vols. New York: Abaris Books, 1978–.

Trevelyan 1930: Trevelyan, George Macaulay. *England under Queen Anne: Blenheim.* London: Longmans, Green & Co., 1930.

Turner 1989: Turner, Nicholas. "Guido Reni." *Print Quarterly* 6, no. 2 (1989):190–94.

Uffenbach 1934: Uffenbach, Zacharias Conrad von. *London in 1710.* Translated and edited by W. H. Quarrell and Margaret Mare. London: Faber & Faber, 1934.

Villiers 1939: Villiers, Marjorie. *The Grand Whiggery.* London: John Murray, 1939.

Viatte 1974: Viatte, Françoise. *Dessins de Stefano della Bella 1610–1664.* Musée du Louvre, Cabinet des Dessins, *Inventaire général des dessins italiens,* vol. 2. Paris: Editions des Musées Nationaux, 1974.

Von Holst 1963: Von Holst, Niels. *Creators, Collectors and Connoisseurs: the anatomy of artistic taste from antiquity to the present day.* Translated by Brian Battershaw. New York: G. P. Putnam's Sons, 1967.

Waals 1984: Waals, Jan van der. "The Print Collection of Samuel Pepys." *Print Quarterly* 1, no. 4 (1984): 236–57.

Waddingham 1960: Waddingham, Malcolm R. "Herman van Swanevelt in Rome." *Paragone* 11, no. 121 (1960):37–50.

Waddingham 1964: Waddingham, Malcolm R. "Andries and Jan Both in France and Italy." *Paragone* 15, no. 171 (1964):13–43.

Wallace 1979: Wallace, Richard W. *The Etchings of Salvator Rosa.* Princeton: Princeton University Press, 1979.

Ward-Jackson 1967: Ward-Jackson, Peter. "Some Main Streams and Tributaries in European Ornament from 1500 to 1750." *Victoria and Albert Museum Bulletin* 3, no. 2–4 (1967):58–70, 90–104, 121–34.

Washington 1980: Washington, National Gallery of Art. *Gods, Saints, & Heroes: Dutch Painting in the Age of Rembrandt.* Washington: National Gallery of Art, 1980.

Washington 1986: Washington, National Gallery of Art. *The Age of Correggio and the Carracci.* Washington: National Gallery of Art, 1986.

Wegner 1989: Wegner, Susan E. "Passion and Piety: Mattia Preti's *Martyrdom of St. Bartholomew.*" *Currier Gallery of Art Bulletin* (Fall 1989):26–53.

Weigert 1953: Weigert, Roger-Armand. "Le Commerce de la gravure au XVIIᵉ siècle en France: les deux premiers Mariettes et François Langlois, dit Ciartres." *Gazette des Beaux-Arts* 6 per., 46 (1953):167–88.

Weigert 1969: Weigert, Roger-Amand. "Graveurs et marchands d'estampes flamands à Paris sous le règne de Louis XIII." *Nouvelles de l'Estampe* no. 10 (1969):445–56.

Weisner 1964: Weisner, Ulrich. "Die Gemälde des Moyses van Uyttenbroeck." *Oud-Holland* 79 (1964):189–228.

Wessely: Wessely, J. E. *Jan de Visscher und Lambert de Visscher. Verzeichnis ihrer Kupferstiche.* Leipzig: Rudolph Weigel, 1866.

Whitfield 1984: Whitfield, Clovis. "Claude and a Bolognese Revival." *Studies in the History of Art* 14 (National Gallery of Art, Washington, 1984):83–91.

Wintermute 1990: Wintermute, Alan. *Claude to Corot: The Development of Landscape Painting in France.* New York: Colnaghi, 1990.

Winternitz 1967: Winternitz, Emanuel. *Musical Instruments and Their Symbolism in Western Art.* London: Faber & Faber, 1967.

Wittkower 1952: Wittkower, Rudolf. *The Drawings of the Carracci in the Collection of Her Majesty the Queen at Windsor Castle.* London: Phaidon, 1952.

Wright 1985: Wright, Christopher. *The French Painters of the Seventeenth Century.* London: Orbis, 1985.

Wurzbach 1910: Wurzbach, Alfred von. *Niederländisches Künstler-Lexikon.* 3 vols. Vienna: Halm und Goldmann, 1910.

Zwollo 1973: Zwollo, An. *Hollandse en Vlaamse veduteschilders te Rome, 1675–1725.* Assen: Van Gorcum, 1973.

DESCRIPTION & CHECKLIST

OF THE ALBUMS

PREFACE TO THE DESCRIPTION AND CHECKLIST
OF THE SPENCER ALBUMS

I AM INDEBTED to Dennis Marnon of the Houghton Library, Harvard University, who provided the description of the albums' bindings and structure.

The Checklist owes much to the work of David P. Becker, former acting curator of prints, Fogg Art Museum, who catalogued the collection when the Spencer Albums were acquired by the Fogg Art Museum. I am very grateful to Alexander Nagel and Kristina Hartzer Nguyen, who proofread the Checklist against the albums and made many useful suggestions concerning the standardization of titles, etc.

I should like also to acknowledge the Fogg Art Museum's great debt to donors who gave monies and prints which made our acquisition of the albums possible. Because of space limitations we have not been able to specify in the Checklist the credit line which has been assigned to each individual print. Here follows the list of donors:

Gift of Melvin R. Seiden

Francis H. Burr Fund
Louise Haskell Daly Fund
Duplicate Print Sales Fund
William C. Heilman Fund
Alpheus Hyatt Fund
Alfred Jaretzki Fund
Richard Norton Fund
William M. Prichard Fund

Bequest of Edwin deT. Bechtel, by exchange
Bequest of Marian H. Phinney, by exchange

Anonymous Gift, by exchange
Gift of Edwin deT. Bechtel, by exchange
Gift of Herrman L. Blumgart, by exchange
Gift of Dr. and Mrs. William N. Bullard, by exchange
Gift of Stuart Denenberg, by exchange
Gift of William Gray from the collection of Francis
    Calley Gray, by exchange
Gift of the heirs of Mrs. Mary Hemenway, by exchange
Gift of Philip Hofer, by exchange
Gift of Mr. and Mrs. Philip Hofer, by exchange
Gift of Edith J. R. Isaacs, by exchange
Gift of Heath Jones, by exchange
Gift of Dr. Arnold Knapp, by exchange

Gift of Roderick K. MacLeod, by exchange
Gift of Prof. Charles Eliot Norton, by exchange
Gift of Belinda L. Randall from the collection of John
    Witt Randall, by exchange
Gift of Franz Röhn, by exchange
Gift of Denman W. Ross, by exchange
Gift of Paul J. Sachs, by exchange
Gift of Agnes Goldman Sanborn, by exchange
Gift of Mrs. William Simes, by exchange
Gift of Mr. and Mrs. Arthur Vershbow, by exchange
Gift of H. B. Warren, by exchange
Gift of Peter A. Wick, by exchange

Transfer from the Department of Architecture, by
    exchange

Francis H. Burr Fund, by exchange
Deknatel Purchase Fund, by exchange
Gray Collection of Engravings Fund, by exchange
Arnold Knapp Fund, by exchange
Miscellaneous Purchase Fund, by exchange
George R. Nutter Fund, by exchange
William M. Prichard Fund, by exchange
Lessing J. Rosenwald Fund, by exchange
Gifts for Special Uses Fund, by exchange

DESCRIPTION OF THE ALBUMS

Refer to fig. 1–3 in the Introduction.

THE SPENCER ALBUMS are nine folio volumes, approximately 568 x 410 mm. They are bound in red goatskin and are tooled in two similar, though not uniform, styles. The covers are tooled in gold with triple fillet borders and small corner decorations. The edges of the boards and the turn-ins are also tooled in gold. The spines have seven gold-tooled bands and eight gold-tooled panels, with titles in the second panel from the top (and volume numbers in the third panel in the Tempesta and Callot volumes). The variations in tooling are found most noticeably on the edges of the boards, turn-ins, and spine panels. Edges are gilt. Each volume has double headbands, worked in red and natural silk, and blue silk markers. The marbled endleaves are a French placard pattern, combed and curled.

The covers, spines, and bottom edges of the boards show wear from abrasion, which on some volumes is considerable. The hinges are cracked but sound in most volumes, exposing early (?) parchment manuscript spine linings. Where sewing can be seen, the gatherings are sewn in twos, all along, with overcasting of several gatherings at the front and rear of each volume.

In the following summary descriptions of the contents of the albums, the numbers in parentheses following the album numbers are shelf-list numbers, two per volume, written on the flyleaf of each volume. The first number, which is written in brown ink and struck through, is also the number written in the Althorp Library inventory taken upon the sale of the large part of that book collection to Mrs. John Rylands in 1892; this inventory is preserved at the John Rylands University Library of Manchester, England. In it the Spencer Albums are listed as books of engravings "left at Althorp," without further description. It should be noted that the pairs of albums containing Callot and Tempesta prints are each assigned only one shelf-list number; thus the inventory, which also records other books of engravings left at Althorp, is not an accurate count of the actual number of volumes of prints formerly in the collection of the Earls Spencer (see Introduction).

Two of the albums retain paper labels on their front covers. These are casually cut antique-laid paper rectangles, approximately 20 x 30 mm, which are mounted at the very top of the cover, centered. The other albums have residues of paper and paste in this location, indicating that all were so labeled at one time. The labels which remain are each inscribed in brown ink with roman capital initials on a first line and a number, preceded by "n°", on a second line. These inscriptions are given in the descriptions of the appropriate volumes, below.

The albums' current volume numbers were assigned relatively arbitrarily when they were first put on deposit at the Fogg Art Museum. The volumes are listed here in shelf-list number order.

Each album's description begins with the transcription of the lettering on the spine, paper label (if any), and title page (except Spencer Album 5). Within the description of the contents themselves, summary headings in French are transcribed from the tables of contents found at the back of each album (except Spencer Album 5) to indicate the compiler's general organization of the albums; these French summaries of sections of the albums are not, however, found in every table of contents. It should be noted that within the albums' tables of contents individual prints are given titles and attributions (usually correct by modern cataloguing standards), and so a heading above a large group of prints by several artists in no way indicates that the compiler believed all the prints below it were by the artist singled out in the heading.

The accession numbers of the prints given in the Spencer Albums Checklist indicate the actual placement of each print within the albums, and so the Checklist should be consulted in tandem with this Description to ascertain the specific mounting sequence of individual prints.

Where pages appear to be missing because folio numbers are skipped over in the descriptions of the albums' contents, it is because pages on which no prints were mounted were counted by the paginator of the albums.

SPENCER ALBUM 1 (8043 [struck through], 1592)

OEUVRE / DES CARACH / ET DES / PEINTRES / DE SON ECOLE

OEUVRES / DES CARRACHES / ET DE Quelques PEINTRES / DE / LEUR ECOLE

Pieces des Carraches.
The Carracci (Agostino, Annibale, and Lodovico) (by and after):
    biblical subjects, fol. 1–23
    saints and other religious subjects, fol. 23–30, 32–40 (Faccini *Saint Francis* fol. 31)
    mythological subjects, fol. 41–46
    genre, landscape, ornament, fol. 49–52

Pieces du Guide & du Pesarese.
Cantarini, Cesio, Lolli, Reni, Scarsello, Sirani, Torri (by and after):
    religious subjects, fol. 57–70
    mythological subjects, fol. 71–74

Pieces des Eleves des Carraches.
Badalocchio, Lanfranco, Mola, Bonzi (called Le Golbo in table of contents), Schedone, Valesio:
    various subjects, fol. 78–86
Guercino:
    Saint Anthony of Padua, fol. 86
Curti, Gatti:
    drawing-book subjects after Guercino, fol. 86–103

Pieces de Carle Maratte.
Maratti (by and after):
    religious subjects, fol. 104–113

SPENCER ALBUM 7 (8047 [struck through], 1591)

OEUVRES / DE / LABELLE

paper label on front cover: G G. / n°32

LES OEUVRES / DE / LABELLE [Below this inscription is drawn a large, ornamental basket of flowers placed on a rise of shaded ground. On the title page of the table of contents are drawn crossed palm fronds (?) tied with a ribbon.]

Della Bella and artists working in his style:
    Battle of the Amalekites, Flights into Egypt, fol. 1–2
    Holy Families and Flights into Egypt, fol. 3–4
    Saint John the Baptists, fol. 5
    portraits of saint and historical personage, fol. 6
    allegories of death, cupids, fol. 7–9
    card games, fol. 10–24
    battle plans, fol. 25–30
    ceremonials, parades, funerals, pageants, theatricals, fol. 31–63
    views of antiquities, gardens, and noted sites, fol. 64–81
    marines and port views, fol. 82–90
    landscapes, fol. 91–96
    four elements, fol. 97

landscapes, fol. 98–108

allegorical representations, including title pages, fol. 109–114

rebuses, fol. 115–116

figure and animal pieces, fol. 117–129

hunts, fol. 130–132

bacchanals, fol. 133–134

figures and animals in landscapes, fol. 135–138

copy of a classical relief, figure on horseback, fol. 138

figures on horseback and other subjects with horses, fol. 139–143

military subjects, fol. 144–146

military subjects and landscapes, fol. 147–149

dwarfs, fol. 150–151

exotic heads, fol. 151bis

drawing exercises, models, and figure pieces, fol. 152–161

four seasons, fol. 161

figure pieces, sketches of figures and animals, monograms, fol. 162–164

vases, fol. 165–166

ornamental panels and reliefs, fol. 167–173

cartouches, fol. 174–185

coats-of-arms and heraldry, fol. 186–189

SPENCER ALBUM 8 (8051 [struck through], 1598)

OEUVRE / DE / TEMPESTE / TOM ∗ I ∗

OEUVRES / DE / TEMPESTE / TOM 1ᵉ

Tempesta:

Old Testament subjects, fol. 1–14

mythological and classical subjects, fol. 15–26

story of the seven infantes of Lara, fol. 27–46

story of the wars between the Romans and Batavians, fol. 47–70

twelve Roman emperors on horseback, fol. 59–70

illustrations to *Jerusalem Delivered*, fol. 71–91

portraits of emperors and kings, fol. 96–99

cavalcades, triumphal processions, etc., fol. 100–105

SPENCER ALBUM 9 (8051 [struck through], 1598)

OEUVRE / DE / TEMPESTE / TOM ∗ II ∗

OEUVRES / DE / TEMPESTE / TOME 2ᵉ

Tempesta:

Metamorphoses of Ovid, fol. 1–19

labors of Hercules, fol. 20–21

landscapes with mythological subjects, fol. 21–25

Orpheus, fol. 26

four seasons, fol. 26–30

mythological subjects, fol. 31–32

four ages of man, fol. 33–34

twelve months, fol. 35–44

battles, fol. 49–59

hunt subjects, fol. 60–96

animal subjects, fol. 99–108

SPENCER ALBUM 5 (8053 [struck through], 1588)

OEUVRE / DE TENIERS / OSTADE / ET AUTRE / FLAMAND [No title page or table of contents was bound into this album; the folios were not numbered.]

Teniers (after):

lowlife and genre subjects, fol. 4–6

Boel after Teniers:

monkey satires, fol. 6–7

Teniers (after):

Temptation of Saint Anthony and lowlife subject, fol. 8

lowlife and genre subjects, fol. 9–11

Ostade (by and after), Bega:

lowlife and genre subjects, fol. 12–27

Miel:

bambocciate, fol. 28–29

Teniers (after), Laer, Bega:

lowlife and genre subjects, fol. 29

Laer (after):

bambocciate, fol. 30–31

Wtenbrouck:

mythological and Old Testament subjects, fol. 32–37

animal subjects, fol. 38

Apocrypha and Old Testament subjects, fol. 39–41

Bisschop after Breenbergh:

Joseph in Egypt, fol. 42

Bronchorst:

figure subjects, fol. 43–44

Roman landscapes, fol. 45–47

Morin:

Italian landscapes, fol. 48–49

Both:

The Five Senses, fol. 52–53

Italian landscapes, fol. 54–58

Waterloo:

landscapes, fol. 59–78

Swanevelt:

animal subjects, fol. 79

Old Testament subjects, fol. 80–81

Italian landscapes, fol. 82–86

landscapes with satyrs, fol. 87

The Story of Adonis, fol. 88–90

Neve:
   pastoral landscapes and mythological subjects, fol.
      91–94
Aken:
   Rhine landscapes, fol. 95–96
Morin and Platte-Montagne:
   landscapes (after Fouquières), fol. 99–104
   round landscapes, fol. 105–106
   landscapes, fol. 107–109
Genoels:
   landscapes, fol. 110–111
Vlieger:
   landscapes with genre subjects, fol. 111–112

SPENCER ALBUM 6 (8058 [struck through], 1594)

OEUVRE / DE DIFFERE / PEINTRE / DITALIE

paper label on front cover: L L / n°38

OEUVRES / DE / LESPAGNOLET / ET DE / BENEDITTE / Aux
   quelles on ajoint un Recueil de pieces choisies, /
   gravées par differens Peintres Italiens, —

Anonymous after Titian:
   landscapes, fol. 1, 3
Grimaldi:
   landscapes, fol. 2, 4–7
Vanni, G.B.:
   Wedding at Cana, fol. 8

Pieces inventées & gravées par le jeune Palme
Palma:
   religious subjects, fol. 9–10
   allegorical subjects, fol. 11–12
   drawing-book subjects, fol. 13–14

Pieces inventées & grav: par Baptiste Franco.
Franco:
   religious subjects, fol. 15–19
Farinati, P.:
   religious subjects, fol. 20–21
Farinati, O.:
   mythological subject, fol. 21

Pieces inven: & grav: Par Jules Carpioni, Venitien.
Carpioni:
   religious subjects, fol. 22–23
Farinati, O.:
   religious subjects and a hunting scene, fol. 25–26
   Venus and Cupid, fol. 27–29
   ornament subjects, fol. 29–31

*Pieces inventées & gravées par le Baroche, le Vannius
   Salembeni, & Vespasien Strada.*
Barocci (by and after), Vanni:
   religious subjects, fol. 35–39
Salimbeni:
   religious subjects, fol. 40–41
Strada:
   religious subjects, fol. 40, 42–44

*Pieces inventées & gravées par Joseph de Ribera, dit
   l'Espagnolet.*
Ribera (and school):
   religious subjects, fol. 48–52
   mythological subjects, fol. 53–54
   drawing-book subjects and heads, fol. 55–56
Caravaggio:
   religious subject, fol. 54
Giordano:
   Saint Anne Received into Heaven, fol. 57

Pieces inventées & gravées par Salvator Rose.
Rosa:
   religious and mythological subjects, fol. 60–65

Pieces inventées & gravées par Jean Benoist Castiglione.
Macé:
   Old Testament subjects (after G. B. Castiglione), fol.
      70–77
Castiglione, G. B.:
   pastoral and religious subjects, fol. 78–82
Macé:
   Old and New Testament subjects (after G. B. Casti-
      glione), fol. 83–86
Castiglione, G. B.:
   religious subjects, fol. 84–90, 96
Castiglione, S.:
   The Raising of Lazarus (after G. B. Castiglione), fol.
      90
Castiglione, G. B.:
   heads, fol. 91–92, 94
   allegorical and mythological subjects, fol. 93, 95–99
Bernard (after G. B. Castiglione):
   A Shepherdess Leading Her Flock, fol. 100

*Pieces inventées & Gravées par Barthelemy Biscaino,
   Genois.*
Biscaino:
   religious subjects, fol. 101–104
Schiamosi:
   Virgin of the Immaculate Conception, fol. 105

SPENCER ALBUM 2 (8059 [struck through], 1593)

OEUVRE / DE PEINTR / DITALIE / DE BOURDON / ET
AUTRES

OEUVRES / DE / DIVERS PEINTRES / D'ITALIE / ET / DE
FRANCE

Testa (no identification of Testa is given in table of
   contents):
   religious subjects, fol. 1–6
   allegorical and classical subjects, fol. 7–18
Grimaldi:
   landscapes, fol. 21–36
Angolo del Moro, Bisi, Borgiani, Passarotti, Passeri,
   Procaccini, Schiaminossi:
   religious subjects, fol. 39–50
Galestruzzi after Polidoro:
   classical subjects and ornament, fol. 51–54
Monogrammist GpP (called Pocetti in table of
   contents):
   Death of Nessus, fol. 55
Bourdon:
   Seven Acts of Mercy (Old Testament subjects), fol.
      59–65
   Jacob Leaves Laban, fol. 66
   tribute to Colbert (after Bourdon?), fol. 66
   religious subjects (largely Madonnas and Flights into
      Egypt), fol. 67–77
   landscapes, fol. 78–89
Prou and others after Bourdon:
   landscapes, fol. 90–96
Corneille:
   religious subjects, fol. 98–101
Claude:
   landscapes, fol. 103–108

SPENCER ALBUM 3 (8062 [struck through], 1595)

OEUURE / DE / CALOT / TOM ∗ I ∗

OEVURES / DE / JACQVES CALLOT / Tome 1ʳ

Lasnes, Custos:
   portraits of Callot, fol. 1
Callot:
   Christian subjects, Judith, fol. 2
   Life of the Virgin, fol. 3
   subjects from the Life and Passion of Christ, fol. 4–9
   Four Banquets, fol. 9bis
   Passion of Christ, fol. 10
   Bearing of the Cross (oval), fol. 11
   Prodigal Son, fol. 11bis
   Seven Deadly Sins, fol. 12
   Penitent Saints, fol. 12bis
   Calendar of Saints and Feasts, fol. 13–37

Martyrdoms of the Apostles, fol. 38
Savior, Blessed Virgin, and Apostles, fol. 39–42
Massacre of the Innocents and other martyrdoms and
   saints, fol. 43–44
Temptation of Saint Anthony, fol. 51
Madonnas, fol. 52
The Tree of Saint Francis, The Crossing of the Red Sea,
   fol. 53
The Little Farm, martyrdoms, other Christian sub-
   jects, fol. 54–55
Altarpieces of Rome, fol. 56–58
Light of the Cloister, fol. 60–61
Life of the Virgin in Emblems, fol. 62–63
Fair of Impruneta, fol. 64–65
landscape views of French and Italian sites, fol. 66–70
Frontispiece of the Assumption of the Virgin, fol. 70
Funeral Decorations for the Emperor Matthias, fol. 70
War of Love, fol. 77–78
Solimano, fol. 78–80
Combat at the Barrier, fol. 81–85
Life of Ferdinando I de' Medici, fol. 90–97
Large Rock, fol. 97
Equestrian Portrait of Louis III, fol. 98
Portrait of Louis de Lorraine, fol. 99
Large Thesis, fol. 101
portraits, fol. 102–104
allegorical frontispieces, fol. 104–105

SPENCER ALBUM 4 (8062 [struck through], 1595)

OEURE / DE / CALOT / TOM ∗ II ∗

OEUVRES / DE / JACQVES CALLOT / Tome 2ʳ

Lasne:
   portrait of Callot, title page
Callot:
   Card Players, Pandora, Review, Two Pantaloni, fol. 1
   Capricci, fol. 2–8
   women, fol. 8bis
   Diverse Figures, fol. 9–10
   Fantasies, fol. 11
   armorial subject, fol. 11
   Military Exercises, fol. 12
   Miseries of War, fol. 13–17
   Gypsies, fol. 18–19
   Slave Market, Tortures, fol. 19bis
   Nobility and other costume subjects (by and after
      Callot), fol. 20–22
   Beggars, fol. 23–26
   commedia dell'arte figures, fol. 27–30
   Hunchbacks, fol. 31–32
   sieges and battles (by and after Callot), fol. 33–63
   landscapes (by and after Callot), fol. 64–71
   coinage, fol. 72–80

CHECKLIST OF THE ALBUMS

INTRODUCTION

IN THE CHECKLIST, the first section under each artist's name gives the standard catalogue numbers of the prints by that artist included in the Spencer Albums. The next section gives series of prints, if any, by the artist in the albums. In several cases series are mounted in the albums in parallel or interspersed with independent prints, and the folio numbers given for their location may be inclusive. The series may be incomplete.

The final section under each artist's name lists the prints individually by title, arranged alphabetically. In this section, the references to standard catalogues are given in full, so that references to and reproductions of prints may be easily located. In the case of multivolume, multi-artist catalogues, the volume and page of the reference are given preceding the actual catalogue number, separated by periods.

Catalogues and other publications referred to in the Checklist:

Andresen: Andresen, Andreas. *Handbuch für Kupfer-stichsammler oder Lexicon des Kupferstecher, Maler-Radirer und Formschneider aller Länder und Schulen.* Leipzig, 1870, 1873.

B.: Bartsch, Adam. *Le Peintre-graveur.* Vienna, 1803–1821.

Bellini: Bellini, Paolo. *L'opera incisa di Simone Cantarini.* Milan, 1980.

Birke: Birke, Veronika. "Towards a Tempesta Catalogue." *Print Quarterly* 2, no. 3 (1985):205–8.

BNIFF17: Bibliothèque Nationale. *Inventaire du fonds français; graveurs du XVIIᵉ siècle.* Paris, 1939–.

Bohlin: Bohlin, Diane De Grazia. *Prints and Related Drawings by the Carracci Family.* Washington, 1979.

Bologna: Bertelà, Giovanna Gaeta. *Incisori bolognese ed emiliani del sec. XVII. Catalogo generale della raccolta di stampe antiche della Pinoteca nazionale di Bologna, Sezione III.* Bologna, 1973.

Brown: Brown, Jonathan. *Jusepe Ribera: Prints and Drawings.* Princeton, 1973.

Cropper: Cropper, Elizabeth. *Pietro Testa, 1612–1650: Prints and Drawings.* Philadelphia, 1988.

DeV.: DeVesme, Alexandre. *Le peintre-graveur italien.* Milan, 1906.

DeV.-M.: DeVesme, Alexandre, and Phyllis Dearborn Massar. *Stefano Della Bella, Catalogue Raisonné.* New York, 1971.

Dutuit: Dutuit, Eugène. *Manuel de l'amateur d'estampes.* Paris, 1881–1888.

H.: Hollstein, F. W. F. *Dutch and Flemish Etchings, Engravings, and Woodcuts, ca. 1450–1700.* Amsterdam, 1949–.

Hollstein: Hollstein, F. W. F. *German Engravings, Etchings, and Woodcuts, ca. 1400–1700.* Amsterdam, 1954–.

LeB.: Le Blanc, Charles. *Manuel de l'amateur d'estampes, contenant le dictionnaire des graveurs de toutes les nations.* Paris, 1854–1890.

L.: Lieure, Jules. *Jacques Callot.* Paris, 1924–1927.

Mannocci: Mannocci, Lino. *The Etchings of Claude Lorrain.* New Haven, 1988.

M.: Meyer, Julius, ed. *Allgemeines Künstler-Lexicon.* Leipzig, 1872–1885.

Meaume: Meaume, Edouard. *Recherches sur les ouvrages de Jacques Callot.* Würtzburg, 1924.

R.-D.: Robert-Dumesnil, A.-P.-F. *Le peintre-graveur français.* Paris, 1835–1871.

TIB: *The Illustrated Bartsch.* W. Straus, general ed. New York, 1978–.

Wessely: Wessely, J. E. *Jan und Lambert Visscher; Verzeichniss ihrer Kupferstiches.* Leipzig, 1866.

In the listing of individual prints, handwritten inscriptions by Pierre Mariette II are given in boldface. Where two inscriptions are indicated for one print, this indicates that the back of the print is visible and there are inscriptions (sometimes with differing dates) on both the front and the back. It should be noted that the backs of the vast majority of the prints are not visible and that inscriptions which may be concealed cannot be read through the heavy mounting paper of the albums' pages. As a significant number of the prints that were removed for exhibition proved to have Mariette inscriptions on their backs, it may be assumed that many prints remaining in the albums also bear these inscriptions.

Prints marked with an asterisk (*) were formerly in the albums but were cut out and sold at auction in 1919 (Christie, Manson & Woods, *Catalogue of Important Etchings by Old Masters Removed from Althorp, the Property of the Rt. Hon. Earl Spencer, K. G.*, London, 25 June 1919). All are listed either by artist alone or by artist and specific title at the appropriate points in the albums' tables of contents. Apart from these losses, there are very few apparent missing prints from the nine albums, notably three or four works from the della Bella album, a Madonna and Child by Bourdon formerly on s2.70, and two prints after landscapes by Antonio Domenico Gabbiani formerly on s2.36. These are listed in the Checklist and described as "missing."

The system of assignment of accession numbers indicates the placement of the prints in the nine Spencer albums. Thus, for example, s1.106.4 is the fourth print reading from the upper left across and down on folio 106 of Spencer Album 1. Album numbers were assigned relatively arbitrarily. Smaller prints are mounted only on the right-hand pages of each opening; larger prints are often drum-mounted as a double-page spread.

THE CHECKLIST

AKEN, Jan van
Dutch, 1614–1661

H.18–21

series:
Views of the Rhine, s5.95.1–s5.96.2

prints:
Travelers on a Bluff at the Right Foreground, after Saftleven (H.I.9.18 iii/vi), s5.95.1
Travelers Resting, after Saftleven (H.I.9.21 iii/vi), s5.96.2
Travelers with Backpacks on a Hill at the Left Foreground, after Saftleven (H.I.9.19 iii/vi), s5.95.2
Travelers with Men Catching Crayfish, after Saftleven (H.I.9.20 iii/vi), s5.96.1

AMATO, Francesco
Italian, c. 1590–?

B.2, 4

prints:
Saint Christopher Reaching Down for the Christ Child (B.XXI.206.4, TIB47.235.4, TIB4719.354.004 S1/2), s6.103.2
Saint Joseph Reading to the Christ Child (B.XXI.205.2, TIB47.233.2, TIB4719.354.002), s6.102.2

ANGOLO DEL MORO, Giovanni Battista d'
Italian, c. 1515–c. 1573

M.19, 61, 63–69; B.5 (Titian)

prints:
Christ Driving the Money Changers from the Temple (M.II.39.61), s2.47.3
Christ Taking Leave of His Mother (M.II.39.63–69), s2.48.2
Entombment (M.II.39.63–69), s2.48.3
Crowning with Thorns (M.II.39.63–69), s2.47.2
Landscape with Saint Theodore and the Dragon, after Titian (B.XVI.99.5 [Titian], TIB32.149.5), s6.3.1
Pietà (M.II.37.19 ii/ii), s2.48.1

ANONYMOUS (after Antonio Domenico Gabbiani)

prints:
Landscape, after Gabbiani, s2.36.1 (missing)
Landscape, after Gabbiani, s2.36.2 (missing)

ANONYMOUS 17th c. (after Stefano della Bella?)

series:
Ballet of Bears with Parrots, s7.52.1–s7.53.6
Ballet of Ostriches, s7.54.1–.6

prints:
Eight Parrot Dancers Fighting in Pairs, s7.53.3
Eight Parrot Dancers in a Circle, Their Parrots in Flight, s7.53.6
Eight Parrot Dancers in a Circle, Their Parrots on the Ground, s7.53.5
Eight Parrot Dancers in Two Rows, s7.53.2
Eight Parrot Dancers in Two Rows with Parrots and an Open Cage, s7.53.4
Eight Parrot Dancers with Parasols, s7.53.1
Four Bear Trainers, s7.52.1
Four Bear Trainers Sprinkling the Ground, s7.52.2
Four Bear Trainers Sweeping the Ground, s7.52.3
Four Bear Trainers with Bears, s7.52.4
Four Bear Trainers with Bears and Lions, s7.52.5
Four Bear Trainers with Bears and Monkeys, s7.52.6
Four Ostriches at the Corners of the Plate, s7.54.2
Four Ostriches in the Center of the Plate, s7.54.3
Six Ostriches Drinking, s7.54.6
Six Ostriches in a Circle, s7.54.5
Six Ostriches in a Line, s7.54.4
Two Ostriches, s7.54.1

ANONYMOUS DUTCH 17th c. (Gillis van Scheyndel?)

H.21–24 (after Swanevelt)

prints:
Landscape with a Traveler on a Donkey in a River Valley, after Swanevelt (H.XXIX.103.21), s5.86.2
Large Wooden Bridge, after Swanevelt (H.XXIX.103.23), s5.87.3
Two Fishermen, after Swanevelt (H.XXIX.103.24), s5.85.2
Two Peddlers on a Path to the Right of a River, after Swanevelt (H.XXIX.103.22), s5.87.4

ANONYMOUS FLEMISH 17th c. (after David Teniers the Younger)

H.36–39, 41; Dutuit 11

prints:
Archers, after Teniers (H.XXIX.190.36), s5.5.1
Couple Dancing before a Farmhouse, after Teniers (H.XXIX.191.38 i/ii), s5.4.4
Five Peasants Gathered around a Barrel, after Teniers (H.XXIX.191.39 i/ii), s5.4.1
Landscape with a Farm on a River, after Teniers (H.XXIX.192.41 ii?/ii), s5.29.1
Men Playing Bowls, after Teniers (H.XXIX.190.37 i/iii), s5.5.4
Temptation of Saint Anthony, after Teniers (Dutuit VI.423.11), s5.8.2

ANONYMOUS FRENCH 17th c.

prints:
Genies Occupied with Various Arts and Crowning the Arms of M. Colbert, Superintendent of the Buildings, Arts, and Manufactures of France, after Bourdon?, s2.66.2

ANONYMOUS FRENCH 17th c. (after Jacques Callot)

L.287; see L.195, 197; Meaume 1209–1212

series:
Four Women (Meaume 1209–1212), s4.22.1–2, s4.22.5–6

prints:
Boarding of the "Bertone," after Callot (reverse copy of L.195), s4.65.2
Capture, after Callot (reverse copy of L.197), s4.65.3
Christ Nailed to the Cross, after Callot (L.287 i/ii), s3.7.2
Two Turks, after Callot (L. appendix, pl.127, fig. 272), s4.8.11
View of a Farm, a Mule Driver at Right, after Callot, s4.65.1
View of a Farm, Chickens in the Foreground, insc. "Veue d'un des Environs de Nancy," after Callot, s4.65.4
Woman with a Basket on Her Arm, after Callot (Meaume 1212, attributed to Henriet), s4.22.6
Woman with a Distaff and Spindle, after Callot (Meaume 1211, attributed to Henriet), s4.22.5
Woman with a Ruff and Fur-Trimmed Jacket, after Callot (Meaume 1209 i/ii, attributed to Henriet), s4.22.1

Woman with Her Hands on Her Hips, after Callot (Meaume 1210, attributed to Henriet), s4.22.2

ANONYMOUS FRENCH 17th c. (after Jacques Callot, attributed to Collignon in Spencer Album table of contents)

Meaume 1103–1120

series:

Diverse Landscapes (Meaume 1103–1120), s4.66.1–s4.68.2, s4.68.4

prints:

Landscape with a Chapel on an Island, a Monk Fishing at the Right, after Callot (Meaume 1111 ii/ii), s4.67.1

Landscape with a Church and an Extensive Vista, after Callot (Meaume 1106 ii/ii), s4.67.2

Landscape with a Church on a Rock, after Callot (Meaume 1109 ii/ii), s4.66.2

Landscape with a Country House, a Wagon Wheel Leaning against Its Wall, after Callot (Meaume 1105 ii/ii, attributed to Henriet), s4.67.5

Landscape with a Country House Surrounded by a Wall and Moat, after Callot (Meaume 1103 ii/ii), s4.67.3

Landscape with a Duck Hunter and a Shepherd, after Callot (Meaume 1120 ii/ii), s4.67.8

Landscape with a Duck Hunter by a Moated Town, after Callot (Meaume 1116 ii/ii), s4.68.1

Landscape with a Farmstead, Its Chimney Topped by a Cross, after Callot (Meaume 1117 ii/ii), s4.66.6

Landscape with a Ferry, after Callot (Meaume 1107 ii/ii, attributed to Henriet), s4.68.2

Landscape with a Fortified Town Guarded by a Round Tower, after Callot (Meaume 1104 iii/iii), s4.67.4

Landscape with a Stag Hunt, after Callot (Meaume 1113), s4.66.8

Landscape with a Strolling Couple Accompanied by a Lutenist and a Poodle, after Callot (Meaume 1114 ii/ii), s4.66.4

Landscape with a Village Square, Pump, and Watering Troughs, after Callot (Meaume 1119 ii/ii), s4.67.6

Landscape with a Walled Village with a Church in the Distance, after Callot (Meaume 1108 ii/ii), s4.66.5

Landscape with Couples Strolling in a Grotto, after Callot, s4.68.4

Landscape with a Large Tree and Travelers by a River Leading to a Seaport, after Callot (Meaume 1112 ii/ii), s4.66.7

Landscape with a Village Church, after Callot (Meaume 1115 ii/ii), s4.66.1

Port Scene with an Inn at the Right, after Callot (Meaume 1110 ii/ii), s4.67.7

Port Scene with Shipping, Rocks in the Foreground, after Callot (Meaume 1118 ii/ii), s4.66.3

ANONYMOUS FRENCH 17th c. (after Jacques Callot or by a follower)

L.264–267

prints:

Landscape with a Dovecote, a Hunter at Left (L.265 i/ii), s4.64.2

Landscape with a Garden, a Well, and Farm Building at Left (L.264 i/ii), s4.64.1

Landscape with a Small Port, Shipping at Left (L.267 i/ii), s4.64.4, **P. mariette 1667**

Landscape with a Watermill, a Bather at Left (L.266 i/ii), s4.64.3

ANONYMOUS FRENCH 17th c. (Jean Mariette?)

R.-D.3

prints:

Holy Family, after Bourdon (R.-D.I.157.3 i/ii, attributed to Mariette, by inference Pierre II), s2.75.2 (attr. in table of contents to Bourdon)

Landscape with a Shepherd and His Flock, after Bourdon, s2.96.1

Rest on the Flight into Egypt with Two Angels, after Bourdon, s2.76.5

Virgin and Child with a Lamb by a Low Wall, after Bourdon, s2.76.1

ANONYMOUS ITALIAN 16th c.

B.4 (Brizio); 6, 7 (Titian)

prints:

Landscape with a Swineherd, after Titian (B.XVI.100.6 [Titian], TIB32.150.6), s6.3.2, **P. mariette 16[76?]**

Landscape with Shepherds (The Flautist), after Titian (B.XVI.100.7 [Titian], TIB32.151.7), s6.1

Virgin with a Pillow, after Annibale Carracci (BXVII.201.4 [Brizio], TIB4003.241.047.s3/3), s1.2.3

ANONYMOUS ITALIAN 17th c.

B.1 (Palma, the younger); 29, 31 (Reni school)

prints:
Nativity, after Palma, the younger (B.XVI.287.1 [copy]), s6.10.4
Saint Michael Fighting the Dragon, after Reni (B.XVIII.324.29 [Reni school], TIB40.241.29), s1.68.3
Studies of Male and Female Torsos, in the manner of Palma, the younger, s6.14.1
Sybil, after Reni (B.XVIII.325.31 [Reni school], TIB40.243.31, Bologna 1052), s1.67.2
Young Boy Overturning the Knitting Basket of an Old Woman in a Landscape, after Annibale Carracci, s1.49.1

ANONYMOUS NETHERLANDISH 17th c.

prints:
Interior with a Smoker, s5.29.2

AUDENAERD, Robert van
Flemish, 1663–1743

M.12, 14–16, 19, 20, 24, 42

prints:
Adoration of the Magi, after Maratti (LEB.18, M.II.384.19), s1.106.3
Agony in the Garden, after Maratti (M.II.384.16), s1.108.3
Christ Crowned with Thorns, after Maratti (LEB.25, M.II.384.17), s1.109.1
Christ on the Cross, after Collignon (LEB.26?, M.II.385.24), s1.109.2
Death of Saint Joseph, after Maratti (LEB.31, M.II.385.42 ii/ii), s1.110.1
Dream of Saint Joseph, after Maratti (M.II.384.15), s1.108.1
Flight into Egypt, after Maratti (LEB.19, M.II.384.20 i/ii), s1.110.2
Marriage of the Virgin, after Maratti (LEB.15, M.II.384.12 i/ii), s1.106.4
Nativity with the Adoration of the Shepherds, after Maratti (M.II.384.14), s1.108.2

BADALOCCHIO, Sisto
Italian, 1581–1647

B.26, 33

prints:
Laocoön, 1606 (B.XVIII.359.33, TIB40.369.33), s1.83
Mystic Marriage of Saint Catherine (B.XVIII.357.26, TIB40.362.26), s1.82.2

BARBIERI, Giovanni Francesco
see Guercino

BAROCCI, Federico
Italian, c. 1535–1612

B.1–4

prints:
Annunciation (B.XVII.2.1, TIB34.9.1), s6.36*
Christ Appearing to Saint Francis in the Chapel of the Portcullis (B.XVII.4.4, TIB34.12.4), s6.38
Madonna in the Clouds (B.XVII.3.2, TIB34.10.2), s6.35.1
Saint Francis Receiving the Stigmata (B.XVII.3.3, TIB34.11.3), s6.35.3

BARTOLI, Pietro Santi, attributed to
Italian, 1635–1700

LEB.56

prints:
Saint John the Baptist Preaching, after Mola (LEB.I.161.56), s1.84.2

BEGA, Cornelis
Dutch, 1620–1664

H.23, 32

prints:
Group at the Fireplace (H.II.217.23 i/ii), s5.17.1
Old Hostess (H.I.226.32 ii?/iv), s5.29.3

BELLA, Stefano della
see della Bella, Stefano

BERNARD, Jacques-Samuel
French, 1615–1687

DEV.-M.1143

prints:
Table of Ornaments to Surround Coats of Arms, 1647, after della Bella (DEV.-M.1143 ii/ii), s7.188

BERNARD, Louis
French, active 1692–1717

LEB.10

prints:

Shepherdess on Horseback with a Flock of Sheep and
Cattle, after Castiglione (LEB.I.290.10 i/ii, M.III.634.10
i/ii), s6.100

BISCAINO, Bartolomeo
Italian, c. 1632–1657

B.4, 7, 22, 31, 35

prints:

Nativity with Angels (large plate) (B.XXI.185.7,
TIB47.198.7), s6.101*

Saint Christopher Kneeling (B.XXI.199.35, TIB47.225.35,
TIB4718.329.035 S2/3), s6.103.1

Saint Joseph Holding the Christ Child (B.XXI.197.31,
TIB47.221.31, TIB4718.325.031 S1/2), s6.102.1

Susannah and the Elders (B.XXI.183.4, TIB47.195.4,
TIB4718.305.004 S1/2), s6.104.1

Virgin Adoring the Christ Child with Saint Joseph
(B.XXI.193.22, TIB47.213.22, TIB4718.319.022 S2/7),
s6.104.2

BISI, Fra Bonaventura
Italian, 1612–1659

LEB.1

prints:

The Holy Family with Saints Elizabeth and John, after
Vasari (LEB.I.348.[1], DEV.1 iii/iii), s2.50

BISSCHOP, Jan de
Dutch, 1628–1671

H.1

prints:

Joseph Distributing Grain in Egypt, after Breenbergh
(H.II.42.1 ii/iii), s5.42, **P. mariette 1660, P. mariette
1668**

BOL, Quiryn
see Boel, Coryn

BOEL, Coryn
Flemish, 1620–1668

H.34, 36–38, 43–48

series:

Monkey Business in the World, s5.6.2, s5.6.4–s5.7.6

prints:

Barber Shop, after Teniers (H.III.13.42), s5.6.4

Fluteplayer, after Teniers (H.III.10.34), s5.10.3

Monkey Singing, Accompanied on the Lute by Another
Monkey, after Teniers (H.III.13.43–48), s5.7.4

Monkey Treating the Wounded Hand of Another Monkey with Sticking Plaster, after Teniers
(H.III.13.43–48), s5.7.2

Smoker in a Tavern, after Teniers (H.III.11.36 ii/ii), s5.9.1

Title page, Monkey Business in the World, after Teniers
(H.III.13.undesc.), s5.6.2

Two Monkeys Eating Oysters, after Teniers
(H.III.13.43–48), s5.7.6

Two Monkeys Playing Backgammon, after Teniers
(H.III.13.43–48), s5.7.1

Two Monkeys Playing Cards, after Teniers
(H.III.13.43–48), s5.7.5

Two Monkeys Smoking, after Teniers (H.III.13.43–48),
s5.7.3

Urine Doctor, after Teniers (H.III.12.37), s5.9.2

Violin Player in a Tavern, after Teniers (H.III.12.38),
s5.8.2

BONZI, Pietro Paolo
Italian, c. 1570/1575–c. 1633/1644

B.2 (Cavedone)

prints:

Madonna and Child with Saints Anthony and Catherine
(B.XVIII.333.2, TIB40.249.2 [Cavedone]), s1.78

BORGIANI, Orazio
Italian, 1577–1620

B.53

prints:

Saint Christopher (B.XVII.320.53, TIB38.412.53), s2.39

BOSSE, Abraham
French, 1602–1676

see L.1418–1427

prints:

Frontispiece to "New Testament" by Callot (see
L.1418–1427), s3.4.2

BOTH, Jan

Dutch, 1610–1652

H.1–15

series:

Environs of Rome, S5.54.1–S5.58.2

The Five Senses, S5.52.1–S5.53.2

Vertical Italian Landscapes, S5.55.1–S5.58.1

prints:

Fishermen at the Tiber near Soracte (H.III.161.9 v/vi), S5.57.2

Hearing, after A. Both (H.III.162.12 ii/iv), S5.52.2

Hinny Drover, Via Appia (H.III.161.6 v/vi), S5.54.2

Large Tree (H.III.159.3 v/vi), S5.55.1

Ox-Cart (H.III.159.2 v/vi), S5.58.1

Ponte Molle (H.III.161.5 v/vi), S5.58.2

Sight, after A. Both (H.III.162.11 ii/iv), S5.52.1

Smell, after A. Both (H.III.162.13 ii/iv), S5.52.3

Taste, after A. Both (H.III.162.14 ii/iv), S5.53.1

Touch, after A. Both (H.III.162.15 ii/iv), S5.53.2

Two Cows near the River, Tivoli (H.III.161.8 v/vi), S5.56.2

Two Hinnies (H.III.159.4 v/v), S5.57.1

View of the Tiber in the Campagna (H.III.161.7 v/vi), S5.55.2

Woman on the Hinny (H.III.159.1 v/vi), S5.56.1

Wooden Bridge at Sulmona near Tivoli (H.III.161.10 v/vi), S5.54.1

BOURDON, Sébastien

French, 1616–1671

R.-D.1–19, 21–40, 42–44

series:

Flight into Egypt, S2.71.1–S2.73.2

Large Landscapes, S2.78–S2.86

Life of the Virgin, S2.68.1–4

Seven Acts of Mercy, S2.59–S2.65

prints:

Angel Counseling Joseph (R.-D.I.145.23 iii/iii), S2.73.1

Annunciation (R.-D.I.137.9 ii/ii), S2.68.4

Annunciation to the Shepherds (R.-D.I.138.11 ii/ii), S2.68.2

Baptism of the Eunuch (R.-D.I.148.30 ii/ii), S2.67

Burying the Dead (R.-D.I.136.8 ii/ii), S2.65

Clothing the Naked (R.-D.I.135.5 ii/ii), S2.62

Feeding the Hungry (R.-D.I.134.2 ii/ii), S2.59

Flight into Egypt (R.-D.I.142.18 ii/iii), S2.74.2

Flight into Egypt (R.-D.I.146.25 ii/ii), S2.73.2

Flight into Egypt (R.-D.I.145.24 ii/ii), S2.71.1

Flight into Egypt (R.-D.I.141.17 ii/ii), S2.70.2

Giving Drink to the Thirsty (R.-D.I.135.3 ii/ii), S2.60

Holy Family with Angels (R.-D.I.147.28), S2.75.1

Holy Family with Saint Catherine (R.-D.I.142.19 i/ii), S2.76.2

Holy Family with the Infant Saint John and a Bird (R.-D.I.143.21 i/ii), S2.74.1

Infant Jesus Trampling the Serpent of Sin Underfoot (R.-D.I.141.16 ii/ii), S2.69.2

Jacob Returning to His Own Country (R.-D.I.133.1 iv?/iv), S2.66.1

Joseph's Dream (R.-D.I.144.22 ii/ii), S2.72.1

Landscape with a Shepherd and His Flock (R.-D.I.150.33 ii/iii), S2.86

Landscape with Christ and the Disciples by a Wheatfield (R.-D.I.154.40 ii/iii), S2.80

Landscape with Joseph in Egypt (R.-D.II.151.34 ii/iii), S2.81

Landscape with Robbers Attacking the Traveler (R.-D.I.152.36 ii/iii), S2.82

Landscape with the Flight into Egypt (R.-D.I.153.39 ii/iii), S2.78

Landscape with the Good Samaritan Bringing the Wounded Traveler to the Inn (R.-D.I.153.38 ii/iii), S2.85

Landscape with the Good Samaritan Tending the Wounded Traveler (R.-D.I.152.37 ii/iii), S2.84

Landscape with the Priest and the Levite Shunning the Wounded Traveler (R.-D.I.151.35 ii/iii), S2.83

Large Landscape, with a Woman on Horseback and a Man on Foot Crossing a Wooden Bridge (R.-D.I.154.42 ii/iii), S2.87

Large Landscape, with Antique Ruins and a Cart Drawn by Two Horses (R.-D.I.155.43 ii/iii), S2.89

Large Landscape, with a Cart Drawn by Four Oxen (R.-D.I.155.44 ii/iii), S2.88

Liberating the Prisoners (R.-D.I.136.7 ii/ii), S2.64

Poor Peasants Resting (R.-D.I.149.31), S2.69.1

Poor Peasants, a Boy Drinking (R.-D.I.150.32), S2.69.3

Rest in Egypt (R.-D.I.146.26 ii/ii), S2.72.2

Rest on the Flight into Egypt with Washerwoman (R.-D.I.147.29 iv?/iv), S2.77

Return from Egypt (R.-D.I.147.27 ii/iii), S2.71.2

Sheltering the Stranger (R.-D.I.135.4 ii/ii), S2.61

Tending the Sick (R.-D.I.136.6 ii/ii), S2.63

Virgin at the Curtain (R.-D.I.139.13), S2.70.1 (missing)

Virgin of 1649 (R.-D.I.140.15 ii/ii), S2.68.3

Virgin with the Book (R.-D.I.140.14 ii/ii), S2.76.3

Virgin with the Bowl (R.-D.I.139.12 ii/ii), S2.76.4

Visitation (R.-D.I.137.10 ii/ii), S2.68.1

Saint Andrew (L.1239 ii/ii), s3.35.12

Saint Andrew (L.1302 ii/iii), s3.40.2

Saint Anne, Mother of the Virgin (L.1058 ii/ii), s3.26.11

Saint Anne, Prophetess (L.1114 ii/ii), s3.29.6

Saint Anselm (L.938 ii/ii), s3.20.11

Saint Anthony (L.859 ii/ii), s3.16.12

Saint Anthony Abbot (L.829 ii/ii), s3.15.1

Saint Anthony of Padua (L.1006 ii/ii), s3.23.19

Saint Antiochus (L.1043 ii/ii), s3.25.16

Saint Apollinarus of Hierapolis (L.817 ii/ii), s3.14.10

Saint Apollonia (L.852 ii/ii), s3.16.5

Saint Apollonius the Apologist (L.934 ii/ii), s3.20.7

Saint Aprus (L.1133 ii/ii), s3.30.6

Saint Arnulf of Metz (L.1047 ii/ii), s3.25.20

Saint Arsenius (L.1049 ii/ii), s3.26.2

Saint Athanasia (L.1087 ii/ii), s3.27.20

Saint Athanasius of Alexandria (L.953 ii/ii), s3.21.6

Saint Augustine (L.1107 ii/ii), s3.28.20

Saint Aurea (L.1100 ii/ii), s3.28.13

Saint Barbara (L.1246 ii/ii), s3.35.19

Saint Barnabas (L.1004 ii/ii), s3.23.17

Saint Bartholomew (L.1101 ii/ii), s3.28.14

Saint Bartholomew (L.1308 ii/iii), s3.42.1

Saint Basil Celebrating Mass (L.44 ii/ii), s3.56.3

Saint Basil the Great (L.1007 ii/ii), s3.23.20

Saint Beatrix (L.1063 ii/ii), s3.26.16

Saint Benedict (L.902 ii/ii), s3.18.15

Saint Benignus (L.1196 ii/ii), s3.33.10

Saint Benjamin (L.914 ii/ii), s3.19.8

Saint Bernard of Clairvaux (L.1095 ii/ii), s3.28.8

Saint Bernardine of Siena (L.979 ii/ii), s3.22.12

Saint Bertin (L.1119 ii/ii), s3.29.12

Saint Bibiana (L.1244 ii/ii), s3.35.17

Saint Birinus (L.1245 ii/ii), s3.35.18

Saint Blaise (L.846 ii/ii), s3.15.19

Saint Blandina and Her Companions (L.993 ii/ii), s3.23.6

Saint Bonaventure (L.1040 ii/ii), s3.25.13

Saint Boniface of Tarsus (L.969 ii/ii), s3.22.2

Saint Briget of Sweden (L.1055 ii/ii), s3.26.8

Saint Bruno (L.1162 ii/ii), s3.31.15

Saint Caesarius of Arles (L.1106 ii/ii), s3.28.19

Saint Callistratus (L.1148 ii/ii), s3.31.1

Saint Callistus (L.1176 ii/ii), s3.32.10

Saint Calliope (L.1001 ii/ii), s3.23.14

Saint Candida (L.1140 ii/ii), s3.30.13

Saint Carpophorus and the Four Crowned Saints (L.1209 ii/ii), s3.34.2

Saint Carpus (L.1173 ii/ii), s3.32.7

Saint Cassian of Imola (L.1086 ii/ii), s3.27.19

Saint Castorius (L.1208 ii/ii), s3.34.1

Saint Castulus (L.909 ii/ii), s3.19.3

Saint Catherine of Alexandra (L.1231 ii/ii), s3.35.5

Saint Catherine of Siena (L.948 ii/ii), s3.21.1

Saint Catherine of Sweden (L.903 ii/ii), s3.18.16

Saint Cecilia (L.1227 ii/ii), s3.34.20

Saint Celestine I (L.922 ii/ii), s3.19.15

Saint Charles Borromeo (L.1201 ii/ii), s3.33.15

Saint Christina (L.1056 ii/ii), s3.26.9

Saint Christina (L.1265 ii/ii), s3.36.18

Saint Clare of Assisi (L.1081 ii/ii), s3.27.14

Saint Clare of Montefalco (L.1091 ii/ii), s3.28.4

Saint Claudius of Besançon (L.997 ii/ii), s3.23.10

Saint Clement I (L.1228 ii/ii), s3.35.1

Saint Cleophas (L.1147 ii/ii), s3.30.20

Saint Columba of Sens (L.1283 ii/ii), s3.37.15

Saint Columbanus (L.1226 ii/ii), s3.34.19

Saint Concordia (L.1083 ii/ii), s3.27.16

Saint Conon (L.882 ii/ii), s3.17.15

Saint Conrad of Constance (L.1234 ii/ii), s3.35.7

Saint Cornelius (L.1131 ii/ii), s3.30.4

Saint Corona (L.971 ii/ii), s3.22.4

Saint Cunegund (L.878 ii/ii), s3.17.11

Saint Cyril of Alexandria (L.839 ii/ii), s3.15.12

Saint Damasus (L.1255 ii/ii), s3.36.8

Saint David, King and Prophet (L.1280 ii/ii), s3.37.13

Saint Demetrius and His Companions (L.1078 ii/ii), s3.27.11

Saint Desiderius (L.982 ii/ii), s3.22.15

Saint Didacus (L.1215 ii/ii), s3.34.8

Saint Digna and Her Companions (L.1082 ii/ii), s3.27.15

Saint Dionysia and Her Son (L.1249 ii/ii), s3.36.2

Saint Dioscorus (L.975 ii/ii), s3.22.8

Saint Dismas (L.907 ii/ii), s3.18.20

Saint Dominic (L.1071 ii/ii), s3.27.4

Saint Donatus (L.1093 ii/ii), s3.28.6

Saint Dorothy (L.849 ii/ii), s3.16.2

Saint Dula (L.906 ii/ii), s3.18.19

Saint Dunstan (L.977 ii/ii), s3.22.10

Saint Dympna (L.972 ii/ii), s3.22.5

Saint Edilburga (L.1031 ii/ii), s3.25.4

Saint Edmund (L.1219 ii/ii), s3.34.12

Saint Edmund of England (L.1224 ii/ii), s3.34.17

Saint Edward the Martyr (L.899 ii/ii), s3.18.12

Saint Egidius (Giles) (L.1112 ii/ii), s3.29.7

Saint Eleutherius (L.1120 ii/ii), s3.29.13

Saint Elias (Elijah), Prophet (L.1050 ii/ii), s3.26.3

Saint Eligius (L.1240 ii/ii), s3.35.14

Saint Elizabeth of Hungary (L.1223 ii/ii), s3.34.16

Saint Elizabeth of Portugal (L.1028 ii/ii), s3.25.1

Saint Elizabeth of Schönau (L.1011 ii/ii), s3.24.4

Saint Elzear (L.1151 ii/ii), s3.31.4

Saints Fusca and Maura (L.857 ii/ii), s3.16.10

Saints Gervase and Protase (L.1012 ii/ii), s3.24.5

Saints Gorgonius and Dorotheus (L.1124 ii/ii), s3.29.17

Saints James the Greater and Christopher (L.1057 ii/ii), s3.26.10

Saints Jonas and Barachisius (L.912 ii/ii), s3.19.5

Saints Julian and Basilissa (L.818 ii/ii), s3.14.11

Saints Julitta and Quiricus (L.1009 ii/ii), s3.24.2

Saints Justus and Pastor (L.1075 ii/ii), s3.27.8

Saints Macedonius and Theodulus (L.1129 ii/ii), s3.30.2

Saints Martial and Saturninus (L.1178 ii/ii), s3.32.12

Saints Maurus and Placid (L.824 ii/ii), s3.14.17

Saints Maxentius and Leander (L.1256 ii/ii), s3.36.9

Saints Mennas and Hermogenes (L.1254 ii/ii), s3.36.7

Saints Nazarius and Celsus (L.1061 ii/ii), s3.26.14

Saints Nicasius and Eutropia (L.1261 ii/ii), s3.36.14

Saints Nicostratus and Antiochus (L.980 ii/ii), s3.22.13

Saints Pamphilus and Porphyrius (L.992 ii/ii), s3.23.5

Saints Perpetua and Felicity (L.883 ii/ii), s3.17.17

Saints Peter and John Heal the Cripple at the Golden Gate (L.38 ii/ii), s3.57.7

Saints Peter and Paul (L.26 ii/ii), s3.57.5

Saints Peter and Paul (L.1022 ii/ii), s3.24.15

Saints Philip and James the Lesser (L.952 ii/ii), s3.21.5

Saints Philoteus and Theotimus (L.1204 ii/ii), s3.33.17

Saints Placid and Flavia (L.1161 ii/ii), s3.31.14

Saints Polyanus and Nemesian (L.1126 ii/ii), s3.29.19

Saints Potamioena and Marcella (L.1021 ii/ii), s3.24.14

Saints Primus and Felician (L.1002 ii/ii), s3.23.15

Saints Probus and Andronicus (L.1171 ii/ii), s3.32.5

Saints Quirinus and Balbina (L.915 ii/ii), s3.19.7

Saints Reparata and Benedicta (L.1167 ii/ii), s3.32.1

Saints Romanus and Barulas (L.1221 ii/ii), s3.34.14

Saints Rufina and Secunda (L.1035 ii/ii), s3.25.8

Saints Sabinus and Venustian (L.1281 ii/ii), s3.37.14

Saints Secundus and Alexander (L.1105 ii/ii), s3.28.18

Saints Seraphia and Erasma (L.1117 ii/ii), s3.29.9

Saints Sergius and Paul (L.1257 ii/ii), s3.36.11

Saints Simon and Jude (L.1192 ii/ii), s3.33.5

Saints Susanna, Marciana, and Palladia (L.983 ii/ii), s3.22.16

Saints Theodora and Didymus (L.945 ii/ii), s3.20.18

Saints Thyrsus and Callinicus (L.1263 ii/ii), s3.36.16

Saints Tiburtius and Valerian (L.930 ii/ii), s3.20.3

Saints Vitalis and Agricola (L.1202 ii/ii), s3.33.13

Saints Vitalis and Valeria (L.946 ii/ii), s3.20.19

Saints Vitus, Modestus, and Crescentia (L.1008 ii/ii), s3.24.1

Saints Zacharia and Elizabeth (L.1203 ii/ii), s3.33.16

Saints Zeno and Zenas (L.1016 ii/ii), s3.24.9

Salamander in Flames (L.627 ii/ii), s3.62.1

Salvator Mundi (L.18 ii/iii), s3.58.8

Salvator Mundi (L.1090 ii/ii), s3.28.3

Scapino and Captain Zerbino (L.390 i/ii), s4.29.4

Scaramucia and Fricasso (L.389 i/ii), s4.29.3

Seated Beggar, Eating (L.502 i/ii), S.4.23.5

Second Naval Combat (L.158 i/ii), s3.96.2

Sermon on the Mount (L.1421 ii/ii), s3.4.6

Seven Sleepers of Ephesus (L.1059 ii/ii), s3.26.13

Shepherd Playing His Flute, 1617 (L.250), s4.3.4

Shepherd Playing His Flute (L.464 i/ii), s4.8.4

Shepherds Protecting Their Flocks (L.602 ii/ii), s3.60.4

Ship Navigating among Rocks (L.628 ii/ii), s3.62.3

Shooting Renegades, 1633 (L.1350 ii/iii), s4.15.4

Siege of Breda (lower center), 1628 (L.593 (2) i/ii), s4.37

Siege of Breda (lower left), 1628 (L.593 (1) i/ii), s4.36

Siege of Breda (lower right), 1628 (L.593 (3) i/ii), s4.38

Siege of Breda (upper center), 1628 (L.593 (5) i/ii), s4.34

Siege of Breda (upper left), 1628 (L.593 (4) i/ii), s4.33

Siege of Breda (upper right), 1628 (L.593 (6) i/ii), s4.35

Siege of La Rochelle (lower center) (L.655 ii/ii), s4.49

Siege of La Rochelle (lower left) (L.655 ii/ii), s4.48

Siege of La Rochelle (lower right) (L.655 ii/ii), s4.50

Siege of La Rochelle (upper center) (L.655 ii/ii), s4.46

Siege of La Rochelle (upper left) (L.655 ii/ii), s4.45

Siege of La Rochelle (upper right) (L.655 ii/ii), s4.47

Siege of the Citadel of Saint-Martin on L'Ile de Ré (lower center) (L.654 ii/ii), s4.60

Siege of the Citadel of Saint-Martin on L'Ile de Ré (lower left) (L.654 iii/iii), s4.59

Siege of the Citadel of Saint-Martin on L'Ile de Ré (lower right) (L.654 ii/ii), s4.61

Siege of the Citadel of Saint-Martin on L'Ile de Ré (upper center) (L.654 ii/ii), s4.57

Siege of the Citadel of Saint-Martin on L'Ile de Ré (upper left) (L.654 ii/ii), s4.56

Siege of the Citadel of Saint-Martin on L'Ile de Ré (upper right) (L.654 ii/ii), s4.58

Siren between Two Ships (L.615 ii/ii), s3.61.5

Slave Market, 1629 (L.369 ii/vi), s4.19.2

Sloth (L.355 i/ii), s3.12.8

Sly Beggar, Seated (L.491 i/ii), S.4.24.4

Small Port, Shipping at Left (L.267 i/ii), s4.64.4, **P. mariette 1667**

Smaraolo Cornuto and Ratsa di Boio (L.382 i/ii), s4.28.8

Snake and Its Skin (L.607 ii/ii), s3.60.9

Soldier in a Circus Ring, 1617 (L.256), s4.4.10

Soldier in a Circus Ring (L.470 i/ii), s4.7.2

Solimano, Act I, 1620 (L.364), s3.80.1

Solimano, Act II, 1620 (L.365), s3.80.2

Solimano, Act III, 1620 (L.366), s3.79.1

Solimano, Act IV, 1620 (L.367), s3.79.2

Woman Playing a Guitar, between Two Men (L.1375 i/ii), s4.11.13

Woman Spinning and Woman Winding Yarn (L.536 ii/ii), s4.8.10

Woman Wearing a Hat with Four Plumes, Her Hands on Her Hips, between Two Men (L.1378 i/ii), s4.11.7

Woman Wearing a Hat with Two Plumes, Her Hands on Her Hips, between Two Men (L.1384 i/ii), s4.11.6

Woman with a Feather in Her Hair, Seen from the Back, between Two Men (L.1373 i/ii), s4.11.10

Woman with a Full Dress, 1617 (L.233), s4.2.5

Woman with a Full Dress (L.447 i/ii), s4.6.4

Woman with a Long Cloak on Her Right Shoulder, between Two Men (L.1383 i/ii), s4.11.8

Woman with a Short Fur-Trimmed Cloak, between Two Men (L.1381 i/ii), s4.11.3

Woman with Three Feathers in Her Hat, Seen in Profile, between Two Men (L.1374 i/ii), s4.11.11

Woman, Bareheaded, between Two Men (L.1379 i/ii), s4.11.4

Woman, Her Left Fist on Her Hip, Seen from the Front, between Two Men (L.1376 i/ii), s4.11.9

Woman, Her Right Fist on Her Hip and Her Left Hand Extended, between Two Men (L.1380 i/ii), s4.11.5

CANTARINI, Simone (Il Pesarese)
Italian, 1612–1678

B.1–9, 11–13, 15, 18, 20 (copy), 21, 23–31, 34

prints:

Adam and Eve (B.XIX.122.1, Bellini 18, TIB42.65.1), s1.57.1

Bearing of the Cross (B.xix.133.20 [copy], Bellini 13 [Copy A], TIB42.90.20-copy), s1.64.1

Fortuna, after Reni (B.xix.143.34 i/ii, Bellini 5 i/ii, TIB42.109.34-I), s1.71.2

Guardian Angel (B.XIX.138.28, Bellini 29, TIB42.101.28), s1.68.1

Holy Family (B.XIX.129.11, Bellini 8, TIB42.78.11), s1.62.2

Holy Family (B.XIX.130.13, Bellini 32 i/ii, TIB42.81.13), s1.58.7

Holy Family with Saints Elizabeth and John the Baptist (B.XIX.127.9, Bellini 11, TIB42.75.9), s1.60.1

Holy Family with the Infant Saint John the Baptist (B.XIX.130.12, Bellini 31, TIB42.80.12), s1.58.5

Holy Family with the Infant Saint John the Baptist, after Reni? (B.XIX.131.15, Bellini 34 iii/iii, TIB42.83.15), s1.58.6

Jupiter, Neptune, and Pluto Offering Their Crown to the Arms of Cardinal Borghese (B.XIX.139.29 ii?/iv, Bellini 35 ii/iv, TIB42.102.29-I), s1.73

Madonna and Child with a Bird (B.XIX.133.18 ii/ii, Bellini 4 ii/ii, TIB42.86.18), s1.61.3

Mercury and Argus (B.XIX.142.31 i?/ii, Bellini 37 i/ii, TIB42.105.31), s1.72.2

Rape of Europa (B.XIX.141.30 i?/ii, Bellini 6 i/ii, TIB42.104.30), s1.72.1

Rest on the Flight into Egypt (B.XIX.127.8, Bellini 7, TIB42.74.8), s1.58.3

Rest on the Flight into Egypt (B.XIX.126.7, Bellini 16, TIB42.74.7), s1.58.4

Rest on the Flight into Egypt (B.XIX.124.3, Bellini 23 i/ii, TIB42.68.3-I), s1.59.1

Rest on the Flight into Egypt (B.XIX.126.6, Bellini 30 ii/ii, TIB42.72.6), s1.59.2

Rest on the Flight into Egypt (B.XIX.122.2 ii/ii, Bellini 22 ii/ii, TIB42.66.2-II), s1.60.2

Rest on the Flight into Egypt (B.XIX.125.5, Bellini 19, TIB42.71.5), s1.62.1

Rest on the Flight into Egypt (B.XIX.125.4, Bellini 15, TIB42.69.4), s1.64.3

Saint Anthony of Padua Holding the Christ Child (large plate) (B.XIX.136.25, Bellini 26 i/iii, TIB42.97.25-I), s1.69.3

Saint Anthony of Padua Holding the Christ Child (small plate) (B.XIX.137.26, Bellini 20, TIB42.99.26), s1.69.2

Saint Benedict Exorcising a Demon, after Lodovico Carracci (B.XIX.138.27 i/ii, Bellini 10 i/iv, TIB42.100.27), s1.66

Saint John the Baptist in the Desert, after Lodovico Carracci (B.XIX.135.23, Bellini 17 ii?/ii, TIB42.94.23), s1.67.1

Saint Sebastian (B.XIX.136.24, Bellini 25, TIB42.95.24), s1.68.2

Virgin Crowned by Two Angels (B.XIX.134.21, Bellini 28 i/iii, TIB42.91.21), s1.61.2

CARAVAGGIO, Michelangelo Merisi da
Italian, 1569–1609

DEV.1

prints:

Denial of Saint Peter, 1603 (DEV.1), s6.54.2

CARPIONI, Giulio
Italian, 1613–1679

B.2, 5, 8, 11

prints:

Agony in the Garden (B.XX.178.2 ii/iii, TIB45.68.2-II, TIB4504.95.002 S2/3), S6.24

Holy Family with the Virgin Reading (B.XX.181.5 ii/ii, TIB45.72.5, TIB4504.98.005 S2/3), S6.22.2

Nativity (B.XX.183.8 ii/ii, TIB45.75.8, TIB4504.100.008 S2/3), S6.23

Saint Anthony of Padua (B.XX.185.11 ii/ii, TIB45.78.11, TIB4504.101.011 S3/4), S6.22.3

CARRACCI, Agostino

Italian, 1557–1602

B.20, 21, 23, 28, 30, 34, 43, 48–63, 65–68, 74–76, 78, 79, 89, 95, 96–98, 102, 105, 107, 109, 110, 116–118, 121, 122, 125, 129, 130, 152–154, 161, 260

series:

Lascivie, S1.46.1–4

Santini, S1.7.1, S1.37.1

Savior, the Virgin, Saint John the Baptist, and the Apostles, S1.24.1–9, S1.25.1–6

prints:

Aeneas and His Family Fleeing Troy, 1595, after Barocci (B.XVIII.99.110, TIB39.152.110, Bohlin 203), S1.42, **P. mariette 1668**

Andromeda (B.XVIII.107.125, TIB39.167.125, Bohlin 179), S1.46.2

Apollo and the Python (Perseus and the Dragon), after Buontalenti/Boscoli (B.XVIII.107.122, TIB39.164.122-I, Bohlin 154 ii/iii), S1.50.1

Coat of Arms of a Bishop (B.XVIII.123.159, TIB39.200.159-I, Bohlin 201 ii/ii), S1.51.1

Coat of Arms of Cardinal Cinzio Aldobrandini (B.XVIII.124.161, TIB39.202.161-I, Bohlin 198 i/ii), S1.51.2

Cordons of Saint Francis, 1586 (B.XVIII.98.109, TIB39.149.109, Bohlin 141), S1.33

Crucifixion, after Veronese, 1582 (B.XVIII.50.21, TIB39.70.21, Bohlin 107), S1.19

Crucifixion ("The Great Crucifixion"), after Tintoretto, 1589 (B.XVIII.51.23, TIB39.72.23, Bohlin 147 ii/ii), S1.21

Ecce Homo, after Correggio, 1587 (B.XVIII.49.20, TIB39.69.20, Bohlin 143 i/ii), S1.18

Harmony of the Spheres, after Buontalenti/Boscoli (B.XVIII.106.121, TIB39.163.121-I, Bohlin 153 ii/iii), S1.50.2

Headpiece in the Form of a Fan ("The Fan") (B.XVIII.149.260, TIB39.280.260-II, Bohlin 193 ?/ii [trimmed]), S1.52

Holy Family, 1597 (B.XVIII.63.43, TIB39.93.43, Bohlin 208 ii/iv), S1.6.2

Holy Family with Saints John the Baptist, Catherine, and Anthony Abbot, after Veronese, 1582 (B.XVIII.89.96, TIB39.135.96, Bohlin 103 ii/iii), S1.9

Madonna and Child Seated on a Crescent Moon, after Ligozzi, 1589 (B.XVIII.58.34, TIB39.84.34, Bohlin 150), S1.6.1, **P. mariette 1679**

Madonna of Saint Jerome, after Cort/Correggio, 1586 (B.XVIII.87.95 ii/ii, TIB39.134.95-II, Bohlin 142 iii/iv), S1.10

Mars Driven Away from Peace and Abundance by Minerva, after Tintoretto, 1589 (B.XVIII.105.118, TIB39.160.118-II, Bohlin 148 ii/iv), S1.41.1

Martyrdom of Saint Justina of Padua, after Veronese, 1582 (B.XVIII.78.78, TIB39.120.78, Bohlin 105 iii/v), S1.39

Mercury and the Three Graces, after Tintoretto, 1589 (B.XVIII.104.117, TIB39.159.117, Bohlin 149 i/iii), S1.41.2, **P. mariette 1667, P. mariette 1667**

Mystic Marriage of Saint Catherine, after Veronese, 1582 (B.XVIII.90.98, TIB39.137.98, Bohlin 104 i/ii), S1.40, **P. mariette 1707**

Mystic Marriage of Saint Catherine, after Veronese, 1585 (B.XVIII.89.97, TIB39.136.97-II, Bohlin 133 ?/iv [damaged]), S1.37.2, **P. mariette 1667**

Omnia Vincit Amor, 1599 (B.XVIII.103.116, TIB39.158.116, Bohlin 210), S1.45.1

Orpheus and Eurydice (B.XVIII.107.123, TIB39.165.123, Bohlin 178 ii/ii), S1.46.1

Parable of the Devil Sowing Tares in the Field (B.XVIII.55.28, TIB39.78.28-II, Bohlin 19 ii/ii), S1.49.2

Pietà, after Veronese, 1582 (B.XVIII.93.102 i/ii, TIB39.142.102-I, Bohlin 102 i/iii), S1.22

Portrait of Giovanni Gabrielli, Called "Il Sivello" (B.XVIII.120.153, TIB39.194.153, Bohlin 212 ii/ii), S1.44.1

Portrait of the Legendary Prester John, King of Ethiopia, after van Mander (B.XVIII.120.152, TIB39.193.152, Bohlin R46 ii/ii [Ciamberlano]), S1.44.2

Portrait of Titian, after Titian, 1587 (B.XVIII.121.154, TIB39.195.154, Bohlin 145 [before inscription]), S1.43, **P. mariette 1666/7***

Saint Andrew, 1583 (B.XVIII.68.52, TIB39.100.52, Bohlin 116), S1.24.5

Saint Bartholomew, 1583 (B.XVIII.68.56, TIB39.102.56, Bohlin 112), S1.25.3

Saint Francis Adoring the Crucifix (B.XVIII.70.66, TIB39.109.66, Bohlin 126 ii/ii), S1.25.8

Saint Francis Consoled by the Musical Angel (Saint

Francis in Ecstasy), after Vanni, 1595 (B.XVIII.70.67, TIB39.110.67, Bohlin 204 i/ii), S1.30.2

Saint Francis Receiving the Stigmata, 1583 (B.XVIII.70.65, TIB39.108.65, Bohlin 124), S1.25.7

Saint Francis Receiving the Stigmata, after Lodovico Carracci, 1586 (B.XVIII.72.68 i/iii, TIB39.111.68-I, Bohlin 140 i/iv), S1.29

Saint James the Greater, 1583 (B.XVIII.68.53, TIB39.101.53, Bohlin 119), S1.24.6

Saint James the Lesser, 1583 (B.XVIII.68.59, TIB39.104.59, Bohlin 118), S1.24.8

Saint Jerome (B.XVIII.75.74 ?/ii, TIB39.116.74-II, Bohlin 205 ?/ii [trimmed]), S1.26.1

Saint Jerome (B.XVIII.75.75 ii/ii, TIB39.117.75-II, Bohlin 213 iv/iv), S1.27

Saint John the Baptist, 1583 (B.XVIII.67.50, TIB39.99.50, Bohlin 109), S1.24.3

Saint John the Evangelist, 1583 (B.XVIII.68.54, TIB39.101.54, Bohlin 117), S1.24.7

Saint Judas Thaddeus, 1583 (B.XVIII.69.61, TIB39.105.61, Bohlin 123), S1.25.6

Saint Lucy (B.XVIII.79.79, TIB39.121.79, Bohlin 52 ?/iii [trimmed]), S1.36.1

Saint Matthew, 1583 (B.XVIII.68.57, TIB39.103.57, Bohlin 115), S1.25.2

Saint Matthias, 1583 (B.XVIII.69.62, TIB39.105.62, Bohlin 120), S1.25.5

Saint Peter, 1583 (B.XVIII.67.51, TIB39.100.51, Bohlin 114), S1.24.4

Saint Philip, 1583 (B.XVIII.68.55, TIB39.102.55, Bohlin 122), S1.25.1

Saint Simon, 1583 (B.XVIII.69.60, TIB39.104.60, Bohlin 121), S1.25.4

Saint Thomas, 1583 (B.XVIII.68.58, TIB39.103.58, Bohlin 113), S1.24.9

Savior ("Salvator Mundi"), 1583 (B.XVIII.67.48, TIB39.98.48, Bohlin 110), S1.24.2

Temptation of Saint Anthony, after Tintoretto, 1582 (B.XVIII.69.63, TIB39.106.63, Bohlin 101 i/ii), S1.32

Three Graces (B.XVIII.108.130, TIB39.172.130, Bohlin 183), S1.46.4

Venus (B.XVIII.108.129, TIB39.171.129, Bohlin 181), S1.46.3, **P. mariette 1666**

Veronica Holding the Sudarium, 1581 (B.XVIII.84.89, TIB39.130.89, Bohlin 43), S1.37.1

Virgin Appearing to Saint Jerome, after Tintoretto, 1588 (B.XVIII.77.76, TIB39.118.76, Bohlin 146), S1.28, **P. mariette 1707***

Virgin Mary, 1583 (B.XVIII.67.49, TIB39.99.49, Bohlin 111), S1.24.1

Virgin of the Annunciation, 1581 (B.XVIII.56.30, TIB39.79.30, Bohlin 41), S1.7.1

Virgin Protecting the Members of a Confraternity, after Veronese, 1582 (B.XVIII.95.105, TIB39.145.105, Bohlin 106 iii/iii), S1.7.2

CARRACCI, Annibale
Italian, 1560–1609

B.1–4, 6–9, 11, 13–17

prints:

Adoration of the Shepherds, (B.XVIII.181.2 ii/iii, TIB39.386.2-I, Bohlin 22 ii/iii), S1.4.2

Christ Crowned with Thorns, 1606 (B.XVIII.182.3 ii/ii, TIB39.388.3-I, Bohlin 21 ii/iv), S1.2.6

Holy Family with Saint John the Baptist, 1590 (B.XVIII.187.11 i/ii, TIB39.397.11-I, Bohlin 11 i/iii), S1.3.2

Madonna and Child with an Angel (B.XVIII.184.7 ii/ii, TIB39.392.7-II, Bohlin 15 ii/ii), S1.2.5

Madonna and Child with Saints Elizabeth and John the Baptist, 1606 (B.XVIII.186.9 ii/ii, TIB39.395.9-I, Bohlin 20 ii/iii), S1.4.1

Madonna Nursing the Christ Child, (B.XVIII.184.6, TIB39.391.6, Bohlin 5 ii/ii), S1.2.4

Madonna of the Swallow, 1587 (B.XVIII.185.8, TIB39.394.8, Bohlin 9), S1.2.2

Mary Magdalen in the Wilderness, 1591 (B.XVIII.191.16, TIB39.403.16-I, Bohlin 12 i/iv), S1.36.2, **P. mariette 1668**

Pietà ("Christ of Caprarola"), 1597 (B.XVIII.182.4 ii/iii, TIB39.389.4-I, Bohlin 18 v/vii), S1.4.3

Saint Francis of Assisi, 1585 (B.XVIII.191.15, TIB39.402.15, Bohlin 7), S1.30.1

Saint Jerome (B.XVIII.189.13, TIB39.399.13, Bohlin 4), S1.25.9

Saint Jerome in the Wilderness (B.XVIII.190.14 ii/ii, TIB39.400.14-II, Bohlin 13 iii/iv), S1.26.2

Susanna and the Elders (B.XVIII.180.1 ii/ii, TIB39.385.1-II, Bohlin 14 ii/iv), S1.1, **P. mariette 1666**

Venus and a Satyr (Jupiter and Antiope), after Agostino Carracci, 1592 (B.XVIII.192.17, TIB39.404.17, Bohlin 17), S1.45.2

CARRACCI, Lodovico

Italian, 1555–1619

B.1–4

prints:

Holy Family under an Arch (B.XVIII.26.4, TIB39.46.4, Bohlin 1 i/iv), S1.11

Madonna and Child with Angels (B.XVIII.24.2, TIB39.44.2, Bohlin 3 i/iii), S1.5.1

Madonna and Child with Saint John the Baptist, 1604 (B.XVIII.25.3, TIB39.45.3, Bohlin 4 ii/ii), S1.5.3

Madonna Nursing the Christ Child, 1592 (B.XVIII.24.1, TIB39.42.1, Bohlin 2 ii/ii), S1.5.2

CASTIGLIONE, Giovanni Benedetto

Italian, 1609–1664

B.1–7, 9–12, 14–18, 21–53,

series:

Large Heads, S6.91.5, S6.92.1–4

Small Heads, S6.91.1–4, S6.91.6–9, S6.94.1–4, S6.94.6–9

prints:

Adoration of the Shepherds (B.XXI.14.9, TIB46.23.9, TIB4602.22.009), S6.88.1

Allegory of Transience, 1655 (B.XXI.25.27, TIB46.40.27, TIB4602.40.027 S2?/5), S6.93.1

Angel Awakening Joseph (B.XXI.15.10, TIB46.24.10, TIB4602.22.010 S3/4), S6.87.1

Christ Child Adored by Two Angels (B.XXI.11.3, TIB46.17.3, TIB4602.16.003 S2/2), S6.96.2

Circe with the Companions of Ulysses Transformed into Animals (B.XXI.21.22, TIB46.35.22, TIB4602.33.022 S2/2), S6.97.2

Diogenes in Search of an Honest Man (B.XXI.20.21, TIB46.34.21, TIB4602.32.021 S2/2), S6.93.2

Discovery of the Bodies of Saints Peter and Paul (B.XXI.17.14, TIB46.28.14, TIB4602.26.014), S6.90.2

Entry of the Animals into the Ark (B.XXI.10.1, TIB46.15.1, TIB4602.15.001), S6.82

Entry of the Animals into the Ark (B.XXI.10.2, TIB46.16.2-II, TIB4602.15.002 S2/5), S6.96.1

Feast of Pan before the Altar of Terminus (B.XXI.18.16, TIB46.30.16, TIB4602.28.016 S3/3), S6.97.1

Flight into Egypt (B.XXI.16.12, TIB46.26.12, TIB4602.23.012 S3/4), S6.88.2

Flock of Sheep Surrounding a Laden Donkey (B.XXI.26.29, TIB46.42.29, TIB4602.43.029 S2/2), S6.78.2

Four Scholars among Tombs (B.XXI.23.25, TIB46.38.25, TIB4602.38.025 S2/4), S6.99.1

Genius of Benedetto Castiglione (B.XXI.22.23, TIB46.36.23, TIB4602.35.023 S1/3), S6.95

Laban Searching for Idols (B.XXI.11.4, TIB46.18.4, TIB4602.16.004 S2/4), S6.80

Man Facing Left with Open Mouth, Wearing a Plumed Turban (B.XXI.30.41, TIB46.48.41, TIB4602.54.041), S6.94.6

Man Holding a Large Scroll and Wearing a Fur Headdress (B.XXI.32.46, TIB46.50.46, TIB4602.56.046 S2/3), S6.91.8

Man in Profile Facing Left, Wearing a Plumed Fur Headdress (B.XXI.33.49, TIB46.52.49, TIB4602.58.049 S2/2), S6.92.4

Man in Profile Facing Right, Wearing a Plumed Turban (B.XXI.28.33, TIB46.45.33, TIB4602.48.033), S6.94.4

Man Wearing a Cap with a Large Plume ("Self-Portrait") (B.XXI.27.31[53], TIB46.44.31, TIB4602.47.031 S1/3), S6.94.5

Man Wearing a Plumed Fur Cap and a Scarf (B.XXI.33.52, TIB46.55.52, TIB4602.61.052 S3/3), S6.91.5

Man with a Beard Facing Left, Wearing a Plumed Headdress (B.XXI.33.51, TIB46.54.51, TIB4602.59.051 S3/3), S6.92.2

Man with a Beard Facing Right, Wearing a Fur Headdress (B.XXI.27.32, TIB46.45.32, TIB4602.48.032), S6.94.1

Man with a Beard in Profile Facing Right, Wearing a Plumed Headdress and Fur Cap (B.XXI.32.48, TIB46.51.48, TIB4602.57.048), S6.92.1

Marsyas and Olympus (B.XXI.17.15, TIB46.29.15, TIB4602.26.015 S2/5), S6.96.4

Melancholy (B.XXI.24.26, TIB46.39.26, TIB4602.39.026 S2/4), S6.96.3

Nativity with God the Father and Angels Adoring the Christ Child (B.XXI.13.7, TIB46.21.7, TIB4602.19.007), S6.89

Nativity with God the Father, the Dove of the Holy Spirit, and Two Angels Adoring the Christ Child (B.XXI.15.11, TIB46.25.11, TIB4602.23.011 S2/2), S6.87.2

Old Man in Profile Facing Left, His Head Bent, Wearing a Fur Headdress (B.XXI.29.38, TIB46.47.38, TIB4602.53.038 S2/2), S6.91.9

Old Man in Profile Facing Right, Wearing a Turban (B.XXI.29.36, TIB46.46.36, TIB4602.52.036 S2/2), S6.94.7

Old Man with a Beard Facing Three-Quarters Right, Wearing a Plumed Turban (B.XXI.29.37, TIB46.46.37, TIB4602.52.037), S6.94.2

Old Man with a Beard Facing toward the Left and Looking Down, Wearing a Fur Headdress (B.XXI.31.45, TIB46.49.45, TIB4602.56.045), S6.94.9

Old Man with a Beard in Profile Facing Left, Wearing a Plumed Turban (B.XXI.30.40, TIB46.47.40, TIB4602.54.040 S1/2), S6.94.3

Old Man with a Beard, His Head Bent Forward, Wear-

ing a Small Cap (B.XXI.33.50, TIB46.53.50,
TIB4602.59.050 S2/2), s6.92.3

Old Woman in Profile Facing Right, Wearing a Turban
(B.XXI.28.34, TIB46.45.34, TIB4602.50.034 S2/2),
s6.91.6

Pan Seated near a Vase (B.XXI.19.18, TIB46.32.18,
TIB4602.31.018), s6.98.2

Raising of Lazarus (B.XXI.12.6, TIB46.20.6,
TIB46.18.006), s6.79.2

Satyr Seated beside a Term (B.XXI.19.17, TIB46.31.17,
TIB4602.31.017 S2/3), s6.99.2

Shepherds Following Their Flock (B.XXI.26.30,
TIB46.43.30, TIB46.45.030 S2/4), s6.81

Theseus Finds His Father's Weapons, 1645 (B.XXI.23.24,
TIB46.37.24, TIB4602.37.024 S3/3), s6.98.1

Tobit Burying the Dead (B.XXI.12.5, TIB46.19.5,
TIB46.18.005), s6.79.1

Young Herdsman on Horseback (B.XXI.25.28,
TIB46.41.28, TIB46.42.028 S2/2), s6.78.1

Young Man Facing Right, His Eyes Lowered, Wearing a
Cap with a Plume (B.XXI.28.35, TIB46.46.35,
TIB4602.50.035 S2/2), s6.91.7

Young Man Facing Three-Quarters Left, Blowing a
Trumpet (B.XXI.31.44, TIB46.49.44, TIB4602.55.044),
s6.94.8

Young Man Facing Three-Quarters Right, Wearing a
Fur Headdress with a Plume, Jewel, and Headband
(B.XXI.29.39, TIB46.47.39, TIB4602.53.039 S2/3),
s6.91.4

Young Man in Three-Quarters View Looking Down
and to the Right, Wearing a Plumed Turban
(B.XXI.31.43, TIB46.48.43, TIB4602.55.043), s6.91.2

Young Man with His Head Lowered to the Left, Wearing
a Turban (B.XXI.30.42, TIB46.48.42, TIB4602.55.042
S2/2), s6.91.3

Young Woman in Profile Facing Right, Wearing a High
Plumed Turban (B.XXI.32.47, TIB46.50.47,
TIB4602.57.047 S2/2), s6.91.1

CASTIGLIONE, Salvatore
Italian, 1620–after 1676

B.1

prints:
Raising of Lazarus (B.XXI.43.1, TIB46.68.1,
TIB4603.130.001), s6.90.1

CESIO, Carlo
Italian, 1626–1686

B.3

prints:
Martyrdom of Saint Andrew, after Reni (B.XXI.104.3,
TIB47.34.3, TIB4705.85.033 S1/3), s1.70

CHAUVEAU, François
French, 1613–1676

DEV.-M.1142

prints:
Table of Battle Dress and Devices, (DEV.-M.1142 iii/iii),
s7.189

CLAUDE GELLEE, Le Lorrain
French, 1600–1682

R.-D.1, 5–16, 18, 21–24

prints:
Artist Sketching outside the Walls of a Seaport
(R.-D.i.13.9 ii/v, Mannocci 36 iiib/v), s2.107.3

Brigands in a Landscape, 1633 (R.-D.i.16.12 v?/viii, Mannocci 11 vb/ix), s2.108.1

Cattle Fording a River (R.-D.i.13.8 iii/iii, Mannocci 18),
s2.10–.–*

Country Dance (large plate), 1637 (R.-D.i.28.24 ii/iii,
Mannocci 20 ii/iv), s2.103.1

Dance by the River (R.-D.i.11.6 iii/iii, Mannocci 13),
s2.10–.–*

Dance beneath the Trees (R.-D.i.14.10 iii/iv, Mannocci
19), s2.10–.–*

Departure for the Fields (R.-D.i.20.16 iii/iii, Mannocci 34
iiic/iv), s2.107.1

Flight into Egypt (R.-D.I.7.1, Mannocci 9 i/iv), s2.107.2

Herd on the Move in Stormy Weather, 1651 (R.-D.i.22.18
iii/iii, Mannocci 40), s2.10–.–*

Rape of Europa (R.-D.I.26.22 ii/iii, Mannocci 14),
s2.102.2*

Roman Forum (Campo Vaccino), 1636 (R.-D.I.27.23 v/v,
Mannocci 17 v/ix), s2.102.1

Seaport with a Lighthouse (R.-D.I.15.11 iii/iii, Mannocci
37), s2.10–.–*

Seaport with a Round Tower (R.-D.I.17.13 iii/iv, Mannocci 39), s2.10–.–*

Seaport with Rising Sun (R.-D.I.19.15 iv/v, Mannocci 15),
s2.10–.–*

Shepherd and Shepherdess Conversing in a Landscape
(R.-D.I.25.21, Mannocci 41), s2.103.2*

Shipwreck (R.-D.I.12.7 ii/ii, Mannocci 35 iiic/v), s2.104.1

Tempest (R.-D.I.10.5 iv/v, Mannocci 6 iv/vi), s2.104.2

Wooden Bridge (R.-D.I.18.14 ii/ii, Mannocci 38),
s2.10–.–*

COCHIN, Nicolas
French, 1610–1686

DEV.-M. 1141

series:
Holy House of Loreto, s7.74.1–s7.77.2

prints:
Heraldry Explained, 1645, after della Bella (DEV.-M.1141 ii/ii), s7.186
Interior Walls, Holy House of Loreto, s7.77.2
Midy, Holy House of Loreto, 1649, s7.77.1
Occident, Holy House of Loreto, s7.75.1
Orient, Holy House of Loreto, 1649, s7.74.2
Plan, Holy House of Loreto, s7.76
Septentrion, Holy House of Loreto, s7.75.2

COLLIGNON, François
French, 1609–1659

See also Anonymous French 17th c.

DEV.-M. 1058, 1061–1073, 1093–1100, 1102–1109, 1146–1156

series:
Collection of a Dozen Cartouches, s7.184.2–s7.185.6
First Suite of Four Landscapes, s7.104.1–4
Humorous Inventions of Love and War,
  s7.150.1–s7.151.6
Marine Views, s7.88.1–s7.89.3, s7.90.1, s7.90.3
Second Suite of Four Landscapes, s7.103.1–4

prints:
Boat Full of Passengers Departing from Land for a Ship,
  pl. 5, 1639, after della Bella (DEV.-M.1106), s7.89.3
Cartouche Flanked by Garlands of Fruit, above a Ram's
  Skull, pl. 6, after della Bella (DEV.-M.1150), s7.184.6
Cartouche Flanked by Putti and Sheep's Heads Decked
  with Flowers, pl. 2, after della Bella (DEV.-M.1146),
  s7.184.2
Cartouche Flanked by Winged Chimeras with Dragon's
  Tails, pl. 5, after della Bella (DEV.-M.1149), s7.184.5
Cartouche Flanked by Winged Nymphs with Serpent's
  Tails, pl. 3, after della Bella (DEV.-M.1147), s7.184.4
Cartouche Surmounted by a Cluster of Flowers, Fruit,
  and Leaves and Flanked by the Heads of Fauns in
  Profile, pl. 11, after della Bella (DEV.-M.1155), s7.185.5
Cartouche Surmounted by a Putto's Head and Flanked
  by Clusters of Leaves and Flowers, pl. 4, after della
  Bella (DEV.-M.1148), s7.184.3
Cartouche with Grotesque Lions' Heads at the Upper

Corners and Surmounted by a Shield, a Coronet
  Above, pl. 12, after della Bella (DEV.-M.1156), s7.185.6
Cartouche, above a Grotesque Head, pl. 7, after della
  Bella (DEV.-M.1151), s7.185.1
Cartouche, above a Ram's Head, pl. 9, after della Bella
  (DEV.-M.1153), s7.185.3
Cartouche, above the Head of an Old Man Looking
  Down, pl. 8, after della Bella (DEV.-M.1152), s7.185.2
Cartouche, above the Heads of Two Lions in Profile
  Linked by Scrolls of Foliage, pl. 10, after della Bella
  (DEV.-M.1154), s7.185.4
Coastal Scene with a Sailor Cooking, pl. 1, after della
  Bella (DEV.-M.1097), s7.103.1
Dedication Page with a Boy Carrying a Chest, Marine
  Views, pl. 1, 1639, after della Bella (DEV.-M.1102),
  s7.88.1
Dwarf Couple Dancing, after della Bella (DEV.-M.1065
  i/iii), s7.150.6
Dwarf Couple Promenading, after della Bella
  (DEV.-M.1066 i/iii), s7.150.4
Dwarf Couple Seated on the Ground, after della Bella
  (DEV.-M.1067 i/iii), s7.150.3
Dwarf Drummer, after della Bella (DEV.-M.1072 i/iii),
  s7.151.1
Dwarf Firing a Gun, after della Bella (DEV.-M.1071 i/iii),
  s7.151.2
Dwarf Flautist, after della Bella (DEV.-M.1073 i/iii),
  s7.151.5
Dwarf Halberdier, after della Bella (DEV.-M.1068 i/iii),
  s7.151.4
Dwarf in an Elaborately Pleated and Buttoned Costume
  Bows to a Female Dwarf, after della Bella (DEV.-
  M.1062 i/iii), s7.150.5
Dwarf Pikeman, after della Bella (DEV.-M.1069 i/iii),
  s7.151.6
Dwarf Playing a Guitar and Female Dwarf Playing a
  Tambourine, after della Bella (DEV.-M.1064 i/iii),
  s7.150.7
Dwarf Standard Bearer, after della Bella (DEV.-M.1070
  i/iii), s7.151.3
Dwarf Wearing Spectacles Makes a Declaration of Love
  to a Female Dwarf, after della Bella (DEV.-M.1063
  i/iii), s7.150.2
Harbor Scene with Ship at Anchor, Two Men Seated at
  Right, pl. 4, 1639, after della Bella (DEV.-M.1105),
  s7.89.1
Harbor Scene with Small Boat in Center, a Galley at
  Left, and Shipping at Right, pl. 8, 1639, after della
  Bella (DEV.-M.1109), s7.90.3
Harbor Scene with Three Men at Center, pl. 3, 1639, after
  della Bella (DEV.-M.1104), s7.88.3

Harbor Scene with Three Turks and an Italian Gentleman at Right, pl. 2, 1639, after della Bella
(DEV.-M.1103), s7.88.2

Landscape with a Cottage, Herdsmen, and Grazing
Cows and Horses, pl. 3, after della Bella
(DEV.-M.1099), s7.103.3

Landscape with a Windmill and a Wayside Cross, pl. 3,
after della Bella (DEV.-M.1095), s7.104.3

Landscape with an Angler, Cows to the Left, pl. 1, after
della Bella (DEV.-M.1093), s7.104.1

Landscape with an Open Carriage and a Church, pl. 2,
after della Bella (DEV.-M.1098), s7.103.2

Landscape with Herd and Herdsman, a Low Church
with a Round Apse in the Distance, pl. 2, after della
Bella (DEV.-M.1094), s7.104.2

Landscape with Windmills, Resting Travelers at the
Left, pl. 4, after della Bella (DEV.-M.1096), s7.104.4

River Scene with a Barge and a Long Wooden Bridge,
pl. 4, after della Bella (DEV.-M.1100 i/ii), s7.103.4

Sea Battle, pl. 7, 1639, after della Bella (DEV.-M.1108),
s7.90.1

Seascape with a Man Firing a Rifle at Left, pl. 6, 1639,
after della Bella (DEV.-M.1107), s7.89.2

Title page, Humorous Inventions of Love and War, after
della Bella (DEV.-M.1061 i/iii), s7.150.1

Triumphal Chariot of Louis XIV, after della Bella (DEV.-
M.1058), s7.111

CORIOLANO, Giovanbattista
Italian, 1590–1649

B.1

prints:
Christ Crowned with Thorns, after Lodovico Carracci
(B.XIX.37.1, TIB41.133.1), s1.17

CORNEILLE, Michel-Ange
French, 1642–1708

R.-D.15, 20–22, 24

prints:
Christ and the Virgin Appearing to Saint Francis ("La
Portioncule") (R.-D.VI.301.24 iii/iii), s2.101

Flight into Egypt with the Holy Family Embarking in a
Boat (R.-D.VI.296.15 iii/iii), s2.98

Saint Andrew Adoring His Cross of Martyrdom
(R.-D.VI.298.20 iii/iv), s2.99

Saint Anthony of Padua (R.-D.VI.299.21 ii/ii), s2.100.1

Saint Francis of Assisi (R.-D.VI.300.22 ii/ii), s2.100.2

CURTI, Francesco
Italian, 1603–1670

Bologna 500–518

series:
Drawing Book, s1.88.1–s1.97.2

prints:
Bust of a Bearded Man Wearing a Crown and Holding a
Trident, after Guercino (Bologna 518), s1.89.2

Bust of a Bishop, after Guercino (Bologna 512), s1.91.1

Bust of a Boy Facing Left and Holding a Round Object,
after Guercino (Bologna 516), s1.95.1

Bust of a Boy Facing Right and Holding a Staff, after
Guercino (Bologna 506), s1.95.2

Bust of a Boy Leaning His Head upon His Left Hand,
after Guercino (Bologna 509), s1.92.2

Bust of a Boy Reading, after Guercino (Bologna 511),
s1.92.1

Bust of a Man Facing Left, with His Right Arm Out-
stretched, after Guercino (Bologna 502), s1.93.1

Bust of a Man in Profile Facing Right and Wearing a
High Cap, after Guercino (Bologna 501), s1.91.2

Bust of a Soldier Facing Right with His Arm Out-
stretched, after Guercino (Bologna 507), s1.96.2

Bust of a Soldier Wearing Armor and Carrying a Furled
Banner, after Guercino (Bologna 515), s1.93.2

Bust of a Woman Facing Right, after Guercino (Bologna
504), s1.97.2

Bust of a Young Boy Facing Left and Wearing a High
Cap, after Guercino (Bologna 500), s1.90.1

Bust of a Young Boy Looking Down and Wearing a
High Cap, after Guercino (Bologna 503), s1.90.2

Bust of a Young Child Holding a Chicken, after Guercino (Bologna 505), s1.94.1

Bust of a Young Man Wearing a Broad-brimmed Hat
with Plumes, after Guercino (Bologna 510), s1.88.2

Bust of a Young Woman Facing Left, Her Hair Loose on
Her Shoulders, after Guercino (Bologna 517), s1.97.1

Bust of a Young Woman, Her Head and Shoulders
Draped, after Guercino (Bologna 508), s1.88.1

Bust of an Angel Holding a Basin of Flowers, after Guercino (Bologna 514), s1.94.2

Bust of an Old Man Looking Down and to the Left, after
Guercino (Bologna 513), s1.89.1

Frontispiece, Drawing Book (Bologna 499), s1.96.1

CUSTOS, Raphael

German, c. 1590–1651

Hollstein 14

prints:

Portrait of Jacques Callot (Hollstein VI.186.14), S3.1.2

DASSONVILLE, Jacques

French, 1619–1670

R.-D.4, 6

prints:

Looking for Fleas (R.-D.I.173.6), S5.6.1
Old Woman and Two Children (R.-D.I.172.4), S5.6.3

DELLA BELLA, Stefano

Italian, 1610–1664

DeV.-M.1, 3–14, 16, 17, 20, 23–26, 28, 30, 33, 38, 42–50,
53–61, 64, 66–68, 70–77, 83–91, 93, 101–151, 156, 157,
159, 162–181, 184–186, 188–192, 205, 211, 213–272,
274–277, 292, 293, 295, 297–301, 303–310, 312, 314–320,
323–331, 333, 334, 336–355, 364–393, 395, 396, 398–410,
412, 414–417, 419, 422–424, 426, 431, 433, 434, 442, 457,
459, 460, 462–465, 467, 468, 472, 474–479, 481,
489–719, 719(.1), 720–740, 743, 743(.1), 744–749,
749(.1), 750–755, 755(.1), 756, 757, 757(.1), 758–760,
760(.1), 761–763, 763(.1), 764–766, 766(.1), 767–784,
787–809, 818, 819, 819(.1), 820–852, 855, 858, 863, 868,
871, 878–882, 919–925, 937–942, 946, 949–952, 952(A),
953, 953(A), 955, 956, 960, 979–1050, 1058–1073,
1093–1100, 1102–1109, 1115, 1141–1144, 1146–1156

series:

Agreeable Diversity of Figures, S7.135.1–10, S7.164.15
Caprices, S7.117.1–13
Collection of Various Caprices, S7.174.1–S7.181.3
Collection of Various Plates of Use in the Art of Portrai-
ture, S7.152.1–11, S7.153.1, S7.153.3, S7.153.11, S7.154.1,
S7.154.3–4, S7.154.11, S7.156.1, S7.156.3, S7.156.5, S7.161.1,
S7.161.3, S7.162.5, S7.162.12, S7.163.8, S7.164.1, S7.164.3,
S7.164.14, S7.164.16
Collection of Various Sketches and Impressions,
S7.161.5–7, S7.161.10–13, S7.162.1–2, S7.162.4, S7.162.8–9,
S7.162.13–16, S7.163.1, S7.164.5–7, S7.164.11, S7.164.13
Collection of Vases, S7.165.1–3
Combat and Ballet on Horseback, S7.43–S7.45
Diverse Landscapes I, S7.98.1–4
Diverse Landscapes II, S7.99.1–S7.102.3
Diverse Views of Remarkable Sites in Italy and France,
S7.78.3–S7.79.3

Drawing Book, S7.153.4, S7.153.6–8, S7.154.5–6, S7.154.12,
S7.156.2, S7.156.4, S7.156.6–7, S7.156.9–10
Eagles, S7.128.1–S7.129.3
Entry of the Polish Ambassador into Rome,
S7.32.1–S7.34.2
Five Deaths, S7.8.2–3, S7.9.1, S7.9.3
Four Elements, S7.97.1–4
Four Seasons, S7.161.15–18
Friezes, Foliages, and Grotesques, S7.169.1–8
Funeral of Emperor Ferdinand II, S7.37.2–S7.38.2
Game of Famous Queens, S7.14.1–S7.17.14
Game of Geography, S7.10.1–S7.13.13
Game of Mythology, S7.21.1–S7.24.12
Game of the Kings of France, S7.18.1–S7.20.16
Gara delle Stagioni, S7.47.1–S7.51.2
Heads of Animals, S7.122.1–S7.123.3
Holy House of Loreto, S7.74.1
Hunts of Various Animals, S7.130.1–S7.132.3
Landscapes and Ruins of Rome, S7.107.1–S7.108.6,
S7.138.1
Landscapes and Seaports, S7.105.1–6
Landscapes with Peasants, S7.136.1–S7.137.6
Large Views of Rome and the Campagna, S7.64–S7.67,
S7.95–S7.96
Mirame, S7.59–S7.63
Mondo Festeggiante, S7.40–S7.41, S7.46
Negro, Polish, and Hungarian Knights, S7.138.3–S7.141.2
New Inventions of Cartouches, S7.182.1–S7.183.6
Night of the Gods, S7.55.2–S7.58.2
Ornaments and Friezes, S7.170.1–S7.173.4
Ornaments and Grotesques, S7.167.1–S7.168.6
Pastoral Landscapes, S7.106.1–6
Port Scenes, S7.83.1–8
Principles of Drawing, S7.157.1–S7.160.6
Seascapes, S7.82.1–7
Second Collection of Various Sketches and Impressions,
S7.155.2, S7.155.12, S7.161.2, S7.161.8, S7.161.9, S7.161.14,
S7.162.3, S7.162.7, S7.162.11, S7.163.2, S7.163.7, S7.164.4,
S7.164.9, S7.163.10, S7.163.11, S7.163.15
Several Heads in Persian Dress, S7.151bis.1–9
Some Maneuvers of Troops, Artillery, and Attacks on
Towns, S7.145.1–12
Upright Landscapes, S7.91–S7.94
Various Animals, S7.124.1–S7.127.6
Various Caprices, S7.118.1–S7.121.6
Various Caprices on Military Subjects, S7.146.1–6
Various Cavalry Exercises, S7.142.1–S7.143.9, S7.144.13
Various Embarkations, S7.84.1–8
Various Figures, S7.137bis.1, S7.147.1–8, S7.155.3–9
Various Figures and Landscapes, S7.137bis.2–8
Various Figures and Sketches, S7.154.8, S7.155.1, S7.155.5,

Landscape with a Horseman Fording a River, pl. 5 (DEV.-M.132 iii/iv), S7.118.5

Landscape with a Horseman Leading Another Horse, pl. 11 (DEV.-M.138 iii/iv), S7.120.5

Landscape with a Horseman Talking to a Man on Foot, pl. 6 (DEV.-M.133 iii/iv), S7.118.6

Landscape with a Man Walking beside a Woman on a Horse Descending a Road, 1656 (DEV.-M.743 ii/ii), S7.105.1

Landscape with a Mounted Herdsman Viewed from the Rear, pl. 24 (DEV.-M.151 iii/iv), S7.119.6

Landscape with a Peasant Driving a Pig, pl. 10 (DEV.-M.778), S7.136.4

Landscape with a Peasant Family on the March, the Man with a Bundle on His Shoulder, pl. 3 (DEV.-M.771), S7.137.3

Landscape with a Peasant with a Basket on His Back, pl. 11 (DEV.-M.779), S7.136.5

Landscape with a Polish Gentleman and a Horse Covered with a Pelt, pl. 15 (DEV.-M.142 iii/iv), S7.121.3

Landscape with a Ruined Square Tower, pl. 6 (DEV.-M.774), S7.137.6

Landscape with a Satyr and a Bathing Nymph, 1656 (DEV.-M.746 ii/ii), S7.105.3

Landscape with a Seated and a Standing Traveler Conversing, pl. 12 (DEV.-M.780), S7.136.6

Landscape with a Seated Man and a Dog, a Standing Woman Observing Them, pl. 1 (DEV.-M.769), S7.137.1

Landscape with a Seated Traveler, pl. 11 (DEV.-M.114 ii/ii), S7.117.11

Landscape with a Seated Woman and Child Conversing with a Standing Woman Carrying Two Children, 1649 (DEV.-M.169), S7.137bis.6

Landscape with a Seated Woman and Child, a Dog Sleeping at Their Feet, pl. 9 (DEV.-M.112 ii/ii), S7.117.9

Landscape with a Traveler Leaning on His Staff, a Building at Left, pl. 9 (DEV.-M.777), S7.136.3

Landscape with a Traveler with Pack and Staff, a Building on a Hill at Left, pl. 7 (DEV.-M.775), S7.136.1

Landscape with a Triple Cascade, pl. 7 (DEV.-M.825 ii/ii), S7.108.1

Landscape with a Waterfall (DEV.-M.749), S7.98.1

Landscape with a Waterfall, Animals and Herdsmen Resting in the Foreground, pl. 10 (DEV.-M.828 ii/ii), S7.108.4

Landscape with a Windmill, pl. 10 (DEV.-M.766 ii/ii), S7.102.1

Landscape with a Woman and Child Listening to a Violin Player, 1649 (DEV.-M.171), S7.137bis.7

Landscape with a Woman and Child Seated under a Tree, 1649 (DEV.-M.170), S7.137bis.2

Landscape with a Woman and Cows Fording a River, pl. 2 (DEV.-M.129 iii/iv), S7.118.2

Landscape with a Woman Carrying a Baby and Talking to a Child, pl. 7 (DEV.-M.110 ii/ii), S7.117.7

Landscape with a Woman Carrying a Basket, pl. 8 (DEV.-M.776), S7.136.2

Landscape with a Woman Carrying a Basket, pl. 13 (DEV.-M.140 iii/iv), S7.121.1

Landscape with a Woman Carrying a Basket and a Bundle with Another Bundle on Her Head, 1649 (DEV.-M.166), S7.137 bis.3

Landscape with a Woman Carrying a Basket and Another Carrying a Bundle on Her Head, pl. 5 (DEV.-M.773), S7.137.5

Landscape with a Woman Carrying a Child on Her Back, a Church in the Background, pl. 10 (DEV.-M.113 ii/ii), S7.117.10

Landscape with a Woman Carrying a Child, Herdsmen in the Distance, pl. 21 (DEV.-M.148 iii/iv), S7.119.3

Landscape with a Woman on Foot and a Woman on Horseback Fording a River, pl. 2 (DEV.-M.770), S7.137.2

Landscape with Artist Sketching Antique Ruins, pl. 12 (DEV.-M.768 ii/ii), S7.102.3

Landscape with Cattle and Women Fording a River, a Cow in the Foreground, pl. 12 (DEV.-M.716), S7.106.6

Landscape with Cattle, a Woman with a Bundle on Her Head at Right, pl. 4 (DEV.-M.772), S7.137.4

Landscape with Cows and Herdswoman Approaching a Bridge, pl. 9 (DEV.-M.136 iii/iv), S7.120.3

Landscape with Figures, the Left Figure Seated on an Upturned Capital, pl. 6 (DEV.-M.109 ii/ii), S7.117.6

Landscape with Frolicking Satyrs (DEV.-M.719), S7.106.1

Landscape with Goats, pl. 12 (DEV.-M.115 ii/ii), S7.117.12

Landscape with Herds and Flocks, a Shepherdess Spinning at the Right, pl. 11 (DEV.-M.767 ii/ii), S7.102.2

Landscape with Horseman and Herd, a Riderless Horse in the Foreground (DEV.-M.715), S7.106.4

Landscape with Horseman and Man Walking Carrying a Rifle, pl. 5 (DEV.-M.108 ii/ii), S7.117.5

Landscape with Horseman in a Plumed Hat, pl. 4 (DEV.-M.107 ii/ii), S7.117.4

Landscape with Horses, Cattle, and a Mounted Herdsman, pl. 7 (DEV.-M.134 iii/iv), S7.120.1

Landscape with Ladies Watching Bathers, 1649 (DEV.-M.167), S7.137bis.8

Landscape with Pan and a Young Satyr Playing with a Goat, pl. 23 (DEV.-M.150 iii/iv), S7.119.5

Landscape with Polish Gentlemen and Other Elegantly Dressed Figures, 1649 (DEV.-M.172), S7.137bis.4

Two Friezes, in the Upper Trophies of Arms, Two Leopards and Two Dogs, in the Lower Trophies of Arms and Two Eagles, pl. 6 (DEV.-M.992 iii?/vi), S7.171.2

Two Hands, pl. 23 (DEV.-M.329), S7.152.4

Two Hands and a Foot, pl. 25 (DEV.-M.331), S7.152.9

Two Hands Grasping a Stick, the Left Hand Resting on the Right, and Three Other Hands, pl. 4 (DEV.-M.367 ii?/ii), S7.157.4

Two Heads of a Bearded Soldier in a Helmet, Both with Shading, pl. 10 (DEV.-M.373 ii?/ii), S7.158.3

Two Heads of a Bearded Soldier in a Helmet, One with Shading, pl. 8 (DEV.-M.371 ii?/ii), S7.158.1

Two Horsemen, One by a Fountain where His Horse is Drinking from the Basin (DEV.-M.477), S7.155.11

Two Horses, the Left in Profile (DEV.-M.730 i/ii), S7.123.1

Two Horses, the Right in Profile, pl. 3 (DEV.-M.728 ii/ii), S7.123.3

Two Lions and a Lioness, pl. 4 (DEV.-M.729 ii/ii), S7.122.3

Two Men Skinning a Horse (DEV.-M.245), S7.143.7

Two Mounted Soldiers Skirmishing with Swords (DEV.-M.176 i/iv), S7.147.3

Two Pikemen at Drill (DEV.-M.219), S7.144.4

Two Profiles of Nose, Mouth, and Chin, a Nose, and Three Mouths (DEV.-M.295), S7.156.7

Two Riders Passing a Flock of Sheep, 1656 (DEV.-M.836 i/ii), S7.96

Two Riflemen and a Drummer (DEV.-M.222), S7.144.6

Two Seated Women with Infants, a Laden Horse at Right, pl. 6, 1642 (DEV.-M.122 ii–iii/v), S7.135.6

Two Soldiers Talking near the Corpse of a Horse Being Eaten by Two Dogs, pl. 7 (DEV.-M.252 iii/iii), S7.145.11

Two Views of a Child's Head, pl. 2 (DEV.-M.347), S7.152.11

Two Views of a Grotto (DEV.-M.841 i/ii), S7.68

Venus, 1644 (DEV.-M.504 iv/v), S7.21.3

Venus and Adonis, 1644 (DEV.-M.525 iv/v), S7.24.6

Vertumnus and Pomona, 1644 (DEV.-M.498 iv/v), S7.22.9

View of a Corner of Calais (DEV.-M.795), S7.83.8

View of Amsterdam with a Tower (DEV.-M.799), S7.83.4

View of Amsterdam with Shipping (DEV.-M.798 ii/ii), S7.83.7

View of Nancy (DEV.-M.855), S7.78.1

View of the Italian Coast (DEV.-M.801), S7.83.6

Virgin and Child in a Circle, 1641 (DEV.-M.6 ii/ii), S7.3.2

Virgin and Child in a Landscape, 1641 (DEV.-M.4 ii/iii), S7.3.3

Virgin and Child in a Room, 1641 (DEV.-M.7 ii/ii), S7.3.5

Virgin and Child in an Octagon (DEV.-M.5), S7.3.4

Virgin and Child in an Oval, 1641 (DEV.-M.8 ii/ii), S7.3.1

Virgin and Child with Saint John, 1641 (DEV.-M.9 iii/iii), S7.3.6

Virgin and Child with Saints John and Elizabeth, 1641 (DEV.-M.10 iii/iv), S7.4.1

Virginia (DEV.-M.586 ii or iii/iv), S7.11.14

Vulcan and Thetis, 1644 (DEV.-M.524 iv/v), S7.24.7

Water, pl. 2 (DEV.-M.754 ii/iii), S7.97.3

Water Buffaloes, pl. 13, 1641 (DEV.-M.702 ii/iii), S7.126.1

Wild Boar, pl. 19, 1641 (DEV.-M.708 ii/iii), S7.127.1

Wild Boar Hunt, a Boar at Bay at the Left (DEV.-M.733), S7.130.1

Wild Boar Hunt, a Deer Hunt in the Background (DEV.-M.736), S7.131.1

Winter (DEV.-M.86), S7.161.18

Woman and Child on Horseback Surrounded by Sheep and Followed by a Camel (DEV.-M.475), S7.163.4

Woman Carrying Two Children with a Child Walking Beside, pl. 22 (DEV.-M.149 iii/iv), S7.119.4

Woman on Horseback, a Large Oak at Left (DEV.-M.783 ii/iv), S7.91

Woman Riding a Donkey, a Large Oak behind Her (DEV.-M.782), S7.93

Woman with Her Arms around a Child on a Donkey, to the Left a Satyr Watches (DEV.-M.464), S7.163.12

Woman's Head and Shoulders from the Back (DEV.-M.340), S7.156.1

Wooded Landscape with Cattle between Ruined Walls, pl. 6 (DEV.-M.824 ii/vi), S7.107.6

Yucatan (DEV.-M.588 ii or iii/iv), S7.11.12

Zanzibar (DEV.-M.562 ii or iii/iv), S7.13.10

Zenobia (DEV.-M.636 ii/iv), S7.14.11

FACCINI, Pietro
Italian, 1562–1602

B.1

prints:
Saint Francis Holding the Infant Christ in the Presence of the Virgin (B.XVIII.272.1, TIB40.144.1, TIB4004.272.001), S1.31, **P. mariette** 1668

FANTETTI, Cesare, attributed to
Italian, 1659?–?

prints:
Presentation of the Virgin, after Maratti, S1.105.2

FARINATI, Orazio
Italian, 1559–after 1616

B.3, 5

prints:
Angels with the Instruments of the Passion, after Paolo Farinati (B.XVI.171.5, TIB32.273.5), S6.21.2
Madonna and Child with Saint John, after Paolo Farinati (B.XVI.169.3 ii/ii, TIB32.271.3), S6.20.1

FARINATI, Paolo
Italian, 1524–1606

B.3, 4

prints:
Charity (B.XVI.165.4, TIB32.262.4), S6.20.2
Saint John the Evangelist (B.XVI.165.3 ii/ii, TIB32.261.3), S6.21.1

FIALETTI, Odoardo
Italian, 1573–c. 1638

B.1, 2, 7–16, 21, 36, 43–52

series:
Hunts, S6.25.2
Sports of Love, S6.27.1–S6.29.2
Various Designs after Polifilo Zancarli, S6.29.3–S6.31.4

prints:
Bear Hunt (B.XVII.276.36, TIB38.230.36), S6.25.2
Cupid Brings Arrows to Refill His Quiver Lying at Venus's Feet (B.XVII.268.12, TIB38.210.12), S6.28.2
Ornament with a Chimerical Man and a Centaur Fighting, a Putto Above, after Giancarli (B.XVII.280.50, TIB38.240.50), S6.31.1
Ornament with a Male and a Female Satyr Attacked by Chimerical Monsters, after Giancarli (B.XVII.280.51, TIB38.241.51), S6.30.2
Ornament with a Satyr Holding a Vase and Two Putti Teasing a Dragon, after Giancarli (B.XVII.279.44, TIB38.234.44), S6.30.3
Ornament with a Satyr Holding a Vielle, a Putto Holding a Panpipe, and a Triton Holding Two Panpipes, with Another Putto Standing above Holding a Bird, after Giancarli (B.XVII.279.46, TIB38.236.46), S6.30.4
Ornament with a Triton and Four Putti Carrying Off a Dolphin, after Giancarli (B.XVII.280.48, TIB38.238.48), S6.31.4
Ornament with a Triton Attacking a Lion Who is At-tacking Another Triton, a Putto Above, after Giancarli (B.XVII.280.49, TIB38.239.49), S6.31.2
Ornament with a Triton Embracing a Nereid Seated on a Sea Monster, a Putto and a Dragon Above, after Giancarli (B.XVII.280.52, TIB38.242.52), S6.31.3
Ornament with Putti, Triton, Tortoise, Dog, and Horned Chimera, after Giancarli (B.XVII.279.47, TIB38.237.47), S6.29.3
Ornament with Tritons, Putti, and a Panther Attacking a Dragon Lying on a Sea-Monster, after Giancarli (B.XVII.279.45, TIB38.235.45), S6.30.1
Title Page, Various Designs after Polifilo Zancarli, after Giancarli (B.XVII.279.43, TIB38.233.43), S6.29.4
Venus and Cupid Kiss and Embrace (B.XVII.268.9, TIB38.207.9), S6.27.3
Venus and Cupid Sleeping (B.XVII.268.11, TIB38.209.11), S6.28.1
Venus Chides the Sobbing Cupid (B.XVII.269.14, TIB38.212.14), S6.28.4
Venus Combs Cupid's Hair (B.XVII.268.10, TIB38.208.10), S6.27.4
Venus Covers the Sleeping Cupid (B.XVII.267.8, TIB38.206.8), S6.27.2
Venus Holds Cupid's Arrow (B.XVII.267.7, TIB38.205.7), S6.27.1
Venus Spanks Cupid (B.XVII.269.15, TIB38.213.15), S6.29.1
Venus Teases Cupid with His Bow (B.XVII.268.13, TIB38.211.13), S6.28.3
Venus Blindfolds Cupid (B.XVII.269.16, TIB38.214.16), S6.29.2
Venus, from "The Four Divinities," after Pordenone (B.XVII.271.21, TIB38.219.21), S6.22.1
Virgin and Child with Saint John on a Cloud (B.XVII.264.1, TIB38.199.1), S6.25.1
Wedding at Cana, after Tintoretto (B.XVII.264.2, TIB38.200.2), S6.26, **P. mariette 1676**

FRANCO, Giovanni Battista
Italian, c. 1510–1561

B.5, 8, 11, 19, 27, 31

prints:
Adoration of the Shepherds (B.XVI.121.8 i/ii, TIB32.164.8-1), S6.15
Christ Bearing the Cross (B.XVI.123.11 i/ii, TIB32.167.11-1), S6.19.2
Entombment (B.XVI.125.19, TIB32.175.19), S6.18
Holy Family with Saint John (B.XVI.128.27, TIB32.183.27), S6.17

Melchizedek Offering Bread and Wine to Abraham
(B.XVI.120.5 ii/ii, TIB32.161.5), S6.16

Saint Joseph Presenting a Bird to the Infant Jesus
(B.XVI.130.31, TIB187.31), S6.19.1

GALESTRUZZI, Giovanni Battista
Italian, 1615/18–after 1669

B.3–8, 16–20, 47–52

series:
Roman History, S2.52.1–S2.53.2
Story of Niobe, S2.53.3–S2.54.2
Trophies of Arms and Vases, S2.51.1–6, S2.52.4

prints:
Apollo and Diana Attacking Niobe's Children, 1656,
after Polidoro da Caravaggio (B.XXI.59.19,
TIB46.88.19), S2.53.2

Bust of a Woman in a Niche between Two Vases, 1660,
after Polidoro da Caravaggio (B.XXI.64.49,
TIB46.106.49), S2.51.2

Castration of Uranus, after Polidoro da Caravaggio
(B.XXI.53.3, TIB46.78.3), S2.52.3

Coat of Mail with a Bandolier between Two Vases, 1660,
after Polidoro da Caravaggio (B.XXI.64.50,
TIB46.107.50), S2.51.5

Cuirass between Pairs of Shields and Vases, 1660, after
Polidoro da Caravaggio (B.XXI.63.47, TIB46.104.47),
S2.51.4

Family of Darius at the Feet of Alexander, after Polidoro
da Caravaggio (B.XXI.54.7, TIB46.80.7), S2.52.1

Large Coat with Fringe between Two Vases, 1660, after
Polidoro da Caravaggio (B.XXI.64.51, TIB46.108.51),
S2.51.6

Lycurgus and Numa Pompilius Giving the Laws to the
Romans, after Polidoro da Caravaggio (B.XXI.53.5,
TIB46.79.5), S2.52.2

Niobe Adored on the Altar, 1656, after Polidoro da Caravaggio (B.XXI.59.18, TIB46.88.18), S2.53.3

Procession of Suppliants, 1656, after Polidoro da Caravaggio (B.XXI.59.16, TIB46.87.16), S2.53.1

Rape of the Sabine Women, after Polidoro da Caravaggio (B.XXI.53.4, TIB46.78.4), S2.52.6

Short Dress Coat with a Sash between Pairs of Shields
and Vases, 1660, after Polidoro da Caravaggio
(B.XXI.63.48, TIB46.105.48), S2.51.1

Slaughter of Niobe's Children, 1656, after Polidoro da
Caravaggio (B.XXI.59.20, TIB46.89.20), S2.54.2

Soldiers of Cyrus Tearing Apart the Army of Spargabise,
after Polidoro da Caravaggio (B.XXI.54.6, TIB46.79.6),
S2.52.5

Statues of Three Ancient Romans, 1660, after Polidoro
da Caravaggio (B.XXI.64.52 [left], TIB46.109.52 [left]),
S2.52.4

Statues of Three Ancient Romans, 1660, after Polidoro
da Caravaggio (B.XXI.64.52 [right], TIB46.109.52
[right]), S2.51.3

Suppliants Taking Gifts to Niobe, 1656, after Polidoro da
Caravaggio (B.XXI.59.17, TIB46.87.17), S2.54.1

Two Senators Speaking to the Vanquished Kings, after
Polidoro da Caravaggio (B.XXI.54.8, TIB46.80.8),
S2.52.7

GATTI, Oliviero
Italian, active 1602–1628

B.118–139

series:
Book of the Principles of Drawing, S1.86.2–S1.87.3,
S1.98.1–S1.103.3

prints:
Bust of a Man with a Mustache, after Guercino
(B.XIX.31.134, TIB41.125.134), S1.98.1

Bust of a Young Man in Profile Facing Right, after Guercino (B.XIX.31.129, TIB41.120.129), S1.100.2

Bust of a Young Man Leaning on His Left Hand, after
Guercino (B.XIX.31.136, TIB41.127.136), S1.98.3

Bust of a Young Man Looking upward and toward the
Right, after Guercino (B.XIX.31.133, TIB41.124.133),
S1.101.3

Bust of a Young Woman Holding an Open Book, after
Guercino (B.XIX.31.135, TIB41.126.135), S1.98.2

Busts of a Young Man and an Old Man, after Guercino
(B.XIX.31.137, TIB41.128.137), S1.99.1

Busts of an Old Man, a Boy, and a Young Woman, after
Guercino (B.XIX.31.131, TIB41.122.131), S1.101.1

Four Eyes and Two Mouths-and-Noses, after Guercino
(B.XIX.30.120, TIB41.111.120), S1.87.2

Frontispiece, Book of the Principles of Drawing, 1619,
after Guercino (B.XIX.30.118, TIB41.109.118 S1/2),
S1.86.2

Girl Lighting a Lamp, after Guercino (B.XIX.32.138,
TIB41.129.138), S1.99.2

Man in Half Length, with His Arms Crossed across His
Chest, after Guercino (B.XIX.32.139, TIB41.130.139),
S1.99.3

Man's Leg and the Bust of a Child Holding a Veil, after
Guercino (B.XIX.31.128, TIB41.119.128), S1.100.1

Man's Torso and His Arms, after Guercino (B.XIX.31.125,
TIB41.116.125), S1.103.1

Parts of Four Faces, a Mouth, and a Mouth-and-Nose, after Guercino (B.XIX.30.122, TIB41.113.122), S1.102.1

Six Ears, after Guercino (B.XIX.30.121, TIB41.112.121), S1.87.3

Six Eyes, after Guercino (B.XIX.30.119, TIB41.110.119), S1.87.1

Study of the Body of a Man Shooting an Arrow, after Guercino (B.XIX.31.132, TIB41.123.132), S1.101.2

Three Hands, after Guercino (B.XIX.30.124, TIB41.115.124), S1.102.3

Torso of a Man, after Guercino (B.XIX.31.130, TIB41.121.130), S1.100.3

Two Feet of a Man, after Guercino (B.XIX.31.126, TIB41.117.126), S1.103.2

Two Hands with One Holding a Balance Scale, after Guercino (B.XIX.30.123, TIB41.114.123), S1.102.2

Two Legs of a Man in a Kneeling Position, after Guercino (B.XIX.31.127, TIB41.118.127), S1.103.3

GENOELS, Abraham

Flemish, 1640–1723

H.66–68

prints:

Landscape with Two Trees, with Crossed Trunks (H.VII.99.67), S5.110.2

Rocky Landscape with a Pool (B.IV.366.68, H.VII.99.68), S5.111.2

Rocky Landscape with Two Figures (H.VII.99.66), S5.110.1

GERARDIN, Jean

French, active 1661–65

prints:

Copernican System ("Mens Agitat Molem"), after della Bella (DEV.-M.1060), S7.110

GIORDANO, Luca

Italian, 1634–1705

B.6

prints:

Saint Anne Received into Heaven by Christ and the Virgin (B.XXI.177.6 i/ii, TIB47.191.6, TIB4717.006 S2/4), S6.57

GOIRAND, Claude?

French, 1610–1664

series:

Agreeable Diversity of Figures, S7.135.9bis (missing), S7.135.11

prints:

Soldier Carrying a Pike on Horseback, after della Bella (DEV.-M., p.71 [12]), S7.135.11

Two Pikemen Walking to the Right, after della Bella (DEV.-M., p.71 [12]), S7.135.10 (missing, identification speculative)

GRIMALDI, Giovanni Francesco

Italian, 1606–1680?

B.1–8, 12, 14, 15, 19, 21, 23–26, 33, 34, 40–44, 52–55,

series:

Horizontal Landscapes, S2.32

Large Horizontal Landscapes, S2.21–S2.24, S6.4–S2.7

Round Landscapes, S2.25–S2.28

Small Horizontal Landscape, S2.29–S2.30

Vertical Landscapes, S2.33–S2.35

prints:

Colossal Bust (B.XIX.86.1, TIB42.11.1), S2.27.1

Horsemen Approaching a Thatched Cottage (B.XIX.87.4, TIB42.14.4), S2.28.1

Landscape with a Bird Perched on a Tree Stump (B.XIX.106.40 i/ii, TIB42.47.40), S2.24, S2.31

Landscape with a Column Shaft (B.XIX.89.8, TIB42.18.8), S2.25.2

Landscape with a Crawling Man (B.XIX.87.3, TIB42.13.3), S2.25.1

Landscape with a Luteplayer, after Titian? (B.XIX.116.54, TIB42.62.54), S6.5

Landscape with a Man Standing near Two Seated Men (B.XIX.96.21, TIB42.28.21), S2.29.2

Landscape with a Man Standing near Two Seated Men, after Titian? (B.XIX.115.53, TIB42.61.53), S6.7

Landscape with a Small Boat (B.XIX.95.19, TIB42.27.19), S2.30.1

Landscape with a Standing Man, Seated Woman, and Child, 1643 (B.XIX.107.41, TIB42.48.41-I), S2.22

Landscape with a Stunted Tree (B.XIX.103.34, TIB42.41.34), S2.32.2

Landscape with a Town near a Cascade (B.XIX.98.24, TIB42.31.24), S2.29.1

Landscape with Brickworks (B.XIX.108.42, TIB42.49.42), S2.23

Landscape with Five Men and Two Women
(B.XIX.99.26, TIB42.33.26), S2.30.3

Landscape with Four Dice Players, after Titian?
(B.XIX.116.55, TIB42.63.55), S6.4

Landscape with Nymphs and Satyrs, after Titian
(B.XIX.109.44, TIB42.51.44), S6.2

Landscape with Three Men, after Titian? (B.XIX.114.52
ii/ii, TIB42.60.52), S6.6

Landscape with Three Men Conversing (B.XIX.88.6,
TIB42.16.6), S2.26.2

Landscape with Three Small Boats on a River
(B.XIX.102.33, TIB42.40.33), S2.32.1

Landscape with Two Fighting Goats (B.XIX.92.14,
TIB42.23.14), S2.34

Landscape with Two Horsemen Entering a Small Fort
(B.XIX.88.7, TIB42.17.7), S2.28.2

Landscape with Two Men on a Hillock (B.XIX.91.12,
TIB42.21.12), S2.33

Landscape with Two Men Seated on a Hillock
(B.XIX.97.23, TIB42.30.23), S2.29.3

Landscape with Two Men Standing near a Seated Man
(B.XIX.98.25, TIB42.32.25), S2.30.2

Penitent Magdalen (B.XIX.108.43, TIB42.50.43), S2.21

Pyramid (B.XIX.87.2, TIB42.12.2), S2.27.2

Rest on the Flight into Egypt (B.XIX.92.15, TIB.42.24.15),
S2.35

Two Horsemen on the Road to a Castle (B.XIX.88.5,
TIB42.15.5), S2.26.1

GUERCINO (Barbieri, Giovanni Francesco)
Italian, 1591–1666

B.1

prints:
Saint Anthony of Padua (B.XVIII.362.1, Bologna 10 i/ii),
S1.86.1

GUIDO
see Reni, Guido

HENRIET, Israel, attributed to
French, c. 1590–1661

L.appendix, pl. 99, fig. 208

prints:
Woman and Young Girl (L. appendix, pl. 99, fig. 208
ii/ii), S4.22.3

LAER, Pieter van
Dutch, 1599–1642

H.15

prints:
Family, after Wyck (H.X.7.15), S5.29.4

LANFRANCO, Giovanni
Italian, 1582–1647

B.30, 31

prints:
Roman General Addressing His Soldiers (B.XVIII.348.30,
TIB40.333.30), S1.80

Triumph of a Roman Emperor (B.XVIII.349.31 ii?/ii,
TIB40.334.31-I), S1.81

LASNE, Michel
French, 1592–1635

L.664; BNIFF17.263, 314

prints:
Portrait of Bernard de Foix de La Valette, 1627, partially
after Callot (BNIFF17.VII.134.314 i/ii), S3.102, **P. mariette 1679**

Portrait of Jacques Callot, 1626 (BNIFF17.VII.113.263
ii/ii), S3.1.1, S4.1a

Portrait of Louis XIII, 1634, partially after Callot (L.664
ii/ii), S3.98

LOLI, Lorenzo
Italian, c. 1612–1691

B.6

prints:
Madonna and Child with Saints Anne and John the
Baptist, after Giovanni Andrea Sirani? (B.XIX.168.6,
TIB42.132.6), S1.58.1

LOLI, Lorenzo, attributed to
Italian, c. 1612–1691

B.4 (Reni School)

Madonna and Child with Saint John the Baptist
(B.XVIII.315.4, TIB40.221.4, TIB42.131.5), S1.58.2

LUCHINI, Antonio-Francesco
Italian, c. 1610–?

prints:
View of Pisa with the Tournament on the Bridge, 1634,
after della Bella (DEV.-M.1059 i/iii), S7.36

MACE, Charles
French, 1631–after 1665

R.-D.112–123

series:
Subjects from the Old and New Testaments, after Castiglione, R.-D.112–123

prints:
Abraham and Sarah Voyaging to Egypt, after Cas-
tiglione (R.-D.VI.279.113 iii/iii, TIB4602.114.37?), S6.70
Abraham Dismissing Hagar, after Castiglione
(R.-D.VI.280.115 iii/iii, TIB4602.113.1), S6.73
Angel Commands Noah to Enter the Animals into the
Ark, after Castiglione (R.-D.VI.279.112 ii/ii,
TIB4602.113.2 or TIB4602.114.38), S6.72
Blessing by God of Abraham and Sarah, after Cas-
tiglione (R.-D.VI.280.114 ii/iii, TIB4602.114.37?), S6.71
Crucifixion, after Castiglione (R.-D.VI.283.123 iii/iii,
TIB4602.115.48), S6.84
Departure of Rebecca in Search of Isaac, after Cas-
tiglione (R.-D.VI.280.116 ii/ii, TIB4602.114.42), S6.74
God the Father Appearing to the Madonna and Child,
after Castiglione (R.-D.VI.283.122 iii/iii,
TIB4602.115.46?), S6.83
Jacob Returning to His Father, after Castiglione
(R.-D.3.VI.281.118 ii/ii, TIB4602.114.44), S6.77
Jacob Returning from Mesopotamia Sends Messengers
to His Brother Esau, after Castiglione
(R.-D.VI.282.119 iii/iii, TIB4602.115.45), S6.76
Moses and His Family Departing Egypt, after Cas-
tiglione (R.-D.VI.283.121 iii/iii, TIB4602.114.40), S6.86
Moses Found by the Daughter of Pharaoh, after Cas-
tiglione (R.-D.VI.282.120 iii/iii, TIB4602.114.39?), S6.85
Rachel's Journey to Her Husband Jacob, after Cas-
tiglione (R.-D.VI.281.117 iii/iii, TIB4602.114.43), S6.75

MARATTI, Carlo
Italian, 1625–1713

B.1–13

series:
Life of the Virgin, S1.105.1, S1.105.3–S1.106.2

prints:
Adoration of the Magi (B.XXI.91.5, TIB47.15.5,
TIB4703.28,005 S3/3), S1.106.1
Annunciation (B.XXI.90.2, TIB47.12.2, TIB4703.25.002
S2/2), S1.105.3
Assumption of the Virgin (B.XXI.92.8, TIB47.18.8,
TIB4703.30.008 S2?/3), S1.106.2
Birth of the Virgin (B.XXI.89.1, TIB47.11.1,
TIB4703.24.001 S2/2), S1.105.1
Christ and the Samaritan Woman at the Well, after
Annibale Carracci, 1649 (B.XXI.92.7, TIB47.17.7,
TIB4703.29.007.S3/3), S1.15
Expulsion of Heliodorus, after Raphael (B.XXI.94.13,
TIB47.24.13, TIB4703.35.013 S3/7), S1.104
Holy Family with Angels (B.XXI.90.4, TIB47.14.4,
TIB4703.27.004 S1/3), S1.111.1
Madonna and Child with the Young Saint John the Bap-
tist (B.XXI.92.9, TIB47.19.9, TIB4703.31.009 S4/4),
S1.111.4
Madonna with the Young Christ Sleeping and Mary
Magdalen (B.XXI.91.6, TIB47.16.6, TIB4703.29.006
S2/4), S1.111.3
Martyrdom of Saint Andrew, after Domenichino
(B.XXI.93.11, TIB47.21.11, TIB4703.34.011 S2/5), S1.112
Mystic Marriage of Saint Catherine (B.XXI.93.10,
TIB47.20.10, TIB4703.33.010 S5/5), S1.111.2
Saint Charles Borromeo Praying to Liberate Milan from
the Plague, after Domenico Cerrini (B.XXI.94.12,
TIB47.22.12, TIB4703.35.012), S1.113, **P. mariette 1695**
Visitation (B.XXI.90.3, TIB47.13.3, TIB4703.26.003 S2/2),
S1.105.4

MARIETTE, Jean
French, 1660–1742

see Anonymous French 17th c.

MASSE, Charles
see Macé, Charles

MIEL, Jan
Dutch, 1599–1633

H.11–13

prints:
Old Woman Combing the Hair of a Boy (B.I.340.2,
H.XIV.34.12), S5.28.1
Shepherd with a Bagpipe (B.I.339.1, H.XIV.34.11), S5.28.2

Youth Extracting a Spine from His Foot (B.I.340.3, H.XIV.35.13), S5.29.5

MOLA, Pier Francesco
Italian, 1612?–1668?

B.3

prints:
Madonna and Child (B.XIX.204.3, TIB42.179.3), S1.84.1

MOLA, Pier Francesco, attributed to
Italian, 1612?–1668?

B.1

prints:

Joseph and His Brothers (B.XIX.203.1, TIB42.177.1–II [trimmed]), S1.85

MONOGRAMMIST CpP (see Monogrammist GpP)

MONOGRAMMIST GpP (called Pocetti in SA table of contents)
Italian, active c. 1650

B.4

prints:
Death of Nessus (B.XIX.185.4, TIB42.161.4), S2.55, **P. mariette** 1707

MONOGRAMMIST IS (superimposed)
see Monogrammist SI (superimposed)

MONOGRAMMIST SI (superimposed)
Flemish, 17th c.

H.1–4

prints:
Man and Woman Dancing, after Teniers (H.XIII.67.1–4, Dutuit VI.427.33 i/ii), S5.4.3
Man Speaking with a Woman at a Cottage Door, after Teniers (H.XIII.67.1–4, Dutuit VI.427.35), S5.5.2
Three Villagers Conversing, after Teniers (H.XIII.67.1–4, Dutuit VII.428.36), S5.5.3
View of a Village, after Teniers (H.XIII.67.1–4, Dutuit VI.427.34), S5.4.2

MONTAGNE, Matthieu
see Platte-Montagne, Matthieu

MORIN, Jean
French, c. 1600–1666

R.-D.89–108

series:
Four Vertical Landscapes, S5.99–S5.102
Round Landscapes, S5.105.1–S5.106.2
Ruins in the Campagna, S5.49.1–S5.49.3
Two Horizontal Landscapes, S5.103, S5.104

prints:
Fishermen in a River (R.-D.II.70.89), S5.105.2
Grotto of the Nymph Egeria, after Poelenburch (R.-D.II.74.100, LeB.III.57.106), S5.49.3
Harvesters in a Wheat Field, after Fouquières (R.-D.II.77.107, H.VII.6.10), S5.104
Landscape with a Carriage and Travelers, after Fouquières (R.-D.II.76.105, H.VII.6.9), S5.108.1
Landscape with a Cowherd, after Fouquières (R.-D.II.76.104, H.VII.6.8), S5.109.2
Landscape with Duck Hunters, after Fouquières (R.-D.II.75.103, H.VII.6.7), S5.109.1
Old Woman Seated, after Poelenburch (R.-D.II.74.101, LeB.III.57.107), S5.49.1
Roman Monuments, after Poelenburch (R.-D.II.76.106, LeB.III.75.107), S5.48.2
Ruined Fortress with a Round Tower (R.-D.II.71.91), S5.105.3
Ruins of an Aqueduct, after Claude (R.-D.II.75.102, LeB.III.57.108), S5.48.1
Ruins with a Mother and Child Seated in the Foreground (R.-D.II.71.92), S5.105.1
Seated Cowherd, after Poelenburch (R.-D.II.73.99, LeB.III.57.105), S5.49.2
Travelers on the Road in a Wooded Landscape, with a Farmhouse on the Left, after Fouquières (R.-D.II.77.108, H.VII.6.11), S5.103
Travelers on the Road, with a Large Tree at the Left, after Fouquières (R.-D.II.72.95, H.VII.6.3), S5.99
Travelers on the Road, with a Large Tree at the Left and an Extended Landscape (R.-D.II.71.93), S5.106.1
Travelers on the Road, with a Large Tree at the Right, after Fouquières (R.-D.II.75.97, H.VII.6.3–6), S5.102
Travelers on the Road, with a Large Tree at the Right and a Cottage at the Left, after Fouquières (R.-D.II.73.98, H.VII.6.6), S5.101
Travelers with a Cart on the Road, with Trees at the

prints:
Smokers in an Inn (H.XV.69.c), S5.21.3

PALMA, Jacopo, the younger
Italian, 1544–1628

B.2, 7, 9, 12, 13, 17–27,

series: Rules for Learning to Draw, S6.9.1–S6.13.3, S6.14.1,
S6.14.3

prints:
Christ and the Woman Taken in Adultery (B.XVI.292.20,
TIB33.143.20), S6.10.2
Doubting Thomas (B.XVI.292.22, TIB33.145.22), S6.10.3
Fame (B.XVI.291.18, TIB33.141.18), S6.11.1
Joseph and Potiphar's Wife (B.XVI.294.27, TIB33.150.27),
S6.9.1
Judith with the Head of Holofernes (B.XVI.294.25,
TIB33.148.25), S6.9.3
Madonna and Child with Saint Jerome, Saint Francis,
and Another Saint (B.XVI.292.21, TIB33.144.21), S6.9.2
Painting and Sculpture (B.XVI.291.17, TIB33.140.17),
S6.12.2
Saint John the Baptist (B.XVI.291.19, TIB33.142.19),
S6.10.5
Samson and Delilah (B.XVI.294.26, TIB33.149.26), S6.10.1
Studies of Eyes, Noses, Mouths, and Ears (B.XVI.288.2,
TIB33.125.2), S6.13.2
Studies of Female Torsos and a Head (B.XVI.290.12,
TIB33.135.12), S6.13.3
Studies of Heads (B.XVI.290.13, TIB33.136.13), S6.13.1
Studies of Men's Arms (B.XVI.289.7, TIB33.130.7), S6.14.3
Studies of Men's Legs (B.XVI.289.9, TIB33.132.9), S6.14.2
Tutelary Goddess of Rome (horizontal) (B.XVI.293.24,
TIB33.147.24), S6.11.2
Tutelary Goddess of Rome (vertical) (B.XVI.293.23 ii/ii,
TIB33.146.23), S6.12.1

PALMA IL GIOVANE, Jacopo
see Palma, Jacopo, the younger

PASSAROTTI, Bartolomeo
Italian, 1529–1592

B.2, 4

prints:
Virgin and Child with Saint John the Baptist
(B.XVIII.4.4, TIB39.14.4), S2.47.1
Visitation, after Salviati (B.XVIII.3.2, TIB39.12.2), S2.46

PASSARI, Bernardino
Italian, c. 1540–c. 1590

B.70

prints:
Rest on the Flight into Egypt, 1583 (B.XVII.36.70,
TIB34.107.70), S2.49

PESARESE, IL
see Cantarini, Simone

PLATTENBERG, Mathijs van
see Platte-Montagne, Matthieu

PLATTE-MONTAGNE, Matthieu
Flemish, c. 1608–1660

R.-D.1, 6, 24–26

series:
Round Landscapes, S5.106.3, S5.106.4

prints:
Road on the Edge of a Wood (R.-D.V.122.24 i/ii,
H.XVII.131.24), S5.107.1
Seaport with a Round Tower (R.-D.V.110.1 i/iii,
H.XVII.126.1), S5.106.3
Skaters (R.-D.V.112.6 i/iii, H.XVII.126.6), S5.106.4
Village in a Wood (R.-D.V.123.26 i/ii, H.XVII.132.26),
S5.107.2
Winter Landscape, after Fouquières (R.-D.V.122.25 i/ii,
H.XVII.132.25), S5.108.2

PROCACCINI, Camillo
Italian, 1550–1629

B.1–5

prints:
Rest on the Flight into Egypt (B.XVIII.19.1, TIB39.36.1-I),
S2.42.2
Rest on the Flight into Egypt, 1593 (B.XVIII.19.2,
TIB39.37.2), S2.40.1
Rest on the Flight into Egypt (B.XVIII.20.3, TIB39.38.3),
S2.40.2, **P. mariette 1667**
[Saint Francis Receiving the Stigmata, 1593 (B.XVIII.21.5,
TIB39.40.5), S2.40A; this print, found inserted loosely
into the album at folio 40, was not originally a part of
the album]
Transfiguration (B.XVIII.20.4 i/ii, TIB39.39.4), S2.41

PROU, Jacques
French, c. 1639–after 1686

LEB.4?, 5?

series:
Large Landscapes after Bourdon, s2.90–s2.94
Landscapes after Bourdon, s2.95–s2.96

print:
Large Rocky Landscape with the Flight into Egypt, after Bourdon (LEB.III.257.4?), s2.90
Large Rocky Landscape with Cart and Oxen, after Bourdon (LEB.III.257.4?), s2.93
Large Rocky Landscape with Family and Soldier, after Bourdon (LEB.III.257.4?), s2.94
Large Rocky Landscape with Hermit Saints (?), after Bourdon (LEB.III.257.4?), s2.91
Large Rocky Landscape with Two Figures by a Tablet, after Bourdon (LEB.III.257.4?), s2.92
Rocky Landscape with Shepherd and Seven Sheep, after Bourdon (LEB.III.257.5?), s2.95.1
Rocky Landscape with Women Washing Clothes, after Bourdon (LEB.III.257.5?), s2.95.2
Rocky Landscape with a Coastal View and Waterfall, after Bourdon (LEB.III.257.5?), s2.96.2

RENI, Guido
Italian, 1575–1642

B.1, 4, 6, 9–11, 13, 15, 16, 45, 50, 51

prints:
Angels in Glory, 1607, after Cambiaso (B.XVIII.299.45, TIB40.196.45, TIB4005.324.028 s3/3), s1.74
Allegory of Learning, (B.XVIII.289.16, TIB40.167.16, TIB4005.311.024), s1.71.1
Infant Christ and the Young Saint John the Baptist on a Hill, after Annibale Carracci? (B.XVIII.287.13, TIB40.163.13, TIB4005.321.027 s2/2), s1.69.1
Holy Family with a Scene of Moses Striking the Rock (B.XVIII.284.9 i/ii, TIB40.157.9, TIB4005.287.004 s1/2), s1.63.4
Holy Family with Saint Clare, after Annibale Carracci (B.XVIII.303.50 i/iii, TIB40.201.50, TIB4005.349.041XX s1/4), s1.3.1, **P. mariette 1666**
Holy Family with the Young Saint John the Baptist and a Vase (B.XVIII.286.11, TIB40.159.11, TIB4005.290.006), s1.63.1
Holy Family with Two Angels (B.XVIII.285.10, TIB40.158.10, TIB4005.287.005 s2/2), s1.63.3
Madonna and Child with Saint Joseph in the Back-

ground (B.XVIII.278.1 i/ii, TIB40.147.1, TIB4005.328.029 s2/5), s1.63.2
Madonna and Child at a Table with the Young Saint John the Baptist (B.XVIII.282.6, TIB40.153.6, TIB4005.343.034), s1.61.1
Madonna and Child in Round Format (B.XVIII.280.4, TIB40.150.4, TIB4005.330.030 S?/2 [trimmed]), s1.64.2
Madonna Nursing the Christ Child, after Annibale Carracci (B.XVIII.303.51, TIB40.202.51, TIB4005.355.043XX), s1.2.1
Saint Jerome (B.XVIII.288.15, TIB40.165.15, TIB4005.348.038), s1.68.4

RIBERA, Jusepe de
Spanish, 1591–1652

B.1, 3–9, 13, 15–17

prints:
Drunken Silenus, 1628 (B.XX.84.13, TIB44.282.13–II, Brown 14 ii/iii), s6.53.2, **P. mariette 1672**
Lamentation (B.XX.79.1, TIB44.269.1, Brown 17 ii/ii), s6.50.1
Large Grotesque Head (B.XX.82.9, TIB44.277.9–I, Brown 11 i/ii [rejected]), s6.55.4
Martyrdom of Saint Bartholomew, 1624 (B.XX.81.6, TIB44.274.6, Brown 12 i?/ii), s6.49, **P. mariette 1667, P. mariette 1670**
Penitence of Saint Peter (B.XX.81.7, TIB44.275.7, Brown 6), s6.48, **P. mariette, 1670***
Saint Jerome Hearing the Trumpet of the Last Judgment, 1621 (B.XX.81.5, TIB44.273.5, Brown 4), s6.51
Saint Jerome Hearing the Trumpet of the Last Judgment (B.XX.80.4, TIB44.272.4, Brown 5), s6.52, **P. mariette***
Saint Jerome Reading (B.XX.80.3, TIB44.271.3, Brown 13), s6.50.2
Small Grotesque Head, 1622 (B.XX.82.8, TIB44.276.8, Brown 10 ii/ii), s6.55.3
Studies of Ears (left half), 1622 (B.XX.86.17, TIB44.286.17, Brown 7 iiia/iii), s6.56.3
Studies of Ears (right half), 1622 (B.XX.86.17, TIB44.286.17, Brown 7 iiib/iii), s6.56.4
Studies of Eyes (left half) (B.XX.85.15, TIB44.284.15, Brown 8 iiia/iii), s6.56.1
Studies of Eyes (right half) (B.XX.85.15, TIB44.284.15, Brown 8 iiib/iii), s6.56.2
Studies of Noses and Mouths (left half) (B.XX.86.16, TIB44.285.16, Brown 9 iiia/iii), s6.55.1
Studies of Noses and Mouths (right half) (B.XX.86.16, TIB44.285.16, Brown 9 iiib/iii), s6.55.2

RIBERA, Jusepe de, circle of
Spanish, 1591–1652

B.10–12

prints:
Centaur and Triton Fighting (B.XX.83.11, TIB44.279.11,
    Brown 19), s6.54.1
Cupid Whipping a Satyr (B.XX.83.12, TIB44.280.12,
    Brown 18), s6.54.3
Poet (B.XX.83.10, TIB44.278.10, Brown 3 [accepted]),
    s6.53.1

ROSA, Salvator
Italian, 1615–1673

B.1, 2, 17–20

prints:
Albert, Companion to Saint William, 1661 (B.XX.269.2,
    TIB45.241.2, TIB4512.336.002), s6.60
Apollo and the Cumaean Sibyl (B.XX.274.17,
    TIB45.258.17, TIB4512.357.018 s2/3), s6.62
Ceres and Phytalus (B.XX.275.19, TIB45.260.19,
    TIB4512.362.020 s1/2), s6.61
Glaucus and Scylla (B.XX.275.20, TIB45.261.20,
    TIB4512.364.021 s2/3), s6.63
Jason and the Dragon (B.XX.275.18, TIB45.259.18,
    TIB4512.360.019), s6.64
Saint William of Maleval, 1661 (B.XX.268.1, TIB45.240.1,
    TIB4512.335.001 s1/2), s6.65

SALIMBENI, Ventura
Italian, 1567/8–1613

B.1–4, 7

prints:
Annunciation, 1594 (B.XVII.192.4 i–ii/ii, TIB38.12.4),
    s6.40.1
Betrothal of the Virgin, 1590 (B.XVII.191.2, TIB38.10.2),
    s6.41.1
Destiny of the Virgin, 1590 (B.XVII.191.3 i?/ii, TIB38.11.3),
    s6.41.4, **P. mariette 1666**
Saint Agnes, 1590 (B.XVII.194.7, TIB38.15.7), s6.41.3
Vision of Joachim and Anna, 1590 (B.XVII.190.1 i/ii,
    TIB38.9.1), s6.41.2

SCARSELLO, Gerolamo
Italian, before 1645–after 1670

B.6

prints:
Fortuna, after Reni (B.XIX.253.6 ii?/ii, TIB42.258.6-1),
    s1.71.3

SCHEDONI, Bartolomeo
Italian, 1578–1615

B.1

prints:
Holy Family (B.XVIII.206.1, TIB40.11.1, TIB4001.17.001
    s1/3), s1.82.1

SCHENDEYL, Gillis van
Dutch, active 1622–1650s

See Anonymous Dutch 17th c.

SCHIAMINOSSI, Raffaello
Italian, c. 1570–c. 1620

B.29, 31, 36, 57, 91

prints:
Elevation of Saint Mary Magdalen, 1612, after Cambiaso
    (B.XVII.232.91, TIB38.113.91), s2.42.1
Madonna Teaching the Infant Christ to Walk, 1614, after
    Cambiaso (B.XVII.219.31 i/ii, TIB38.80.31), s2.45
Rest on the Flight into Egypt, 1612, after Barocci
    (B.XVII.218.29, TIB38.78.29), s2.44
Stoning of Saint Stephen, 1608, after Cambiaso
    (B.XVII.226.57, TIB38.98.57), s2.43
Virgin of the Immaculate Conception, 1603, after
    Castello (B.XVII.222.36, TIB38.85.36), s6.105

SILVESTRE, Charles-François de
French, 1667–?

LEB.1

prints:
Descent from the Cross, after Callot (LEB.III.505.1),
    s3.7.3

SILVESTRE, Israel
French, 1621–1691

prints:
Frontispiece, Diverse Views of Rome and Environs,
    s7.78.2
Louvre and the Tuileries (with della Bella) (DEV.-
    M.863), s7.79.1

SIRANI, Giovanni Andrea, attributed to
Italian, 1610–1670

B.1 (Reni school)

prints:
Judith with the Head of Holofernes, after Reni
(B.XVIII.314.1 [Reni school], TIB40.218.1), S1.57.2

SPAGNOLETTO, LO
see Ribera, Jusepe de

STEEN, Franciscus van der
Flemish, 1625–1672

H.34, 35, 37–39

prints:
Drinker and His Wife, Reading a Letter, after Teniers
(H.XXVIII.60.35), S5.10.2
Gold Weighers, after Teniers (H.XXVIII.60.34), S5.11.1
Man with Jug, after Teniers (H.XXVIII.60.37), S5.10.1
Two Men, One Smoking, after Teniers (H.XXVIII.60.38),
S5.11.2
Woman with a Bottle, a Man behind Her, after Teniers
(H.XXVIII.61.39), S5.11.3

STRADA, Vespasiano
Italian, c. 1582–1622

B.2–4, 6, 7, 9, 12, 14–17

prints:
Dead Christ with Angels (B.XVII.304.4, TIB38.341.4),
S6.43.4
Ecce Homo (large plate) (B.XVII.304.3, TIB38.340.3),
S6.44.2
Ecce Homo (small plate) (B.XVII.304.2, TIB38.339.2),
S6.44.1
Madonna and Child on the Clouds (B.XVII.307.12,
TIB38.349.12), S6.40.3
Madonna and Child on the Crescent (B.XVII.306.7,
TIB38.344.7), S6.42.2
Madonna and Child with a Rose (B.XVII.306.9,
TIB38.346.9), S6.40.2
Madonna and Child with Cherubs (B.XVII.305.6,
TIB38.343.6), S6.43.2
Madonna and Child with Saint Catherine, 1595
(B.XVII.310.17 iii/iii, TIB38.354.17), S6.42.1
Madonna and Child with Saint John the Baptist in a
Landscape (B.XVII.309.15, TIB38.352.15), S6.43.3
Mystic Marriage of Saint Catherine (B.XVII.309.16,

TIB38.353.16), S6.42.3, **P. mariette 1666, P. mariette
1667**
Virgin with Saints (Holy Kinship) (B.XVII.308.14,
TIB38.351.14), S6.43.1

SUYDERHOEF, Jonas
Dutch, 1613–1689

H.21, 22, 26, 27

prints:
Interior with Dancing Couple, after Ostade
(H.XXVIII.215.27 i/iii), S5.14
Peasants About to Brawl, after Ostade (H.XXVIII.214.26
iii/iv), S5.15
Three Crones, after Ostade (H.XXVIII.211.21 i?/vi), S5.19.1
Three Peasants around a Bench in an Interior, after
Ostade (H.XXVIII.212.22 iv/vi), S5.18.1

SWANEVELT, Herman van
Dutch, c. 1600–1655

H.1–5, 18–23, 26–29, 50–62, 110–116

series:
Diverse Views in and near Rome, S5.82.1–S5.86.3,
S5.87.4–5
Landscapes with Animals, S5.79.1–7
Landscapes with Satyrs, S5.87.1–2, S5.87.5–6
The Story of Adonis, S5.88.1–S5.90.2

prints:
Abraham and the Three Angels (H.XXIX.50.1 i/ii), S5.81.3
Angora Sheep (H.XXIX.99.115 i?/iii), S5.79.3
Balaam and the Ass (H.XXIX.52.5 iv/viii), S5.80.2
Baths of Caracalla, 1652 (H.XXIX.75.52 i/iii), S5.83.3
Birth of Adonis, pl. 1, 1654 (H.XXIX.60.18), S5.88.1
Camels (H.XXIX.97.110 i/ii), S5.79.1
Church of Saint Adrian on the Via Flamina, 1653
(H.XXIX.77.56 i/iii), S5.82.3
Cows (H.XXIX.97.111 i/iii), S5.79.5
Dancing Satyr (H.XXIX.64.27 i/ii), S5.87.6
Death of Adonis, pl. 5, 1654 (H.XXIX.61.22), S5.90.1
Donkeys (H.XXIX.98.112 i/iii), S5.79.7
Elijah in the Wilderness (H.XXIX.51.4 ii/iv), S5.81.2
Farm beyond the Porta del Popolo, 1653 (H.XXIX.78.57
i/iii), S5.84.3
First View of the Zugro, 1653 (H.XXIX.79.59 i/iii), S5.85.3
Goats (H.XXIX.98.114 ii/iii), S5.79.2
Hagar and the Angel (H.XXIX.50.2 ii/iv), S5.80.1
Inn at the Prima Porta, 1653 (H.XXIX.77.55 i/iii), S5.84.1
Pigs (H.XXIX.99.116 i/iii), S5.79.6

TEMPESTA, Antonio
Italian, 1555–1630

B.187, 234–259, 545–554, 557–607, 618, 636–823, 825, 826, 828–855, 857, 858, 860, 863–902, 904–911, 914–968, 1015–1019, 1021–1065, 1068–1132, 1140–1147, 1147a, 1147b, 1148–1156, 1160, 1162, 1163, 1166, 1168–1171, 1208–1247, 1329–1357, 1388–1427, 1453–1459

Wild Bull Hunt with a Bull Pursuing Dogs in the Background (B.XVII.168.1148–1157, TIB37.54.1155), S9.63.1

Wild Bull Hunt, the Bull Shot with Arrows and Speared (B.XVII.164.1027–1074, TIB36.285.1041), S9.84.2

Wild Dog Hunt (B.XVII.164.1027–1074, TIB36.298.1054), S9.81.5

Wild Oxen (or Buffalo) Hunted with Spears, 1602 (B.XVII.165.1085, TIB36.329.1085), S9.74.3

Winter, 1592 (B.XVII.152.807, TIB36.105.807), S9.30.2

Winter, 1592 (B.XVII.153.811, TIB36.109.811), S9.30.1

Wolf and Stag Hunt, pl. II (B.XVII.167.1141, TIB37.38.1141), S9.61.1

Wolf Hunt with a Dead Ram Dragged as Bait (B.XVII.164.1027–1074, TIB36.288.1044), S9.83.2

Women and Children Observe Civilis Battling the Romans, pl. 8, 1611 (B.XVII.145.567, TIB35.296.567), S8.51.2

Wreck of Ceyx's Ship, pl. 107, 1606 (B.XVII.151.744, TIB36.63.744), S9.14.3

TESTA, Pietro
Italian, 1612–1650

B.2–4, 9, 13–15, 18–25, 27, 30, 32, 33, 35

prints:

Achilles Dragging the Body of Hector Around the Walls of Troy (B.XX.221.22, TIB45.143.22, TIB4506.149.022 S1/6, Cropper 121), S2.11

Adoration of the Magi (B.XX.215.3, TIB45.124.3, TIB4506.138.003 S3/3, Cropper 63), S2.4

Allegory of the Arrival of Cardinal Franciotti as Bishop of Lucca (Faith, Hope, and Charity), 1637 (B.XX.224.30, TIB45.152.30, TIB4506.158.030 S2/2, Cropper 36), S2.7

Altro diletto ch'imparar non trovo ("I find delight only in learning"; Youth in the Service of Virtue and the Sciences) (B.XX.225.32, TIB45.154.32, TIB4506.159.032 S2/3, Cropper 101), S2.18

Birth and Infancy of Achilles, (B.XX.220.21, TIB45.142.21, TIB4506.148.021 S2/4, Cropper 118), S2.12

Dream of Joseph (B.XX.216.4, TIB45.125.4, TIB4506.139.004 S1/2, Cropper 25), S2.3

Garden of Charity (horizontal plate) (B.XX.222.27, TIB45.149.27, TIB4506.156.027 S1/2, Cropper 9), S2.6.2

Holy Family with Saint John the Baptist (B.XX.217.9, TIB45.130.9, TIB4506.142.009 S1/2, Cropper 1), S2.1.1

Martyrdom of Saint Erasmus (B.XX.218.14, TIB45.135.14, TIB4506.144.014 S2/5, Cropper 6), S2.5

Sacrifice of Iphigenia (B.XX.221.23, TIB45.145.23–II, TIB4506.151.023 S2/3, Cropper 61), S2.13, **P. mariette 1694**

Sacrifice of Isaac (B.XX.215.2, TIB45.123.2, TIB4506.138.002, Cropper 71), S2.1.2

Saint Jerome in the Desert (B.XX.219.15, TIB45.136.15, TIB4506.145.015 S3/3, Cropper 8), S2.2

Sinorix Carried from the Temple of Artemis (B.XX.220.19, TIB45.140.19, TIB4506.147.019 S2/2, Cropper 53), S2.10

Suicide of Cato, 1648 (B.XX.220.20, TIB45.141.20, TIB4506.148.020 S1/4, Cropper 116), S2.8

Symposium, 1648 (B.XX.220.18, TIB45.139.18, TIB4506.146.018 S2/6, Cropper 114), S2.9

Three Luchese Saints Interceding with the Virgin for the Victims of the Plague (B.XX.218.13, TIB45.134.13, TIB4506.144.013 S2/3, Cropper 7), S2.6.1

Triumph of Painting on Parnassus (B.XX.226.35, TIB45.160.35, TIB4506.164.035 S2/2, Cropper 73), S2.16, **P. mariette 1664**

Triumph of the Virtuous Artist on Parnassus (B.XX.225.33, TIB45.156.33–II, TIB4506.163.033 S2/3, Cropper 102), S2.17

Venus and Adonis (B.XX.222.25, TIB45.147.25, TIB4506.152.025 S1/3, Cropper 16), S2.14

Venus Giving Arms to Aeneas (B.XX.221.24, TIB45.146.24, TIB4506.152.024 S1?/2, Cropper 59), S2.15

TORRI, Flaminio
Italian, 1621–1661

B.4

prints:

Virgin in Glory and the Patron Saints of Bologna, after Reni (B.XIX.215.4, TIB42.193.4), S1.65

UYTTENBROUCK, Moyses van
see Wtenbrouck, Moyses van

VALESIO, Giovanni Luigi
Italian, 1583?–1633

B.7, 104, 105, 107

prints:

Dedication to Marie de' Medici for R. Campeggi, "Le lagrime di Maria Vergine," 1617 (B.XVIII.240.105, TIB40.103.105, TIB4002.51.040 S1/2), S1.79.3

Frontispiece to R. Campeggi, "Le lagrime di Maria Vergine," 1617 (B.XVIII.240.104, TIB40.102.104, TIB4002.51.039), S1.79.4

Title Page to G. A. Magini, "Tabula Novae," with Coat of Arms of Cardinal Carlo de' Medici, 1619

(B.XVIII.241.107, TIB40.105.107, TIB4002.54.043 S1/3), S1.79.2

Twelve Principal Movements of the Head (B.XVIII.216.7, TIB40.18.7, TIB4002.144.167), S1.79.1

VANNI, Francesco
Italian, 1563–1610

B.2, 3

prints:

Saint Catherine of Siena (B.XVII.196.2, TIB38.17.2), S6.35.2, **P. mariette 1668**

Saint Francis in Ecstasy (B.XVII.196.3, TIB38.18.3), S6.35.4

VANNI, Giovanni Battista
Italian, 1599–1660

B.17

prints:

Christ at the Wedding of Cana, 1637, after Veronese (B.XX.118.17, TIB44.329.17), S6.8, **P. mariette 1670, P. mariette 1670**

VILLAMENA, Francesco
Italian, 1566–1626

LeB.28, 36

prints:

Descent from the Cross, 1606, after Barocci (LeB.IV.124.28 i/iv), S6.37, **P. mariette 1666**

Saint Francis Receiving the Stigmata, 1597, after Barocci (LeB.IV.125.36), S6.39

VISSCHER, Cornelis
Dutch, 1619–1662

Dutuit 76, 79

prints:

Beggars, after Laer (Dutuit VI.488.74 ii/ii), S5.30

Stable, after Laer, (Dutuit VI.489.76 iii/v), S5.31

VISSCHER, Jan de
Dutch, c. 1600–1667

Dutuit 530(3), 531(1), 531(2); Wessely 54, 55

prints:

Dance in a Barn, after Ostade (Dutuit VI.531[1] ii/ii, Wessely 57), S5.25.2

Dance outside an Inn, after Ostade (Dutuit VI.530[3] ii/ii), S5.24.2

Interior of an Inn, after Ostade (Wessely 54), S5.24.1

Interior of an Inn, after Ostade (Wessely 55), S5.25.1

Music Making, after Ostade, S5.21.5

Village Wedding, after Ostade (Dutuit VI.531[2] ii/iii), S5.23

VLIEGER, Simon de
Dutch, c. 1601–1653

B.8–10

prints:

Fisherfolk at Scheveningen (B.I.29.10, TIB1.26.10-II, Dutuit VI.537.10 ii/ii), S5.111.1

Inn in the Ruins (B.I.27.8, TIB1.24.8-III, Dutuit VI.535.8 iii/iii), S5.112.2

Market Town (B.I.28.9, TIB1.25.9, Dutuit VI.535.9 iii/iii), S5.112.1

WATERLOO, Anthonie
Dutch, 1618–1677

Dutuit 105, 107, 108, 111, 112, 114–116, 119–131, 134–136

series:

Six horizontal landscapes, S5.77.2, S5.78

Six landscapes with mythological subjects, S5.63–S5.68

Six landscapes with Old Testament subjects, S5.59–S5.62

Six vertical landscapes, S5.69–S5.74

Six wooded landscapes, S5.72–S5.76

prints:

Landscape with a Dog Drinking from a Stream (Dutuit VI.611.120 ii/ii), S5.69

Landscape with a Farm by the Water (Dutuit VI.608.116 ii/ii), S5.77.2

Landscape with a Hunchback (Dutuit VI.611.121), S5.74

Landscape with a Mill (Dutuit VI.610.119 ii/ii), S5.71

Landscape with a Path through the Woods (Dutuit VI.607.115 ii/ii), S5.78.2

Landscape with a Small Wooden Bridge (Dutuit VI.612.124), S5.70

Landscape with a Woman and Child on a Bridge (Dutuit VI.607.114 ii/ii), S5.78.1

Landscape with a Woman and Three Children (Dutuit VI.611.122 ii/ii), S5.73

Landscape with Alpheus and Arethusa (Dutuit VI.612.125 ii/ii), S5.67

Landscape with Apollo and Daphne (Dutuit VI.613.126 ii/ii), S5.68

Landscape with Elijah Fed by Ravens (Dutuit VI.616.136 ii?/iii), S5.60

Landscape with Mercury and Argus (Dutuit VI.613.127 ii/ii), S5.65

Landscape with Pan and Syrinx (Dutuit VI.613.128), S5.66

Landscape with the Circumcision of Moses' Son (Dutuit VI.616.135), S5.59

Landscape with the Death of Adonis (Dutuit VI.614.130), S5.64

Landscape with the Expulsion of Hagar (Dutuit VI.614.131), S5.61

Landscape with Tobias and the Angel (Dutuit VI.616.134), S5.62

Landscape with Two Travelers Resting (Dutuit VI.612.123), S5.72

Landscape with Venus and Adonis (Dutuit VI.613.129), S5.63

Wooded Landscape: Couple Crossing a Stream (Dutuit VI.604.109 iii/iii), S5.77.1

Wooded Landscape: the Forest Entrance at the Little Wooden Bridge (Dutuit VI.603.107 ii?/iii), S5.75.2

Wooded Landscape: the Trimmed Groves (Dutuit VI.604.108 ii/ii), S5.75.1

Wooded Landscape: Travelers Resting (Dutuit VI.605.111 ii/ii), S5.76.2

Wooded Landscape: Two Men in a Hollow (Dutuit VI.606.112 ii/ii), S5.76.1

WILLEMSENS, Sidrach

Flemish, 1626–?

Andresen vol.2, p. 738

prints:

Temptation of Saint Anthony, after Teniers (Andresen II.738), S5.10.4

WTENBROUCK, Moyses van

Dutch, c. 1595–1646/1647

B.2–4, 6, 8–10, 12–17, 22, 24, 27–33, 38–42, 44, 45, 47–49, 52

series:

The Story of Hagar, S5.33.3–S5.40.1

The Story of Mercury and Argus, S5.34.3–S5.36.3

The Story of Tobias, S5.40.2–S5.41.2

prints:

Abraham Preparing to Sacrifice Isaac, 1620 (B.V.90.9, TIB6.64.9, TIB605.65.009 S3/3), S5.39.3

Arcadian Shepherds (B.V.108.45, TIB6.99.45, TIB605.83.045 S1/4), S5.34.5

Bacchus and Ariadne (B.V.101.30, TIB6.85.30, TIB605.77.030 S2/3), S5.33.2

Bather Stepping from a Forest Pool (B.V.106.39, TIB6.93.39, TIB605.80.039 S2/2), S5.33.1

Bathsheba at Her Bath (B.V.91.12, TIB6.67.12, TIB605.67.012 S3/3), S5.34.2

Battus Reveals Mercury's Hiding Place for Apollo's Horses (B.V.99.27, TIB6.82.27, TIB605.76.027 S2/2), S5.36.3

Cows and Other Animals beside a Wall (B.V.107.41, TIB6.95.41, TIB605.81.041 S1/3), S5.38.3

Diana Chastening Callisto (B.V.102.31, TIB6.86.31, TIB605.77.031 S2/2), S5.35.1

Dismissal of Hagar, 1620 (B.V.86.2, TIB6.60.2, TIB605.57.002 S3/4), S5.40.1

Donkeys and Other Animals beside a Wall (B.V.108.44, TIB6.98.44, TIB605.82.044 S1/5), S5.38.4

Hagar and Ishmael Walking in the Desert (B.V.88.6, TIB6.63.6, TIB605.64.006 S1/2), S5.33.4

Hagar Comforted by the Angel (B.V.89.8, TIB6.63.8, TIB605.64.008 S2/2), S5.33.3

Hagar Comforted by the Angel, 1620 (B.V.87.4, TIB6.62.4, TIB605.62.004 S2/3), S5.39.2

Hagar's Departure (B.V.86.3, TIB6.61.3, TIB605.60.003 S3/4), S5.39.1

Horses and Other Animals beside a Wall (B.V.107.42, TIB96.42, TIB605.81.042 S1/5), S5.38.1

Landscape with a Laden Donkey (B.V.112.52, TIB6.106.52, TIB605.88.052 S1/3), S5.41.3

Mercury Accuses Battus (B.V.101.29, TIB6.84.29, TIB605.76.029 S2/2), S5.36.2

Mercury Lulls Argus to Sleep (B.V.97.22, TIB6.77.22, TIB605.75.022 S1/2), S5.34.3

Mercury Lulls Argus to Sleep (B.V.98.24, TIB6.79.24, TIB605.75.024 S2/3), S5.35.2

Mercury Provokes Battus for His Indiscretion (B.V.100.28, TIB6.83.28, TIB605.76.028 S2/2), S5.36.1

Nude Woman and Child Kneeling before an Old Man (B.V.109.47, TIB6.101.47, TIB605.83.047 S2/2), S5.32.2

Pastoral Couple Taking Refuge from a Storm (B.V.110.49, TIB6.103.49, TIB605.85.049 S4/4), S5.37.2

Return of the Holy Family from Egypt (B.V.94.17, TIB6.72.17, TIB605.72.017 S3/4), S5.33.6

Sacrifice of Isaac, 1620 (B.V.90.10, TIB6.65.10, TIB605.65.010 S3/3), S5.32.1

Shepherd and Shepherdess in an Idyllic Landscape (B.V.110.48, TIB6.102.48, TIB605.83.048 S2/4), S5.37.1

Sleeping Silenus (B.V.103.33, TIB6.88.33, TIB605.77.033 S1/2), S5.34.4

PRINTED BY THE STINEHOUR PRESS

IN THE NORTHEAST KINGDOM, LUNENBURG, VERMONT

COMPOSED IN ADOBE MINION AND TRAJAN TYPES

BOOK DESIGN BY CHRISTOPHER KUNTZE